Linguistics in Britain

Personal Histories

Publications of the Philological Society, 36

Linguistics in Britain

Personal Histories

Edited by

Keith Brown and Vivien Law

Publications of the Philological Society, 36

Oxford UK & Boston USA

Copyright © The Philological Society 2002

ISBN 0–631–23476–4

First published 2002

Blackwell Publishers
108 Cowley Road, Oxford, OX4 1JF, UK

and
350 Main Street,
Malden, MA 02148, USA.

British Library Cataloguing in Publication Data
A catalogue record for this publication is available from the British Library

Library of Congress Cataloging-in-Publication Data
Applied for

Typeset by Joshua Associates Ltd., Oxford
Printed in Europe by
the Alden Group, Oxford

CONTENTS

PREFACE

The latter half of the twentieth century was a remarkable time for linguistics in Britain. Prior to the Second World War the only established posts in linguistics were specialist Chairs of Comparative Philology at Oxford, Cambridge and a few other universities and of Phonetics at University College London. In 1944 J. R. Firth was appointed to the Chair of General Linguistics in the School of Oriental and African Studies in London, where he was Head of the Department of Phonetics and Linguistics. During the 1950s and 1960s linguistics expanded rapidly in both the old and the new universities. In 2001 there were 69 higher education institutions offering 645 courses with linguistics as part of an undergraduate degree; these included 19 single-subject linguistics honours degrees on offer at 16 institutions.

The new linguistics teachers in Britain had to learn about their subject during their first years of appointment. They had to deal with the subject as a whole as well as with the particular theories held by their few seniors, such as Daniel Jones and Firth. They had no prior qualifications specifically in linguistics, since degree courses in linguistics were mostly set up in the 1960s and later. This generation had to find its own way in the subject and establish and articulate it for various degree syllabuses, while at the same time establishing themselves as teachers and research workers.

The beginning of a new millennium seems to be an opportune moment to look back over the achievements of the previous half-century. The Council of the Philological Society decided to mark the occasion with a volume of personal reminiscences by some of those most centrally involved in linguistics in that period. Contributors were asked to reflect on how and why they went into linguistics, what branches of the subject attracted them, what formative influences they were exposed to and how they reacted to them. They were also asked to reflect on the part they had played in the intellectual development of linguistics and how they had contributed to its institutional development. Subject to these loose guidelines, contributors were encouraged to shape their contributions as they preferred: consequently the contributions are not written to a standard pattern. This volume is not an academic history of linguistics in Britain, but rather a collection of personal memoirs. In some cases, different contributors have participated in the same events and inevitably see them from different perspectives: we have not attempted to harmonize their accounts. We have tried to ensure that dates are correct but cannot always check them because we do not have access to the appropriate records.

R. H. Robins, the then emeritus President of the Society, Vivien Law, at the time a member of Council, and Keith Brown, the Publications Secretary, were asked to act as editors. R. H. Robins played a significant part in planning this volume, but sadly died soon after it was under way. Fortunately, he left his own 'personal history'. Vivien died while the book was in press, her health having deteriorated during the latter stages of the editing. Keith Brown, on behalf of Vivien and Bobby, would like to record gratitude to all the contributors for their co-operation.

JEAN AITCHISON

AITCHISON, Jean Margaret; Rupert Murdoch Professor of Language and Communication, University of Oxford, since 1993; Fellow, Worcester College, Oxford, since 1993; *b.* 1938, *m.* 2000 John Robert Ayto; *Education:* Wimbledon High School; Girton College, Cambridge, BA 1st cl. Hons Classics 1960, MA 1964; Radcliffe College, Harvard, AM Linguistics 1961; *Career:* Assistant Lecturer in Ancient Greek, Bedford College, University of London, 1961–5; Lecturer in Linguistics, London School of Economics, University of London, 1965–82, Senior Lecturer 1982–92, Reader 1992; Reith Lecturer, BBC, 1996; Member LAGB, LSA, Philological Society; Member board of consulting editors *Linguistics* 1991–7; Member editorial board *International Journal of Lexicography* 1988–; Editor *Cambridge Approaches to Linguistics* (Cambridge University Press series 1990–). *Major Publications: Linguistics* 1972 [5th ed. 1999]; *The Articulate Mammal: An Introduction to Psycholinguistics* 1976 [4th ed. 1998]; *Language Change: Progress or Decay?* 1981 [3rd ed. 2001]; *Words in the Mind: An Introduction to the Mental Lexicon* 1987 [2nd ed. 1994]; *The Seeds of Speech: Language Origin and Evolution* 1996; *The Language Web: The Power and Problem of Words* (Reith lectures) 1997.

* * *

'Look, gee-gees!' said the visitor as, on my third birthday, I showed her my new toy farm, with its miniature horses in their own stable.

'We call them *horses*', I solemnly informed her.

This was reportedly a typical conversation in my early childhood. According to my mother, I was fascinated by the idea that the same object could have different names.

Age five, I tried to write poems, enticed by rhyme:

> O look and behold
> The autumn leaves are turning gold

ran one early effort.

Words were my concern from an early age. I was always asking about them: 'What does *curtainly* mean?' I enquired, age six. Nobody knew. After I'd finally pointed out the strange word to an adult, it turned out I was misreading – and so mispronouncing – *certainly*. I liked arithmetic too – but those numbers didn't have the luscious enchantment of words.

Greek books belonging to my father lured me on in my early teens: I wanted to be able to read all those funny letters. So I leaped at the opportunity to learn Greek at school, especially as other languages, Latin and French, were my favourite subjects.

I found Latin and French fairly easy, and won a prize I didn't know existed, the Winifred Margaret Matthews prize for the girl with the highest mark in GCE A-level Latin (University of London exam board). Greek I found harder, but I always preferred it: the Greeks seemed a much livelier bunch than Caesar with his Gallic wars, and Propertius with his moans about unrequited love.

Then I pulled a book out of the school library which contained an account of how the Frenchman Champollion had deciphered the Egyptian hieroglyphs. I too would decipher a mystery script, I decided, the strange symbols found on ancient Cretan tablets, then known as Linear B. In fact, Linear B was deciphered within a year, by Michael Ventris. The language was an early type of Greek, now known as Mycenaean. Far from this disappointing me, I was delighted. Greek! I was already learning Greek! If I could go to Cambridge University, I could find out more about Mycenaean: John Chadwick, Ventris's collaborator, worked there (Ventris himself was killed in a car crash soon after the decipherment). I was awarded an Exhibition to Girton College, Cambridge, to read classics.

In my final year, I predictably selected the 'philology' option, alongside a number of others who also later went into university teaching, including John Wells (another contributor to this book). Indirectly, I owe a debt to John and several of the other males who took this option. They were sympathetic and patronizing to me as one of the only two females on this course: 'Poor you! It must be very hard being a woman classicist at Cambridge! We men have been learning Latin and Greek for many more years!' I worked hard to overcome this supposed deficit (though it was unfashionable to admit one worked, and I pretended I didn't!), and (much to my surprise and delight!) ended up with the best degree result of the 'philology' students that year.

The philology option covered chunks of comparative philology (Greek, Latin and Sanskrit); the history of Greek and Latin; Greek, Latin and Sanskrit phonology; and Greek and Latin inscriptions, including Mycenaean. It also included an exam paper in linguistics, taught by W. S. Allen, then the Professor of Comparative Philology.

Digidzimaritsu, meaning 'they couldn't get him to move', ran my notes from Professor Allen's first linguistics lecture. This was my attempt at writing down a sequence from Abaza, a Caucasian language. My version contained too many vowels, I discovered, Abaza being one of those strange languages with congealed chunks of consonants. Numerous other fascinating languages were out there, which behaved quite differently from the few I knew, I began to realize.

I read the various books recommended on linguistics, Bloomfield (1933),

Sapir (1921), Saussure (1916), Sturtevant (1917) – though the more I read, the less I felt I understood language. So I applied to go to the USA, to do a graduate course in linguistics.

Well, lucky me! I was awarded an English Speaking Union and Radcliffe College (now part of Harvard) Joint Fellowship, and a Fulbright Grant to pay my fare. So off I went to the USA.

In those days, only lecturers went by air; graduate students slummed it on the ocean. On my trip across on the Cunard liner *Mauretania*, a stewardess woke me each morning, telling me my bath was ready, then breakfast, then deck quoits, then I was tucked up on deck with a book by the deck steward, then lunch. . . . This idyllic existence faded a bit when the sea became horrendously rough about two-thirds of the way over. How that boat creaked! Passengers were forbidden to go on deck as waves crashed down. We had apparently moved into the edge of the disturbance created by hurricane Donna, one of the major hurricanes of those years. (This was 1960.)

Eventually, I arrived safely at Radcliffe Graduate Center. And it was noses to the grindstone at Harvard in Cambridge, Mass. Graduate courses were more supervised, with more tests and continuous written work than I was used to at Cambridge, England. To be told to 'read pages 14–92 before Thursday when you will be tested' was dreary in the extreme, whether the book was Charles Hockett's *Course in Modern Linguistics* (1958) or Kenneth Pike's *Phonemics* (1947). But it was all very useful: left to my own devices, I would undoubtedly have been more selective and less thorough in my reading.

I hadn't expected to work so hard. Partly, this was my choice of courses. As well as the basic linguistic courses, I tried to learn more old languages. Elementary Sanskrit required swallowing up a lot of grammar, and Hittite (ably taught by Calvert Watkins) involved memorization of cuneiform, all those little wedges splayed out at odd angles. I took to smoking – nobody in those days realized puffing at cigarettes was harmful, at least at Harvard. I (briefly) set a sofa on fire as I prepared for a Hittite exam: I'd accidentally stubbed out the cigarette on the cushion beside me, instead of the ashtray.

But it wasn't all slog. I found time to go sailing on the river Charles, to hear Tom Lehrer sing, and to listen to Robert Frost reading his poems. And some courses were inspirational. I was mesmerized by Roman Jakobson, whose course on 'Historical Phonology' was one of the high spots of my Harvard days: 'My friends, everybody treats language change like dive bombs, boom, boom', he would say, staring round the room, his two eyes apparently looking in different directions. One eye was supposedly sightless, but I never discovered which: nor did one of my female friends, who claimed to fancy the great man. She could never decide which side of the room to sit to be noticed. 'But ze dive bomb idea is wrrrong', he continued. 'If you look at ze language at any one time, eet eez nevair neat and tidy. Eet eez like a photo of people as they move around. Some of zem would have one foot up like zis.' Here he stood on one leg, and waved the other around in the air. 'Many people assume zat ze language eez like a posed family photo, but eet eez not. Eet eez always moving.'

Some of his pronouncements were superficially baffling: 'My friends, why did zis Czech sound alter into zat one?', he would ask, scribbling illegible phonetic symbols on the blackboard. 'Ze answer eez simple: zis one eez compact, and ze other eez diffuse', he concluded with triumph, ensuring that his audience would hurry off to libraries to read about acoustic distinctive features, one of the 'in' topics of that time. And his writing on historical phonology (1949) I still find inspiring.

But not all courses were so inspirational. I yawned my way through one of the papers set for the main graduate course in linguistics, taught by Karl Teeter: 'A critical essay identifying and discussing the fundamental similarities and differences in the linguistic work of Leonard Bloomfield and Edward Sapir'. 'Not as insightful as I should have wished' was the polite comment on my pedestrian effort. But I loved writing the next paper required for this course: a book review of a recent major book, either Martinet (1955) or Whorf (1956). I chose Martinet, *Economie des changements phonétiques*. The idea of a search for equilibrium via 'drag chains' and 'push chains' excited me, as these movements seemed to explain those shifting Greek dialects which had been my concern in Cambridge, England. In fact, Sidney Allen had been the first to rouse my interest in Martinet, and I was picking up on ideas he had already put forward in a paper about the Greek vowel system (Allen 1959).

Karl Teeter included Chomsky's *Syntactic Structures* (1957) in our course reading, and provided a synopsis in a lecture. He advised us to go and hear Chomsky talking at MIT: 'It's the "in thing"', he said, 'you might get something out of it – but it's too soon to know whether his ideas will catch on.'

Chomsky's lectures I found incomprehensible: he talked very fast, I wasn't used to his accent, he was in places inaudible, and he often turned his back on the audience, as he scribbled unreadable bits and pieces on the board. Chunks of what he was saying (this is 1960–1) eventually turned up in *Aspects of the Theory of Syntax* (1965). Going along to hear Chomsky was more of a social occasion, a group of friends getting the MTA (subway) from Harvard Square along to MIT, and staring at this velvet-jacketed gabbler waving his arms around. Only when (belatedly) I read Robert Lees's insightful review of *Syntactic Structures* in *Language* (1957) did I begin to realize how important Chomsky's ideas would be for linguistics.

In early 1961 my future was quite undecided. My scholarship to Harvard was for one year, for an MA course. Did I want to apply for further scholarships, to extend my time in the USA to complete a PhD in linguistics? Did I want to come back to GB and do research on Greek? Or what did I want?

At this point, Alison Duke, my ex-tutor at Cambridge, wrote enclosing details of a job I might like to apply for, an Assistant Lectureship in Ancient Greek, at Bedford College, University of London. I reasoned that it would be impolite not to apply, when she had spent time sending me this information, but that I clearly would not be offered such a post, as I would be unable to go for interview, and, in any case, had done far too little postgraduate work to qualify.

Imagine my astonishment when I was offered the job! I was offered it for one year, with a possibility of extension to four years. Well, I thought, what a marvellous opportunity to pay off my debts. (I still owed money to my parents from Girton days. Much is said about current student debts. We all owed quite as much in those days, especially if like me you were an avid book-buyer.)

Once in London, I discovered the heady excitement of scrabbling around in sections of old Greek, and finding out things which maybe nobody had noticed before. My first published article – the first one I ever wrote – was entitled 'Homeric *ánthos*' (1963) (*ánthos* being the classical Greek word for 'flower', as in *chrysanthemum*, *anthology*). I had noticed that *ánthos* certainly could not mean 'flower' in all the passages where it occurred in Homer. It was cognate with Sanskrit *andhas*, something horses ate in the Rig Veda. In several places in Homer, *ánthos* appeared to mean 'upward growth', as opposed to *rízda* 'root, downward growth'. So 'young men having the flower of youth' was a mistranslation; it really meant 'young men having the upward growth of youth', that is, young men beginning to sprout hair on their faces. The phrase 'flower of youth' was (wrongly) treated as a meta-phor, borrowed into Latin, and became a cliché which crept into English poetry, as 'They were in the flower of youth and beauty' (Mary Howitt, 1853), where it could even refer to women: 'A simple maiden in her flower / Is worth a thousand coats of arms' (Tennyson, 1830). I felt I had 'arrived' academically when I found my article referred to in the first fascicle of *Lexicon der frühgriechischen Epos*! My other Greek articles of this era (1964a, 1964b) gave me similar feelings of elation, that I had perhaps illuminated some small corner of Greek prehistory.

At this time, I was fascinated by Greek, the language, and I liked the students personally. But teaching Greek I found dreary. Dreariest of all were tutorials on Greek prose, still obligatory in those days. Most of the time was spent pointing out problems with Greek irregular verbs, and explaining the use of Greek particles. And when it came to marking literature essays, I thought I would scream loudly if I read one more essay about Oedipus from an 18-year-old pouring out her life's hopes and fears (all the Bedford students were women in those days).

I did not worry overmuch, because I knew my post was a four-year one (unrenewable). In those days, it was considered useful to have a turnover of lecturers, though such temporary posts were later abolished. But as the end of my four years drew near, I decided I did not want to continue in classics. So what next?

Linguistics I had kept up in a minor way. I went to London University Linguistics Circle meetings organized at Bedford by Vivian Salmon: I particularly remember a good paper by Jimmy Thorne. I read work on historical linguistics, to back up the research I was doing on Ancient Greek, and I still corresponded with some of my Harvard friends, who told me about their PhD projects.

But I was fairly hazy about my future. One possibility (I thought) might be journalism, because I had friends who were journalists. Some of them gave me the occasional conference to write up, or books to review, and I thoroughly enjoyed the challenge of turning out a readable, snappy account of a conference on, say, computers (which were new in those days), after listening to several hours of lectures. A number of conferences on applied linguistics also came my way, with information on language laboratories, then fairly new.

As the months went by, I applied for various jobs, knowing I had to find some way of existing: academic posts, publishing, journalism were all possibilities, I thought. I almost accepted a job exploring the teaching of Latin in schools (I wrote a correspondence course on O-level Latin and marked O-level Latin exam scripts one year in order to pay for car repairs, and had formed views on how it might be taught).

One of the more interesting jobs I applied for was a Lectureship in Linguistics at the London School of Economics (University of London). I applied, though not particularly hopefully, because I assumed that dozens of qualified people would apply. I didn't hear anything for some months, so assumed that the post had been filled.

Suddenly, I received a summons to an interview at LSE. Norman Denison (head of the Department of Language Studies) told me that LSE would be teaching for a new London University degree in linguistics and a language, and the advertised post was to be the beginning of a major expansion in linguistics.

My linguistics (apart from historical linguistics) was rusty after several years lecturing in Greek, I explained. He said the students would not be arriving for a year. In short, he convinced me that I could keep one jump ahead if I rolled up my sleeves, and started reading.

In order to get my act together on introductory linguistics, I agreed to give a course on the topic at a London evening institute (City Literary Institute). Among the audience were an American couple, psychology lecturers in Tennessee. They quizzed me non-stop about language, then invited me to come and stay with them in USA. 'But I couldn't afford the fare' I replied.

'Write a *book*', they said. 'That's how we manage to globe-trot, we write books! You've already told us there is no "introduction to introductions to linguistics" on the market. *Write* one.'

Could my evening class really turn into a book? I pondered. What publisher would be interested in a plain, clear, short course in linguistics? How about the Teach Yourself series? So I sent off a prospective first chapter and contents outline to the series' publishers (then English Universities Press). To my delight, they decided that they would indeed commission such a book – though for a fixed fee. Their market research suggested the book would sell at most 3,000 copies, they informed me, so they would give me a flat fee of £300. I tried to argue for a percentage royalty, based on advice from publishing friends: the most EUP would agree to was a royalty if book sales exceeded 100,000, an impossible figure.

So I wrote my first book, originally called *General Linguistics*, later just *Linguistics*, which after numerous delays, both in my completion of the manuscript, and in their publishing of it, came out in 1972. (It's still in print, now in its fifth edition, which in its first year sold 7,000 copies.) My general aim in writing it was to bridge the gap between real beginners and the best introduction on the market, at that time John Lyons's *Introduction to Theoretical Linguistics* (1968), which beginning students found hard going.

At LSE, we were the first institution in GB to offer a first degree (or rather half a first degree) in linguistics: linguistics was combined with a language, either French or German. Due to bureaucratic delays other University of London colleges (UC, SOAS) in fact started a year later. Dr Norman Denison, then in charge of the Language Studies Department, unexpectedly took a post abroad, and I was left organizing linguistics at LSE. I remember working every day one year, even on Christmas Day! I tried very hard to arrange for the students to attend lectures elsewhere, for those topics (such as phonetics) for which we did not have expertise at LSE. And our results were excellent! In those early years, our students achieved a greater proportion of first class degrees than any other college, and several of them went on to become teachers of the subject. Jenny Cheshire, one of our earliest intake, is now a Professor at Queen Mary College, University of London, and is the author of one of the earliest books on the sociolinguistic study of morphology (Cheshire 1982). Shula Chiat, a few years later, is now a Lecturer at University College London, and the author of a book about children with language problems (Chiat 2000).

For a time, I tried to continue linguistic work on Ancient Greek (e.g. Aitchison 1976), but eventually I turned to more modern linguistic matters. As student numbers swelled at LSE, I still had a cloud-cuckooland idea that if I found out enough about psycholinguistics, I would discover why language changes. So I agreed to teach psycholinguistics to final year students, in addition to historical linguistics, my main speciality. In order to prepare for this, I arranged to give a University Extension evening course entitled 'Language and Mind'. A large, enthusiastic audience turned up, among them a senior publisher. Eventually, she asked me to a meal at a

Greek restaurant (my favourite type of food, at that time) and asked me if I would consider writing up my lectures as a book. I hesitated.

She repeated the invitation to a Greek meal a few months later. On my fifth quail, and towards the end of our bottle of retsina, I said that if I *were* to write such a book, I had found a good title: 'The Articulate Mammal' from Ogden Nash:

> I find my position as an articulate mammal
> bewildering and awesome.
> Would to God I were a tender apple blawssom.

But, I said, I really couldn't write it unless the advance covered my existing debts (about twice the normal advance at that time). I assumed I was protecting myself from having to write it.

Later that week, I got a phone call: 'You're on, you can have the title and the advance you want!' So, as I was due (at last) a sabbatical term, one term per seven years, I set to work, and wrote it, a chapter a week. My aim was to write an introduction to psycholinguistics from the point of view of a linguist (all previous introductions had been written by psychologists). I particularly wanted to link Chomsky's linguistic ideas with psycholinguistic work by psychologists, since I felt both needed to be properly understood by anyone seriously concerned with 'language and mind'. Psycholinguistics was a fairly small field in those days, and I was reasonably satisfied that I had perused everything of importance!

Once it was published, complete silence followed. Nobody reviewed it, at first. Several months later, an enthusiastic review appeared in *York Papers in Linguistics* (Green 1977.) (Thank you, John Green, that really cheered me up.) Then an American Science publisher spotted it. He bought it for his US label (Universe), and sold the paperback rights on to McGraw-Hill. Then it was named as one of the 'Significant Science Books, 1976–7' by *American Scholar*; as one of the 'Outstanding Academic Books' of the year by *Choice* (American library journal); it was an American Behaviorist book club choice; and eventually (in GB) an Open University set text. *Scientific American*, *Washington Post* and other journals all said encouraging things about it in reviews. In 1998 it came out in a fourth edition, now published by Routledge – though psycholinguistics has exploded to such an extent in the intervening years that I can no longer be sure I have read everything significant.

Then Fontana (the publisher) asked me to edit a new introductory series on linguistics, a series eventually taken over by Cambridge University Press. Fontana asked me to write one of the books myself, eventually *Language Change: Progress or Decay?* (1981), now in its third edition (2001). My metier, I decided, was to write reliable, readable and up-to-date introductions, but to keep my research going by writing articles, whose content could get built into my books.

For *Language Change*, I was writing about my original deep interest, historical linguistics. But by this time, the field had split into two. Traditional historical linguistics dealt with changes in the dim, distant past. Meanwhile, sociolinguists such as William Labov had started to look at changes in progress. I decided to try and pull both strands together in a single book.

But to do that, I myself wanted to explore some changes in progress. I realized that pidgin languages (restricted languages used by people with no common language) changed into creoles (full languages) relatively fast. So I applied for a grant to go to Papua New Guinea, in order to probe into the pidgin (Tok Pisin) which had in several areas become a creole. I was helped enormously by anthropologists who lent me Tok Pisin audio-tapes, and by Peter Mühlhäusler, at that time probably Tok Pisin's foremost scholar (e.g. Mühlhäusler 1979), who generously lent me numerous books and articles.

In Papua New Guinea, I was lucky enough to be given lodgings by the University at Lae among a group of first generation creole speakers. My recordings of their speech formed the basis of a series of articles on creolized Tok Pisin (Aitchison 1989, 1990, 1992, 1996). These also enabled me to hone my own ideas about how language change worked (e.g. Aitchison 1995), and provided sections of my book *Language Change* (1981/2001). And when reviews of the book came out, I was pleased to find comments such as: 'This . . . is the first book I have come across on language change which gives up-to-date references to current research and yet which is not aimed at specialists in linguistics . . . the difficult balancing act between accuracy and simplicity of presentation is deftly managed' (*Journal of Linguistics* 1983).

By now, I had started work on the mental lexicon, the link, I hoped, between language change and psycholinguistics. Various publishers invited me to write books. I proposed my mental lexicon idea to Philip Carpenter, Blackwell's publishing director. He said 'OK, but it's such a minor topic, we wouldn't't allow anyone else except you to write on it.' *Words in the Mind: An Introduction to the Mental Lexicon* was eventually published in 1987, and received some friendly reviews. My favourite ran: ' "Leider nicht von mir" ("wish it were mine") Johannes Brahms regretfully remarked when he first heard Johann Strauss's waltz "An der schönen blauen Donau". I felt quite the same way when I read this book for the first time, and I admire it still' (from *Yearbook of Morphology* 1988). I am now preparing the third edition of that book, whose topic has become an important one within linguistics. I have also continued doing research and writing articles on the lexicon (e.g. Aitchison and Chiat 1981; Aitchison and Straf 1981), some of the recent ones jointly with my talented research assistant Diana Lewis (e.g. Aitchison and Lewis 1995, 1996). And I keep trying to write up a research project of some years ago, on the vocabulary of 11–14-year olds, so far only summarized (Aitchison 2000). My interest in the lexicon is undoubtedly helped by the fact that my long-term partner, now my husband, John Ayto, is a lexicographer, and the author of several books about words (e.g. Ayto 1990, 1993/2000, 1998, 1999).

As time went by, linguistics was discontinued at LSE, except as a subsidiary subject, in spite of excellent exam results from students. LSE decided that at a time of economic hardship, they should concentrate on economics, and discontinue irrelevant extras. At first I moped, like a mother hen without her chickens, as the serious students faded away: I had put so much effort into establishing that course, worked so hard to prepare clear and informative lectures, etc., etc.

Then I cheered up. I could accept far more invitations to lecture in other parts of the world than when I was trodden underfoot by numerous students. Eventually I taught only optional subjects at LSE, mainly to anthropologists, psychologists and sociologists. But that turned out to be a bonus! I got the pick of the bunch: self-selected, really bright students. Linguistics had a reputation for being difficult, so only the cleverest and most hard-working applied.

The anthropologists' interest in language origin led me to start collecting information on the topic, which became the basis for my book *The Seeds of Speech: Language Origin and Evolution* (eventually, CUP 1996, also CUP's Canto imprint 2000).

One day, now in 1992, I sat gloomily at home, contemplating the sad reality of university cuts: I had to write a separate letter for any book which I requested for LSE library costing more than £25. What a waste of time! Then I heard a tinkle-tinkle sound. Not a fairy godmother, but my new cordless phone, with a disembodied voice asking if I would like to be considered for a newly endowed Chair at Oxford University, the Rupert Murdoch Professorship of Language and Communication. I was offered and accepted this post. What a fascinating challenge! Then the BBC asked me to give the 1996 Reith lectures, on the topic of language (Aitchison 1997). Again, what a fascinating challenge! So just as I despaired, it all changed into an exciting new world.

At Oxford, my post is in the Faculty of English Language and Literature – so I am building up knowledge of stylistics (language of literature) and the language of newspapers. I am beginning to write articles on these topics (e.g. Aitchison, Lewis and Naylor 2000) – and I am starting to get ideas about another new book I might write . . .

So what might I have contributed to linguistics in GB? Some things are the same as everybody else's: the organization of a good linguistics programme, care and accuracy in my research, and clarity in my teaching, I hope. Three things, I would claim, are less usual among linguists.

First, I have attempted to link together subsections of linguistics. So many scholars polish their own square inch of ivory (often beautifully), but sometimes fail to explain how their piece of ivory attaches to other pieces.

In my books and teaching, I have tried to present a broader overview, and to link together strands of language that are related.

Second, I have always cared enormously about intelligibility: I often spend hours rearranging a lecture or chapter so it ends up in a clear, coherent order. This passion for clarity started when I was a student. At that time, I resented bitterly having to plough through sludgy and incomprehensible books and articles, when I could be playing tennis, or chatting to friends. In my room at Girton, I had various quotations pinned up on a noticeboard. One was: 'If one is not a genius, it is best to be intelligible' (Anthony Hope, 1894). If I ever get into any position of responsibility, I used to think, I shall make sure that I express things clearly. Much of the linguistics I have read has not been difficult, though sometimes technical. But it has often been badly written, or put in the wrong order. I wanted to help others to get to the kernel of ideas as quickly as possible. I also tried to get across some of the interest and excitement of words, the lusciousness of language, that I discovered as a child. I have, I hope, led some people more quickly into the 'charmed circle' of linguistics than would have happened if they had not been exposed to my books or teaching.

Third, and especially more recently, I have tried to explain to a wider audience what linguistics is all about, and why it is important.

My overall aims, then, have been to find out more about language; to link sections of it together; and to present to others findings and ideas in an interesting and coherent way. A quotation from Joseph Addison comes to mind. He wished 'to make hard Things intelligible, and to deliver what is abstruse of it self in such easy Language as may be understood by ordinary Readers' (Joseph Addison, 1712). Addison was talking about poetry, I'm talking of language about language. I hope I have succeeded, at least some of the time.

REFERENCES

AITCHISON, JEAN, 1963. 'Homeric *ánthos*', *Glotta* 41, 271–8.
AITCHISON, JEAN, 1964a. 'The Achaean homeland: Achaiía or Achaiís?', *Glotta* 42, 19–28.
AITCHISON, JEAN, 1964b. '*Telamōnios Aías* and other patronymics', *Glotta* 42, 132–8.
AITCHISON, JEAN, 1972/1999. *Linguistics*, 1st ed., London: English Universities Press 1972; 5th ed., London: Hodder and Stoughton 1999. Also pub. as *Linguistics: An Introduction*, 2nd ed., London: Hodder and Stoughton 1999.
AITCHISON, JEAN, 1976. 'The distinctive features of ancient Greek', *Glotta* 54, 173–201.
AITCHISON, JEAN, 1976/1998. *The Articulate Mammal: An Introduction to Psycholinguistics*, 1st ed., London: Hutchinson 1976; 4th ed., London and New York: Routledge 1998.
AITCHISON, JEAN, 1981/2001. *Language Change: Progress or Decay?*, 1st ed., London: Fontana 1981; 3rd ed., Cambridge: Cambridge University Press 2001.
AITCHISON, JEAN, 1987/1994. *Words in the Mind: An Introduction to the Mental Lexicon*, 1st ed. 1987, Oxford: Blackwell; 2nd ed., Oxford and New York: Blackwell 1994.
AITCHISON, JEAN, 1989. 'Spaghetti junctions and recurrent routes: some preferred pathways in language evolution', *Lingua* 77, 151–71.

AITCHISON, JEAN, 1990. 'The missing link: the role of the lexicon', in J. Fisiak (ed.), *Historical Linguistics and Philology*, Berlin: Mouton de Gruyter, 11–28.

AITCHISON, JEAN, 1992. 'Relative clauses in Tok Pisin: is there a natural pathway?', in M. Gerritsen and D. Stein (eds), *Internal and External Factors in Linguistic Change*, Berlin: Mouton de Gruyter, 295–316.

AITCHISON, JEAN, 1995. 'Tadpoles, cuckoos and multiple births: language contact and models of change', in J. Fisiak (ed.), *Linguistic Change under Contact Conditions*, Berlin and New York: Mouton de Gruyter, 1–13.

AITCHISON, JEAN, 1996. 'Small steps or large leaps? Undergeneralization and overgeneralization in creole acquisition', in H. Wekker (ed.), *Creole Languages and Language Acquisition*, Berlin: Mouton de Gruyter, 9–31.

AITCHISON, JEAN, 1996/2000. *The Seeds of Speech: Language Origin and Evolution*, Cambridge: Cambridge University Press 1996. Also pub. under Canto imprint, with added introduction, 2000.

AITCHISON, JEAN, 1997. *The Language Web: The Power and Problem of Words. The 1996 BBC Reith Lectures*, Cambridge: Cambridge University Press.

AITCHISON, JEAN, 2000. 'Shuddering halt or sudden spurt? The linguistic development of (pre-)adolescents', in H. W. Kam and A. Pakir (eds), *Recent Developments in Applied Linguistics: A Collection of SAAL (Singapore Association of Applied Linguistics) Lectures*, Singapore: EPB, 97–111.

AITCHISON, JEAN & CHIAT, SHULAMUTH, 1981. 'Natural phonology or natural memory: the interaction between phonological processes and recall mechanisms', *Language and Speech* 24, 311–26.

AITCHISON, JEAN & LEWIS, DIANA, 1995. 'How to handle wimps: incorporating new lexical items as an adult', *Folia Linguistica* 29 (1–2), 7–20.

AITCHISON, JEAN & LEWIS, DIANA, 1996. 'The mental word web: forging the links', in J. Svartvik (ed.), *Words*, KVHAA Konferenser 36, Stockholm: Swedish Academy, 39–47.

AITCHISON, JEAN & STRAF, MIRON, 1981. 'Lexical storage and retrieval: a developing skill?', *Linguistics* 19, 751–95. Repr. in A. Cutler (ed.), *Slips of the Tongue and Language Production*, The Hague: Mouton 1982.

AITCHISON, JEAN, LEWIS, DIANA & NAYLOR, BRONWEN, 2000. ' "Car murder hubby caged" and other murderous headlines', *English Today* 16.1 (January), 23–30.

ALLEN, W. SIDNEY, 1959. 'Some remarks on the structure of Greek vowel systems', *Word* 15, 240–51.

AYTO, JOHN, 1990. *Bloomsbury Dictionary of Word Origins*, London: Bloomsbury.

AYTO, JOHN, 1993/2000. *Bloomsbury Dictionary of Euphemisms*, London: Bloomsbury, 1st ed. 1993; rev. ed. 2000.

AYTO, JOHN, 1998. *Oxford Dictionary of Slang*, Oxford: Oxford University Press.

AYTO, JOHN, 1999. *Twentieth Century Words*, Oxford: Oxford University Press.

BLOOMFIELD, LEONARD, 1933. *Language*. New York: Holt, Rinehart and Winston.

CHESHIRE, JENNY, 1982. *Variation in a British Dialect: A Sociolinguistic Study*, Cambridge: Cambridge University Press.

CHIAT, SHULAMUTH, 2000. *Understanding Children with Language Problems*, Cambridge: Cambridge University Press.

CHOMKSY, NOAM, 1957. *Syntactic Structures*, The Hague: Mouton.

CHOMKSY, NOAM, 1965. *Aspects of the Theory of Syntax*, Cambridge, MA: MIT Press.

GREEN, JOHN, 1977. 'Review of Jean Aitchison, *The Articulate Mammal*', *York Papers in Linguistics* 7, 247.

HOCKETT, CHARLES F., 1958. *A Course in Modern Linguistics*, New York: Macmillan.

JAKOBSON, ROMAN, 1949. 'Principes de phonologie historique', appendix in N. S. Troubetzkoy, *Principes de phonologie*, Paris: Klincksieck.

LEES, ROBERT B., 1957. 'Review of Noam Chomsky, *Syntactic Structures*', *Language* 33, 375–408.

LYONS, JOHN, 1968. *Introduction to Theoretical Linguistics*, Cambridge: Cambridge University Press.

MARTINET, ANDRÉ, 1955. *Economie des changements phonétiques*, Berne: Francke.

MÜHLHÄUSLER, PETER, 1979. *Growth and Structure of the Lexicon of New Guinea Pidgin*, Pacific Linguistics C-52, Canberra: Australian National University.

PIKE, KENNETH, 1947. *Phonemics*, Ann Arbor: University of Michigan Press.

SAPIR, EDWARD, 1921. *Language: An Introduction to the Study of Speech*, New York: Harcourt Brace.

SAUSSURE, FERDINAND DE, 1916. *Cours de linguistique générale*, Paris: Payot.

STURTEVANT, EDGAR H., 1917. *Linguistic Change: An Introduction to the Historical Study of Language*, Chicago: University of Chicago Press,

WHORF, BENJAMIN LEE, 1956. *Language, Thought and Reality: Selected Writings of Benjamin Lee Whorf*, Cambridge, MA: MIT Press.

W. SIDNEY ALLEN

ALLEN, William Sidney, FBA 1971; Fellow of Trinity College, Cambridge, since 1955; *b.* 1918, *m.* 1955 Aenea; *Education:* Christ's Hospital; Trinity College, Cambridge (Classical Scholar); Porson Scholarship, 1939; *Career:* War of 1939–45: RAC and General Staff (Intelligence) (dispatches); Lecturer in Phonetics, 1948–51, and in Comparative Linguistics, 1951–5, School of Oriental and African Studies, University of London; dialect research in India, 1952; Fellow of Rockefeller Foundation, USA, 1953; Professor of Comparative Philology in the University of Cambridge, 1955–82; British Council visitor, University of West Indies, 1959; Linguistic Society of America's Professor, 1961; Collitz Professor, Linguistic Institute, USA, 1962; Ida Beam Lecturer, University of Iowa, 1983; President, Philological Society, 1965–7; Honorary Fellow, Society for Cycladic Studies (Athens), 1977. Chairman, Editorial Board, Cambridge University Press linguistics series, 1969–82; Editor, *Lingua*, 1963–85. *Major Publications: Phonetics in Ancient India*, 1953; *On the Linguistic Study of Languages* (inaugural lecture), 1957; *Sandhi*, 1962; *Vox Latina*, 1965; *Vox Graeca*, 1968 [3rd edition 1987]; *Accent and Rhythm*, 1973.

* * *

My entry into the field of linguistics was through a classical education, and the classical languages continued frequently to provide material for my work.

From an LCC primary school, where no languages were taught, I won a scholarship in 1929 to Christ's Hospital, a charitable foundation originally located in London but by then a public school occupying a splendid site in West Sussex. It is now the wealthiest school in the country, but virtually all its endowments are devoted to enabling poorer scholars to achieve their potential. There I started to learn Latin, and two years later Greek. From the beginning my interests were more linguistic than literary, though we were expected to read vast amounts of the main classical authors. My principal form-master, Derrick Macnutt, was also 'Ximenes', the setter of the fiendish *Observer* cryptic crossword, and was himself a highly skilled composer of Latin and Greek prose and verse, who passed his enthusiasm on to his pupils. This exercise is now, regrettably, largely defunct, but it underpinned one's feeling for the structure, including the metrical patterns, of the languages.

From Christ's Hospital in 1937 I gained a major scholarship in classics to

Trinity College, Cambridge. In those days Part I of the Classical Tripos, occupying two years, consisted almost entirely of translation and composition – simply an extension of one's school work; so that someone who had come up with a major scholarship could be virtually certain of sailing through to a first class in the examination with a minimum of further work. This meant that in my second year I was able to devote most of my time (when not rowing) to attending the classes and doing the reading for Part II, which I was due to take in my third and final year. Of the various specialized options in Part II I naturally chose the language option ('Group E'), which was primarily concerned with the comparative and historical study of Indo-European, and included set texts, for linguistic comment, in Latin, the Greek dialects, and Sanskrit (including Vedic).

My teachers were Professor N. B. Jopson (whom I later succeeded in the Chair of Comparative Philology) and Professor (Sir) Harold Bailey (the Professor of Sanskrit). Jopson, an enthusiastic and encouraging teacher, tended towards the 'Old Curiosity Shop' school of linguistics, though he was thoroughly competent in the essentials of comparative Indo-European (his main specialization had been in Balto-Slavonic, particularly Lithuanian).

Bailey was formidably knowledgeable over the whole Indo-Iranian field, and his lectures on the Vedic texts were models of detailed exposition. But for me the most inspiring and influential part of his teaching was his acquaintance with the relatively new 'laryngeal theory', in fact dating back ultimately to Ferdinand de Saussure's *Mémoire* of 1879. To simplify the matter somewhat – Saussure had been struck in effect by the apparent existence of two types of Indo-European verbal root, the more common involving a structure in which a 'full' (accented) form $*CVRC$ (where $R = a$ 'sonant', i.e. a liquid, nasal or semivowel) alternated with a 'weak' (unaccented) form $*C\underset{\circ}{R}C$ (with a syllabic R), and another, apparently disparate type in which a full $*C\bar{V}C$ alternated with a weak $*C\partial C$ (where $*\partial$ was traditionally posited to account for a correspondence of Greek a to Sanskrit i). The revolutionary proposal by Saussure was that the two types could be brought under the same formula if the long vowel of the second type was analysed as representing a contraction of a short vowel with a following (lost) component functioning in the same role as one of the 'sonants' of the first type, which Saussure therefore termed a 'coefficient sonantique'. So (using Saussure's A for the 'lost' element) $*C\bar{V}C < **CVAC$ and $*C\partial C < **C\underset{\circ}{A}C$: as a corollary $*A$ was later usually indicated as $*\underset{\circ}{\partial}$, implying a consonantal form of the vowel $*\partial$. Since the long vowel of $*C\bar{V}C$ varied in quality, these variations were accounted for by recognizing different values of ∂: in the 'classical' formulation of Emile Benveniste (1935: ch. ix) three such values were posited $(*\partial_1, \partial_2, \partial_3)$, and these could also be used as initials to account for the different qualities of vowel in those roots which were traditionally assumed to lack an initial consonant (so e.g. $*ag- < **\partial_2 eg-$).

As envisaged by Saussure the 'coefficients' were theoretical constructs, though some later scholars, espousing an original unity of Indo-European and Hamito-Semitic ('Nostratic'), notably Albert Cuny and Hermann Möller, were disposed to identify these with the 'laryngals' of the latter family – e.g. the glottal stop and the pharyngal fricatives of Arabic: hence the term 'laryngeal' later applied to the theory.

In 1917 the Czech scholar Bedřich Hrozný had succeeded in deciphering the cuneiform Hittite texts and showing that the language was related to Indo-European. Then in 1927 the Polish scholar Jerzy Kuryłowicz showed that Hittite displayed some hitherto unknown consonants (transcribed with the phonetically suggestive ḫ) in places posited for the coefficients of Saussure's theory. The history of the theory is thus similar to the discovery of the planet Pluto, whose existence had been assumed by Lowell in 1915 to explain certain perturbations in the movement of Uranus, and which later, in 1930, was actually observed in the predicted place.

It was from Kuryłowicz's work, more particularly vol. I (1935) of his *Etudes indo-européennes*, that Bailey had gleaned most of his information on the theory. I was later frequently to meet Kuryłowicz and become an admiring friend of his. I have devoted much space to this subject, since it made a strong impression on me at the time and constituted my first introduction to a 'structural' approach to linguistic material.

In 1939, having done little specific preparation, I took Part I of the Classical Tripos and had no difficulty in gaining a first class. But thereafter my whole career underwent a sea-change.

In the course of my general reading for Part II I had come across references to the 'conservatism' of the modern Icelandic language, from which I had gathered that it has undergone little change since the time of settlement (870–930 AD). I was already becoming somewhat obsessed with the idea of probing the 'actuality' of ancient languages, and was fascinated by the possibility of experiencing such a language in a living form. So in the summer of 1939 I set off with two (non-linguist) friends from Trinity on the then somewhat arduous journey to Iceland by the smallest and cheapest ship of the Iceland Steamship Company. This sailed from Leith and arrived off eastern Iceland after five somewhat nauseous days; it then proceeded round the eastern, northern and western coasts calling at numerous small ports and eventually arriving at the capital, Reykjavík. After exploring the immediate vicinity of the south-west we moved, towards the end of August, to Great Geysir, from where we hired ponies and tents and set off for the uninhabited interior, which in those days involved a complete loss of communication with the outside world. Returning to Geysir in early September, we learned that we were now at war. The Icelanders, unable to afford the war-risks insurance on their ships, had laid them up for the duration, and it was only through the good offices of the Norwegian consul in Reykjavík that we were able to secure a passage on a small Norwegian vessel to Bergen, and thence to Newcastle. From there I was able to return to Cambridge just in time for the beginning of the Michaelmas term.

I now continued reading for Part II of the Tripos, and also took the opportunity of attending classes in phonetics offered by Professor Arthur Lloyd-James, University Professor at the School of Oriental and African Studies in London, who had then been evacuated to Cambridge. This was my first introduction to practical phonetics. But having been a member of the 'Mechanized Cavalry' squadron of the OTC, I was obliged to report to the recruiting office, and during November 1939 I was called up to join an Armoured Corps officer-cadet training unit, the Westminster Dragoons. I then had six months' training in the various aspects of tank warfare, and in May 1940 was commissioned into a battalion of the Royal Tank Regiment.

But shortly after joining my unit I was summoned to the War Office. They had (untypically) heard of my visit to Iceland, and it soon became apparent that, after our defeat in Norway, there were plans to occupy Iceland in order to maintain a northern base, and the services were required of anyone with local knowledge of the country. So I returned to Iceland, as a 'local intelligence officer' attached to the HQ of the 49th (West Riding) Division, which had recently been evacuated from Norway. My duties were pleasingly vague but involved a good deal of travel disguised as 'reconnaissance'. After about a year the Americans took over the main defence of the island, and with the intention of preparing the division for a possible arctic role, a Winter Warfare School was set up in northern Iceland in winter 1941/2. I was sent as HQ representative on the first, instructors' course – which developed more into a training for arctic exploration than a serious military operation. I thoroughly enjoyed it, and in due course returned to my HQ, where I was now a junior staff officer (and incidentally 'instructor in snow living to headquarters personnel' – which inevitably led sometimes to my being called 'The Abominable Snowman').

But in April 1942 we returned to the UK with no clear role. After assorted vicissitudes, in winter 1943 I was given command of a photographic intelligence section being assembled in London to work with General Dempsey's Second Army HQ in the planning of Operation Overlord, the landing in Normandy, in collaboration with a reconnaissance wing of the Royal Canadian Air Force. I continued in this role with the Second Army in Normandy and beyond, and my active war came to an end on Lüneburg Heath on 4 May 1945, from where we were operating when the armistice in north-west Europe was signed there. After various interim sinecures I returned to Cambridge just in time for the Michaelmas term 1945.

After six years away from any academic study I was disinclined to settle down to undergraduate work for a Part II of which I had already absorbed the essentials. I had a lot of time to make up and was, I suppose, though not by choice and not quite in his sense, what F. M. Cornford termed 'a young man in a hurry'. I already had a 'War BA', based on Part I, and I now registered for the PhD. This degree was almost ignored, and even despised, by classical scholars at that time, but I had to be registered for some degree in order to qualify for an ex-service grant. My subject was a study of ancient views (as expressed in Greek, Latin and Sanskrit sources) on various aspects of language. My supervisor was to be one A. J. Beattie, of Sidney Sussex College, an expert on Ancient Greek dialects. When I announced that I would be working on a subject intermediate between classics and linguistics, his discouraging comment was, 'What *is* linguistics? Isn't it just bad philology?' Beattie's main claim to fame was his lifelong refusal to accept the clear evidence (adduced by Ventris and Chadwick) that the language of the Mycenaean Linear B tablets was an early form of Greek (he was, somewhat ironically, nicknamed 'Linear Beattie'); he later became Professor of Greek at Edinburgh. By tacit mutual agreement we saw little of one another, and I duly received my degree in 1949: I had presented my dissertation in September 1948, and my examiners were John Brough (then Professor of Sanskrit in the University of London) and (Sir) Peter Noble (then Professor of Humanity at Aberdeen).

I saw rather little of Jopson during my PhD work, but he knew of my growing interest in general linguistics and phonetics, and mentioned this to J. R. Firth, who had been appointed University Professor of Linguistics at SOAS in 1944 and was Head of the Department of Phonetics and Linguistics there. Firth was in the process of building up the Department, and came to meet me in Cambridge. I subsequently had an interview with the Director of SOAS, Sir Ralph Turner, renowned for his work on the comparative and historical study of the Indo-Aryan languages (he was later, in retirement in 1966, to complete his massive *Comparative Dictionary*). The outcome of these meetings was that I was offered a Lectureship in Phonetics at SOAS as from September 1948. My knowledge of the subject at that time was minimal, but the department provided intensive training in both the theoretical and practical aspects of linguistics and phonetics. At the same time I took the opportunity of extending my knowledge into the modern Indo-Aryan field by attending classes in Hindi.

A close colleague of mine at that time, a fellow trainee, was Robert ('Bobby') Robins, with whom I shared a room at SOAS for the next seven years. As my phonetic knowledge grew, I revised the part of my PhD dissertation concerned with the work of the Sanskrit phoneticians in the light of modern phonetics. The outcome was my first book, *Phonetics in Ancient India* (1953a), which constituted volume I of the London Oriental Series. In turn, the section of this (3.10ff) on 'Word and Morpheme Junction' I later (1962) developed into a more technical full-length monograph under the title of *Sandhi*.

At SOAS in those years one was entitled, and encouraged, to spend one year in four on study leave abroad. I had decided to make a study of the various Rajasthani dialects, largely unwritten, and to this end I was funded to engage, for the academic year 1950–1, a Brahmin from the city of Bundi, a speaker of one of the less well-known dialects, Hāṛautī, who was to work with me as my 'informant'. I then spent the calendar year 1952 in India, extending my studies into the other main dialects, principally Mārwārī and Mewāṛi, aided by a rather cumbersome tape-recording apparatus ('Sound-mirror'). Fieldwork of this type was then a normal part of a linguist's training and research – in fact there was a good deal of overlap between the work of linguists and social anthropologists. In a general way my visit was fascinating, and I retain vivid memories of my time amongst the people, villages and towns of the Indian desert (long before its recent invasion by tourism). Linguistically, however, the dialects presented rather little of excitement, being on the whole typical of what one might have expected in a modern Indo-Aryan language located geographically between Gujarati and Hindi, with some influence from Sindhi in the north-west. However, I did produce a few articles on various aspects of the dialects, and I might single one out as of more general interest – a kind of latter-day 'Grassmann's Law', in my 'Aspiration in the Hāṛautī nominal', published in a Special Volume of the Philosophical Society entitled *Studies in Linguistic Analysis* (1957c). Like my colleagues at that time, I had been considerably influenced by Firth's 'prosodic' approach to phonology (e.g. Firth 1948), which emphasized the syntagmatic as against the paradigmatic aspects of sound-structure, and I employed this, perhaps to excess, in my article. A more traditional description of the phenomenon appeared in Allen (1957b) and more fully in (1977).

Later a Cambridge research student from Oriental Studies largely followed my footsteps in Rajasthan, though his interests were more in the oral literature than on the linguistic side: Dr J. D. Smith is now University Lecturer in Sanskrit in Cambridge. I handed my recordings over to him, and parts of the open-reel paper tapes have been successfully transferred to modern cassettes.

Soon after my return from India I was contacted by the Rockefeller Foundation, which was then fostering interest in Indian studies amongst American scholars. The idea was for me to attend as an observer at the graduate Linguistic Institute organized by the Linguistic Society of America being held in summer 1953 at the University of Indiana in Bloomington. I was given a fellowship to finance my visit both there and, more briefly, at a rival Institute held that year at Ann Arbor, Michigan. I was also given ample funds for visits to other universities – UCLA, Berkeley, Chicago, Cornell, Harvard and Yale. It was hoped that my visits would help to alert American scholars to the opportunities for linguistic research in the Indian field. In turn I had the opportunity of meeting and establishing personal relations with many of the leaders of pre-Chomsky American linguistics, including Bernard Bloch, Murray Emeneau, Mary Haas, Robert A. Hall Jr, Zellig Harris, Charles Hockett, Harry Hoijer, Martin Joos, John Lotz, Kenneth

Pike, Tom Sebeck, George Trager, and the Voegelins, as well as fellow visiting scholars, including E. M. ('Bob') Uhlenbeck (from Holland) and H. J. Uldall (from Denmark, the close associate of Louis Hjelmslev, founder of the 'glossematic' school).

For my own part, I had felt that the most useful purpose to which I could put my Rajasthani material would be in the field of comparative Indo-Aryan studies. My idea was that one might compare these and other modern dialects to reconstruct earlier stages of the language, in the same way as one compared the earlier Indo-European languages, but with the difference that here we already knew the answers whereby our hypotheses could be tested, since we had continuous records, from Old Indian (Sanskrit/Vedic), through the Middle Indian Prakrits and the 'Apabhraṃśas'. I was able to experiment with this approach, with some enlightening results, in a few articles (e.g. 1953b: 66ff, 106ff, and later particularly 1978a: 92ff).

In connection with this work I had considerable contact with the Norwegian scholar Georg Morgenstierne, who had worked on the Kafiri dialects of the Indo-Iranian borderlands, which exhibited certain characteristics typical neither of Iranian nor Indo-Aryan but rather of an assumed earlier Indo-Iranian unity. His highly readable reports (1926, 1932) had already provided me with a role-model and inspiration for fieldwork in remote areas before I set out for Rajasthan.

With a view to this proposed line of work I had already in 1951 persuaded the university to change the title of my lectureship from Phonetics to Comparative Linguistics. This soon turned out to be something of a prophetic move. In 1954 Jopson, who would have been due to retire in 1957, decided to retire two years early, and the Chair of Comparative Philology at Cambridge was advertised. At that time I would not have considered myself as a serious candidate for the post. I was still young by Cambridge standards (36), and moreover six years had been spent away from academic work and a further seven away from the traditional comparative-historical field; and I had a pretty thin record of publication, little of it immediately relevant to the post. However, I was encouraged by Sir Ralph Turner to put in an application; he was one of the Electors to the Chair and John Brough was another (later, on Bailey's retirement from the Sanskrit Chair at Cambridge in 1967, I was one of the Electors who appointed Brough!). In 1955, to my astonishment, I was elected – I could only assume that the university felt a new broom was needed and they were prepared to take a risk.

So in October I moved to Cambridge, and to a fellowship at my old college. I was of course responsible for continuing the necessary teaching for the existing Part II syllabus, ably supported by my colleague John Chadwick, of Linear B fame. But at the same time I was determined to remedy the existing situation in Cambridge by providing what I saw as the essential underpinning of this and other similar 'philological' syllabuses by imparting to these some elements of general linguistics and phonetics. As the only representative of these disciplines I was giving the basic lectures, open to all relevant faculties, which were well attended by students (and occasional staff) from Classics, Modern and Medieval Languages, Oriental Studies and Anthropology. Conspicuous by their absence were any representatives of English. However, I could not continue alone to provide all the necessary teaching in addition to the traditional comparative philology. It was some time, though, before this position was improved.

On my arrival back in Cambridge I was asked to supervise the work of a commencing research student in the Classical Faculty – John Lyons, who had in mind a semantic study of intellectual terminology in Plato. Influenced by the work of J. R. Firth[1] – notably his article 'The technique of Semantics' (1935) – which sought to define the meanings of words in terms of their 'privileges of occurrence' with other words, I suggested that Lyons might start out along this 'collocational' line. This he did with great assiduity, but after some time we both realized that in one important respect we were at something of an impasse. He had a mass of material, but I was unable to suggest how formally to connect items occurring in different grammatical structures which one intuitively felt to belong together, and so to bring the material into manageable shape. In 1956 I saw a pre-print of Noam Chomsky's first major work, his *Syntactic Structures* published in 1957. It seemed to me that this, with its transformational-generative approach, might provide a solution to Lyons's problem – and so it proved to be. He successfully adapted and refined Chomsky's basic ideas to his own ends, his dissertation was duly completed in 1961 and was published in a revised form by the Philological Society in 1963.

In 1957 Lyons was appointed to my former Lecturership at SOAS, where he came under the supervision of Robins for the rest of his PhD work. Meanwhile I had been lobbying members of the General Board at Cambridge with a view to establishing posts in linguistics and phonetics here, and in 1961 Lyons was appointed to a University Lecturership in General Linguistics, and during the three years up to 1964 (when he was elected to the chair of General Linguistics at Edinburgh), he succeeded in putting the subject on a firm footing in Cambridge. A post in phonetics had also been established, and plans were afoot for the formation of a Department of Linguistics within the Faculty of Modern and Medieval Languages, overseen by an interfaculty committee, one of whose members, (Sir) Edmund Leach (Reader in Social Anthropology 1957–72, Professor 1972–8), was a particularly influential supporter of developments in linguistics (by contrast, one of the most entrenched opponents of our plans was Dorothy Whitelock, Professor of Anglo-Saxon 1959–69). For a long time the committee had been convinced of the need for a Chair of Linguistics, but this was long in coming. I suppose in some ways I was my own worst enemy in this connection, since I had been teaching the subject ever since my return to Cambridge, and it was difficult to persuade the General Board of the difference between traditional comparative philology and modern linguistics (including phonetics). Only after a quarter of a century, in 1980, was an election made, and under the able leadership of Professor Peter Matthews the subject and the department have flourished.

I return now to a rather more detailed account of some of my own work. In the months before my return to the UK, I had the opportunity of working on one of the more exciting projects of my career. Sir Harold Bailey had encountered a certain Major Huseyin Kumuz [q'ə́məz], a former Circassian cavalryman, a native speaker of Abaza, a member of the north-western group of Caucasian languages, closely allied to Abkhaz and to Kabardian. Bailey's main interest was in the fact that these languages reportedly had certain suggestive resemblances in their phonological systems to the more recent ideas about Proto-Indo-European, which posited an increase in the number of consonants (notably the 'laryngeals') and a diminution in the number of vowels, as proposed, for example, in Winfred Lehmann's *Proto-Indo-European Phonology* of 1952. However, as Bailey himself was the first to acknowledge, he was an 'eye-philologist' with no great phonetic ability. Consequently he was baffled by the complexities of Abaza, and asked Eugénie Henderson (University Reader in Phonetics, later Professor, at SOAS) if she would care to take on the task. She was, however, otherwise occupied at the time and passed Kumuz over to me. I obtained funding from SOAS to engage him to work with me for 100 hours, and we set about the task of analysis.

In tackling this I had some advantage in having worked earlier (1950) on the phonetics of Eastern Armenian. This is, of course, an Indo-European language, but (like the Iranian Ossetic) has acquired a phonological system closely similar to those of South Caucasian, more particularly in regard to glottalized consonants.

Kumuz proved to be a perfect informant – straightforward, not inclined to offer his own explanations, and with extremely clear diction. It was also an advantage that he could not write his language (there is a Russian-based orthography, but it is structurally inadequate in several respects). At the end of the allotted time I had succeeded in establishing the phonology and basic morphology, and in 1956 my results were published in *TPhS*. Among the more striking features was the number of distinct consonant phonemes (64, including 'laryngeals' galore), by contrast with a minimal vowel system (at most 2, 'open' /a/ and 'close' /ə/), and the verbal structure. There is no system of cases in the noun (by contrast with their proliferation in the north-eastern Caucasus). Each noun belongs to a particular class ('gender') having a characteristic marker (usually a single consonant) which appears in the (sentence-final) verb and by its place therein indicates the grammatical function of the noun to which it refers. By way of illustration one might take the verb form $y.g^{y}.s.z.d.m.l.rə́.t.d.$ (with points indicating morpheme divisions) – 'I couldn't get them to give it to her', i.e. 'it.*neg¹*.I.*pot*.them.*neg²*.her.*caus*."give".*aor*', in which the actual verbal root is simply *t*. The complex is rendered pronounceable by the insertion of 'anaptyctic' vowel sounds of predictable position and quality. The markers refer in this example to the nouns *a.lá* 'the.dog', *á.cʸ'.kʷ'.n.cʷakʷa* 'the.boy.*pl*' and *a.phʷə́spa* 'the.girl' occurring earlier in the sentence.

While I was preparing my article for press there was published in Moscow a monograph by one A. N. Genko, *Abazinskij Jazyk* (1955). Genko had lived in the Caucasus during the 1930s, but had refused to follow the party line in linguistic matters and his work had long remained unpublished. He died in the siege of Leningrad, but his manuscript survived and was now published in the relatively liberalized linguistic atmosphere of the 1950s. I awaited its appearance with some trepidation, since my own study had been based on the speech of a single informant, long separated from his fellow speakers. But to my surprise and relief Genko's account agreed with my own down to the smallest details (e.g. the systematically surprising absence of a pulmonic, as opposed to glottalic, palatalized uvular plosive) – a tribute to the linguistic representativeness and retentiveness of my informant. I later (1960) published a review of Genko's book; in 1965(b) I also published, in a Caucasological journal, a text with analysis and translation of a 'Nart' folk-take recited by Kumuz: another such text remains unpublished (both have been transferred to cassettes from the original shellac discs produced in the SOAS phonetics laboratory).

In my own 1956 article (170ff) I had suggested that, albeit by a somewhat innovative phonological approach, it might be possible to reduce the vowel system to one, and there are indications in Genko's work that he was also thinking along these lines. In 1965(c) I published an article elaborating this idea. Hardly surprisingly it was received with scepticism in some quarters, amongst others by Roman Jakobson (as contravening his principles of binary oppositions) and Oswald Szemerényi (out of simple ignorance of the facts). But among those who have actually worked on the languages of the north-western Caucasus the idea has occurred independently with remarkable frequency: thus, apart from Genko on Abaza, Prince Trubetz-koy on Adyghe (1939: 87), Hans Vogt on Ubykh (1963: 22ff) and Aert Kuipers on Kabardian (in this last writer's words [1960: 47], 'The notation with ə somehow misses, at every step, the "genius of the language"').

In the following years some of the remarkable features of this language provided examples to enliven my lectures on other subjects, and one of my pupils, George Hewitt, became sufficiently 'hooked' to enrol at the University of Tbilisi and to visit the north-western Caucasus – subsequently marrying an Abkhazian fellow-student and now occupying the Chair of Caucasian Languages at SOAS.

After taking my Chair at Cambridge, I followed the then customary practice of delivering an inaugural lecture, in March 1957, under the title *On the Linguistic Study of Languages*. It was published in that year by the University Press and was subsequently reprinted elsewhere (1966, 1973). It took as its leitmotiv the concluding words of Saussure's *Cours de linguistique générale*: 'Linguistics has but one proper subject – the language-system viewed in its own light and for its own sake.' Its polemical tone was not to everyone's liking. One sentence in particular seemed scandalous in some quarters, namely that 'There are no facts in linguistics until the linguist has made them.' But the need for such an uncompromising form of expression in the Cambridge of that era has been well recognized by John Lyons in particular (1991: 48f; cf. Allen 1966b: 4).

During my tenure of the Chair I published a score or so of articles mainly concerned with new approaches to problems of Indo-European phonology, with occasional excursions into fields of very marginal interests, such as Aegean cartography and Icelandic Bibles. I also continued to be attached to the idea of 'actualizing' ancient languages in the sense of a practical reconstruction of their phonetics. The first of my books devoted to this subject, *Vox Latina* (1965a), found a ready audience amongst classical schoolteachers in particular, and was followed by its companion *Vox Graeca* in 1968. In subsequent editions both books seem to have established themselves as the standard reading on these matters in schools and universities. A particular source of satisfaction to me was the publication in 2000 of an excellent Modern Greek translation of the third edition of *Vox Graeca* by the Aristotelean University of Thessaloniki – satisfying because traditionally the Greeks had adopted a glottocentric attitude to the subject, in the sense of pronouncing Ancient Greek literature in the Modern Greek manner – to the complete disruption of the original phonetic and metrical textures. For this gratifying development I have largely to thank my former pupil Anastasios ('Tasos') Christidis, now Professor of Linguistics at Thessaloniki.

The metrical aspects of ancient literature had in fact always held a prominent place in my thinking, in so far as they reflected the phonological patterns of the languages; and it was suggested that I might bring together my 'prosodic' writings (in both the metrical and phonological senses of the term) into a single volume of reprints. But I preferred, for reasons explained in detail in a preface, to write a completely new and substantial book, *Accent and Rhythm* (1973). It appeared as volume 12 in the Cambridge Studies in Linguistics, which had been founded a few years earlier by Michael Black, of Cambridge University Press, and myself (I was Chairman of the Editorial Board from 1969 to 1982, in which time 37 volumes had appeared).

In 1982 the university was offering an attractive early retirement package to any of its officers who wished to take advantage of it. I had already been occupying the Chair for 27 years, and I decided to take up the offer (though my Fellowship at Trinity continues for life, and I have been residing there since my wife's death in 1996). The Chair was held 'on ice' until 1985, when I would have been due to retire normally, and was then readvertised (unlike the Chair of Sanskrit, which was suppressed after the death of John Brough in 1984). In 1985 my colleague Robert Coleman was elected to the Chair, and it is now occupied by a former pupil of us both, Geoffrey Horrocks.

In my retirement I also returned to my old love of Modern Icelandic, with frequent nostalgic visits to that country. Compared with their violent manifestations in a language like Abaza, the phonological distinctions of Icelandic are of a more subtle kind, and have tended to be described in rather impressionistic terms: in an article of 1995 I attempted to give a more down-to-earth characterization of some of these.

In 1963 I had been invited to become an editor of the international journal *Lingua*, in succession to A. W. de Groot, with Anton Reichling and E. M. Uhlenbeck as co-editors. I retired from this position in 1985.

From 1965 to 1967 I was President of the Philological Society (having earlier been its Secretary for Publications). In this capacity I revived the custom of delivering a Presidential Address, under the title of 'Prosody and prosodies in Greek' (1966a), in which I proposed a hypothesis about patterns of (non-phonemic) stress in Ancient Greek. Whilst not universally accepted, it has been widely agreed that this 'most revolutionary enquiry' (in the words of *Current Trends*: Householder & Nagy 1972: 745ff) provides, if correct, an immediate and simple solution to a number of apparently unconnected restrictions on word-boundaries ('bridges') in a variety of spoken Greek metres. This was further developed in some detail in my *Accent and Rhythm* (1973: 274–334). It provides an explanation of, amongst others, the notorious 'Porson's Law' – named after Richard Porson, the great classical scholar (Fellow of Trinity 1782–92) – of which it was once said, 'Yet was no "law" human or divine ever so isolated or unintelligible.' This application of my hypothesis was particularly gratifying to me personally because as an undergraduate in 1939 I had been awarded the university's Porson Scholarship in Classics, and breaches of the 'Law' had been considered particularly reprehensible in the days of one's schoolboy compositions (though Porson himself had committed such breaches as an undergraduate!).

In 1971 I was elected a Fellow of the British Academy. At that time there was no section devoted to linguistics, and my election was due largely to the efforts of Sir Harold Bailey, supported by the Oriental and classical sections, in which areas most of my work had been conducted. After my election I was asked by the Secretary to advise Council on the possible development of a special linguistics section, to consist initially of philologists and other appropriate scholars seconded from other sections. The first Fellow to be elected specifically to the new section was John Lyons in 1973. In 1974 the Academy elected as Corresponding Fellows Roman Jakobson,

Jerzy Kuryłowicz (both long overdue) and Noam Chomsky. The present Section H4 (Linguistics and Philology) now numbers 31 members (plus 7 'secondary' members from the sections of their 'primary allegiance').

NOTE

1 For an external view of Firth's wide-ranging influence on the 'London School' see particularly Langendoen (1968).

REFERENCES

ALLEN, W. SIDNEY, 1950. 'Notes on the phonetics of an Eastern Armenian speaker', *TPhS* 180–206.

ALLEN, W. SIDNEY, 1953a. *Phonetics in Ancient India*, London Oriental Series, vol. 1, Oxford: Oxford University Press (repr. 1961, 1965).

ALLEN, W. SIDNEY, 1953b. 'Relationship in comparative linguistics', *TPhS* 52–108.

ALLEN, W. SIDNEY, 1956. 'Structure and system in the Abaza verbal complex', *TPhS* 127–76.

ALLEN, W. SIDNEY, 1957a. *On the Linguistic Study of Languages* (inaugural lecture), Cambridge: Cambridge University Press (repr. with foreword in *Five Inaugural Lectures*, ed. P. Strevens, Oxford: Oxford University Press, 1966, and in *Edinburgh Course in Applied Linguistics*, I, Oxford: Oxford University Press, 1973.

ALLEN, W. SIDNEY, 1957b. 'Some phonological characteristics of Rājasthānī', *BSOAS* xx (in honour of Sir Ralph Turner), 5–12.

ALLEN, W. SIDNEY, 1957c. 'Aspiration in the Hāṛautī nominal', *Studies in Linguistic Analysis*, Philological Society, 68–86.

ALLEN, W. SIDNEY, 1960. 'Review of Genko 1955', *Phonetica* 5, 212–17.

ALLEN, W. SIDNEY, 1962. *Sandhi: The Theoretical, Phonetic and Historical Bases of Word-Junction in Sanskrit* (Janua Linguarum, series minor, Nr. 17), The Hague: Mouton. (reprinted 1972).

ALLEN, W. SIDNEY, 1965a. *Vox Latina: A Guide to the Pronunciation of Classical Latin*, Cambridge: Cambridge University Press (2nd ed. 1978).

ALLEN, W. SIDNEY, 1965b. 'An Abaza text', *Bedi Kartlisa* xix–xx, 159–72.

ALLEN, W. SIDNEY, 1965c. 'On one-vowel systems', *Lingua* xiii.2, 111–24.

ALLEN, W. SIDNEY, 1966a. 'Prosody and prosodies in Greek' (presidential address), *TPhS* 107–48.

ALLEN, W. SIDNEY, 1966b. See 1957a.

ALLEN, W. SIDNEY, 1968. *Vox Graeca: A Guide to the Pronunciation of Classical Greek*, Cambridge: Cambridge University Press (2nd ed. 1974, 3rd ed. 1987).

ALLEN, W. SIDNEY, 1973. *Accent and Rhythm: Prosodic Features of Latin and Greek: A Study in Theory and Reconstruction* (Cambridge Studies in Linguistics, vol. 12), Cambridge: Cambridge University Press.

ALLEN, W. SIDNEY, 1974. See 1968.

ALLEN, W. SIDNEY, 1977. 'The PIE aspirates: phonetic and typological factors in reconstruction', *Studia Linguistica et Philologica* 4 (offered to Joseph Greenburg), Saratoga, 237–47.

ALLEN, W. SIDNEY, 1978a. 'The PIE velar series: neogrammarian and other solutions in the light of attested parallels', *TPhS*, Philological Society Neogrammarian Volume, 87–110.

ALLEN, W. SIDNEY, 1978b. See 1965a.

ALLEN, W. SIDNEY, 1987. See 1968.

ALLEN, W. SIDNEY, 1995. 'On "tenseness" in Modern Icelandic', *TPhS* 93.1, 1–16.

ALLEN, W. SIDNEY, 2000. *Vox Graeca: i proforá tis Ellinikís tin klasikí epochí* (Modern Greek translation of Allen 1987 by Maria Karali and G. M. Parasoglou), Aristotelean University of Thessaloniki.

BENVENISTE, EMILE, 1935. *Origines de la formation des noms en indo-européen*, Paris: Adrien-Maisonneuve.

CHOMSKY, NOAM, 1957. *Syntactic Structures* (Janua Linguarum, No. IV), The Hague: Mouton.
FIRTH, JOHN RUPERT, 1935. 'The technique of Semantics', *TPhS* 36–72.
FIRTH, JOHN RUPERT, 1948. 'Sounds and prosodies', *TPhS* 127–52.
GENKO, A. N., 1955. *Abazinskij Jazyk: grammatičeskij očerk narečija Tapanta,* Moscow: Akademija Nauk SSSR.
HOUSEHOLDER, FRED W. & NAGY, GREGORY, 1972. 'Greek', in Thomas A. Sebeok (ed.), *Current Trends in Linguistics,* vol. 9 (*Linguistics in Western Europe*), The Hague: Mouton, 735–816.
KUIPERS, AERT H., 1960. *Phoneme and Morpheme in Kabardian* (Janua Linguaram, No. VIII), The Hague: Mouton.
KURYŁOWICZ, JERZY, 1927. 'ə indo-européen et ẖ hittite', in *Symbolae Grammaticae in honorem Ioannis Rozwadowski,* vol. I, Cracow: Polska Akademja.
KURYŁOWICZ, JERZY, 1935. *Etudes indo-européennes,* vol. 1, Cracow: Polska Akademja.
LANGENDOEN, E. TERENCE, 1968. *The London School of Linguistics: A Study of the Linguistic Theories of B. Malinowski and J. R. Firth* (MIT Research Monograph No. 46), Cambridge, MA: MIT Press.
LEHMANN, WINFRED P., 1952. *Proto-Indo-European Phonology,* Austin: University of Texas Press and Linguistic Society of America.
LYONS, JOHN, 1963. *Structural Semantics* (Publication of the Philological Society, xx), Oxford: Blackwell.
LYONS, JOHN, 1991. *Natural Language and Universal Grammar,* Cambridge: Cambridge University Press.
MORGENSTIERNE, GEORG, 1926. *Report on a Linguistic Mission to Afghanistan,* Oslo: Instituttet for Sammenlignende Kulturforskning, série CI-2.
MORGENSTIERNE, GEORG, 1932. *Report on a Linguistic Mission to North-western India,* Oslo: Instituttet for Summenlignende Kulturforskning, série CIII-1.
SAUSSURE, FERDINAND DE, 1879. *Mémoire sur le systeme primitif des voyelles dans les langues indo-européennes,* Leipzig: B. G. Teubner.
SAUSSURE, FERDINAND DE, 1916. *Cours de linguistique générale,* Lausanne and Paris: Payot.
TRUBETZKOY, PRINCE NIKOLAI, 1939. *Grundzüge der Phonologie (TCLP* 7), Prague: Cercle Linguistique de Prague.
TURNER, SIR RALPH, 1966. *A Comparative Dictionary of the Indo-Aryan Languages,* Oxford: Oxford University Press.
VOGT, HANS, 1963. *Dictionnaire de la langue oubykh,* Oslo: Instituttet for Sammenlignende Kulturforskning, série B:LII.

R. E. ASHER

ASHER, Ronald E., Professor Emeritus, University of Edinburgh, since 1993; *b.* 1926; *m.* 1960 Chin, 2 s; *Education:* King Edward VI GS Retford, Notts; University College London; University of London BA 1950, PhD 1955; University of Edinburgh DLitt 1992; *Career:* Assistant of French, UCL 1951–3; Lecturer, Linguistics and Tamil, SOAS, University of London, 1953–65; Senior Lecturer, Department of Linguistics, University of Edinburgh, 1965–70, Reader 1970–7, Professor of Linguistics 1977–93, Dean of Faculty of Arts 1986–9, Vice-Principal 1990–3, Curator of Patronage 1991–3, Director, Centre for Speech Technology Research, 1994, Hon. Fellow, Faculty of Arts, 1993–9, 2001–; Visiting Professor of Tamil, University of Chicago, 1961–2, of Linguistics, University of Illinois, 1967, of Tamil and Malayalam, Michigan State University, 1968, of Linguistics, University of Minnesota, 1969, of Dravidian Studies, Collège de France, Paris, 1970, of Linguistics and International Communication, International Christian University, Tokyo, 1994–5, of 20th-Century Malayalam Literature, Mahatma Gandhi University, Kottayam, 1995–6; Fellow of the Kerala Sahitya Akademi (Kerala Academy of Letters) 1983, Gold Medal of the Akademi for distinguished services to Malayalam language and literature; FRAS 1961; Medal of the Collège de France 1970; FRSE 1991; President International Association of Tamil Research 1983–90; Council, Philological Society, 1980–6, 1989–94, 1996–2001; Member of the General Council, Tamil Sahitya Academy, Chennai, India, 2000–. *Major Publications: A Tamil Prose Reader* (with R. Radhakrishnan) 1971; *Aspects de la littérature en prose dans le sud de l'Inde* 1972; *Some Landmarks in the History of Tamil Prose* 1973; '*Me Grandad 'ad an Elephant!'* (trans. from Malayalam of three novels by V. M. Basheer) 1980; *Towards a History of Phonetics* (ed. with E. J. A. Henderson) 1981; *Tamil* 1982; *Malayāḷa bhāṣā sāhitya paṭhanaṇṇaḷ* (Malayalam: *Studies on Malayalam Language and Literature*) 1989; *National Myths in Renaissance France* 1993; *Scavenger's Son* (trans. from Malayalam of novel by Thakazhi Sivasankara Pillai) 1993; *Atlas of the World's Languages* (ed. with C. Moseley) 1994; *The Encyclopedia of Language and Linguistics* (ed.-in-chief) 1994; *Concise History of the Language Sciences* (ed. with E. F. K. Koerner) 1995; *Malayalam* 1997; V. M. Basheer, *Svatantryasamara kathakaḷ* (Basheer, *Stories of the Freedom Movement*; ed.) 1998; *Baṣīr: malayāḷattinṟe sargavismayam* (Malayalam: *Critical Essays on the Novels and Stories of V. M. Basheer*) 1999.

* * *

There's a divinity that shapes our ends,
Rough-hew them how we will.

This is to say that there is some obscurity about how I come to have spent
most of my academic life in linguistics. Certainly chance played a role at a
number of points along the way to this destination, and long-term
planning has not been a defining feature of my career development. I
recall enjoying doing exercises in the village school in the parsing of
sentences – not unlike what I was to know in a slightly more sophisticated
form many years later as IC-analysis – as part of the preparation for the
scholarship examination (the ancestor of what was later to be called the
eleven-plus), but it would be exceedingly romantic to claim this as the
beginning of a passion for language. The best parts of life at grammar
school were mathematics, literature (English, Latin, French and German)
and – once we moved beyond 1066 and all that into the study of such
topics as benevolent despotism, revolutionary France and Napoleon, and
reform movements in the nineteenth century – history. There was some
study of English syntax in preparation for the School Certificate examinations, and something slightly akin to semantics in a non-examined course
on 'clear thinking' in the sixth form. Otherwise, any language study there
was merely a means to an end – that of the better appreciation of
literature. In my pre-sixth-form years the strongest fascination was for
mathematics and I proposed to continue the subject up to Higher School
Certificate and perhaps at university. Unfortunately, the idea proved too
impractical. In those days, on a supposedly decreasing scale of intellectual
challenge, one studied classics, modern languages, or science, and one was
expected to set out clearly on one of these paths by the age of 12 or 13.
Mixing languages and mathematics in the most senior forms was unheard
of, and I soon found that timetable problems made the idea unworkable.
Thus it was that my proposed study of advanced mathematics was to be
done only vicariously by my two sons, David and Michael, when they
went to Cambridge.

   Undergraduate study at University College, London, in French, with
some German (which provided the great good fortune of being taught by
(Elizabeth) Mary Wilkinson (1909–2001)), found me taking no classes in
linguistic analysis apart from a compulsory paper on the history of the
development of Latin into Modern French, for which the important sources
were Nyrop, Brunot and Bruneau, Wartburg, and Mildred K. Pope, and the
emphasis was therefore strongly philological. However, this subject and
medieval French were taught by Brian Woledge, one of several fine teachers
in the department of which he was head, and he pointed those who were
interested to a broader study of language that went beyond the strict
confines of the syllabus. This led some of us to a familiarity with Whitney,
Sapir and Bloomfield among others. Any attraction they had, which was

considerable, was nevertheless insufficient to divert me from my plan to work for a PhD in Renaissance French, with a double focus on historical writing and poetry.

During my first year of research I also took steps to improve the quality of my spoken French by studying for the UCL Certificate in the Phonetics of French. As anyone who had the privilege of knowing Hélène Coustenoble (1894–1962) will know, this experience was not only valuable, but quite unique. The practical side of the course was dominant over the theoretical, but one did learn something about Jonesian phonemics, for, despite her assertion 'Je m'intéresse à ce qui *est*', Coustenoble was not indifferent to theoretical issues, provided that the theory did not involve an attack on Daniel Jones's work. Though he had by that time retired, arrangements were made by Coustenoble for favoured students to meet her hero. The French phonetics course also brought one into contact with her junior colleagues and the pleasure of being taught by A. C. Gimson (1917–85) and (Emma) Marguerite Chapallaz (1906–91). The interest in phonetics that this course generated stayed with me and gave me the confidence 30 years later to edit a book jointly with Eugénie Henderson (1914–85) on the history of phonetics, and 20 years later still to join John Laver in his project for an encyclopedic dictionary of speech. Performance classes came into their own on such occasions as when I decided that a laureation address in honour of the singer and writer Anne Lorne Gillies should be delivered in Gaelic, a language which, to my shame, I have never studied. Ear-training classes proved invaluable when I embarked on linguistic fieldwork in South India.

As I progressed through the second year of my research I began to feel that some employment that went beyond that of a part-time temporary assistantship would be in order, and I started to apply for assistant lecture-ships in Renaissance French and, once I became aware of the scarcity of such posts and of the consequent strength of competition for them, other types of post also. One of my developing interests throughout my student years had been India, and I found some attraction in a training post at the School of Oriental and African Studies which was intended to lead to a lectureship in Tamil. The appointment would entail spending three or four years in the Department of Phonetics and Linguistics there, dividing one's time between courses on linguistic theory and courses on Tamil language, before moving to a permanent lectureship in the Department of India, Pakistan and Ceylon. A move into such a post, if offered, would clearly be something of a shot in the dark but would equally have some advantages over unemployment. In due course I received an offer of the post, simul-taneously with the offer of one in the Department of French at the new University College of North Staffordshire. Not without hesitation, I opted for SOAS.

So I became a member of J. R. Firth's department. Before taking up the appointment I had a number of fascinating conversations with Firth (1890–

1960). Now, inevitably, I can remember only a few unrelated details of my chats with him. There was his statement that nowadays the way forward for publication in linguistics lay in the writing of articles rather than books. There was his pleasure in discovering that on returning to my village in the northernmost tip of Nottinghamshire I always used my native dialect (which was not unlike his). There were discussions of his own publications, including *Speech*, part of his pride in which lay in the fact that it was published in 'Benn's *Sixpenny* Library'. There was mention of linguistic fieldwork – already – in the course of which he referred to his delight in the fact that his lecturer in comparative linguistics had done work with informants on unwritten languages in Rajasthan. Firth struck me as a man who would take a very fatherly interest in his younger colleagues. Indeed, when he met my parents some three years later, he told my father that he might be my biological father, but that he, Firth, was my intellectual father.

Thus, even before joining Phonetics and Linguistics at SOAS, I was already learning that there were sides to the study of language that had escaped my attention at UCL. The only clearly distinguishable continuous thread was that of the importance of phonetics as the indispensable foundation if one was to do serious descriptive work. The stress on theory was new to me as, of course, was the theoretical stance of the department. What immediately appealed to me in all this was that, no matter how abstract the theorizing, there must always be the possibility of 'renewal of connection with experience' of actual language use. A strong impression left with me from my conversations with Firth and from listening to his lectures was that he did not see linguistic theory and the description of languages as belonging to two separate domains, with work in one being able to proceed in isolation from the other; good descriptive work is possible only in the context of a sound theoretical approach, and theorizing is empty without some reference to descriptive material. This simple point has, it seems to me, become more apparent since the later years of the twentieth century with the increasing interest in language typology and linguistic universals. Such topics cannot be discussed in either a theoretical or a descriptive vacuum. The balance in Firth's work was obviously in the direction of theory. I like to believe that my own emphasis on the descriptive side would not have disappointed him.

Of particular interest to me when I joined Firth's department, given the specifics of the post, were the courses given by Eileen Whitley (1910–88) on the phonology of Dravidian languages, which at the time of my appointment were limited to Kanarese and Malayalam, her course on Tamil being developed only after the arrival of my language informant, R. Radhakrishnan, from South India. Mrs Whitley's strongest enthusiasm, it always seemed to me, was for Malayalam, which to her was obviously – in the words of K. P. Mohanan in the dedication to his mother tongue of his 1986 book on *The Theory of Lexical Phonology* – 'a phonologist's paradise'.

Work with Radhakrishnan soon made it clear that the Tamil of everyday conversation was far removed from the modern written Tamil that I was learning in classes put on by Captain C. S. K. Pathy (1895–1976). Though we had no ready word for the phenomenon, Charles Ferguson's 1959 article not yet having appeared, it was clear that I should need to learn to understand something about the nature of Tamil diglossia. Before I had walked far along this path, my first year of leave in South India was fixed for 1955–6.

This led me to touch the edges of panic with regard to my still unfinished doctoral research, for it seemed to me that, if I did not complete it before setting sail for India, I might find it difficult to pick up the threads after 12 months out of touch. Less than a month before I was due to board the Colombo-bound SS *Oranje* at Southampton, I managed to submit a thesis, and helpful examiners made it possible for me to set sail with a successful oral examination behind me. That particular story did not, however, end there, for I was determined to publish a book on material used for the thesis – an ambition which seemed to be equally shared by my supervisor, D. P. Walker (1914–85), who throughout the previous five years, when we had met in the Museum Tavern for my supervision sessions, had always asked me, 'How is your *book* coming along?' When the euphoria of passing the doctoral milestone had worn off, however, I was able to recall my awareness of gaps in my material that time constraints had prevented me from filling. So, like a man who marries but keeps in regular touch with a former girlfriend, I continued for years to take time off from Tamil in the summer to work on printed and manuscript Renaissance texts in libraries in Paris. Time passed, and 43 years after I started the research, the book was published. This fact, yet to be recorded in the *Guinness Book of Records*, was not lost on a reviewer, who noted that the book was the 'bilan d'une recherche qu'il a poursuivie avec persévérance depuis des années, et dont il a livré par le passé plusieurs témoignages'. More remarkably to me, he also felt able to conclude his review, after a further reference to '[l]e caractère tardif de la publication', by speaking of 'l'actualité du livre de R. E. Asher dans l'Europe d'aujourd'hui'. Such are the blessings of procrastination.

Knowing that within a year of returning from India I was expected to enter a department concerned with the literatures as well as the languages of South Asia, I aimed while there to divide my time between fieldwork on colloquial Tamil and the study of both classical and modern literature. This, for lack of suitable experts on literature, could not be managed during the first half of my leave, which was spent in the village of Chengam in North Arcot District, for Firth had wisely advised that I should begin my year in a place where I should unavoidably find myself somewhat immersed in a variety of language that was free from influences of a literary style. I was fortunate in having as my principal informant a schoolteacher, M. K. Dharmeswaran, from whom I found it easy to elicit genuine colloquial forms – a fact that was confirmed by conversations with friends I made who were totally illiterate, including the 4-year-old Dakshinamurtti who, fascinated by the fact that I had one of the few clocks in the village, crossed the street to see me several times a day to ask the time. I was later to find that a really good informant was no small blessing, when others I tried to recruit in Batticaloa (former Ceylon) claimed, quite falsely of course, that they never used this 'low' variety of Tamil. Other problems entailed by fieldwork in those days were of a very practical kind, such as how to transport one's recording equipment. The Ferrograph recorder provided by SOAS was packed, along with tapes and accessories, in a strong wooden crate and the whole thing weighed 169 lb. Once unloaded from the ship, this had to be transported by train, bus and bullock cart (and how I hated the spine-crunching effect of those unsprung wheels as they rolled along unmetalled roads!). One of the many miracles of my trip was seeing the slightly built conductor of the bus walk up the ladder at the back of the vehicle with the crate on his head so that he could stow it on the roof. Almost a year later, when I took a plane from Madras to Jaffna, two seats had to be removed from the aircraft, a sturdy old Dakota, to make room for it.

In Madras for the second half of my year's research leave I was fortunate to have as my guru Professor Mu. Varadarajan (1912–74), a prolific author who was a distinguished novelist as well as a commentator on classical Tamil poetry and a writer on general linguistic topics. With his help, and with that of some of his students to guide me in both the colloquial and literary language, I felt reasonably well prepared on my return to London for the move from the 'third floor', the label that was in familiar usage attached to Firth's domain, to the Department of the Languages and Cultures of India, Pakistan and Ceylon.

Reminded by such things as Murray Emeneau's masterly talk to the Philological Society on Toda in 1956 that there was work needing to be done in the field of comparative Dravidian, I decided in due course, partly through the encouragement provided by Eileen Whitley's lectures, to broaden my own knowledge of the family by devoting some of my attention to Malayalam. Tuition of a different sort was provided by a Malayali postgraduate, Joseph Minattur, who took me through a series of readers prepared for the primary classes in schools in Kerala.

In those days, fieldwork trips ('study leave') were at SOAS not just a privilege but an obligation, and my second year in India was planned for 1963–4. Though considerably less well equipped then in Malayalam than I had been in Tamil in 1955, I decided to spend the second half of the year in Kerala doing research into the spoken language. Unwilling to neglect the written language in a state where, untypically for any part of South Asia at that time, the majority of people, women included, were literate, I again sought guidance on the current literary scene. This brought me into contact, and later close friendship, with Kerala's two greatest novelists, Thakazhi

Sivasankara Pillai (1912–2000) and Vaikom Muhammed Basheer (1908–94), and the study and translation of their work has been one of my constant preoccupations since then.

Between my Indian excursions, there had been a year in the South Asia Center at the University of Chicago, where I had the good fortune to be in at the beginning of the Chicago Linguistic Circle, at meetings of which, held at Northwestern University, the regulars included Edward Dimock, Edwin Gerow, Eric Hamp, Norman McQuown, James Sledd and Norman Zide. The environment at the Center was very stimulating in that it provided an interdisciplinary setting in which literature specialists, theoretical and descriptive linguists and social anthropologists, among others, could exchange ideas. Apart from establishing courses in Tamil language, one of my obligations was to prepare a Tamil prose reader for more advanced students – to be produced under a National Defence Education Act grant, an important source of funding in those days, particularly for work on languages that had not traditionally been on the curriculum of American universities. My collaborator on this project was my former assistant at SOAS, Radhakrishnan. Perhaps it was in Chicago that the idea developed that practically the whole of my career might not after all (as envisaged when I joined SOAS) be spent in one institution.

Though I took no active steps towards a change of allegiance, quite suddenly in 1965 a number of doors were opened before me. In a conversation after a meeting of the Philological Society, John Lyons encouraged me to apply for a post in the new Department of General Linguistics that he was setting up in the University of Edinburgh. Then, before I had made up my mind about the post that was subsequently offered, I also had offers of two posts for which I had not formally applied: one in Dravidian languages at the University of Pennsylvania and one in Renaissance French at my former department at UCL. Faced with three attractive possibilities, I might well have opted for the status quo, but the excitement of being in on something new in the end determined the issue.

So it was that at the age of 39 it came about that my definitive academic career was to be in linguistics. Obstinately, I still did not drop my other interests in Renaissance historiography and the Malayalam novel. If called on to justify these, I would on the one hand point to the work of some of my Renaissance authors on issues of language, and on the other argue that, if we do research into language because it is language above all that distinguishes man from other species, then it is the creative use of language in literature that illustrates the fullest extent of this distinction. It was with this thought in mind that I did not appreciate the comment in a review of Firth's 1957 *Papers in Linguistics* that '[a]t times the author seems lost to linguistics, as in his generous quotations from Swinburne and the 18th-century letter writers in *Modes of Meaning*'. At the same time, I have to admit that I have still to achieve a proper integration in my mind of linguistic theory and the analysis of literary texts.

Finding myself in a small department in Edinburgh in which my colleagues were John Lyons, Erik Fudge, Keith Brown and Mitzi MacGregor was more than enough to make me happy with my decision to move north, especially as our student body on the postgraduate diploma course was soon to include such people as Michael Garman, Peter Trudgill, Mary Tay, John Christie, Jim Miller, Patrick Griffiths, and others mentioned below by Peter Trudgill. I had a special interest in Mike Garman, for he became the first of seven students to complete a doctoral thesis on a Dravidian language under my supervision. It is hard to remember that at that stage there were no undergraduate courses in linguistics at Edinburgh, and that because of the caution felt about establishing them the first undergraduate degree (MA) that we felt able to propose was a joint one with French. Undergraduate study in phonetics had a longer history in Edinburgh, even though not as a subject of an honours degree, in the form of an 'Ordinary' course. Such courses formed one-third of the study required for the first or second year of undergraduate study; only in third and fourth years is there full concentration in the older Scottish universities on the chosen honours subject(s).

Theoretical linguistics was not new in Edinburgh in the 1960s. Angus McIntosh had held a Chair of English Language and General Linguistics since 1948, and in the School of Applied Linguistics there had been courses by Michael Halliday, Firth (after his retirement) and a number of distinguished Americans, including Martin Joos. The setting up of the Chair of General Linguistics and an associated department was nevertheless a significant step forward. The story of what followed can be read in John Lyons's account.

The successive amalgamations in the 1960s, with Phonetics and with Applied Linguistics, produced a single Department of Linguistics with an academic staff complement of what now seems an incredible 24. Since those days a decrease in staff numbers has, as elsewhere, been followed by an increase in the range of courses and in student numbers. There have been other changes. Amalgamation had been accompanied by an agreement that there should be a three-year rotating headship, to be held in turn by the heads of the three components. After this had resulted in a John Lyons, Pit Corder (1918–90), David Abercrombie (1909–92) sequence, some members of the department had the revolutionary idea that the Head of Department should be elected. Somewhat reluctantly accepted – for Linguistics only – by the Dean, this principle has since become commonplace, if not quite the norm, in the university. Thus it was that I fell into the position (though, following John Lyons's move to Sussex, the result was in fact the same as it would have been under the old order).

It was a tradition that Professors and Heads of Department provided academic leadership, though how this was to be defined was not always clear. Certainly it was not understood by any of us in Linguistics as being a lead in a certain unified theoretical direction. My own tendency was to see the role of an academic administrator as being largely an enabling one, that is to say one of finding ways of making it possible for colleagues with good ideas to put them into practice. This often means selling the idea to individuals or groups who have power to block or permit the realization of dreams.

Two such ideas, in my two separate spells as Head, were put to me. The first came from Clive Criper and other colleagues in applied linguistics as a proposal to set up an Institute of Applied Language Studies which, along with providing much-needed income for the subject and for the university, would strengthen the research capacity of that part of the department's interests. It is fair to say that the Institute has flourished. The second idea was a proposal from John Laver to establish some sort of centre that would make it easier to obtain external funding for research with a phonetics base. We were encouraged by the then Principal of the University, Dr (later Sir) John Burnett, to drop our preferred label 'Language Technology' and instead set up a Centre for Speech Technology Research. With John Laver as Director, this succeeded in its aim far beyond what our imagination had foreseen, with the £5,000,000 Alvey project on speech recognition, which had six principal investigators spread over the areas of phonetics, syntax, psychology, artificial intelligence and electrical engineering.

Simultaneously with this, there were other developments in which Linguistics had an interest, the most important of which was the change of the interdisciplinary School of Epistemics into a (teaching) Department of Cognitive Science. My own hope was that this could be part of a single unit with Linguistics. Efforts to achieve this, much to my disappointment, failed – and for reasons which I regarded as unsound from a strictly academic viewpoint, having more to do, I thought, with university politics. Happily, co-operation between Linguistics and Cognitive Science remains encouragingly strong, particularly through the Human Communications Research Centre.

It was at the time of these initiatives that I found myself drawn into major administrative roles outwith my department, first as Dean of the Faculty of Arts and then as Vice-Principal of the University. During most of my tenure of these offices, the university was struggling to emerge from a financial crisis, a factor which ensured that the roles were some distance from being sinecures. When I took on the first, linguistics seemed likely for me to fade into the background.

Just the same, there seemed time at least to accept an invitation to join in discussions on the possible viability of a multi-volume encyclopedia of linguistics, the brainchild of Alan Steele of Pergamon Press and Angus

McIntosh. If the outcome of talks was positive, the work would be a joint publication of Pergamon and Aberdeen University Press, both at the time part of the Maxwell empire. The group of discussants increased by stages, and at each stage there was enthusiastic support for the venture. A decision was therefore taken to proceed with it, at which point it emerged that I had been thought of as the possible editor-in-chief. In the circumstances in which I found myself, it was clear that it would be a foolhardy and unrealistic decision to accept. Equally clearly, it was not an offer to turn down lightly. In the course of my thinking – very briefly – about what I should do, it occurred to me that there was, as regards the task ahead, some degree of appropriateness in the fact that my academic interests had always been broad. Persuading myself that the proposed good number of subject editors would ensure that the job would not become impossibly burdensome, I adopted a Wildean approach to the temptation that had been put before me. After the finished work was released, and perhaps even before then, I reflected on Thomas Mann's (English) postscript on the making of *Der Zauberberg*: 'If a writer had before him from the start all the possibilities and all the drawbacks of a projected work, and knew what the book itself wanted to be, he might never have the courage to begin.'

It was decided that, to launch the project, there should be a meeting of as many subject editors as could be signed up by the time agreed for it. The group would convene at whatever spot in the world seemed to be in the geographical centre in relation to its members' institutions. This having been judged to be the Channel Islands, we met at a hotel in Jersey in April 1988.

By the time of that meeting, one or two problems had already arisen, the chief of which was that work had already started on a large-scale encyclopedia of linguistics to be published by Oxford University Press and edited by William Bright, a friend and colleague whom I had first met at the Annamalai University in South India 30 years earlier when we were both apprentice Dravidianists, and of whose editorial competence I was very much aware. The consensus when this was discussed by our group was that the market would be able to stand two competing encyclopedias in a discipline as important as linguistics.

From the start it had been agreed that the Pergamon encyclopedia should seek to display four characteristics: it should be authoritative, international in authorship and content, comprehensive, and up to date. Its authority would derive from having leading figures in the various branches of linguistics and related disciplines as members of the Executive Editorial Board (made up of the set of subject editors), as members of the Honorary Advisory Board (jointly chaired by Angus McIntosh and Dwight Bolinger (1907–92)) and as authors. The international requirement speaks for itself. A publication that would be up to date required as short a time as possible between the commissioning of articles and their publication. I therefore enunciated the principle that it was easier to produce a work of five million

words within four or five years than over a longer period. Comprehensiveness was perhaps the most difficult feature to achieve. Good organization
and competent editorial work could ensure that the *commissioning* had this
quality, especially as it had been agreed in Jersey that there should be no
rigid demarcation between the work of different editors; all should feel free
to propose articles to fill perceived gaps. Added to this were suggestions
made by members of the Advisory Board, most of whom were very
conscientious in giving valued advice rather than assuming that their only
function was to grace the prelims of the work with their name. The risk in
the policy of freedom to commission outside one's own area was that there
could be duplication. Avoiding this became one of the many tasks of the co-
ordinating editor, and we were lucky indeed to have the coolly efficient and
exceptionally knowledgeable J. M. Y. Simpson for this role. The principal
difficulty in achieving comprehensiveness was therefore in execution, for
there was no way of ensuring that 1,000 authors would all meet their
deadline. A further characteristic of the work was that it should aim to be
informative rather than polemical or sectarian. It should as far as possible
provide information on any subject that might seem relevant to a person
interested in any aspect of the serious study of human language. It was this
that motivated the decision to have as its title *The Encyclopedia of **Language
and Linguistics*** (*ELL*).

The whole enterprise was made easier than it might have been by the
attitude and expertise of the publishers. Put at its simplest, Pergamon were
very experienced and skilled in the mechanics of producing encyclopedias.
No less importantly, they readily accepted the editor's view that academic
quality was a necessary partner of commercial success. To ensure this
success, they were willing to invest considerable sums in advance of the
time when they could sell the work. These sums included not only piece-
work payments to editors and authors but also the cost of setting up and
maintaining a well-staffed editorial office in Edinburgh in premises rented
from the university.

So the work proceeded. The editors proved that they could combine
impressive scholarship with organizational skills and dedication. There were,
it is true, a few editorial problems, stemming mainly from the fact that some
of the obvious people in some fields were not free to be involved. One
solution was to spread commissioning among existing editors – as was done
with typology and universals, and with sociolinguistics. When no other way
out seemed to offer itself, as for example in the cases of animal communication and of the history of linguistics outside Europe and America, I
blithely took on the subject area myself (with regular advice on the former
from Aubrey Manning of our Science Faculty). One effect of assuming these
additional tasks was that I fell behind in the one area that I had decided to be
responsible for from the start, that of the language situation in the countries
of the world. Fortunately, ready help with this problem was available in the

person of the project's very talented Executive Secretary, Alison Bowers, who found authors for the last 20 per cent or so of the entries required.

When the ship had sailed more than half the way to its destination, there came the shock of Robert Maxwell's decision to sell Pergamon, with the prospect of our discovering that years of hard work might be wasted. However, the new owners, Elsevier, declared that they were keen to support the project to its intended conclusion, but with the condition of an accelerated completion rate and a very strict production timetable. One part of this was that there would a precise deadline for the submission of the text of every article – noon on a certain day, depending on the alphabetic position of the first word of the title, with absolutely no exceptions made. The comprehensiveness principle seemed destined to take at least a few knocks as a result of this draconian ruling. One device to overcome the problem was that of retitling delayed articles so that they came lower in the alphabetic sequence and so would have a later deadline. This, of course, had limited possibilities, and I devised another contingency plan, which involved identifying danger spots and then writing articles myself for insertion into the production chain where necessary at the last minute. Fortunately, in most cases my calculations proved too pessimistic and only a few of the drafts were used.

Somehow, there was no overall slippage, and towards the end of 1993 it was possible to turn to the planning of the launch. Throughout the years of toil (for, no matter how exciting and rewarding the project was, it did involve a lot of hard work) I had cherished the secret ambition of making the Encyclopedia as 'autobiographical' as possible – a strange notion, no doubt, in relation to such an impersonal work. Thus India and the European Renaissance were both very well represented, though this, of course, is hardly conspicuous, given the importance of both in the history of linguistic speculation. A place was assured in the set of biographies for any of my teachers whose presence could be justified. I made a point of thinking up relevant topics that would allow me to invite contributions from colleagues and friends in related disciplines, notably anthropologists and historians, whose work I had admired. I even found a pretext to represent one of my schoolboy enthusiasms by including an essay on Ludwig Koch, who did such remarkable work on the study and recording of bird song in the 1930s. It was in this frame of mind that I conceived the idea that the launch of ELL should be in a relationship with two institutions that had been important to me in my academic career. Hence the function, by kind permission of the college authorities, was held (in January 1994) in the Flaxman Gallery of UCL, and in association with a meeting of the Philological Society, the regular meetings of which by a happy coincidence were at the time being held at the college. The then President of the Society, Peter Matthews, helpfully gave his enthusiastic approval to my proposal.

Eight years later, I remain reasonably satisfied with the outcome of a task that took up much more of my time than any other single assignment had done. *ELL* was generally favourably received both by reviewers and by users. All those involved – publisher, editors and contributors – will have taken pleasure in comments such as the one made by William Bright, the person most qualified by experience to understand the nature and size of the task, that 'This is now the definitive and indispensable scholarly reference publication, on all branches of linguistics, for any library where linguistics is taken seriously.' One thoughtful review, it is true, showed some dissatisfaction with the design of the work, expressing the view that 'elle appelle soit une refonte qui résolve les problèmes d'intégration et de biaisement [anglo-saxon] ... pour devenir vraiment une encyclopédie des sciences du langage, reposant sur un travail de réflexion et de consensus scientifique, à plus long terme et plus général; soit un nouvel ouvrage, autrement conçu'. Most reviewers, however, seem to have taken the view that the editorial team's conception of what was needed was right and concentrated their criticism more on matters of detail, finding, for instance, that names were missing from the set of biographees or noting, with good reason, that the tenth volume (made up of indexes and other appended matter) was, through the failure to correct a number of mistakes, not quite up to the standard of the other volumes. It is the natural claim of Seumas Simpson and myself that if the unbelievably tight schedule had allowed time for us to have sight of the proofs, the errors would all have been eliminated. This, however, is the only small shadow on a publisher/academic relationship that was and still is a very happy one. The total experience was exceptionally rewarding and I am deeply indebted to the many subject editors and their chosen authors who made it so.

In one respect, work on *ELL* continues – through the publisher's decision to bring out a series of spin-off volumes, for which I act as consulting editor (and in one case as actual editor). These, generally under the title of *Concise Encyclopedia of X*, bring together all the *ELL* entries in a given subject area, which are updated and also supplemented by newly commissioned articles. So far eight books have been published and two are in progress.

One adverse effect of my having to devote so much time to *ELL* was that work on another project, begun earlier, namely my *Atlas of the World's Languages*, fell behind schedule, and it became necessary to take on a joint editor, Chris Moseley, to help finish the task. His single-mindedness meant that *ELL* and the *Atlas* came out almost simultaneously.

By the time of their publication, I had passed the end of my contract with the University of Edinburgh. The Department, which with the reunification in 1999 of Linguistics and Applied Linguistics has become the Department of Theoretical and Applied Linguistics, kindly tolerates my occasional presence as I try to complete writing projects that proved to be incompatible with administrative duties earlier. My main research effort has continued to be in descriptive linguistics, for I remain committed to the value and importance of work in this field. In being so, I remember some of my conversations with Firth on linguistic theory, which always seemed to return to the joint topics of the language *of* description and the language *under* description; I take theoretical linguistics as having two inseparable purposes, discovering more about language in general and discovering more about particular languages. I also seem to have continued, though not as a matter of deliberate policy, the practice exemplified by my Renaissance studies of letting extended periods of research lead first only to articles, with books waiting perhaps for decades. In this way my 1955/6 fieldwork on spoken Tamil found its way into books with publication dates of 1982 and 2002, while the 1964 work on Malayalam led to a book only in 1997. Happily I can find a good precedent for this in the fact that the major descriptive work (on Toda) produced by Murray Emeneau, the highly regarded doyen of Dravidian linguists of the second half of the twentieth century and now honorary member of the Philological Society, came out more than four decades after his three years' research leave in India as a young man in 1936–9.

Returning to my opening theme, I am led to wonder how much of my life in linguistics was predictable. Perhaps the general diversity of my interests made a broad vision of the subject, reflected for instance in the structure and content of *ELL*, inevitable. I have difficulty in seeing any one aspect of the serious study of language as being intrinsically more exciting than any other; all of them, whether located in language structure or language use, seem to me endlessly fascinating. Yet one question still intrigues me: what sort of linguist would I have become if I had pursued my schoolboy love of mathematics?

REFERENCES

ASHER, R. E., 1982. *Tamil*, Lingua Descriptive Studies series, Amsterdam: North-Holland.
ASHER, R. E., 1993. *National Myths in Renaissance France: Francus, Samothes and the Druids*. Edinburgh: Edinburgh University Press. Reviewed by Claude-Gilbert Dubois, *Bibliothèque d'Humanisme et Renaissance* 55 (1993), 61–4.
ASHER, R. E., (ed.) 1994. *The Encyclopedia of Language and Linguistics*, 10 vols, Oxford/New York/Seoul/Tokyo: Pergamon Press. Reviewed by S. Auroux, E. Lazcano & J. Léon, *Bulletin de la Société de Linguistique de Paris* 90/2 (1995), 34–49; and by William Bright, *Journal of Linguistics* 30 (1994), 551–5.
ASHER, R. E. & ANNAMALAI, E., 2002. *Colloquial Tamil*, London/New York: Routledge.
ASHER, R. E. & HENDERSON, EUGÉNIE J. A., (eds.) 1981. *Towards a History of Phonetics*, Edinburgh: Edinburgh University Press.
ASHER, R. E. & KUMARI, T. C., 1997. *Malayalam*, London/New York: Routledge.
ASHER, R. E. & MOSELEY, CHRISTOPHER, (eds.) 1994. *Atlas of the World's Languages*, London/New York: Routledge. Japanese translation: Tokyo, Toyo-shorin, 2000.
ASHER, R. E. & RADHAKRISHNAN, R., 1971. *A Tamil Prose Reader: Selections from Contemporary Tamil Prose with Notes and Glossary*, Cambridge: Cambridge University Press.
BASHEER, VAIKOM MUHAMMED, 1980. *'Me Grandad 'ad an Elephant!' Three Stories of Muslim Life in South India*, tr. R. E. Asher and Achamma Coilparampil, Edinburgh: Edinburgh University Press.

BRIGHT, WILLIAM, (ed.) 1992. *International Encyclopedia of Linguistics*, 4 vols, New York/ Oxford: Oxford University Press.

EMENEAU, M. B., 1957. 'Toda, a Dravidian language', *TPhS* 15–66.

EMENEAU, M. B., 1984. *Toda Grammar and Texts*, Philadelphia: American Philosophical Society.

FERGUSON, CHARLES A., 1959. 'Diglossia', *Word* 15, 325–40.

FIRTH, J. R., 1930. *Speech*, London: Benn.

FIRTH, J. R., 1957. *Papers in Linguistics 1934–1951*, London: Oxford University Press. Reviewed by Einar Haugen, *Language* 34 (1958), 498–502.

KOERNER, E. F. K. & ASHER, R. E., (eds.) 1995. *Concise History of the Language Sciences: From the Sumerians to the Cognitivists*, Oxford/New York/Tokyo: Pergamon Press and Elsevier.

MANN, THOMAS, 1996. *The Magic Mountain*, tr. H. T. Lowe-Porter, with a postscript by the author 'on the making of the Magic Mountain', London: Minerva.

MOHANAN, K. P., 1986. *The Theory of Lexical Phonology*, Studies in Natural Language and Linguistic Theory, Dordrecht/Boston/Lancaster/Tokyo: D. Reidel.

SIVASANKARA PILLAI, THAKAZHI, 1993. *Scavenger's Son (Tottiyute makan)*, tr. R. E. Asher, Oxford: Heinemann.

JOHN BENDOR-SAMUEL

BENDOR-SAMUEL, John Theodore, *b.* 1929; *m.* 1955 Pamela Moxham; *Education:* Christ Church, Oxford, Fell Exhibitioner, BA 1952, MA 1957; SOAS, University of London, PhD 1958; *Career:* Director, SIL-UK, 1958–83; Director, SIL-Africa, 1962–83; Executive Vice-President, SIL International, 1984–91; Director SIL-UK 1992–9; Director Emeritus 1999–; Member of Council of West African Linguistics Society 1967–99; Editor *Journal of West African Languages* 1982–93. *Major Publications: The Niger-Congo Languages* (ed.) 1989.

* * *

I count myself fortunate that my first linguistics teachers were K. L. Pike and J. R. Firth. They could hardly have been more different both in temperament and in their linguistic theories but they had a sincere respect for each other. I recall Firth commenting to me that Pike was the only American who had taken the trouble to understand him. Apparently he'd been across the Atlantic to give a paper at one of the Summer Linguistic Institutes and had come across Pike there. Pike, for his part, welcomed what he perceived was Firth's rejection of the rigid Bloomfieldian formalism which dominated linguistics in the US in the 1940s and 1950s. Both men were unashamed students of meaning.

My path into linguistics was, to a large degree, accidental. After history at Oxford and some postgraduate education and theology at London, I was preparing to go overseas, thinking of teaching biblical studies and theology. In 1953, out of the blue I saw in the press an announcement of a summer training course to help missionaries learn non-European languages. In common with three million others after the Second World War, I had been privileged to see something of the wider overseas world, courtesy of His Majesty. National Service had given me an opportunity I would not otherwise have had of experiencing other cultures. It did not take much acumen on my part to perceive that learning the local language was an essential element in effective communication. So I applied for this training. I knew I needed it, for up to that point my language study had been dismal and depressing – equally to me and my teachers. I had endured Latin and German only to the level where I could scrape into Oxford and cope with Responsians, so that I could get on with my real study!

Not surprisingly then, I was looking forward to the summer with some apprehension. Kenneth Pike and his wife, together with George Cowan, himself a very competent linguist–Bible-translator, were the principal teachers of what was the first such course offered by the Summer Institute of Linguistics (SIL) in the UK. Very soon fascination and excitement replaced the attitudes of fortitude and endurance with which I had begun the summer.

Pike was quite unlike any teacher I had previously had – a whirlwind of energy and full of illustrations from his own fieldwork but at the same time very approachable, and indeed he treated neophytes like me as if we were his equals, eager to debate every point of linguistic analysis. I had no idea whatsoever that he was an eminent linguist and blush to think of my ignorant boldness in arguing with him on various occasions. By the end of this stimulating summer, instead of dreading languages, I came away enjoying linguistics, having found to my genuine surprise that I could, after all, cope with languages.

The SIL training covered five subjects of instruction: phonetics, phonemics, morphology, syntax and field problems (an introduction to cultural anthropology coupled with preparation for living in the jungle!). For each subject there was an hour's lecture every day and the equivalent of an hour's practical 'homework'. All the lectures were fully illustrated with actual language data drawn very largely from the field research SIL members were conducting, and the 'homework' was an exercise working out the analytical procedures taught in class that day on actual language data. For the last three weeks of the 11-week course, we 13 students were divided up into small groups of three or so and worked with an informant, learning and analysing his language. So it was that my first contact with an African language was Ewe.

Pike was in the midst of developing his tagmemic theory; only at that stage he called these units of grammar 'grammemes' – subsequently (1958) renamed 'tagmemes'. He had found the etic–emic distinction useful in his early work on phonology and extended the concept to grammar. Already he had large parts of his magnum opus, *Language in Relation to a Unified Theory of the Structure of Human Behaviour*, in draft. A preliminary edition was in fact published the next year, 1954, though it was not until 1967 that the revised and much enlarged work was finally published in its entirety – 762 large pages. He used some of this material in his teaching. I still remember his analysis of an ordinary breakfast, a behavioural unit where once again etic and emic came into focus, being applied to the events as well as the language used at the breakfast table!

The next summer, three of us who had done well were invited back as apprentice teachers. Certainly one of the best ways to learn any subject is to teach it to others! I taught syntax. Again, I thoroughly enjoyed the summer and decided to join SIL and its sister organization, the Wycliffe Bible Translators (WBT). It made sense, too, in terms of my previous thinking

– after all, how could you teach biblical studies to people when they didn't have a Bible in a language they could understand!

As soon as I joined SIL, Ken Pike urged me to study with Firth at SOAS. With Pike's recommendation and on the strength of two summers at SIL, Firth accepted me as a graduate student and indeed acted as my supervisor for the first period of this study. So I began a year at SOAS. All students and most, if not all, staff attended Firth's Wednesday morning lectures. Scintillating, witty and iconoclastic are some of the words I would use to describe them. At the time, I felt that Firth was more succesful in demolishing all the current linguistic theories than he was in explaining his own theory of language. In retrospect I think that was probably a reaction arising from the fact that the SIL initial training I had received was so thoroughly practical, grounded with masses of actual language data.

That year I completed the necessary preliminaries to be registered as a PhD student and, on the advice of SIL and with the approval of Firth, in the summer of 1955 my wife and I set out for Peru to begin linguistic research on an Amazonian language, Jebero, located in the jungles of eastern Peru between the confluence of the Marañon and Huallaga rivers. Pam and I had met at the first SIL, she coming to it with a much better preparation than I had, having read a degree in Latin and Greek at London University. She also taught in the summer of 1954 and we got married just before leaving for Peru.

That year, September 1955 through to September 1956, was a honeymoon for us both in a double sense, not only for our marriage but for our initiation into the delights of linguistic fieldwork. We can thoroughly recommend Amazonia on both counts! We could hardly have been in a more remote place – three weeks by river travel from the SIL Centre at Yarinacocha just outside Pucalpa. Fortunately that long journey was reduced to two-and-a-half hours in the small plane SIL had.

We didn't take much with us to the little town of Jebero. The small, single-engined plane that took us to a landing strip outside Jebero couldn't carry much in addition to us, but we thought we were well equipped with our battery-operated reel-to-reel tape-recorder and an Olympia typewriter with some of its keys modified with some commonly used phonetic symbols, together with our one enamel mug and plate apiece and our mosquito net and safari bed! I smile now, as I think of the laptops and solar panels we use in our linguistic research today.

We lived alongside the villagers, eating local food and taking our daily bath as they did, in the main stream which flowed along the edges of the little town. Such living gave us good opportunities to learn their language and study their culture. Painstakingly over the months that followed we began to speak Jebero.

One of the foundational elements of our study of Jebero was a collection of over 100 stories of all kinds that we recorded: stories of everyday activities, fables about the jungle animals, especially the puma, accounts of Jebero history, time-honoured legends, and so on. With the indispensable assistance of our Jebero friends, we translated these texts and discussed them in detail, drawing out many of the phonological and grammatical features of the language. Together we devised a (more or less) phonemic alphabet. How they loved to see their language in writing for the first time and enjoyed learning to read it!

Our interest in them and their language was very well received. On one occasion when we were visiting the home of one of the leading men, he embarrassed us by asking one of the Peruvian traders, who had spent many years coming and going to the little town and had married a Jebero girl, how much Jebero he knew. When the trader confessed that he hadn't learnt any because it was too difficult, our host pointed to us and exclaimed, 'There's Don Juan, he's only been here three months and he knows our language!' We pardoned the gross exaggeration, realizing it expressed his appreciation that we were studying his language, whereas most Peruvians despised it.

Part of the time we worked in the little town of Jebero, and the rest of the time at the SIL Research Centre a few miles out of Pucalpa. The year passed swiftly and by the time we left, in addition to the embryonic linguistic analysis and a card file with some 3,000 entries, there were some literacy materials and even a few Bible stories – the Christmas and Easter stories – in Jebero. Not much to repay our Jebero friends who had so enriched us with the fascinating data of a previously unknown language.

The following 18 months were spent in analysis and reanalysis, as we hammered out a description of the 'verbal piece' in Jebero. For this, my supervisor was the late Professor R. H. Robins. I can't speak too highly of his contribution to this process. The discussions I had with him were stimulating and balanced. He was always accessible and quick to respond to drafts of chapters – a real encourager and a master of linguistic common sense.

My thesis attempted to apply some of insights of prosodic theory to both the phonological and grammatical structure of Jebero. After it was completed in 1958 we returned to fieldwork, studying the Terena language in the Mato Grosso in Brazil. Prosodic analysis illuminated the structures and systems of Terena even more clearly than Jebero.

The Firthian concept that categories of phonology are realized over more than one phonological segment of structure and his postulation of prosodic features in contradistinction to phonematic units illuminated Terena phonology clearly. The phonological system lends itself to a description of five hierarchical levels (syllable, word, phrase, clause and sentence) each marked by specific prosodic features. Thus the phonological syllable comprises one or more phonematic units and one of three prosodies (i-, u- or -prosody) and the phonological word comprises one or more syllables and one of three other prosodic features (N-, Y- or Z-prosody).

Another attractive feature of such an analysis in Terena is that it facilitates the statement of certain congruencies between the phonological and grammatical systems of the language. Thus the phonetic exponents of the grammmatical categories of first, second and third person can be stated as being realized by one of the word level prosodies, as illustrated in the table.

Z-prosody		N-prosody		Y-prosody	
'owoku	'his house'	'õwõŋgu	'my house'	'yowoku	'your house'
'piho	'he went'	'mbiho	'I went'	'pihe	'you went'

In 1962 we began our involvement with African languages, moving to Ghana that autumn. For the next 20 years we followed the basic pattern of living and working in Africa for eight months of the year, with some three months running the SIL summer programme in the UK.

In contrast to the Kwa languages of southern Ghana, very little attention had been paid to the Gur languages of the north, so we focused on these. Being based at the newly established Institute of African Studies at the University of Ghana just outside Accra at Legon gave interaction with scholars of African languages, including Gilbert Ansre, J. M. Stewart and W. A. A. Wilson. Later, as SIL work in Africa expanded, we lived in Nigeria and began to get acquainted with Benue-Congo languages.

The 1960s were an exciting time for language study in West Africa. New universities were founded and Departments of Linguistics established. The West Africa Linguistics Society (WALS) was founded in 1965 and I served on its Council until 1999. WALS provided an annual congress to stimulate the study of African languages. Those Congresses, though now on a two-yearly cycle, continue to this day. The Society published a journal, the *Journal of West African Languages*, with two issues every year. I served as editor for 12 years (1982–93) and have been pleased to see both the steadily improving quality of articles submitted to the *Journal* and a significant increase in the number of articles published that were written by African scholars working in West African institutions. A new generation of Africans, competent in linguistics and enthusiastically committed to the study of the languages of their countries, was growing up and it was an inspiration to work with them.

My own work shifted to giving guidance and encouragement to SIL colleagues working in quite a range of African languages. We missed the more intensive study of specific languages but gained a broader understanding of languages in the whole vast Niger-Congo language family and also in Chadic. With over 1,600 distinct languages in Niger-Congo grouped in eight main sub-families, not to mention the 250 languages in Chadic, it will be many years before linguists exhaust the incredible richness of their linguistic structures.

All through these years, our involvement with the annual SIL 11-week training programmes in the UK continued. We both enjoyed the teaching summer by summer. The numbers attending the courses grew steadily. By 1957 we had over 100 students, in 1958 I was appointed Director and I continued in this role until 1983. They were 25 good summers and we enjoyed introducing the fascinating study of language to a wide range of people who came not only from the UK but from many other countries.

The summer linguistics programme was organized in two courses. The first was a Language Learning course designed to give appropriate training to those who would need to learn a language in which there would be very little, if any, material available to assist them and no language school. This six-week course focused on preparing them to recognize and reproduce unfamiliar sounds and to handle non-European grammatical systems. The syllabus comprised an introduction to phonetics, grammar and language learning techniques. There was a strong emphasis on practical application, e.g. phonetic drills every day, at the end of which every student had a reproduction session with the instructor. We also included an hour a day covering sociolinguistic topics such as the role of language in society, bilingualism and bilingual education.

For the final two weeks the participants worked in small groups with a speaker of a non-European language, preferably from a part of the world to which they were going, putting into practice the skills they had acquired. For the majority of students, in addition to the technical skills, they also gained an appreciation of and respect for other languages and a measure of confidence in their ability to learn them. They were usually surprised how much they could learn in those last two weeks. Our view was that these attitudinal changes were just as important as the technical skills and indeed, in the long run, they would determine success or failure in language learning and adaptation to another culture.

The second course was an 11-week general introduction to linguistic analysis designed for those who were preparing to carry out linguistic research in a hitherto unstudied language. Its syllabus included all the material taught on the Language Learning course but with extensive material on phonological and grammatical analysis. There was the same emphasis on practical application, with a range of examples taken from many different languages which illustrated the specific aspects of phonological and grammatical analysis being taught. There was also some introductory material on cultural anthropology. The last three weeks similarly ended with participants working in small groups with a speaker of a non-European language, but with the focus on making a brief initial description of its phonology and certain elements of its grammatical system.

By 1962 we had introduced a more advanced 11-week course which concentrated on phonological and grammatical analysis and also introduced semantics and translation principles to the students who had already completed the first year general course or its equivalent. This more advanced course also gave students a more extended opportunity to apply linguistic theory to a non-European language, as they worked for a large part of the day over a six-week period with a native speaker, usually an overseas student free during the summer vacation.

By the early 1960s, it became clear that this informal summer linguistics programme was here to stay, so the decision was made to set up SIL on a legal basis as an academic institution in the UK in 1964. As this was being done, we recognized the value of a link with a university which had an active programme in linguistics, preferably within a reasonable geographical distance so as to facilitate contact. At that time the courses were being run at Merstham on the border of Surrey and Sussex, so we established a link with the University of Sussex. When in 1972 SIL acquired a training centre near High Wycombe, we developed an association with the University of Reading and subsequently a significant number of our staff studied in the Department of Linguistics and, more recently, in other Departments – in Education and Agricultural Extension and Rural Development.

In the early 1970s, we introduced a Literacy Specialists' course which gave students an introduction to developing literacy materials and organizing literacy programmes.

By the mid-1970s, these various courses attracted some 200 students to SIL each summer. Many came from overseas, with over half the student body coming from a wide range of European countries. SIL became a truly international school with students from over 20 countries participating each year.

In the late 1970s, we began to develop courses outside of the summer period, and by the mid-1980s, a regular all-the-year-round programme was established. The introductory courses (the Language Learning course and General course) continued to be offered in the summer but the more advanced training and specialist courses, such as the Literacy course, were offered in the autumn and spring. This pattern has continued evolving, with more specialist courses, like biblical Hebrew, being added. Since the early 1990s, we have seen increasing use of computers in linguistic analysis, and students are introduced to the growing number of programs which are available.

From the start it was recognized that, useful as the SIL training was for those beginning linguistic research, it needed to be taken further through study programmes at Departments of Linguistics in our universities. SIL members who demonstrated ability in linguistic analysis were encouraged to pursue postgraduate studies. Such studies were undertaken at a wide range of universities, for example the School of Oriental and African Studies and

University College at London, at Reading, at Edinburgh and at Manchester. In the 1960s, for instance, some seven staff members completed their PhD studies and a similar number completed MA work.

This policy of encouraging competent staff to pursue advanced training has continued, with an additional 25 SIL members in the UK completing PhDs and over 50 others studying at the Masters level. More recently, in addition to staff continuing to take advanced degrees in linguistics, the range of studies has broadened to reflect the wide scope of language development, sociolinguistics, bilingual education and translation work undertaken by SIL members. Studies have been carried out at the institutions mentioned above and others, such as the Institute of Education at London and at the Universities of Lancaster, Sheffield, Southampton, Warwick and York.

From the beginning and all through the programmes offered by SIL, the teaching at the courses has been handled on team lines, with a field-experienced and qualified (usually PhD- or MA-level) Head of Department briefing a team of three or four less experienced staff, discussing each lesson in detail with them. In this way, junior staff deepen their grasp of linguistics as part of the process of teaching the introductory courses. We also had weekly seminars in which senior staff and linguists from the various universities gave papers. R. H. Robins was a regular visitor for many years.

Field research too was organized so as to utilize the experience and qualifications of more senior staff, who served as consultants to new and less experienced staff, meeting regularly with them and discussing the analysis of the language which each staff member was learning and analysing. Personnel from the UK numbered only about 8 per cent of the worldwide body of SIL members but contributed a higher percentage of consultants and training staff.

With the leaders of the SIL courses having been trained at many different Departments of Linguistics, no one linguistic model dominated the teaching approach. In the early years particularly, we benefited from insights from Pike's tagmemic model, but it was never the exclusive or even main model used in the courses. Insights from Firthian prosodic analysis, for example, were incorporated into the teaching.

Indeed, in the 1960s and 1970s I attempted to utilize the concept of stating phonological structures in terms of segmental phonematic units and prosodic features extending over more than one place in the structure in looking at some grammatical features in the same way. This syntagmatic approach to grammar, sometimes called 'structure–function', abstracted grammatical features whose domain extended over more than one grammatical unit.

This broadly hierarchical approach to grammar and phonology owed much to scholars like Pike and Halliday, whose 1961 article, 'Categories of the theory of grammar', was particularly influential. Several of our staff used the structure–function model that we utilized for our grammar courses in their analysis and description of West African languages; see for example the PhD theses of Adive (1989), Clark (1969), Naden (1973), Stanford (1967) and Thomas (1969).

Later we attempted to introduce some of the concepts both of the generative approach and of functional grammar. Staff members have been encouraged to study in various linguistic schools, so that the insights they have gained from their studies may be included in the continued development of our courses.

As has happened to many other linguists, I became more and more involved in the administration of the institution under which I served, and in 1984 I became the Chief Executive Officer of SIL International. After that, I carried out a similar role for SIL and WBT in the UK. Inevitably, it was a struggle to maintain involvement in the study of African languages. Field research became impossible and my contribution was severely limited to editing and consultant work. In addition to editing the *Journal of West African Languages*, I also served as organizer and editor of a kind of 'state-of-the-art' book entitled *The Niger-Congo Languages*, published in 1989. In that volume, some 23 contributors provided an overview of each of the main branches of that huge family of languages. More recently, my linguistic writing has been confined to articles for encyclopedias and the like.

As the field of linguistics has proliferated and it has become increasingly difficult to keep up with all the developments in linguistic theory, not to mention the many kinds of hyphenated linguistics, my conviction has deepened that the foundation of all linguistic study must be good descriptions of specific languages. In this I see a continuing worthwhile role for SIL, both in its field research and in its training programmes. With over half of the world's 6,800 languages still without any description, there's plenty of scope for linguistic analysis and description. Then, too, the potential of modern technology makes it realistic to contemplate that many descriptions of languages that have not yet been published will soon become available in electronic format. SIL is committed to using these new means of making its research available to other scholars. We have come a long way from battery-operated, reel-to-reel recorders. Unquestionably, the next 40 years will be as exciting as the last and hopefully our knowledge of the world's languages will continue to expand with equal velocity.

REFERENCES

ADIVE, JOHN R., 1989. 'The verbal piece in Ebira', in *Summer Institute of Linguistics and University of Texas at Arlington Publications in Linguistics* 85, Dallas: SIL and UTA.

BAZELL, C. E., 1966. *In Memory of J. R. Firth*, London: Longman.

BENDOR-SAMUEL, JOHN T., 1961. 'The verbal piece in Jebero', supplement to *Word* 17, New York: Linguistic Circle of New York.

BENDOR-SAMUEL, JOHN T., 1963. 'A structure–function description of Terena phrases', *Canadian Journal of Linguistics* 8, 59–70.

BENDOR-SAMUEL, JOHN T., 1966. 'Some prosodic features in Terena', in C. E. Bazell (ed.), *In Memory of J. R. Firth,* London: Longman, 30–9.

BENDOR-SAMUEL, JOHN T., 1970. 'Syntagmatic features or grammatical prosodies', in Alexandru Graur et al. (eds.), *Actes du Xe Congrès International des Linguistes,* vol. 2, Bucharest: Académie de la République Socialiste de Roumani, 901–10.

CALLOW, JOHN C., 1962. *The Apinaye Language: Phonology and Grammar.* Unpublished PhD dissertation, University of London, School of Oriental and African Studies.

CLARK, DAVID J., 1969. *A Grammatical Study of Ekpeye.* Unpublished PhD dissertation, University of London, School of Oriental and African Studies.

HALLIDAY, MICHAEL A. K., 1961. 'Categories of the theory of grammar', in *Word* 17, New York: Linguistic Circle of New York, 241ff.

HUDDLESTON, R. D., 1965. 'Rank and depth', *Language* 41, 574ff.

NADEN, ANTHONY J., 1973. *The Grammar of Bisa: A Synchronic Description of the Lebir Dialect (Ghana).* PhD dissertation, University of London.

PIKE, KENNETH L., 1967. *Language in Relation to a Unified Theory of the Structure of Human Behaviour,* The Hague: Mouton.

STANFORD, RONALD, 1967. *The Bekwarra Language of Nigeria: A Grammatical Description.* PhD dissertation, University of London, School of Oriental and African Studies.

THOMAS, ELAINE, 1969. *A Grammatical Description of the Engenni Language.* PhD dissertation, University of London.

GILLIAN BROWN

BROWN, Gillian, CBE 1992; Professor of English as an International Language, University of Cambridge, since 1988; *b.* 1937; *m.* 1959 Keith Brown, 3 d.; *Education:* Perse School for Girls, Cambridge, Girton College, Cambridge (Exhib.), BA 1959, MA 1962; University of Edinburgh PhD 1971; University of Cambridge LittD 1997; *Career:* Lecturer in English Language, University College of Cape Coast, Ghana, 1962–4; Assistant Lecturer, 1965–7, then Lecturer in Phonetics and Linguistics, University of Edinburgh, 1967–80, Reader in Linguistics, 1980–3; Professor of Applied Linguistics, University of Essex, 1983–8; Dean, School of Social Sciences, Member of Council, Senate, etc., University of Essex 1985–8; Director of the Research Centre for English and Applied Linguistics, Fellow of Clare College, Syndic of the University of Cambridge Local Examinations Syndicate, since 1988; Member General Board, Chairman of Work and Stipends Committee, 1992–7; Dr Honoris Causa, University of Lyon, 1987; Member: National Foundation for Education and Research, English Steering Committee, 1983–8, SSRC Education and Human Development Committee 1983–7, Board of Management, British Institute in Paris, since 1986 (Chair: Academic Board since 1995), Kingman Committee of Inquiry into the Teaching of English in Schools 1987–8, Council ESRC (Chair, Research Grants Board) 1987–91, University Grants Committee (UGC Arts Sub-committee) 1987–9, Council of the Philological Society 1988–96, Universities Funding Council 1989–91, Board of the School of Advanced Studies, University of London, since 1994, University of London Council since 1998; Member of the Philological Society since 1983, Linguistics Association of Great Britain since 1975, British Association of Applied Linguists since 1978; Editorial Boards *Journal of Semantics* 1987–95, *Journal of Applied Linguistics* since 1985, *Journal of Second Language Acquisition Research* since 1989, *Linguistics and Education* 1989–97, *Issues and Developments in Applied Linguistics* 1989–97. *Major Publications: Phonological Rules and Dialect Variation: The Phonology of Lumasaaba* 1972; *Listening to Spoken English* 1977 [2nd ed. 1990]; *Discourse Analysis* 1983 (with George Yule); *Speakers, Listeners and Communication* 1995; *Performance and Competence in Second Language Acquisition* (ed. with K. Malmkjaer and J. N. Williams) 1996.

* * *

1 ENGLISH AT CAMBRIDGE

In the late 1950s, the English Tripos at Cambridge offered few papers in English language. My Director of Studies, the distinguished Elizabethan scholar Muriel Bradbrook, had a markedly low opinion of those who had been blessed with exhibitions to enable them to study the thinking of great literary minds and chose instead to opt for tinkering with what she dismissed as 'the mere mechanics' of language. Despite her disapproval, I took optional papers in Anglo-Saxon and Early Norse and the history of the English language (where history came to an end in 1550). These papers were taught within the confines of a traditional paradigm, with close study of individual texts yielding apparently *ad hoc* sets of grammatical and lexical categories which happened to arise in a given text, some of which recurred in a changed form in later texts or in contemporary texts from different dialect areas. The focus of attention was the text as a linguistic object. The texts themselves were in most cases interesting, exciting, sometimes moving, to read. What was lacking was any overview of the grammar of the language or of the nature of language change. The most mysterious aspect of all was what was called 'sound change', a term which referred to different spellings of the same word. One alphabetic letter shape, say 'o', would change into another letter shape, say 'a'. I have no doubt, in retrospect, that those who taught these courses had a sound knowledge of traditional articulatory phonetics, but it was certainly the case that students taking these courses were not offered preliminary training in phonetics; hence for most of them the relationship of the phonology to the orthography was opaque, and the 'sound changes' which occurred in the texts which we happened to study were reduced to arbitrary lists of variant spellings learned by rote.

No doubt the method of teaching, by detailed study of a range of different types of features of language as they occurred sequentially in particular texts, was not conducive to generalization. However, I suspect that those teaching were also inhibited by the knowledge that most senior members of the Faculty abhorred the very idea of systematic teaching about 'the mere mechanics' of language, above all of generalizations about language which were not immediately applied to illuminate a reading of a literary text. In the late 1970s, I met Muriel Bradbrook in Edinburgh and asked her whether, now that linguistics had become an established discipline, the English Tripos might contain options from linguistics, and she replied 'over my dead body'. This aesthetic reaction to the study of language was nicely described to me at about the same time by a Scottish HMI as a fear of 'taking the bloom off the peach'.

2 PHONETICS AT EDINBURGH

In 1964, I went to Edinburgh to study for the Diploma in Phonetics. That it should be Edinburgh was as fortuitous as that the Diploma should be in Phonetics. For the previous two years my husband, Keith Brown, and I had been teaching at the new University of Cape Coast, in Ghana. Keith had been appointed as a Lecturer in English Literature, and I was later appointed as a Lecturer in English Language, a subject I knew rather little about. In the event, we shared the literature and language teaching. Keith worked particularly on the phonetics of English and local Ghanian languages and I constructed what now seems a curious, but I then found absorbing, course on semantics, largely based on the only locally available books which seemed at all relevant: Ziff (1960), *Semantic Analysis*, Ullmann (1957), *Principles of Semantics*, and Nida (1949), *Morphology*. During the UK winter, a number of UK professors visited the Ghanaian coastal universities, ostensibly to advise the Ghanaian government on staff recruitment. When they chanced upon people who were doing a reasonable job, they urged them to return to Britain for formal training. Thus it came about that Keith and I were invited first to Leeds by Peter Strevens to work in applied linguistics, and then to Edinburgh by David Abercrombie. David spent a week in Cape Coast, staying with a lecturer in French, Eric Clavering. Eric had only a rudimentary cook, whereas we had a very good one, so David, a gourmet, and Eric dined with us every evening. David was feeling expansive, having just learned that he had been promoted to a personal Chair in Phonetics, and somehow, during this week, it was settled that we would go to Edinburgh. Keith and I discussed which of us would study for the Diploma in General Linguistics as opposed to the Diploma in Phonetics. We had, by then, three daughters aged 1, 2 and 3, and we were going to be living on a constrained budget. I opted for the Diploma in Phonetics, which could be taken over two years.

The Department of Phonetics was, in the mid-1960s, situated in the basement of Minto House in Chambers Street. It consisted of a rabbit warren of rather small, ill-lit rooms. In those days, professors were absolutely powerful, seconded by charming, intimidating, Scottish secretaries. The first year course, shared by undergraduates, was highly structured and very well taught. It contained a brief introduction to the historical basis of phoneme theory but it was almost exclusively concerned with general phonetics: articulatory phonetics, practical perceptual phonetics, experimental phonetics and acoustic phonetics, some of it also distinctly historical in flavour. John Laver gave a course on experimental phonetics, working with basic tools. We went off to the dental hospital at the end of Chambers Street and had casts made of our palates. Then we practised palatography, first spraying the roof of the mouth with a mixture of cocoa and charcoal, then articulating, then photographing the area of wipe-off on the palate, which could eventually be calibrated with the cast palate. Kymography involved working in a dank, cold, smelly cupboard on the turn of the basement stairs, hands and feet freezing, and articulating powerfully against a tambour constructed from a male contraceptive, while voicing energetically enough for the rather weak throat microphone to pick up the signal, then dipping the recording, which consisted of a fragile impression on a charcoal-covered paper strip, into shellac, to fix it, and hanging the dripping shellacked strip with clothes pegs on a string behind the door. These gruesome procedures did teach one quite a lot about lingual articulation and voice onset time, but the procedures themselves were extraordinarily time-consuming. We were allowed, towards the end of the course, to progress to working with the sound spectrograph, which seemed, then, a huge technological advance.

At the end of the first year, I was appointed by David Abercrombie to an Assistant Lectureship in Phonetics, as was Alan Kemp, who had also been following the first year of the Diploma. The power of professors is well illustrated by these appointments, since we were both appointed apparently without any consultation and certainly without an appointing committee – indeed, to my astonishment, David offered me the post one evening as I sat next to him at dinner. At the same time, Keith was offered a Lectureship in General Linguistics (but John Lyons, himself recently elected to the Chair in General Linguistics, went through proper modern procedures of advertisement, shortlisting and appointing committee). Those were the days of decently funded expansion of universities.

In the second year, the numbers on the Phonetics Diploma were reduced to six, all postgraduate, with two of us working as Assistant Lecturers; the second year included Alan Kemp, who spent his entire career teaching in the Department (and its later amalgamations), Robin Thelwall, who went off to lecture in the Sudan before moving to a Chair at Coleraine, and Henning Wode, now a distinguished Professor of Second Language Acquisition in Germany. The second year seemed a much less highly structured course, but it did include far more instruction on a historical view of phonology. David Abercrombie gave an immensely informative course which began with early nineteenth-century phoneticians, then explored the phonological ideas of Henry Sweet, Baudouin de Courtenay and Ferdinand de Saussure before moving into structuralist phonology in Europe (Trubetskoy, Jakobson, Martinet) and in the US (Sapir, Twadell, Bloomfield, Pike), eventually emerging into Firthian prosodic analysis. Ken Albrow and John Kelly, in different courses, each introduced us to practical aspects of Firthian prosodic analysis. One enterprising lecturer, Klaus Kohler, did, this being 1965, begin to give us a lecture course (called English Phonology) on new-fangled Chomskian phonology, which was being taught regularly by Erik Fudge to students of general linguistics only three streets away. However,

Klaus's subsequent lectures were cancelled (he left the Department at the end of the year), so we emerged from the Diploma without knowing what was currently going on in phonology in the wider world.

3 PHONOLOGY AT EDINBURGH

In the next year or so, a series of events shaped my career interests. First, David Abercrombie invited me to take over the teaching of phonology and phonetics to the Diploma in Applied Linguistics. I enjoyed lecturing to a course of some 30 enthusiastic teachers of English drawn from many different countries, whose experiences frequently overlapped with my own experience in attempting to articulate and to understand spoken languages, English as well as local, in Uganda and Ghana. Many of the students were far more experienced than I was in the problems of language learners, so I learned a great deal from teaching the course and, in doing this, laid the foundations of a career-long interest in the problems of foreign students listening to English spoken by speakers with different accents and with varying degrees of articulatory explicitness. I eventually wrote up some of this work in my 1977 book *Listening to Spoken English*. Within applied linguistics, the area which came to be called 'listening comprehension' hardly existed at that time, and the book made a surprising and enduring impression which has led to many invitations to lecture in Europe and overseas.

A couple of years after our arrival, the Department of Phonetics amalgamated with the Department of General Linguistics and moved from the troglodyte existence of Minto House to the new, utilitarian, Adam Ferguson Building in George Square, where we shared accommodation with our new colleagues. Most members of the newly amalgamated Department employed a speaker of an exotic language who visited them frequently for 'informant sessions'. I, too, acquired an informant whom I began to work with on a regular basis. Since we had lived in Uganda for two years after leaving Cambridge, I decided to work on the phonology of a Ugandan language, and I was fortunate to work with Florence Wamanga, a primary schoolteacher studying at Moray House College of Education. She spoke a language which its speakers call Lumasaaba (though under the British Protectorate it was renamed 'Lugisu'). Lumasaaba is a language spoken right up on the Bantu northern border, projecting up into non-Bantu country on three sides, only abutting on Bantu-speaking areas at the southern and south-western tip. Perhaps because it had been so comprehensively isolated over the centuries, Lumasaaba retained a large number of what Purvis (1907), Johnston (1919/22) and Doke (1945) believed to be archaic and 'original' features of the Bantu languages, notably full double prefixes. I managed to obtain from Makerere University a photocopy of

Purvis's (1907) pamphlet, the only extended description of Lumasaaba. It quickly became clear that Mrs Wamanga spoke a different dialect from the one described by Purvis. Although the phonetic content of his description is limited, he certainly had a good ear for a voiced/voiceless opposition, and it was evident that there were differences at phonological, morphological and lexical levels.

In the summer of 1968, I left Keith with our daughters and their grandmothers, and spent two months in Uganda, undertaking a dialect survey in Bugisu (this was a *quid pro quo* for Keith's spending two months in Ghana collecting Akan data in 1967). I chuntled around Bugisu in a stripped-down Renault 4 with slung canvas seats which was light enough to be picked up and carried like a sedan chair when it became bogged down in the unmade-up murrum tracks during the rains. Everyone who asked me for a lift, and often there were as many as eight people draped in and around the small car, provided me with autobiographical details and a 1,000-word list recorded on my Uher tape-recorder. No compulsion was necessary; it turned out to be a popular and prestigious way to pass the time. Hans Speitel, of the Scottish Linguistic Survey, had advised me to ask people from each area in what way the speech of people in the next area was different or strange, a remarkably insightful and successful technique since this largely illiterate population seemed particularly sensitive to linguistic variation ('largely illiterate' because Lumasaaba did not exist in written form, and many Bagisu failed to complete primary school education, which was conducted in what was for many an unintelligible language, Luganda). It soon became obvious that there were two large dialect areas, one to the north and one to the south of the spur of Mount Elgon which juts out across Bugisu. Within each major area were three clearly distinct accent areas. (I write 'were' because, as I left, in September 1968, the predatory Amin was assuming power, a savage regime soon to be followed by the dreadful incursions of AIDS, and I have no current information about whether the relatively small numbers of speakers of the less populous accents have survived.)

Initially, I had intended to describe the phonology of Lumasaaba within a Firthian framework, but those in Edinburgh actually working in this framework almost immediately departed, Ken Albrow for Bangor and John Kelly for York, which left me as a neophyte in an area where many distinguished publications existed, typically written in a numinous style appropriate for other members of the in-group but difficult for a non-member to crack without help. It was unclear to me how it would be possible to make a succinct and systematic statement of the relationships between the six accents of Lumasaaba, since I could find nothing in the Firthian literature which attempted to compare such a variety of related accents. I turned to generative phonology, particularly, to begin with, Halle (1959; 1964) and Chomsky & Halle (1965). Then, as time passed, more papers and books began to appear, notably Stanley (1967), Chomsky & Halle (1968), Postal (1968) and Kiparsky (1968). I read in this area for a year, without formal instruction in this model since Erik Fudge had also departed, having been appointed to a Lectureship in Cambridge, which left the Department temporarily without a phonologist. At this point, the value for me of the amalgamation of the departments became clear, since John Lyons encouraged me to teach the phonology course for the Diploma in General Linguistics. I suppose the most efficient, though terrifying, way of learning about a subject is to be in the position of teaching it to outstandingly good students (many of whom are today colleagues, often professors, in departments of linguistics in the UK and around the world); I certainly learned a great deal about generative phonology by teaching it.

My PhD supervisor was Laurie Iles, who used to say that he had published two papers, 'one on *ex*plosives and one on *im*plosives'. He was a former sapper officer, who had been working in the Department of Phonetics since his retirement from the army. He had not worked on Bantu languages nor had he read in generative phonology, but he was the most extraordinarily scrupulous supervisor, who would go over every argument in meticulous detail, checking back over the piles of poorly typed, palely carbon-copied, cut-and-pasted pages which he retained from each of our meetings to ensure that it was coherent with what had been said before. His help was invaluable, and I learned a great deal from him and from his systematic way of working. I learned too, during this period, about the art of writing an academic paper from Peter Matthews. I sent off a discursive early version of what was to become the central theoretical chapter in my thesis to the *Journal of Linguistics*. Peter Matthews had recently taken over the editorship, and he replied swiftly and devastatingly, saying essentially that he didn't see the point of the paper. After the initial shock came a surge of adrenalin and, with steam coming out of my ears, I wrote a brisk reply. To my considerable surprise, I received, almost by return of post, a most generous and detailed letter, encouraging me to rewrite the paper in the forthright terms of my reply to him. This was published in the *Journal* in 1970 and was, apart from a descriptive piece on the dialect situation in Bugisu which appeared in the *Journal of African Languages* in 1968, my first academic paper.

My thesis had been officially registered initially for an MLitt, since David Abercrombie held the view that the PhD was 'not an honourable degree' but 'a jumped-up American invention' which was only necessary for those proposing to work in the USA. However, a further benefit for me of the amalgamation of the departments was that John Lyons was kind enough to read parts of my thesis, and he not only confirmed that it was substantial enough for a PhD but also urged me to send off the completed version to Cambridge University Press, who subsequently published it in 1972.

By this time Roger Lass had joined the Department, and I enjoyed, for the first time, during the few years he was in Edinburgh, the pleasure of daily interaction with a stimulating and immensely knowledgeable colleague who was working in the same fast-developing field. Also I now had a number of PhD students working in phonology (notably Francis Katamba, now Professor at Lancaster); phonology suddenly became fun. Since I was no longer alone responsible for teaching phonological theory to each of the undergraduate years and to each of the three Diplomas (soon all to be called MSc), time became available for new developments and I began to move into an area of phonology which at that time was rather little explored, intonation. In 1975, I applied to the (then) SSRC for funding to work on Scottish intonation in different Scottish accents and its relation to southern English intonation, particularly that of RP, and was awarded a four-year research grant. Karen Currie and Joanne Kenworthy (now at North London University) were just completing their undergraduate degrees and they both worked on the grant throughout its duration. Initially, we were raw recruits in learning how to work together constructively, but eventually we each developed our own area of expertise within an overall framework, greatly helped by the Phonetics laboratory, which assisted with huge amounts of detailed acoustic analysis, as we set about debunking many of the myths which had accumulated about 'English' intonation in the descriptive and pedagogical literature.

A research project on intonation necessarily involved working with conversational English as well as with extended turns where one individual spoke, uninterrupted, for a period of time. I began to work on the relationship of lexico/syntactic packaging of information and the structure of intonation in such data. This led me into the field which later became known as 'discourse analysis' (see section 4 below). The book reporting the outcome of the project (Brown, Currie & Kenworthy 1980) is still cited as a major description of Scottish intonation.

4 DISCOURSE ANALYSIS AT EDINBURGH

Since the late 1960s, I had been part of a team which began to develop a course then called 'Communication Studies' for the Applied Linguistics Diploma (later renamed MSc). The team included, at various times, Henry Widdowson, Patrick Allen, Clive Criper, Pit Corder and Alan Davies, and in the early days I was a fairly peripheral member. The course included a wide selection of material ranging from literary stylistics, through the simplification of pedagogical texts and notions of 'authenticity', to various approaches to conversational analysis, textual cohesion and the analysis of classroom discourse. I contributed a session on differences between written and spoken discourse. As those teaching the course changed, so the content changed. When Patrick Allen left for Toronto in the early-1970s, 'cohesion' disappeared, and when

Henry Widdowson departed to the University of London Institute of Education in the mid-1970s, 'stylistics' disappeared. By the late 1970s, the number of posts in applied linguistics had halved, even though the number of students still grew. I found myself taking on the supervision of applied linguistics PhD students working on aspects of discourse structure, and I was eventually asked to undertake the teaching of what had hitherto been called 'Communication Studies' for the applied linguists, at the same time as I was asked to construct a course on text-linguistics for fourth year undergraduates; I named both courses 'Discourse Analysis'.

Meanwhile, as the research project on Scottish intonation ended, I applied to the SSRC for a further grant to work on intonation and information structure. George Yule, who had just completed the MSc in Applied Linguistics, joined me on this project while researching for his PhD. It was an exciting time in Edinburgh to be working in this area, since the School of Epistemics (later the School of Cognitive Science, now part of Informatics) had recently been established, and was attracting interdisciplinary participation, remarkably able postgraduate students and starry national and international visitors and seminar speakers. Keith and I were both early participants in the School (indeed Keith was, for a year, Director), and when the MSc in Epistemics was established, I taught a discourse analysis course, referring not only to the linguistics input of the MSc but also to the psycholinguistic processing and the philosophy of language courses. When, in 1981, towards the completion of the SSRC 'information' project, George Yule and I wrote *Discourse Analysis* (published 1983), we drew upon this rich interdisciplinary background, as well as the various lecture courses I was giving to different constituents, together with the notion of 'topic' emerging from George's PhD research. This allowed us to construct a strongly linguistic and cognitive account of 'discourse analysis', which has proved remarkably hard-wearing despite the challenge from more sociologically motivated approaches.

In 1979, I had been invited by the National Foundation for Educational Research (NFER) to participate in a conference on teaching and testing oral skills in English and Welsh schools at ages 7, 11 and 15. There seemed to be an excellent opportunity here for applying insights into information structure. This led me into discussions with the Scottish Education Department (SED), who were anxious to find some way of improving and testing the oral capacities of school-leavers who were low academic achievers (in some cases functionally illiterate). A large research project on developing communication skills in academically low-achieving teenagers was funded by the SED from 1980, on which George worked for a while, soon joined by Anne Anderson (now Professor of Psychology at Glasgow). Work on this project provided input as George and I wrote a further book together, drawing on our notion of 'discourse analysis'; *Teaching the Spoken Language* (also published in 1983). As the writing of these two books neared completion,

George left to take up a post as Associate Professor in the Linguistics Department at Minnesota. The SED project was then enlarged to include psychologist Richard Shillcock and cognitive scientist Nigel Shadbolt (now Professor of Computer Science at Southampton).

A characteristic of my research projects has been that we work on spoken data derived from two to four people who need to talk to each other as they co-operate in undertaking a task. In 1975, in the intonation project, we had begun by simply collecting large amounts of spontaneous speech derived from a wide range of speech situations, but we soon found that spontaneous speech corpora, however large and varied, may not yield the particular syntactic, intonational or discoursal data required. For instance, when we wanted to demonstrate the intonational patterns which can occur in pseudo-cleft questions, we discovered that our corpus included no pseudo-cleft questions. We wrestled with various tasks, initially discarding 100 per cent as useless when piloted, but eventually constructed a task which freely and naturally elicits pseudo-cleft questions (cf. Brown et al. 1980). Gradually, over a number of projects, our expertise in task design increased. Towards the end of 1982 the first version of the Map Task was developed, a spectacularly successful task for many reasons (cf. Brown 1995a), which has now, in a variety of forms, been used in many different projects, for different purposes, in the UK and overseas. The development of tightly constructed and extensively pre-tested tasks enables researchers to explore, in children, adolescents and adults, the developing use of particular formal features of a first or second language in well-demarcated contexts as well as the ability of speakers to achieve particular pragmatic effects. The same task-type can be adapted to the different cognitive abilities of subjects in different stages of language development (Brown 1982; 1994; 1995b).

5 APPLIED LINGUISTICS AND COMMITTEES AT ESSEX

In 1983, Keith and I accomplished what a friend at SOAS described as 'a spectacular double salmon leap' and both moved to the University of Essex. I went to a Chair in Applied Linguistics, but felt perfectly at home, since the applied linguistics section was embedded in the overarching Department of Language and Linguistics. I left behind in Edinburgh a new SED-funded project on listening comprehension which was continued by Anne Anderson, and took with me to Essex an ESRC project, with Richard Shillcock (now back at Edinburgh) and Barry Smith (now lecturing in philosophy at Birkbeck) as researchers, and a Leverhulme project with psychologists Gordon Brown (now Professor of Psychology at Warwick) and Peter Wright (now at York) as researchers, all working on aspects of listening comprehension. In these projects, we explored how different aspects of the social setting or different aspects of the construction of the task would lead to problems for the listener in understanding what was said in the way that the speaker intended. The ESRC project began by manipulating the Map Task, to cluster information visually in helpful or unhelpful ways, and moved on to provide landscape features in the maps which would inhibit movement in a given direction and give rise to misleading use of deictic terms, and to the exploitation of features which would receive ambiguous descriptions from subjects. A major development was the introduction of the use of video film, which introduced a complex temporal dimension into tasks which otherwise retained the structure of the Map Task. Groups of subjects exchanged information about scenes which they had witnessed but their listeners had not seen (cf. Brown 1995a). The Leverhulme project meanwhile was examining issues such as the effect of an unclear message being spoken by someone apparently in authority as opposed to a junior speaker, where listeners tend to blame themselves for not understanding the authoritative speaker but blame a junior speaker, who delivers an identical message, for not speaking clearly (cf. Brown, Sharkey & Brown 1987).

In Essex, the disadvantages from the point of view of research of being the only woman Professor in the university were soon apparent, as I was asked to join increasing numbers of committees and, eventually, to become Dean of Social Sciences. At a national level, too, institutions sought women professors for committees, and I joined the ESRC Education and Human Development Committee, the British Council English Advisory Committee, and several others. The most interesting was the 18-month Kingman Inquiry into the teaching of English language in primary and secondary schools (1987–8). This involved many days spent in travelling to, and visiting, primary and secondary schools and university education departments around the country, full-day committee meetings, and the reiterative writing of proposals for the model of English language which was to be recommended. In the event this last task fell largely to me, since Henry Widdowson, the only other person on this large committee of 'experts' who was academically involved with the English language, was unwell for many months during this period. In retrospect, this expenditure of time does seem to have been worthwhile, since the Kingman Report informed the National Curriculum Committee, whose work informed the current National Literacy Strategy, and now, at last, children at school are once again learning something about the English language. In support of this, I have recently (1998–2000) co-authored with a primary school teacher, Kate Ruttle, and with Keith in the area of English grammar, nine primary school textbooks intended not only to draw children into thinking about their language but also to inform teachers, many of whom know little about the English language, of what they need to know to teach each lesson (published as part of the Cambridge Reading Scheme by Cambridge University Press).

6 RETURN TO CAMBRIDGE: APPLIED LINGUISTICS AND MORE COMMITTEES

My move to Cambridge in 1988 consumed a year during which I wrestled with architects and commissioned furniture and fittings, and constructed a basic library for the Research Centre in English and Applied Linguistics while appointing the first two members of staff during 1989 and planning the work of this new institution. Meanwhile I became a member of the University Grants Committee (and later of the Universities Funding Council) and various associated sub-committees, and of the ESRC. For the first four years of its existence I chaired the newly formed ESRC Research Grants Board and fought its corner in the funding Council, which was already into a directed funding mode and looking for extra funds to support its various 'initiatives'. The Research Grants Board's share of the cake steadily increased during my chairmanship. The other cause for which I fought much less successfully, with few allies on Council other than Keith Thomas, was expanding the number of research student grants; the current (underfunded) expansion of universities has revealed a worrying shortage of UK applicants for posts, not only in linguistics but in the social sciences generally.

Within Cambridge over the ensuing years, committee work has mounted steeply in a university dedicated to the representation of both sexes on all major committees but with only a handful of senior women academics. For five years (1992–7), I was a member of the General Board, which is responsible for the academic affairs of the university, which again entailed membership (sometimes as Chair) of a great many sub-committees. When I eventually resigned from the General Board, I also resigned from 13 other committees. Quite a number remain. I have been associated with the British Institute in Paris (an Institute of London University) for 15 years as a member of its Board, also recently as Chair of its Academic Board. Similarly, as Curator of the School of Advanced Studies, and more recently as a member of Council, of the University of London, I have watched, perhaps even contributed to, new, academically exciting institutions emerging from the somewhat apprehensive residue of departments and institutions which remained in the central university after the Sutherland reforms. Participating in committee work of this kind, despite the fact that it is immensely time-consuming, is none the less deeply satisfying when there are clear academic gains. In contrast, dealing with the piles of administrative paperwork which are nowadays generated for all academics, particularly for Heads of Departments, has become utterly destructive of research time with no obvious consequential benefits. Many Heads of Department can only hope to undertake joined-up research during the (shrinking) long vacations. For the last five years, I have been intermittently exploring, using a rich data-bank of material from accumulated research projects, how listeners construct the context within which a linguistic message is interpreted (cf. for example Brown 1999). I hope to complete the book I am writing on this before I retire.

My major focus over the last 12 years has been the development of the Research Centre for English and Applied Linguistics (RCEAL) as a nationally and internationally recognized centre for theoretical research in applied linguistics. Since it seems likely that the Centre will remain a fairly small enterprise (though it has grown from its initial three members of academic staff to, currently, eight), it is vital that its expertise remains sharply focused. The establishment of the Centre offered the opportunity of creating an institution dedicated to research and teaching in those aspects of applied linguistics which rely on linguistics and on cognitive psychology. Besides working in English syntax and semantics/pragmatics, we concentrate on different aspects of the acquisition, development, and discourse processing of first and second languages. We have been fortunate in attracting outstanding research staff. The success of the Centre has also been powered by a unique Master's degree which is aimed at university lecturers and senior language teachers who wish to undertake research in those fields in which we specialize. The reputation of the MPhil now attracts a large application from which we select 10–15 students each year. About 50 per cent go on to undertake PhD research at the Centre, so we have some 20 PhD students at any given time. The Centre also welcomes two or three distinguished Visiting Fellows each year, who contribute to the work of this growing research community.

Today, most applied linguistics in the UK is increasingly to be found located in departments of education, apparently intent on cutting itself off from its roots in linguistics and often embracing postmodernist approaches to language which denigrate the formal analysis of language. The addition of a highly respected research centre to the handful of remaining departments of applied linguistics which assert the relevance of linguistic and psycholinguistic research to issues in first and second language learning and use will, I hope and believe, assume a vital significance for the future of the discipline in this country.

In many ways the Centre is in an enviable position, since it has a foundation endowment (since added to by further fund-raising) which means that it is able to make independent decisions in areas such as staffing and the buying of books and equipment. On the other hand, for some purposes, it is regarded as part of the Faculty of English, for whom it is a strange cuckoo in the nest. The views of the majority in the Faculty about the linguistic study of language have changed little in 40 years. However, since our arrival, despite a number of interim difficulties and misunderstandings, the Faculty of English has generously adapted itself to coping with this anomalous institution whose work is exclusively concerned with 'the mere mechanics' of language.

REFERENCES

BROWN, GILLIAN, 1970. 'Syllables and redundancy rules in generative phonology', *Journal of Linguistics* 6.1, 1–17

BROWN, GILLIAN, 1972. *Phonological Rules and Dialect Variation: The Phonology of Lumasaaba*, Cambridge Studies in Linguistics, 7, Cambridge: Cambridge University Press.

BROWN, GILLIAN, 1977. *Listening to Spoken English*, Harlow: Longman. 2nd ed. 1990.

BROWN, GILLIAN, 1980 (with Karen Currie & Joanne Kenworthy). *Questions of Intonation*, London: Croom Helm.

BROWN, GILLIAN, 1982. 'The spoken language', in R. A. Carter (ed.), *Linguistics and the Teacher*, London: Routledge and Kegan Paul, 75–87.

BROWN, GILLIAN, 1983a (with George Yule). *Discourse Analysis*, Cambridge: Cambridge University Press.

BROWN, GILLIAN, 1983b (with George Yule). *Teaching the Spoken Language*, Cambridge: Cambridge University Press.

BROWN, GILLIAN, 1987 (with Gordon Brown and Amanda Sharkey). 'Factors affecting the success of referential communication', *Journal of Psycholinguistic Research* 16.6, 535–49.

BROWN, GILLIAN, 1994. 'Modes of understanding', in G. Brown, K. Malmkjaer, A. Pollitt & J. Williams (eds.), *Language and Understanding*, Oxford: Oxford University Press, 9–21.

BROWN, GILLIAN, 1995a. *Speakers, Listeners and Communication*, Cambridge: Cambridge University Press.

BROWN, GILLIAN, 1995b. 'Dimensions of difficulty in listening comprehension', in D. Mendelsohn & Joan Rubin (eds.), *A Guide for the Teaching of Second Language Listening*, San Diego: Dominie Press, 59–74.

BROWN, GILLIAN, 1999. 'Context creation in discourse understanding', in K. Malmkjaer & J. Williams (eds.), *Context in Language Learning and Language Understanding*, Cambridge: Cambridge University Press, 171–93.

CHOMSKY, NOAM & HALLE, MORRIS, 1965. 'Some controversial questions in phonological theory', *Journal of Linguistics* 1.2, 97–138.

CHOMSKY, NOAM & HALLE, MORRIS, 1968. *The Sound Pattern of English*, New York: Harper and Row.

DOKE, C. M., 1945. *Bantu*, London: International African Institute.

HALLE, MORRIS, 1959. *The Sound Pattern of Russian*, The Hague: Mouton.

HALLE, MORRIS, 1964. 'Phonology in generative grammar', in J. L. Fodor & J. L. Katz (eds.), *The Structure of Language: Readings in the Philosophy of Language*, Englewood-Cliffs, NJ: Prentice-Hall, 334–53.

JOHNSTON, HARRY, 1919/22. *A Comparative Study of the Bantu and Semi-Bantu Languages*, vols. 1 and 2, Oxford: Clarendon Press.

KIPARSKY, PAUL, 1968. 'Linguistic universals and linguistic change', in E. Bach & R. T. Harms (eds.), *Universals in Linguistic Theory*, New York: Holt, Rinehart & Winston, 171–204.

NIDA, EUGENE, 1949. *Morphology: The Descriptive Analysis of Words*, 2nd ed., Ann Arbor: University of Michigan Press.

POSTAL, PAUL, 1968. *Aspects of Phonological Theory*, New York: Harper and Row.

PURVIS, J. B., 1907. *A Handbook of Lumasaba Grammar*, London: SPCK.

STANLEY, RICHARD, 1967. 'Redundancy rules in phonology', *Language* xliii, 393–436.

ULLMANN, STEPHEN, 1957. *Principles of Semantics*, 2nd ed., Oxford: Blackwell.

ZIFF, PAUL, 1960. *Semantic Analysis*, Ithaca, NY: Cornell University Press.

N. E. COLLINGE

COLLINGE, Neville Edgar, MC 1944; Emeritus Professor Comparative Philology, University of Manchester, since 1987; *b.* 1921; *m.* 1949 Mildred Elizabeth Owen; *Education:* Manchester Grammar School; University of Manchester BA 1942; Cambridge University BA 1947, MA 1952, PhD 1967; *Career:* Lecturer, University of Durham, 1947–59, Senior Lecturer 1959–69; Professor, University of Toronto, 1969–74 (Director of Centre for Linguistic Studies 1971–4), University of Birmingham (and Head of Department of Linguistics) 1974–9, University of Manchester (Mont Follick Professor, Head of Department of Linguistics) 1980–7. Founder Member, Linguistics Association of Great Britain (and President 1962–5), Visiting Faculty Member, University of Pennsylvania, 1962, Yale University 1966, Publications Secretary, Philological Society (and editor of *Transactions*), 1966–9, Council Member 1974–9, President, Societas Linguistica Europaea, 1984–5. Member Editorial Boards *Journal of Linguistics* 1965–70 and 1974–83, *Journal of Indo-European Studies* 1972–93, *Archivum Linguisticum* 1980–1; Panel member DES State Studentship Selection Committee 1983–6 (Chairman 1985–6), President, Cambridge University Linguistic Society, 1990–2.

* * *

Most classical scholars are familiar with the story of the schoolmaster who proclaimed 'this term, boys, you are to have the privilege of reading the *Oedipus Tyrannus* of Sophocles, a veritable treasure-house of grammatical peculiarities'. For many classicists, myself included, explaining the vagaries of Greek and Latin grammar and exploring the linguistic adventurism of ancient authors (especially the poets) was always a mental exercise of delight. Although I lectured and wrote on such things as the structure of Horace's lyric composition and the architecture of Euripides' tragedies, it was the challenge of their language, going along with historical speculation into the genetics of that language ('comparative philology'), which hastened the narrowing of my interest. People like me became heirs to the nineteenth-century tradition and Proto-Indo-European was our goal.

To the classical tongues, plus some knowledge of the Italic languages and of the dialects of Ancient Greece (augmented in 1952–3 by the unveiling of Mycenaean), I added Sanskrit (Vedic and classical) and made the acquaintance of Hittite and its Anatolian cousins and even learnt something of Tocharian. But to swell my data from the remaining stocks of Indo-European I have had to rely on the findings of other scholars.

Yet I, and my historical colleagues, largely ignored such questions as 'how does language basically work?' or 'what licence do native users have to choose, invent, exploit or even apparently misuse the forms of their language?' For the former concern we relied on traditional taxonomy; for the latter we substituted *ad hoc* explanations case by case. The predominance and persistence of the historical approach may be gauged from the retitling of the English translation of Holger Pedersen's 1924 review of nineteenth-century (purely diachronic) work as *The Discovery of Language* as late as the edition of 1962.

In fact, there existed plenty of guides and inspirers to a wider vision. Phonetics turned out (as Abercrombie had shown in 1948) to have been an on-going scholarly concern in England since the seventeenth century; and Daniel Jones soon introduced us (in 1950) to Kruszewski's 'phoneme' – though awareness of the input of Trubetzkoy and the Prague School came more slowly. Linguistic theory and its various aspects began to emerge from the mists. These mists were heavy and long-lasting in England, but not quite dissipated elsewhere: so John W. Spargo had written in 1930 of 'the terror of language study so prevalent in America', and this despite the efforts of such as Edward Sapir a decade before. But gradually 'descriptivism' – to use the fashionable term of the time – made itself known and felt. Bloomfield's *Language* (which did not appear in England until 1935, two years after its publication in America) was supplemented, or even introduced to us, by Al Gleason's *Introduction to Descriptive Linguistics* (1955) and Charles Hockett's *Course in Modern Linguistics* (1958). But possibly my first marked awakening came only with the appearance of the Philological Society's special volume of 1957, *Studies in Linguistic Analysis*. This was notable for, inter alia, Willi Haas's intriguing article on 'zero' in linguistic description (he used to say in later life that his reputation had been 'built on nothing'). Its main content, however, was the editor J. R. Firth's own synopsis of linguistic theory from 1930 to 1955, which was admittedly 'Firthian' in slant and contained much to disagree with (such as his attack, p. 21 and fn. 1, on the correctly reconstructed IE subjunctive and optative as being 'personifications of categories' and 'pseudo-universal' entities, which they have not been claimed to be). Yet he opened our eyes to the work done in England already on the working of grammar as well as of phonology; he put into circulation terms like 'levels', 'context of situation', 'collocation' and 'colligation'; and he offered thought-provoking 'general conclusions' – for instance, that there are in language study 'no brute facts'. The other contributors revealed work, of a London ideology, done on a wide variety of languages. As a result we were prompted to gaze more widely, and writers like Bloch, Benveniste, Hjelmslev, Harris – and then Chomsky – swam into our consciousness. And 'generativism' became the fashionable flavour.

None the less, the great deficiency in those years, for effective exchange of ideas and reinforcement of progress in the subject in this country, was the absence of a relevant and regular learned forum. In the late 1950s Ronald Crossland, Barbara Strang and I formed a linguistic section of the University of Durham Philosophical Society (based in fact in Newcastle). But nationally there was nothing. The Philological Society, with all its merits and long-standing authority, was traditionally geared to presentations of theses on particular languages with a primarily historical slant (although by then a 'London school' approach had introduced some structuralism); moreover, its meetings were (and still are) devoted to single papers, with no annual or six-monthly colloquium at which there might be a menu of contributions and time for fruitful interplay between scholars of differing backgrounds. This lack was effectively made good by the inauguration of a Linguistic Circle at Hull University. This was made possible by collaboration between several of its dons and departments; but it was really the brainchild of one scholar, the Germanist Jeffrey Ellis. He invented the Circle and he held it together during the later 1950s. For four or five years the Hull conferences brought together linguists from London, Manchester, Durham, Newcastle and other centres. Then, at one meeting, J. R. Firth attended as a guest and was pressing in his flattering suggestion that the Circle become a national institution. In 1959 this end was achieved; and the inaugural meeting of the 'Linguistics Association (Great Britain)' – as it was first styled – took place in University College, London. Ellis was elected its first President (1959–62). I was happy, as a regular attender and speaker at Hull, to join in the new venture; and in 1962 I succeeded Ellis as second President (1962–5). Lively papers were presented and argumentative sessions begun by such figures as David Crystal, Erik Fudge, Willi Haas, Michael Halliday (who virtually unveiled there his 1961 'Categories of the theory of grammar'), R. H. Robins, Barbara Strang and Jimmy Thorne. Yet these efforts, when published, appeared in journals relevant to their topics and often abroad, so that inspirational unity was lost. Not surprisingly, therefore, at a meeting at Bangor it was decided to start the Association's own periodical, to be called (I believe by the suggestion of John Lyons, fifth President and first Editor) the *Journal of Linguistics*. I had the honour of signing the contract with Cambridge University Press; and the first fascicule of *JL* appeared in April 1965, published by CUP for what had then become the 'Linguistics Association of Great Britain'. I contributed the first article (1965a). Now *JL* is a major international serial of quality, attracting a wealth of valuable papers and reviews across the world and across the whole spectrum of the subject.

For each of us in the 1950s, 1960s and even 1970s, entry into linguistics, in the institutional sense, was a tortuous process. From bases in established disciplines and departments we tentatively embarked on more or less (commonly less rather than more) joint enterprises. At Durham, where I served the university for 22 years, I was part of a loose consortium which sought to promote general consciousness of the operation of language. My colleagues were from Durham Randolph Quirk and from Newcastle (because what is now the University of Newcastle upon Tyne was then a division of the University of Durham) Ronald Crossland and Barbara Strang. My own linguistic shaping was further affected by two brief spells of service in America, first at the University of Pennsylvania in Philadelphia (1962–3) and then at Yale University (1966). The first visit introduced me to, inter alios, Henry Hiż, Zellig Harris and Haj Ross; the second – though my duties were mainly classical – to Isidore Dyen and Warren Cowgill. The multi-faceted nature of language study was revealed to me, as well as its excitement and its potential for varied strategies. Sadly, the advent of the first version of Chomskyism had already begun to impose a constricting religiosity upon at least the American scholarly world.

Still, starting with the USA, the world was also multiplying its academic bases (university departments, centres or just programmes) for coverage of the newish subject. In 1971 came my own irreversible transfer into it. At the University of Toronto, where I had by then held a Professorship in Classics for two years, I was invited to succeed Martin Joos as director of the Centre for Linguistic Studies. My mandate was to transform a rather heterogeneous collection of people from different subject sources (Al Gleason being, perhaps, the only thoroughbred linguist) into a regular and structured – and financially accountable – department, which it now is. It was an enjoyable stint (1971–4). My immediate co-workers included Jack Chambers, Jonathan Kaye, Peter Reich, Hank Rogers, Peter Salus and Bill Samarin, so that I became aware of bilingualism and societal forces, of Amerindian researches, of stratificational analysis, of Celtic and African problems, and much besides. Quite another programme awaited me when I returned to England to head the newly established Department of Linguistics at the University of Birmingham (1974–9), namely to turn a proposal into a reality and a pilot team (comprising Peter Ricketts, John Payne and later Suzanne Romaine) into a fully fledged and staffed unit. But this hope was dashed by the swingeing cuts in university funding of the early 1980s; and after less than a decade the enterprise had been abandoned, yet not without enriching the mental fare available to students with a flair for the analysis of language. Besides, in an adventurous inter-university scheme with Nottingham we taught some courses to their students (e.g. case grammar and stratificational analysis) and they (notably Chris Butler and Margaret Berry) responded by instructing ours in systemic linguistics. Occasional colloquia were actually three-way, involving also Aston University. My last berth entailed yet another sort of obligation. I was called to Manchester University, and its Mont Follick Chair, to captain an already well-founded and sizeable organization, the department established by Willi Haas with the help and zeal of especially Edward Carney, David Allerton, Alan Cruse and Alan Cruttenden (which meant that philosophy of grammar and lexis was well buttressed by phonetic and phonological expertise). Here my mission (1980–7) was two-fold. For one thing, I had to insinuate linguistics, in varied suitable forms, into Honours programmes jointly with other disciplines and on a wide front: we married not only with English and classics but also with philosophy, psychology, anthropology and sociology, and even education. We also co-operated with UMIST in computational linguistics. For another thing, I had to prompt or assist the release into published form of the research achievements of the Department's team – to produce books, in fact. Success on both fronts meant I was able to bequeath to my successor, Nigel Vincent, a far-reaching and articulate operation, and one which has continued to attract able and lively members. It now forms part of a School of English and Linguistics.

Two other activities worth a mention fell to my lot during the 1980s. I joined the Societas Linguistica Europaea, a brave and indeed successful attempt to bring linguists together through the then still existing Iron Curtain. It has gone from strength to strength, with now two journals, *Folia Linguistica* (1967–) and *Folia Linguistica Historica* (1980–). But it has tended not to catch the interest and participation of very many English scholars. In 1984 Martin Harris and I organized its annual symposium in Manchester and Salford; and in the session 1984–5 I served as President of the Societas. (An abiding memory is that of introducing the Mayor of Toledo to the conference in his own town.) Then I was persuaded by the publishing house Croom Helm, afterwards taken over by Routledge, to edit a volume comprising a multiplex review of past and present work across the discipline (and sub-disciplines) of linguistics. Despite the anguished protestations of myself and the volume's energetic publishing officer, Jonathan Price, the product (1990) was titled *An Encyclopaedia of Language*, even though it was in reality a survey with some inherent eclecticism but much theoretical, critical and (where relevant) historical depth. Encyclopedias, by contrast, are exhaustive but superficial. Yet it was a great pleasure and privilege to act as 'whipper-in' to the authors of its 26 chapters, and I learned enormously from their efforts.

Clearly, my own role has been as much administrative as ideological, and critical rather than creative. Yet I have spoken and written fairly freely. The worth of my publications is for others to judge, and no doubt they have made the assessment. But, for anyone who cares to read further, it will do no harm to list at least those contributions which have seemed to me worthy of a little notice. Besides, it will enable me to voice one or two beliefs, or doubts, which the progress of the subject over the last four decades has nurtured in me.

My corners of linguistics have been four. To list them in order of increasing commitment, they are: (a) pragmatics; (b) theories of grammar; (c) historiography; and (d) comparative-genetic studies. I was attracted to (a) pragmatics after the switch of semantics from concentration on the meaning of words and phrases (lexical semantics) – which seemed a constricting concern even after Stephen Ullmann had introduced us to field theory – to consideration of utterances and their 'force' in situational context, a fascinating can of worms. Firth hinted at it; but the lid was more decisively raised in 1955 by John L. Austin, who was part of the delayed philosophic reaction to logical positivism and the devotion to pure truth values. The can was further shaken by John Searle, who offered to define 'illocutionary force'; after which, speech acts, presuppositions, implicatures and similar notions set linguists and philosophers (and philosophers and philosophers) on delightful collision courses. Paul Grice, with his conversational maxims and the implicatures of their flouting, and Deirdre Wilson (with Dan Sperber), relating the nuances simply to an all-embracing control of 'relevance' – and others, including in this country Leech and Levinson – all made challenging contributions. I did myself, however, wonder (in 1988) whether Ancient Greek was a rather wayward tongue in displaying enmity towards (or, anyhow, avoidance of) presuppositions, a timidity of venturing on purely calculable speech acts, and a preference for making crystal clear on the surface the relevance-link of utterances (using its plethora of sentential particles).

On the second topic, (b) theories of grammar, purely British enterprises are rarer, at least at the level of invention. Possibly we can claim only 'systemics', the later development by Michael Halliday and his school of his original 'scale and category' formulation. Still, Ian Catford's revelation of ergativity as it is to be seen in the North Caucasian languages is perhaps a valid example of British priming of the pump. Other sub-disciplines are of foreign invention – one thinks of case studies, valency theorems, the active–ergative–accusative relation, stratificational analysis and categorial grammar – but all have had their proponents in Britain. I have always been drawn to these, currently non-mainstream, topics. This is not least because each theory has partial blinding success in accounting for actual language data and equally partial simple blindness. Moreover, they clash in maddening ways. Categorial grammar, in whatever version, rests on two basic entities, that of which it can be asked 'does X exist meaningfully?' and that which faces the question 'is Y true?' Respectively, positive input sets up 'noun' and 'sentence', all other categories being derived. So we have an immediate confrontation with any verb-centred approach, such as valency or (largely) case grammar. Now argument as to the theoretical priority of noun or verb engaged the earliest Indian grammarians (see my remarks at 1970: 181) and led Sanctius in the sixteenth century to equate their standing. The issue has yet to be resolved; I am glad of that, for once it ceases to attract people's attention my interest will lapse. My devotion to the topics mentioned above (as in the discussions at 1970: ch 7, 8; 1978b; 1980; 1983) arose from these dilemmas. They reinforced my conviction that languages are such tricky customers that a multiplicity of theories, and not merely of systems (as Firth held), is needed to plot their operation. That a single theory, however complex, may not suffice to handle a language explains my concern to make students cognisant of these partially effective notions (including role and reference grammar, and functional grammar), which were out of the lime-light from 1960 onwards and still are. In my various departments, in other words, I have favoured a policy of eclecticism.

And I remain a non-Chomskian (even a non-Jespersenian) linguist for two further reasons. For one thing, I favour (in general linguistics but not in comparative-historical studies) 'more-or-less' solutions, to quote Sidney Allen, and I prefer a 'hocus-pocus' attitude to a 'God's truth' one, to use Fred Householder's terms. I admired Haj Ross's sliding scales: for example, of 'noun-iness' and 'neg-iness'. Inexactitude is endemic in our trade; as Sapir famously remarked in the year of my birth (1921), 'all grammars leak'. Second, as was said above, my approach has been essentially critical. I have favoured regular testing on a wide front, or what Firth called constant 'renewal of connection with the data'. Hence I have shunned preoccupation with the theoretical base for its own sake. To pick up John Lyons's perhaps overneat divisive terms (as in Lyons 1999), I have preferred linguistic theory to theoretical linguistics. Chomsky in particular has promoted the latter, and has enticed most of the world to accept his attitude (though puzzling his adherents by successive revolutions in his own interpretation of theory). He has also pushed on to centre stage once more consideration of 'der sprechende Mensch' (already in 1878 the seat of language for Brugmann and Osthoff), together with the implied mental processes. Fair enough, as long as we bear in mind that the native speaker, as Saussure saw in his 'sujet parlant', is a muddler and a muddier of categories and a non-respecter of rules. Case-syncretism is a prime example of muddying, as is lack of strictness in use of the unsyncretized cases, where they exist.

Another negative conclusion to which I have been drawn, more gradually, is that there are no such things as grammatical universals. Thirty years ago I noted Hoenigswald's and Cowgill's uncertainties over the assumption of universals in language history (1970: 14 and fn. 3 – the reference is to their reports in Greenberg 1966, a book which inaugurated a lasting fascination with these concepts). One may recall my further words on 'laws' of history (1978a: 73). My own doubts have since grown, to cover the grammatical inventory and operation of languages in the synchronic dimension. (I daresay the constraints of physiology do impose phonetic universals.) Now the Sapir–Whorf hypotheses (on which see Lee 1996) include one which holds that all languages differ uniquely and at arbitrary points, which are numerous and unpredictable as to location. It must follow that in the most idiosyncratic section of language real universals are dangerous things to suppose. Of course, there are two reservations. First, we must accept definitional universals (such as Hockett's famous 'design features', in Green-berg 1966: 8–13), which have to be present in a communication system for it to be a language; only *ad hoc* universals are debatable. Second, I am concerned with absolute universals, and not denying the existence of general laws or principles which are statistically based – that is, which are operative in a preponderance of cases but with exceptions. These are useful guides to speculation, diachronic and synchronic, via a probability calculus. But a single counter-example strips away the label 'universal'; and as time goes by grammatical research never fails to turn up further excipienda. It is notoriously difficult to prove a negative contention: but the onus of proof really rests on those who canvass universals, as several highly rated scholars were doing in the 1980s and 1990s and as is inherent in Optimality approaches (which hopefully include syntax). I doff my cap alike to Sapir's notion of 'drift' and Behaghel's laws of ordering; but remain unhappy with the belief that either language history or grammar contains any absolute *ad hoc* universal.

A positive suggestion I have made (without attracting much attention) concerns the perennial argument about the relation of semantics to grammar and the border, if any, between them. It is simply that it may be at least salutary to distinguish, and this on a language-by-language basis, 'inner' semantics from 'outer' semantics. Outer semantics – including pragmatics – covers the speaker's message in all its aspects. It is often conveyed by syntax and it may pose constraints on syntax. Their border is debatable: negation, for instance, seems to straddle it. Yet outer semantics is separable, and is usually separate, from grammar; it can be conveyed by gestures or illustrations. Inner semantics is not separable, even if entered in the lexicon. It comprises the meanings inextricably encoded in the grammar, in effect in its morphology (by some values of case, for instance, or gender or number or potentiality or tense or aspect). For those who accept the most famous Sapir–Whorf hypothesis, it is the area of language which controls patterns of thought. (For another version of this, using 'prior' versus 'posterior' semantics, see 1983: 68.)

My part in topic (c), mapping the history of the subject, has been rather fuller. It was very much prompted by the support and enthusiasm of Konrad Koerner, but was also reinspired by the notable oeuvre of Vivien Law. In 1963 (and again in 1986a) I puzzled over the odd choices of descriptive categories among the Ancient Greek and Roman language analysts. In 1985, in a more general vein, I tried to shed some limelight on three lesser stars in the galaxy of past linguistic theorists (these being Bhartṛhari, Sanctius and Whitney – 1985b). The neogrammarians have had their share of my attention too. In 1978 the Philological Society's *Transactions* were devoted to celebrating the centenary of their famous breakthrough in historical method; my offering (1978a) enquired into the varied nature of exceptions, in general, to rules and laws. This led on to a description of neogrammarian theoretic disarray when their doctrine of *Ausnahmlosigkeit* came face to face with undesirable but inescapable *Unregelmässigkeit* (to use Verner's term) in the data. I returned to coverage of these historical worthies in the 1994 Asher and Simpson encyclopedia, though this was as part of my evaluative account (1994b) of all the aspects and practitioners of historical linguistics, an account paired in that same publication with a similarly organized review (1994a) of the progress of comparative linguistics. Yet thereafter I returned briefly (1995b) to considering the Greek tradition, in particular the puzzling monograph attributed to Dionysius Thrax, a savant of the second century BC.

Even so, my most considerable input has undeniably been to topic (d), historical-comparative linguistics, especially the genetic inquiry which engenders the construct 'Proto-Indo-European'. First, in 1953, I addressed the presumption that PIE possessed some sub-buccal, 'laryngeal', segments which surfaced in altered form, or were lost with various phonetic traces, in the evidential languages. This hypothesis stemmed from a singularly murky conception in Saussure's 1879 *Mémoire*, but was promoted by Cuny, Couvreur and especially Kuryłowicz in the twentieth century. In effect my (successful) contention was that these reconstructed segments were conso-nants only, no matter how they affected contiguous vowels. I say 'segments' because, in spite of a tongue-in-cheek chapter (5) in my 1970 book which explores the case for assuming just a single specimen, I have really remained loyal to Ronald Crossland's Hittite-based view that there were originally two 'H's, rejecting the (now apparently victorious) idea that there were three. In passing, I have more recently examined the suggested possibility of PIE having had glottalic ejective stops as the source of the widespread, but awkwardly behaved, plain voiced stops as recorded.

A major preoccupation of mine in this field has been with methodological tactics. Koerner was not really fair in declaring (1989: 1) that 'historical linguists have generally tended to be reticent about making theoretical statements regarding the practice of their field': the writings of Henry Hoenigswald have long been a shining contradiction, and more recently Hock, Labov, Lass, McMahon and others have corrected the impression. My contributions have perhaps been rather more practical. They began with reflections on the intricacies attendant on attempts to grapple with historical phonology and syntax (in the 1956 and 1960 volumes of that useful but transitory periodical, *Archivum Linguisticum*). Later I pointed out that our very data may contain well-meaning but quite erroneous testimony (1965b). In 1970 (ch. 4) I offered formulae for calculating the likelihood of there having existed specific items in the cultural and geographic background of speakers of the protolanguage, given degrees of parity of terminology among the daughter tongues. Finally, in 1986b, I forecast those areas of diachronic study wherein general linguistic concepts (such as typology or iconicity) would increasingly provoke dust-disturbing encounters between historical researchers.

Yet possibly the most useful contribution – certainly in intention – from me has been in collecting, codifying and generally glossing the 'laws' so commonly and conveniently (but perhaps mystifyingly) cited by historians with inadequate explanation of their content or seaworthiness. Relevant are my papers of 1975 and 1987. But the first comprehensive listing and discussion constitutes my book (1985a). Mind you, this has already been supplemented by addenda (1994c; 1995a; 1999); for there is no end to the fresh naming of 'laws', whether hopefully as labels for quite new findings or as shorthand devices for referring to hoary old pronouncements previously quoted *in extenso*. In such circumstances any index rapidly becomes out of date; and so such efforts as I feel I can still make are limited to this sphere.

Participation in all these enquiries has been mentally rewarding and has been fun; and I am grateful to all the scholars whose creativity, of ideas or of unexpected interpretations of our data-base, has led us all such a merry dance. I have profited personally from the achievements of my fellow contributors to this volume, as well as of figures like Robert Coleman, Martin Harris and Peter Strevens. If I have been remiss in failing to mention other sources of inspiration, entries elsewhere in the book are sure to remedy the oversight.

REFERENCES

ABERCROMBIE, D., 1948.'Forgotten phoneticians', *TPhS* 47, 1–34.
ABRAHAM, W., (ed.) 1978. *Valence, Semantic Case and Grammatical Relations*, Amsterdam: John Benjamins.
ASHER, R. E. & SIMPSON, J. M. Y., (eds.) 1994. *The Encyclopedia of Language and Linguistics*, Oxford: Pergamon Press.
AUSTIN, J. L., 1962. *How To Do Things with Words*, Oxford: Oxford University Press.
BLOOMFIELD, L., 1933. *Language*, New York: Holt. (British ed. 1935: London: Allen & Unwin.)
BYNON, T. & PALMER, F. R., (eds.) 1986. *Studies in the History of Western Linguistics*, Cambridge: Cambridge University Press.
CARDONA, G. & ZIDE, N. H., (eds.) 1987. *Festschrift for Henry Hoenigswald*, Tübingen: Narr.
COLLINGE, N. E., 1953. 'Laryngeals in Indo-European ablaut and problems of the zero grade', *Archivum Linguisticum* 5, 75–87.
COLLINGE, N. E., 1956. 'The limitations of historical phonology', *Archivum Linguisticum* 8, 111–28.
COLLINGE, N. E., 1960. 'Some reflexions on comparative historical syntax', *Archivum Linguisticum* 12, 79–101.
COLLINGE, N. E., 1963. 'The Greek use of the term "middle" in linguistic analysis', *Word* 19, 232–41.
COLLINGE, N. E., 1965a. 'Some linguistic paradoxes', *Journal of Linguistics* 1, 1–12.
COLLINGE, N. E., 1965b. 'Phonetic information and misinformation in dead languages', *Proceedings of the 5th International Congress of Phonetic Sciences* (1964), 235–8.
COLLINGE, N. E., 1970. *Collectanea Linguistica*, The Hague: Mouton.
COLLINGE, N. E., 1975. 'Lachmann's law revisited', *Folia Linguistica* 8, 223–53 (and 9, 397).
COLLINGE, N. E., 1978a. 'Exceptions, their nature and place – and the neogrammarians', *TPhS* 76, 61–86.
COLLINGE, N. E., 1978b. 'Restructuring of noun-cases in syntax. Why "anti-" will not do', in W. Abraham (ed.), *Valence, Semantic Case and Grammatical Relations*, Amsterdam: John Benjamins, 617–32.
COLLINGE, N. E., 1980. *Case and Space*, LAUT series A: 76, University of Trier.

COLLINGE, N. E., 1983. 'Syntax and space', in S. Rot (ed.), *Languages in Function*, Budapest: Academy, 65–9.

COLLINGE, N. E., 1985a. *The Laws of Indo-European*, Amsterdam / Philadelphia: Benjamins.

COLLINGE, N. E., 1985b. 'Linguistic light from three lesser stars', *Bulletin of the John Rylands University Library of Manchester* 68, 34–52.

COLLINGE, N. E., 1986a. 'Greek (and some Roman) preferences in language categories', in T. Bynon & F. R. Palmer (eds.), *Studies in the History of Western Linguistics*, Cambridge: Cambridge University Press, 11–22.

COLLINGE, N. E., 1986b. 'The new historicism and its battles', *Folia Linguistica Historica* 7, 3–19.

COLLINGE, N. E., 1987. 'Who did discover the Law of the Palatals?', in C. Cardona & N. H. Zide (eds.), *Festschrift for Henry Hoenigswald*, Tübingen: Narr, 73–80.

COLLINGE, N. E., 1988. 'Thoughts on the pragmatics of Ancient Greek', *Proceedings of the Cambridge Philological Society* 214 (n.s. 34), 1–13.

COLLINGE, N. E., (ed.) 1990. *An Encyclopaedia of Language*, London / New York: Routledge.

COLLINGE, N. E., 1994a. 'Comparative Linguistics: History', in R. E. Asher & J. M. Y. Simpson (eds.), *Encyclopedia of Language and Linguistics*, Oxford: Pergamon Press, 629–36 (repr. in E. F. K. Koerner & R. E. Asher (eds.), *Concise History of the Language Sciences*, Oxford / New York / Tokyo: Pergamon Press and Elsevier, 195–202).

COLLINGE, N. E., 1994b. 'Historical Linguistics: History', in R. E. Asher & J. M. Y. Simpson (eds.), *Encyclopedia of Language and Linguistics*, Oxford: Pergamon Press, 1559–67 (repr. in E. F. K. Koerner & R. E. Asher (eds.), *Concise History of the Language Sciences*, Oxford / New York / Tokyo: Pergamon Press and Elsevier, 203–12.)

COLLINGE, N. E., 1994c. 'Sound laws: Named', in R. E. Asher & J. M. Y. Simpson (eds.), *Encyclopedia of Language and Linguistics*, Oxford: Pergamon Press, 4061–3.

COLLINGE, N. E., 1995a. 'Further laws of Indo-European', in W. Winter (ed.), *On Languages and Language*, Berlin / New York: Mouton de Gruyter, 27–52.

COLLINGE, N. E., 1995b. 'Dionusios Anomalos?', in V. Law & I. Sluiter (eds.), *Dionysius Thrax and the Technē Grammatikē*, Münster: Nodus, 55–71.

COLLINGE, N. E., 1999. 'The laws of Indo-European: the state of the art (1998)', *Journal of Indo-European Studies* 27, 355–77.

GLEASON, H. A. Jr., 1955. *An Introduction to Descriptive Linguistics*, New York: Holt, Rinehart & Winston. (Rev. ed. 1961.)

GREENBERG, J. H., (ed.) 1966. *Universals of Language*, 2nd ed., 1st ed. 1963, Cambridge, MA. / London: MIT Press.

HOCKETT, C. F., 1958. *A Course in Modern Linguistics*, New York: Macmillan.

JONES, D., 1950. *The Phoneme: Its Nature and Use*. Cambridge: Heffer.

KOERNER, E. F. K., 1989. 'Comments on reconstruction in historical linguistics', in T. Vennemann (ed.), *The New Sound of Indo-European: Essays in Phonological Reconstruction*, Berlin: Mouton de Gruyter, 1–20.

KOERNER, E. F. K. & ASHER, R. E., (eds.) 1995. *Concise History of the Language Sciences*, Oxford / New York / Tokyo: Pergamon Press and Elsevier.

LAW, V. & SLUITER, I., (eds.) 1995. *Dionysius Thrax and the Technē Grammatikē*, Münster: Nodus.

LEE, P., 1996. *The Whorf Theory Complex*, Amsterdam / Philadelphia: Benjamins.

LYONS, J., 1999. 'Diachrony and synchrony in twentieth century lexical semantics: new wine in old bottles?', *TPhS* 97, 287–329 (esp. 307–13).

ROT, S., (ed.) 1983. *Languages in Function*. Budapest: Academy.

VENNEMANN, T., (ed.) 1989. *The New Sound of Indo-European: Essays in Phonological Reconstruction*. Berlin: Mouton de Gruyter.

WINTER, W., (ed.) 1995. *On Languages and Language*, Berlin / New York: Mouton de Gruyter.

JOSEPH CREMONA

CREMONA, Joseph Anthony, Emeritus Lecturer in Romance Philology, University of Cambridge, since 1989; *b.* 1922; *m.* (i) 1946–62 Joanna Dorothy Collerick, (ii) 1973– Pamela Anne Mason; *Education:* Lycée Chateaubriand, Rome; St Bartholomew's Hospital, London; University College, London, BA Hons 1948; Westfield College, London, PhD 1956; *Career:* Part-time Lecturer in Italian, Westfield College, 1949–50, Assistant Lecturer in Romance Philology, 1950–4, Lecturer 1954–5; Lecturer in Romance Philology, University of Cambridge, 1955–89 (Chairman, Faculty Board of Modern and Medieval Languages, 1981–6). Fellow and Director of Studies in Modern Languages, Trinity Hall, Cambridge, 1966–89, Librarian 1968–89, Vice-Master 1982–6, Emeritus Fellow since 1989; Member of Council, Philological Society, 1972–6; Hon. Founding Senior Research Fellow, Institute of Romance Studies, University of London, since 1990; Member, Institute of Linguistics, University of Malta, since 1988; Member of the Language Committee of the Società Dante Alighieri, Rome, 1966–9; Editorial Board *Journal of Anglo-Italian Studies* since 1997. *Major Publications:* BBC Television language courses in French (*Bonjour Françoise, Répondez s'il-vous-plaît*), Italian (*Parliamo Italiano, Si Dice Così, Conversazioni, Buongiorno Italia!*), Spanish (*Vamos a Ver, Realidades*).

* * *

My first degree, in Modern Languages, was taken at University College, London, in 1948, just after the Second World War: French Honours with subsidiary Spanish. I had earlier studied medicine, from 1940 to 1943, at St Bartholomew's Hospital, which had evacuated its first three teaching years (the pre-clinical years) to Queens' College, Cambridge, for the duration of the war. Several other London University colleges (LSE, Bedford College, London Hospital) were accommodated in Cambridge at the same time. Although I had wished to study medicine from an early age, I slowly became aware, during my second year, that I was not enjoying the course and was having serious doubts about my suitability as a practitioner of the art. Most of my friends at the time were following other disciplines, mostly literary or historical subjects. By 1943, the war had reached a stage which infused me with excitement and made me restless. I decided to interrupt my studies at the end of my third year, join up, and reflect on which career to follow after the three or four years I expected to remain in the forces. I asked to join the Royal Navy and, since it was thought at the time that my languages would not be required, I was recruited as a radio mechanic in their Fleet Air Arm division, specializing in radar. After about a year's training (I believe I have never worked so hard as during that year) and a few months spent at a naval station in Scotland, I was picked out, early in 1945, to start and run a periodical whose function was to keep British naval radar mechanics scattered around the world in touch with the developments in their equipment, which were taking place at an ever increasing pace. The periodical never saw the light of day because the end of the war in Europe was quickly approaching (June 1945), followed closely by the surprise ending of the war in the Far East (August 1945). I spent the remainder of my time in the Navy loaned to the Ministry of Aircraft Production in their research establishment in Malvern, TRE (Telecommunications Research Establishment, later RRE, Radar Research Establishment), writing technical manuals on radar until demobilized in August 1946.

Meanwhile I had decided to try and get a degree as quickly as I could, in two years if possible, since I was already 24 years old. I still had rather vague ideas on which career to embark. The Foreign Office, my father's employer, was in my mind, but I was well aware that it was hard to enter its administrative grades. In order to make sure of obtaining a reasonably good degree in two years, I decided to study modern languages. Several of my friends at Cambridge had been modern linguists, I had done a little private teaching of Italian there and of French in the Navy to help with pocket money, and I had enjoyed the experience.

I should at this stage sketch out my early years and linguistic background. I was born in Rome in August 1922 to Maltese (Gozitan) parents. My father had obtained the post of Assistant to the Press Attaché at the British Embassy in Rome and was to remain in that office until war with Italy broke out in 1940. In 1929 my younger brother and I were sent to the French lycée in Rome, the Lycée Chateaubriand, at first temporarily, until sufficiently old to be sent to an English boarding school, but financial problems created by the 1930 crash resulted in our both having to complete our schooling at the Rome lycée. The linguistic position at home was peculiar. Father, mother and the two Gozitan maids they had brought with them to Rome spoke Maltese with each other. The language all four used with my brother and myself, however, was Italian. This was a common pattern among middle-class families in Malta, especially, as in our case, among those belonging to the legal profession. Maltese thus came to be the language used when the grown-ups did not wish the children to understand what was being said. The children, on the other hand, for reasons of survival, quickly learnt to follow what was being said in Maltese, but without ever giving the game away by using the language themselves. Since French was the language used by all students at the lycée, my brother and I began speaking French with each other after a few months, as we did with our school friends. Three languages were thus commonly spoken at home, Maltese, Italian and French. English was never used, except for a few months with an English governess. My parents had been advised by their English friends in Rome not to speak it with the children because they had an 'accent'. It would be better to leave the learning of it to a later stage, when at boarding school in Britain. Apart from some very imperfect school classes and a few desultory private lessons, I did not, in effect, begin to study English in earnest until after passing my second Baccalauréat in June 1939, when, armed with a British Council scholarship, I came to London to study for matriculation at a 'crammer' in Chancery Lane as a preliminary to entering medical school. Until then, all my reading had been in French or in Italian.

I started at UCL, the London college I had chosen, in October 1946 and took the decision not to read Italian as a subsidiary language to French Honours but to take up a new language. My first choice had been French with Arabic, French because it was familiar, Arabic because the language interested me, not least because of my budding interest in Maltese. However, I was told that the combination was not allowable (I later discovered it was) and so I opted for Spanish in lieu of Arabic. My interest in Spanish had developed during my Cambridge medical years. Spanish had been popular with several of my friends and its study had been much stimulated by the presence in Cambridge of refugees from the Spanish civil war, and by the regular meetings of the University Spanish Society presided over by Professor J. B. Trend in his rooms at Christ's. There was no Spanish department at UCL in the immediate post-war years and we had to cross a good portion of Central London to King's College in the Strand for all Spanish lectures and classes.

The two years I wished to spend reading for the degree had been allowed because of the time I had spent studying medicine and in the Navy, but in effect I only studied for my finals for five of the six terms, since the first term, autumn 1946, was taken up in finishing my work for, and taking, the 'Intermediate' examination in five subjects as required by the regulations in force at the time. The result of finals was a good 2.1, with sufficiently good first class marks in the relevant papers to allow me to proceed to graduate research.

This course had been proposed well before finals by Professor Brian Woledge, the head of the French Department, whose speciality was Old French language and literature and, to a lesser extent, the history of the French language. I found him a most inspiring teacher, particularly in his history of French lectures, and he noticed my interest in the subject. History-of-the-language courses were frequently taught by non-specialists in British universities, usually by lecturers in medieval literature, and this tended to result in the subject becoming unpopular with students. Professor Woledge was an exception: he was well read in general and French historical linguistics and managed to communicate his interest to his students. Practically all my contemporaries at UCL found interest in the study of French linguistic history, an unusual state of affairs, as I later discovered.

Professor Woledge suggested that in view of my interest in historical linguistics and knowledge of French, Italian and, by now, some Spanish, I might be attracted by the prospect of an academic career and research in a topic in Romance Philology. This subject had recently been established at London University and a Chair had been created at Westfield College in 1948, filled by Professor William Dennis Elcock. The full title of the chair was 'Romance Philology and Medieval French Literature', a pairing of two distinct subjects typical of the attitude to linguistics in British Arts Faculties at the time. *The Times* reported Professor Elcock's appointment as being 'to the chair of Romance, Philology and Medieval French Literature at Westfield College', then a college for 'young ladies'!

Dennis Elcock was the product of the Manchester School of Romance Linguistics, which had included Mildred Pope and John Orr, and he had taught in Oxford before coming to London. He was working on Pyrenean dialects and had examined the validity of the theory of substratum influence on a number of phonetic developments in the Romance dialects of those valleys bordering on Basque-speaking regions at either side of the Pyrenees. The results were written up in his *De quelques affinités phonétiques entre l'aragonais et le béarnais* (Elcock 1938). The writing of monographs on single dialects or on phenomena affecting a number of dialects and the preparation of linguistic atlases had been the activity which had occupied the attention of perhaps the majority of Romance linguists during the first half of the twentieth century, so that when Professor Elcock proposed that I followed in those tracks I had little hesitation in taking up his suggestion. After some discussion, we settled on the study of one dialect, that of a Gascon Pyrenean valley, and he suggested the Vallée d'Aure in the Central Pyrenees as a suitable location. I had decided not to take up an alternative suggestion, the study of one of the Alpine Romance dialects, largely because the Pyrenees were closer to my Spanish interests, but also because the Alps were being thoroughly investigated by a formidable school of Swiss linguists who had the advantage of living close to the places being investigated. Elcock had made some contacts in the Vallée d'Aure before the war, although the valley was not included in the terrain covered by *De quelques affinités*. I never had occasion to regret the choice of location in the eight years it took me to write my dissertation. The dialect and the cluster of problems it presented both from the descriptive and from the historical points of view proved an absorbing and frequently a challenging object of study.

In order to prepare myself adequately for the necessary fieldwork, I followed, during the first year of research work, a course in phonetics at UCL. There I had the good fortune of being a pupil in the ear-training classes of Hélène Coustenoble and of meeting Daniel Jones, who was retired. My other teachers included A. C. Gimson and Marguerite Chapallaz. I had found historical phonetics particularly interesting when working for my first degree and some of my phonetics teachers regretted the fact that I had not taken up research in their subject, given the training I had received in anatomy and physiology during my medical years and in electronics when in the hands of the Fleet Air Arm. UCL was located close to the School of Oriental and African Studies, where the only Chair in Linguistics in the country at the time was held by Professor Firth, but I cannot remember any of my UCL teachers suggesting that I went to follow lectures on general linguistics at SOAS. I remember noticing some lack of collaboration between UCL and SOAS at the time, largely due, I suspect, to diffidence on the part of the UCL linguists towards 'Firthian' linguistics.

Only one year, 1948–9, was devoted to full-time research, for in 1949 I began teaching part-time at Westfield College: my assignment was to teach history students who had chosen the Florentine Renaissance period as their special subject to read contemporary Italian texts (Machiavelli, Guicciardini, etc.), but also to teach Modern Italian to students of English. In 1950 I was appointed to a newly created post of Assistant Lecturer in Romance Philology (later upgraded to a lectureship), with more extensive duties. These included teaching together with Dennis Elcock a London intercollegiate course in Romance Philology, a subject that had been added to the options open to undergraduate students in Modern Languages. In addition, from 1950 onwards, I had undertaken to teach a three-year evening course in comparative Romance linguistics at the City Literary Institute in High Holborn, two hours a week for each year of the course (7 to 9 p.m.). These elementary comparative lectures proved to be popular and the first year had to be duplicated at the Marylebone Institute after 1952, so that for a few years I taught two hours in the evening four times a week. The aim was to take students who already had some French and teach them the rudiments of three additional Romance languages, Italian, Spanish and Portuguese, by using a comparative historical method and studying the language of texts that ranged from medieval to modern and included some in the principal dialects. The idea had not been mine. I was following in the tracks of a predecessor who had planned to incorporate Portuguese in the course but had not yet done so. My teaching load during these London years was thus rather heavy. I was able, nevertheless, to devote a good deal of time to research on 'my' dialect, Aurois, and to the reading of Romance topics, though not enough, I thought, to the study of other branches of linguistics.

I had found Dennis Elcock inclined to be sceptical, in his writings and in his teaching, on the question of adopting a theoretical approach to linguistic matters, particularly one based on a structural interpretation of the data. I, on the other hand, had been much influenced by my readings of the Prague School structuralists. For Romance, the authors that had struck me most were André Martinet (the three lectures published by the Philological Society [1949] and his *Economie des changements phonétiques* [1953]) and, later, André Haudricourt and Alphonse Juilland (1949) for French and Emilio Alarcos Llorach (1950) for Spanish. The approach in my dissertation had been distinctly 'structural' and yet Elcock, although he read the whole of it very attentively as it was being written, never commented on points of method or interpretation. When I tried to draw him out on these topics, he would side-step the questions. When he came to write his classic textbook *The Romance Languages* and asked me to read it in typescript for comments, I remember suggesting that a representation of the Latin vowel system on the 'vowel triangle' pattern would make clearer sense in tracing its development in Vulgar Latin and Romance; but he could not see the point and kept to the arrangement of the vowels in alphabetical order, as was the practice in all the Romance textbooks at the time (this defect and others like it have been put right by John Green in the revised second edition). Romance linguists tended to be extraordinarily conservative where linguistic analysis was concerned. I remember beginning a paper on 'Polymorphism in a Pyrenean Dialect' read to the Philological Society at their Oxford meeting in 1956 with the words: 'The great advantages that Romance Philologists enjoy in the study of their subject – a thorough knowledge of the parent language, Latin, and a long tradition of scholarship – are largely offset by their natural consequences: the general mediocrity of their knowledge of other linguistic fields, a mediocrity that only the greatest succeed in avoiding.' (The position is altogether different now, I should add.)

On the question of substratum influence in a number of phonetic developments in the Pyrenees I had reached in my thesis conclusions that were opposite to Dennis Elcock's. The nature of the changes, the way these changes related to the phonetic structure of the Vulgar Latin of Gaul and Spain and their distribution tended to convince me of the strength of the substratum theory for a substantial number of developments in Gascony and Spain. I tended in fact to follow lines taken by André Martinet and especially those of one of his pupils, Fredrick Jungemann. The latter allowed, for instance, the likelihood of the influence of a substratum language as long as it was not the only factor appearing to act on the direction of a particular change (Jungemann 1955). Several of my students at Cambridge quickly noticed the discrepancy between my views on substratum theory and those of more sceptical scholars, and enjoyed teasing me for my allegedly too ready acceptance of substratum action even in those instances where I held that judgement should be suspended for lack of clear evidence one way or the other, as in the case of the Central Italian *gorgia toscana*, ascribed by some to the action of Etruscan.

In my approach to dialectology, I was much influenced by Jean Séguy, who had taken up the chair of Romance Languages at the University of Toulouse just before I began fieldwork in the Vallée d'Aure in the winter of 1948. Séguy was the author of a splendid work on the dialect plant names of the northern, Gascon, side of the Central Pyrenees (1953) and had taken over the awesome task of publishing the linguistic atlas of Gascony, begun by Albert Dauzat, the first of a series of 'second generation' French linguistic atlases, each devoted to a linguistic region (Séguy et al. 1954–73). Séguy soon gathered round him a small group of young, enthusiastic dialectologists who readily accepted me as one of their number and who became firm friends: Jacques Allières, Pierre Bec, Manuel Companys and, a little later, Xavier Ravier and Jean-Louis Fossat. Despite his warm welcome, Séguy at first gave me the feeling of being not a little dismayed at the sight of an inexperienced outsider wishing to describe an unfamiliar dialect. He was firmly of the opinion, as is usual among modern French dialectologists, that it is best for the fieldworker to belong to the region he is investigating and to be familiar, if at all possible, with the dialect being investigated or one close to it. His scepticism grew when he learnt that I proposed to use the International Phonetic Association alphabet in my transcriptions instead of the diacritically rich system then in use among romanists: 'C'est bien simple, on ne vous lira pas', was his blunt comment. Some years later, however, he confessed that it had been a mistake not to adopt the IPA system in producing the new French atlases: the fonts containing diacritics were very prone to breakage in printing and easily led to errors being made; they also imposed a tremendous strain on the eyes of the proofreader. It did not take long for Séguy's first diffident attitude to vanish, despite the awkwardness of communicating at a distance and the infrequency of my visits to Toulouse, dictated by the comparatively high cost of travel in the first post-war decade.

On the question of whether it was preferable to have a 'native' investigating the dialect of a region rather than an outsider, I came to the conclusion that the advantages of being a 'native' were counterbalanced by at least one disadvantage, the fact that a 'native' tended to hear what he or she was prepared to hear rather than what was being said by an informant, thus tending to miss the unexpected should it arise. I had a neat illustration of this phenomenon in the course of investigating Aurois. In my fieldwork, I had noticed that there was a good deal of incipient diphthongization of the open mid vowels under certain conditions, the most important of which was their presence in a stressed syllable. In the course of excursions I was able to make in neighbouring areas, I noticed that these diphthongs were not exclusive to the Vallée d'Aure but a good deal more widespread. No trace of these diphthongs appeared in the first volume of the linguistic atlas of Gascony or in any other transcriptions of local dialects I was able to examine; diphthongs only began to appear in transcriptions after I drew attention to their presence.

The dissertation was completed towards the end of 1955 and the PhD awarded in 1956, with Professor Alfred Ewert from Oxford as external examiner. I never did publish the work despite two offers of publication. The first was from the Philological Society (Sidney Allen was its Publications

Secretary at the time), but on condition that I cut out the lexical chapters; the thesis was indeed very long. The other offer came from the Instituto de Estudios Pirenáicos at Saragossa; in this case the work would have had to be translated into Spanish. I was inclined to accept the Spanish offer since, at the time, I was rather proud of my work on the lexis. Meanwhile, however, a monumental work, very relevant to the lexical and phonological aspects of my thesis, had begun to appear. This was Joan Coromines' etymological dictionary of the Spanish language (Corominas 1954–7). I had studied and incorporated into my own work the findings of the Catalan scholar's extensive review (Coromines 1937) of Rohlfs' *Le Gascon* (1935), and I could see that the publication of Coromines's dictionary obliged me to look again at the lexical component of the dissertation before it could be published, and incorporate all relevant material. My appointment at Cambridge in 1955 prevented me from getting down to this work of revision straight away and by the time I was free to take it on, other interests had taken over.

Just before submitting the dissertation, I had applied for a Lectureship in Romance Philology at Cambridge, and I obtained it in July 1955. The post was a newly created one. There had been a Readership in the subject in the first decades of the century, held from 1900 by Dr E. G. W. Braunholz of King's, but it was discontinued after Braunholz's resignation in 1940 (it was said that he had made the subject unpopular with undergraduates). Teaching in the history of the French language was provided by Professor Lewis Harmer and Dr (later Professor) Peter Rickard, both traditional in their approach to language history and description. A number of other linguistic papers could be offered in Part II of the Modern and Medieval Languages Tripos: History of Spanish, History of Italian, Vulgar Latin and Romance Philology, and General Linguistics. The last paper was entitled at the time 'Principles of Language' and contained questions of the type 'Define "homonymic clash". Give examples from two languages, and show what efforts those languages make to counteract this phenomenon.' The teaching for these papers had been in the hands of Professor Jopson, the polyglot holder of the Chair of Comparative Philology. When Jopson retired in 1955, his successor, William Sidney Allen, did not consider it his responsibility to take on the teaching of the Romance subjects and persuaded the Faculty to resurrect the post in Romance Philology. The new lectureship was assigned to four departments: French, Italian, Spanish and 'Other Languages' (the last because of Vulgar Latin, Provençal, Portuguese and Rumanian, occasionally taken by students). For the first few years at Cambridge much of my time was taken up by the demands of the History of Spanish paper (among the papers for which I was responsible, this was the one which had the greatest number of takers). This went on being the case until 1979, when the Faculty was able to obtain a second post in Romance Philology, an Assistant Lectureship, filled by Christopher Pountain, who relieved me of all teaching in Spanish and Portuguese. Although my university teaching responsibilities did not include the history of French (except from a comparative angle), I was able to keep up with the subject and took on supervision work for the paper.

Two or three years after Sidney Allen's appointment to the Chair of Comparative Philology in the Classics Faculty, he, together with John Trim, a UCL man appointed in 1957 to a newly established Lectureship in Phonetics (another consequence of Sidney Allen's election), myself and one or two others, founded the Cambridge University Linguistics Society. Sidney Allen was its first President, John Trim its first Secretary and I its first Treasurer. The Society became the main focus of inter-faculty activity in linguistics in the university. Unlike Oxford, Cambridge had suffered from an anti-linguistics bias in its English and Modern Languages faculties for some decades, due in part to the antipathy undergraduates felt towards historical linguistics when taught in a pedestrian, neogrammarian style. There was also a deep misunderstanding of what linguistics was about: a distinguished don in the French Department once described the subject to me as consisting in little more than the collection of dialect words. Sidney Allen's appointment placed the study of language, as opposed to the study of languages, on a serious academic footing in the university for the first time. His inaugural lecture had stressed the importance of the independence of linguistics as a discipline (Allen 1957). In the introduction to the reprinted version of his lecture, Sidney Allen wrote, 'In Cambridge in 1957 Linguistics was recognized only by the existence of an optional paper in the Modern and Medieval Languages Tripos, and by the election to the chair of Comparative Philology of one who had served his apprenticeship under the late Professor J. R. Firth at the School of Oriental and African Studies in London' (1966: 5). To Allen's short list, I would add the existence of a linguistics book club, the 'E' Book Club, founded in the nineteenth century and named after Paper 'E' (the philological paper) of the Classical Tripos. This club did sterling service for the subject until the mid-1960s, when books relating to linguistics became too numerous and diverse for the club to function satisfactorily.

It was some years, however, before it could be said that the anti-linguistics bias had disappeared altogether. A few years after my appointment I tried to change the title of the paper 'Vulgar Latin and Romance Philology' to 'Romance Linguistics', but the attempt failed. A Lectureship in Linguistics was created in 1961, first held by John Lyons, but the establishment of a (small) Department had to wait until 1966 before being approved by the university. Before that date, it was my custom to advise bright students wishing to undertake research on a linguistic subject to go to a university such as Reading or Manchester and follow a graduate course in linguistics.

The main contribution I believe I made to the study of the subject during my years at Cambridge was the introduction in the late 1950s of two linguistic papers, one in Italian and one in Spanish, in Part I of the

Tripos. The overt object of these papers was that of introducing students to the historical study of their chosen language as a preparation for the Part II historical paper. In intention and practice, however, the focus was largely on the description of the modern language, with all that this implied, on the grounds that a valid history (as opposed to a simple list of changes) must be preceded by a valid description or attempt at a description. Both papers were reasonably popular and introduced linguistics to a number of students, several of whom are now distinguished academics. The complexities of the Cambridge Tripos system meant that for many years the papers could only be chosen by those students in their second year who had taken up the study of a new language since leaving school (two languages were needed for Part I) and who were thus obliged to spend two years working for the first part of their Tripos in order to reach a sufficient proficiency. This meant that the two linguistic papers had a limited currency, since the majority of students then coming up to read modern languages at Cambridge were about equally proficient in two languages and able to take Part I at the end of their first year. No corresponding paper existed for French, since all students reading French were able to take Part I in their first year. The position has changed in the past few years and now the papers (or their modern equivalents together with a newly introduced one in French) can be selected by all students in their first year.

Soon after coming to Cambridge I was asked to inaugurate a 'Romance Linguistics' section in the *Year's Work in Modern Languages* survey published by the Modern Humanities Research Association. In my article, I attempted to cover relevant works in General Linguistics as a prelude to the Romance survey. I had tried, but unsuccessfully, to convince the editorial committee of the value of having a separate General Linguistics section to the book. Many years were to pass before the section was finally introduced. After two years on my own, I invited Rebecca Posner, then at Cambridge, to join me and we wrote the chapter jointly for another two years; collaboration became difficult, however, after Rebecca's departure to a Chair in Ghana.

At about this time I was approached by Professor T. B. W. Reid, who followed Professor Ewert in the chair of Romance Philology at Oxford, saying that both he and Professor Orr had put forward my name as a suitable person to bring up to date a work that had become a classic of Romance linguistic literature: Iordan and Orr's *Introduction to Romance Linguistics* (1937). Much flattered, I accepted after some misgivings, but it was not long before I found myself bogged down in attempting to write up some of the new work. My biggest stumbling block by far was the theory put forward in Paris by Gustave Guillaume, whose work had been admired by Antoine Meillet and was enjoying a late and remarkable following in France and in French Canada but went practically unheeded elsewhere. I found myself unable to follow his thought as expressed in his writings (chiefly

Guillaume 1919; 1929). I was especially puzzled by the fact that several contemporary French linguists whose work I knew and admired had become converted to Guillaume's way of thinking. One 'convert' in particular, whose intellect and work before meeting with Guillaume had impressed me particularly strongly, was a Hispanist friend, Maurice Molho. Molho had tried to unfold the mysteries of Guillaume's ideas to me, stressing at the same time that one could only follow them properly when expounded in person by the master himself. Early in 1960 Molho arranged for me to attend one of the regular evening meetings Guillaume had been holding with his pupils at his Paris home. Unfortunately, however, this was not to be, for Guillaume died a few weeks before the beginning of the Easter vacation. Other difficulties arose in the revision of Iordan and Orr's book, and in the end I gave up altogether the idea of bringing it up to date. The work was entrusted to Rebecca Posner, who put my efforts to shame by finishing the revision in a remarkably short space of time. The revised edition finally saw the light in 1970.

My interest in the synchronic and diachronic study of languages had generally inclined towards the phonological and the lexical components, and naturally my lectures tended to reflect this. I seldom gave time to syntax in my lectures, reserving the topic to supervision work. The theoretical basis of the treatment of syntax in the traditional works in Romance had left me dissatisfied and at one time, in the early 1950s, I attempted to work out a more satisfactory treatment, if only to fill the gap in my teaching. I hoped that the publication of Lucien Tesnière's book on structural syntax (1959) would alter the position, but the work did not convince me because of what struck me at the time as its static approach, which it shared with earlier treatments. When I came into contact with Noam Chomsky's *Syntactic Structures*, two or three years after its publication in 1957 (an old pupil, Peter Matthews, was the first to draw my attention to the work), and digested it together with the author's subsequent ideas in the course of the 1960s, I could see that the direction being taken would be exciting and productive, but came to the conclusion that to take on transformational grammar at this stage in my life would in practice mean having to abandon virtually all my other linguistic interests (as I had been abandoning my Pyrenean interests), interests such as the history of the Romance lexicon, the medieval external history of the Romance languages, and the development of Romance grammatical treatises in late medieval and Renaissance times. I was much attracted to generative phonology, however, and applied techniques derived from it in an account of the status of palatal consonants in modern Italian in a paper read to the Cambridge Linguistic Department seminar in 1967, left unpublished.

All through the 1960s I had the good fortune to have a remarkably high proportion of very bright students who took to linguistics and, in particular, to Romance linguistics. By 1968 there were enough of them doing graduate work in Cambridge to give the most senior of them, Martin Harris, and myself the idea of organizing regular seminars on Romance topics at which each would take turns to read a paper, to be discussed very informally afterwards. The idea worked very well: in addition to Martin Harris, whose chief languages were French and Spanish, and myself, the regular members of the seminar were Andrew Radford, an Italianist, Christopher Pountain, a Hispanist, and Nigel Vincent, another Italianist. John Green spent hardly any time in Cambridge after his first degree before leaving for York. When the opportunity presented itself we invited outside speakers. We met informally three or four times a year for a few years, even after some of the members went to teaching posts in other universities. In the course of 1972, we decided to open the seminar to all interested persons, to meet once a year only, but for two full half-days, and invite one distinguished speaker. We met for the first time in Trinity Hall in January 1973 with Giulio Lepschy as the distinguished speaker. Martin Harris, by now at Salford University, took on the brunt of the administrative work for the first ten years or so. This was the start of the Cambridge Romance Linguistics Seminar, now in its twenty-ninth year without, so far, changing either format or venue.

The last ten years before retirement were largely taken up by teaching and administrative work in Faculty and College. Since retirement, I have been apportioning my time evenly between the history of Maltese, the Mediterranean Lingua Franca, and the use of Italian in the Mediterranean region since the sixteenth century.

REFERENCES

ALARCOS LLORACH, EMILIO, 1950. *Fonología española, según el método de la escuela de Praga*, Madrid: Gredos.
ALLEN, WILLIAM SIDNEY, 1957, 1966. *On the Linguistic Study of Languages*, Cambridge: Cambridge University Press, 1957; repr. in Peter Strevens (ed.), *Language and Language Learning. Five Inaugural Lectures*, London: Oxford University Press, 1966.
CHOMSKY, NOAM A., 1957. *Syntactic Structures*, The Hague: Mouton.
COROMINAS, JUAN, 1954–7. *Diccionário crítico etimológico de la lengua castellana*, 4 vols., Berne: Francke and Madrid: Gredos.
COROMINES, JOAN, 1937. 'A propos d'un nouveau livre sur le gascon', *Vox Romanica* II, 147–69 and 447–65.
ELCOCK, WILLIAM DENNIS, 1938. *De quelques affinités phonétiques entre l'aragonais et le béarnais*, Paris: Droz.
ELCOCK, WILLIAM DENNIS, 1959. *The Romance Languages*, London: Faber & Faber; 2nd ed., rev. with new intro. by John N. Green, London: Faber & Faber, 1975.
GUILLAUME, GUSTAVE, 1919. *Le problème de l'article et sa solution dans la langue française*, Paris: Maisonneuve.
GUILLAUME, GUSTAVE, 1929. *Temps et verbe. Théorie des aspects, des modes et des temps*, Paris: Champion.
HAUDRICOURT, ANDRÉ GEORGES & JUILLAND, ALPHONSE G., 1949, 1970. *Essai pour une histoire structurale du phonétisme français*, 2nd ed. 1970, Paris: Klincksieck, and The Hague: Mouton.
IORDAN, IORGU & ORR, JOHN, 1937, 1970. *An Introduction to Romance Linguistics, its Schools and Scholars*, Oxford: Blackwell, 1937; 2nd ed. rev. with supp. by Rebecca Posner, Oxford:

Blackwell, 1970. The 1937 edition was a translation, amplification and revision by John Orr of Iorgu Iordan's *Introducere in Studiul Limbilor Romanice*, Jassy: Jassy University Press, 1932.

JUNGEMANN, FREDRICK H., 1955. *Le teoría del sustrato y los dialectos hispano-romances y gascones*, Biblioteca Románica hispánica, Tratados y Monografías 7, Madrid: Gredos.

MARTINET, ANDRÉ, 1949. *Phonology as Functional Phonetics*, Publications of the Philological Society XV, London: Oxford University Press.

MARTINET, ANDRÉ, 1953. *Economie des changements phonétiques*, Bern: Francke.

ROHLFS, GERHARD, 1935. *Le Gascon. Etudes de philologie pyrénéene*, Beihefte zur Zeitschrift für Romanische Philologie 85, Halle/Saale: Niemeyer.

SÉGUY, JEAN, 1953. *Les noms populaires des plantes dans le Pyrénées centrales*, Filología 18, Barcelona: Instituto de Estudios Pirenáicos.

SÉGUY, JEAN, ET AL. 1954–73. *Atlas linguistique et ethnographique de la Gascogne*, 6 vols. and 4 supps., Toulouse: Institut d'Etudes Méridionales de la Faculté des Lettres, and Paris: Centre National de la Recherche Scientifique.

TESNIÈRE, LUCIEN, 1959, 1965. *Eléments de syntaxe structurale*, 2nd ed. 1965, Paris: Klincksieck.

DAVID CRYSTAL

CRYSTAL, David, OBE 1995, FBA 2000; Honorary Professor of Linguistics, University of Wales, Bangor, since 1985; *b.* 1941; *m.* (i) 1964 Molly Irene Stack, (ii) 1976 Hilary Frances Norman; *Education:* St Mary's College, Liverpool; University College, London, BA in English 1962; University of London, PhD in English 1966; *Career:* Research Assistant, Survey of English Usage, 1962–3; Assistant Lecturer in Linguistics, University of Bangor, 1963–5; Lecturer in Linguistic Science, University of Reading, 1965–9, Reader in Linguistic Science 1969–75, Professor of Linguistic Science 1975–85. Hon DSc, Queen Margaret College, Edinburgh, 1997; Hon. FRCSLT (Royal College of Speech and Language Therapists) 1983; Honorary President: National Association of Professionals concerned with Language Impaired Children (1985–), Society of Indexers (1992–5), National Literacy Association (1995–), International Association of Teachers of English as a Foreign Language (1995–); Honorary Vice-President: Royal College of Speech and Language Therapists (1995–), Institute of Linguists (1998–); Member: Linguistics Association of Great Britain (Secretary 1965–70), British Association of Applied Linguistics, Linguistics Society of America, Philological Society; Editorial Boards: *Language and Society*, *English Today*, *International Journal of Lexicography*, *Clinical Linguistics & Phonetics*; Editor: *Journal of Child Language* (1973–85), *Child Language Teaching and Therapy* (1985–96), *Linguistics Abstracts* (1985–96). *Major Publications: Prosodic Systems and Intonation in English* 1969; *Investigating English Style* (with D. Davy) 1969; *Linguistics* 1971; *The English Tone of Voice* 1975; *The Grammatical Analysis of Language Disability* (with P. Fletcher & M. Garman) 1976; *A Dictionary of Linguistics and Phonetics* 1980 [5th ed. 2001]; *Clinical Linguistics* 1981; *Profiling Linguistic Disability* 1982; *The Cambridge Encyclopedia of Language* 1987 [2nd ed. 1997]; *The Cambridge Encyclopedia of the English Language* 1995; *English as a Global Language* 1997; *Language Play* 1998; *Language Death* 2000.

* * *

I was brought up in Holyhead, a port town in the north-west corner of Wales, in the 1940s, and some of my earliest memories are of the linguistic consequences of being part of a bilingual culture. Trilingual even, for Holyhead was the port for Dun Laoghaire, and perhaps a third of the townspeople were Irish, several of whom larded their speech with Irishisms (as they still do) and visited the west of Ireland regularly. My family straddled the divide: I had both Irish and Welsh uncles and aunts, and heard both languages spoken – though chiefly *at* me, for the language of my home was English. Uncle Joe, who was as Welsh as the hills, used to call me 'Dafydd y Garreg Wen' – 'David of the White Rock', a character in Welsh mythology – and from him I picked up a basic sense of what Welsh was all about, and began to speak it a bit. Then in primary school, it was introduced as a second language. By 10 I was confidently semilingual, and fascinated with the language mystery. Is this perhaps an inevitable consequence of being raised in a monolingual home in a bilingual culture?

A move to Liverpool in 1951 brought me into contact with another language, Scouse, and an initial experience of what one might call 'expedited accommodation'. My Welsh accent was so strong that I was immediately dubbed 'Taffy' – a nickname which lasted throughout my secondary schooling, long after the accent was beaten out of me by my newfound classmates. I picked up Liverpudlian perforce, as a matter of survival, and in a matter of days. And I recall enjoying the process, acquiring the aggressive yet jocular verbosity which characterizes so much Liverpool speech. It was very different from the lilting Anglo-Welsh I had previously been used to. We would go back to Holyhead for holidays a couple of times each year, and I remember making my speech change, round about Llanfairpwllgwyngyll, on Anglesey, where the close encounter with its 57 letters acted as an injection of linguistic benzedrine. On the way back, the change worked the other way. I must say I didn't see much difference, at the time, between bidialectism and bilingualism. Identity was everything.

Secondary school brought a varied language experience. There was French, from the outset, and Latin from the second year – the latter taught by a Christian Brother whose methods had a great deal in common with those used by the teachers reported in Aelfric's *Colloquy*, a thousand years before. But they worked, and I learned my cases and genders with an accuracy and confidence that far exceeded the corresponding progress derived from my much gentler French teacher. In the third year, the 'choice' was Greek or German, the former automatic if you were in the alpha stream, the latter in the beta: we were left in no doubt that Greek was a higher class of language. Each lesson our teacher would arrive and make us recite in unison, 'Dei graphein kata tous nomous' ('It is necessary to write according to the laws'), and we would then go through the laws of concord, one by one. 'Concord' was a familiar notion, as those were the days of English language O-level, and that was just one of many grammatical terms and rules which I, along with everyone else in my year, was beginning to dislike thoroughly. The best bit about English was the literature – and also the elocution, which was taught by an inspiring lady who made her voice – and also ours – do things I never dreamed possible.

By the fourth year, the various language experiences had somehow combined to make me a linguist-in-waiting. I know this, because I recall inventing an artificial language in woodwork class (a domain where I had no competence) and forcing classmates who were smaller than me to speak it. It was an amalgam of everything I knew – chiefly, Latin and Greek, with a proliferation of cases and tenses. During that exercise, I began noticing the similarities – some with French and English, some even with Welsh. Might not all these languages have sprung from some common source, which perhaps no longer exists? However, the advice given for choosing subjects at A-level was to do the subjects you were best at – which for me were English, history and geography. I regret now not going into at least one of my other languages in greater depth. But I was never in any doubt about which subject to follow at university – it had to be English, and it had to be a course where there was a language element alongside the literary. I very much wanted both. Apart from anything else, I had started to write primitive fiction, and I was a voracious reader of literature. I loved the set texts we had worked through. I had been to Stratford and seen several plays. I had to find a course which would give me a chance to develop both strands. The syllabus of the English Department at University College, London, was ideal, and I was lucky enough to be accepted, in 1959.

From a linguistic point of view, the first year was a virtual disaster. I studied Old English, Old Norse, Gothic and several other fascinating languages, but they were taught in a curiously distant manner, as purely written texts. The nearest you got to speaking them was through a notion described as 'sound changes'. I remember a dialogue with my tutor when I asked him how the Anglo-Saxon word for 'king', *cyning*, would have been pronounced. He basically refused to say, and gave me a mini-lecture about the antecedents of the high front rounded vowels of Old English. But I had already read the description: what I wanted to hear was how it all sounded – not just the vowel values, but the rhythms and rhymes as well. No one would oblige. 'We know very little about the phonetic realization of the Old English phonemes', was the typical reply. John Dodgson was different, in his approach to linguistic history: he taught us about English place-names the best way, by arranging meetings in country pubs where appropriately oiled locals would be interrogated about the names in their vicinity. His course brought home to me the possibility that the history of the language could be made real. But on the whole, I felt my language interests slipping away during that first year. The matter was clinched when I followed an Introduction to Linguistics taught in the third term, in which we were taken through several of the classics at a rate of knots. *The Meaning of Meaning*, Saussure's *Cours*, Bloomfield, and others, one a week. I understood little, and found it a million miles away from what I thought languages were about. The course was assessed by an essay, and I got a D – a fail. That clinched it. Literary options for me from now on.

But the history of the language class in the second year was obligatory. I remember sitting there not looking forward to it, when in came the lecturer, Randolph Quirk, and one hour later I was a born-again linguist. I can remember very little about that hour, except one thing. He spoke a sentence, then told us to write it down in phonetic transcription. We all looked at each other. What was phonetic transcription? We were harangued. How can anyone study language without being able to do phonetics? Anyone serious about it should get themselves over to the Phonetics Department and sign on for that option right away. This is what I had, without realizing it, been waiting to hear. By the end of the day I was signed up. I found myself, a lone (it turned out) English Department emigré, in the hands of A. C. Gimson and J. D. O'Connor, in a tiny year of three students. The benefits from that small class-size, and the focused teaching (for timetable clashes with my colleagues meant that I was often on my own), were incalculable. By the end of my degree I wanted only to use my phonetics in some way.

That opportunity came through Quirk, who in 1960 was putting together the Survey of English Usage. I graduated in 1962, and – having followed every linguistic option I could find in my three years – had become something of a buff, with my superior phonetics knowledge at a high premium among my more literary-minded classmates (I exchanged it for hints about how to handle the nineteenth-century novel). The UCL English Department turned out to be an excellent linguistic nurturing ground. It was home to the English Place-Name Survey, for example, and it had specialists in palaeography and stylistics, and nearby there were courses in comparative philology (Oswald Szemerenyi) and communication theory. I became a denizen of the linguistics section of the library, and revisited all the books I had found so difficult in my first year. Now that I knew some phonetics, Bloomfield began to make sense. I would never forget that lesson. Theory unrelated to practice can stifle the linguistic spark that I believe is within everyone. I have never met anyone who was not fascinated by some aspect of language – local accents, place-names, children's acquisition, etymologies. . . . The world is full of potential linguists, but it does not take much to put them off. Long before I encountered the phrase in Henry Sweet, I knew that phonetics was the 'indispensable foundation'.

Quirk was looking for research assistants for his Survey, and I was one of two appointed that year. I arrived late, due to an unanticipated bout of TB which had kept me in a north Wales sanatorium for several months. (I had actually taken my finals in the san – including my phonetics oral, fortunately made possible by the nearby arrival on holiday of SOAS's Eileen Whitely.) My role was indeed to use my phonetics – to develop the Survey prosodic transcription so that it would cope with the wider range of intonation patterns and tones of voice that the speech samples were bringing to light. Working closely with Quirk was a formative experience. It involved long hours intensively listening to a range of spoken styles on tape-repeaters, lengthy discussion of phonetic differences, and a parallel track of in-depth grammatical description and debate, as it became increasingly apparent just how different were the realities of everyday spoken English from the traditional grammars on which we had all cut our teeth. I learned how to put a book together, as we slowly hammered out the approach which would be published the next year as Crystal and Quirk, *Systems of Prosodic and Paralinguistic Features in English*. Quirk was insistent that my name should be first, even though I was the least in his kingdom.

The Survey world opened innumerable intellectual doors. As a member of staff, albeit the most junior, I was made immediately welcome by those whom I had previously looked upon with student-like awe. I got to know all the other phoneticians, at the time led by Dennis Fry, and a merrier bunch of academics I have never since met. Gimson asked me to write up the Survey approach for *m.f.* (*Le Maître Phonétique*, distinctive at the time for having all its articles in phonetic transcription), and I reviewed the Daniel Jones memorial volume in its pages (which brought me a treasured thank-you card, in tiny spidery writing, from the great man). The Quirk postgraduate seminars were a high point of the week, attended by students from all over the world, and led by a variety of visiting scholars as well as himself. I learned my generative grammar from one of them, Jim Sledd, whose orientation to linguistics – best described as sceptical enthusiasm – has stayed with me. Michael Halliday was in town, at the time, and I worked through scale-and-category grammar, thinking it the coolest approach to linguistic theory I had so far encountered.

The Survey opened doors of opportunity, too. It gave me the chance to do some teaching, both inside and outside the university, and I realized I liked it, and was apparently quite good at it. I had my first EFL tutoring job, on the London University summer school. That was an intriguing, tempting world, with its immediate involvement with diverse cultures. Quirk pushed us to do some writing, whenever we could, and I found I liked that too. The Survey had to fight its way for recognition, and we all had a mandate to be clear and forceful in our explanations about language matters to the outside world. Invitations to lecture would come in to the Survey, and I would take my turn along with the others in responding to them. 'What is linguistics and is it useful?' was one of the commonest requests. As the person with the widest range of general linguistic interests in the English Department, I often found myself in the back of beyond, cobbling together an answer to this question. By the end of the year, I knew how to answer it, and had tried out the arguments on a variety of audiences. So, when I saw an ad for an Assistant Lecturer in Linguistics at the University of Bangor, it seemed like a sensible move. But having been on the Survey for less than a year I was reluctant to go for it, feeling a sense of immense loyalty to Quirk. He was in no doubt. Go for it. I did – and later that year found myself the latest arrival in Frank Palmer's group at Bangor.

The two years I spent at Bangor were for me an immense broadening of intellectual linguistic horizons. From Frank himself I got a sound sense of descriptive principles in practice. Here, and afterwards at Reading, his insistence on real-language analysis, using informants, put me in intimate touch with a wide range of disparate languages. Never did I bless my phonetics training more. I tried out my newfound thoughts about scales and categories with Peter Matthews, not long returned from a stay in the USA, and retired licking my wounds. This linguistic theory business was going to be more complicated than I had thought. Alan Thomas, the dialectologist, was building up the Survey of Welsh Dialects, and this brought me a welcome renewed contact with Welsh – though a curious one. Having missed out on 10 years of teenager usage since leaving Holyhead, and all the vocabulary learning that goes on in the teenage years, I realized I had become genuinely semilingual, fluent in nursery rhymes and linguistic metalanguage, but precious little else!

My evolving lecturing abilities had not gone unnoticed, and I found myself repeatedly used for introductory courses. For instance, the Department took on an ELT group from South America, but then found that it could not integrate their needs with other courses. I was made their course tutor, with the remit of introducing them to the whole of linguistics. I taught 33 hours a week that term, and by the end of it, there was hardly any topic in linguistics that I had not had to work up. As would happen later so often, I found that the best way of learning a subject is to teach it. The immediate result was an irritation that I had had to do so much work for such an apparently straightforward job. But there were no books to do the job for me. I was not going to fall into the trap of getting my new-to-the-subject students reading Bloomfield, et al. Why were there no motivating introductions to linguistics, to phonetics, to stylistics, to grammar, to semantics – to anything? Why should I feel discomfited when students came up and asked for something easy to read on my subject, and I could not help them? There were introductions to psychology, sociology and other subjects around. Why not linguistics?

Serendipitously, my first chance to try introducing the subject in book form came in 1964, when at a conference I bumped into a representative of the firm of Roman Catholic publishers, Burns and Oates, who wanted a book on religious language for one of their series. The 1960s was a decade of great linguistic turmoil for religious studies, with controversies over biblical translation, theological language (the bishop of Woolwich), the introduction of the Catholic vernacular liturgy (Vatican II), and stylostatistical analysis (the St Paul letters), as well as ongoing waves from earlier controversies, notably those initiated by A. J. Ayer. When my *Linguistics, Language and Religion* came out, it was given a Nihil Obstat and Imprimatur – I think, the only book in linguistics to have such commendations! It was good experience, proving to me that it was possible to reduce linguistics to its bare essentials in a coherent way, and to take linguistic principles and findings and apply them to an entirely different domain. Certainly some very naive notions of language permeated religious thinking of the time, and one did not have to do much to provide a fresh perspective. The welcome I received (in terms of reviews and reactions) for my theolinguistics (as it would later come to be called) was heart-warming. On the other hand, with the enthusiasm of youth I failed to see that it might not be such a good idea to include a chapter critiquing logical positivism, given the influence which proponents of that approach still held at the time. I'm told it cost me two senior jobs later on.

The Bangor experience was a perfect grounding for the move to Reading when it came, two years later (see Palmer's chapter below). With new single-subject and combined degrees to be taught, as well as MA and EFL Diploma courses, it was important to be able to make contributions over a wide range of subject matter at various levels, from first year to postgraduate. The importance of applied linguistics grew. The institutionalization of linguistics as a discipline became more evident during the mid-1960s. I found myself playing an increasingly active role in the newly formed Linguistics Association, first as Assistant Secretary, then as Secretary, and thus came to meet all the country's linguists. The arrival of the *Journal of Linguistics* in our department gave me a first experience of journal (assistant-)editing, and my first introduction to a major publisher, Cambridge University Press. Having completed my PhD (from London) in 1966, on English prosodic systems, and having been advised to publish it, it was a useful contact, for it eventually appeared as the opening volume in the 'blue-backed' Cambridge Studies in Linguistics.

Publishers had begun to realize that Something Was Up, as far as linguistics was concerned. All the leading publishers were sensing the potential of the new subject, especially in ELT, and all wanted introductory material. With relatively few professional linguists about, and only a subset of them willing or able to write at this level, the news that there was a linguist who not only had a hobby-horse about the need for introductory texts but had actually written one (albeit in a somewhat marginal domain) travelled around the publishing stands at the various conferences. Soon, reps were prowling the departmental corridors. In my case, the first outcome was *What is Linguistics?*, the consequence of visit to Edward Arnold, where I had my first experience of what is sometimes euphemistically called a publisher's 'lunch'. I staggered towards Paddington in the late Friday afternoon, having apparently agreed to write an introductory book for schools. There was a train strike, and with several hours available, I started to write it on the platform. Then the project obsessed me, as so many later would do, so that I could not think of anything else, and when that happens there is nothing you can do but finish it as quickly as possible, so that you can get on with something else. I sent a draft off to Arnold's on the Monday, along with my thank-you note for the wine.

I think it was that weekend which convinced me that my first love was writing. I was never happier than when sitting in front of a typewriter. A day passed without something written to me was a wasted day – whether it was a lecture outline, a review, an article, a radio script or a bit of a book. I was rarely proactive. My fault was that I couldn't say no – and there were so many ideas and opportunities around not to say no to. The need to make use of Survey of English Usage materials was an early priority, hence the collaboration with Derek Davy, who had become assistant director of the Survey, to write *Investigating English Style* (1969), which is surprisingly still in print. A collaboration with Whitney Bolton, then professor of English at Reading, produced an edited collection of essays on the history of the language. I think it may have been the coincidental publication in 1969 of three books (these two plus the prosody monograph) which gave me the reputation for being a 'prolific' author. It gained me a Readership, in both senses, anyway. But prolificness has its down side: at the readership panel, I was told quite firmly that my future academic career would be jeopardized if I continued to publish so much. No one was attacking the quality of the work. It was evidently my penchant for popularization which the panel found disturbing. (But times change. And at a later promotions panel, in an increasingly cash-strapped and public-conscious academic world, it was those books and other activities – such as broadcasting – that had achieved the highest public profile for which I was especially commended.)

There was nothing I could do about it, whatever the outcome. These things have a habit of developing a momentum of their own. In 1968 I had been approached by Penguin, who wanted to launch a new domain on linguistics, to parallel their very successful series on psychology. There would be three strands: a series of introductory Pelicans, a series of monographs, and a series of readings. 'How many in each?', I remember asking. No limit, I was told! I still have the outline I made for this vast project, based closely on the psychology one, with over 100 books in it, on all aspects of linguistics. The series was launched, and the first few did actually appear – but then Penguin Education ceased to exist, and with it the grand plans. The Pelican series, however, was robust, and as Editor I had the difficult task of trying to persuade colleagues to take time out from their busy course-planning and teaching schedules (for new courses were prolif-erating in the late 1960s) to write an introductory text on this or that. I find it impossible to act credibly as a Series Editor without having had a writing role myself, and so here, as in several later series, I took on an authorial as well as an editorial involvement, the result being *Linguistics* (1971). That series taught me a Great Truth, which all journal Editors know – that editing work is just as time-consuming and intellectually challenging as authorial work. That is why it is criminal that editorial tasks are not given greater credit by quality assessment bodies.

I am very proud of those introductory series, with contributions from

Palmer, Trudgill, Corder, Leech, O'Connor, Bolinger, Householder and others. The fact that many of the books are still in print, 30 years on, albeit in later editions, suggests that they met a need, and continue to do so. I saw editing as an academic duty, and still do – but it is a rewarding role. Apart from anything else, it makes you read material more closely even than in book-reviewing, because you are in a real interchange with an author. And I had several later opportunities to repeat the editorial role – an applied language studies series for Academic Press, a clinical linguistics series for Edward Arnold (later Whurr Publishers), and the Language Library series for André Deutsch (later Blackwell), where I took over from Simeon Potter as Co-Editor with Eric Partridge, and then as Editor. Some 40 books would emerge as part of the last series, mostly as a result of my invitation, and some of them have given me more pleasure to see in print than anything I have written myself.

The editing had an academic dimension too. At the Florence Child Language Symposium in 1972, Charles Ferguson came up with the idea of a journal to provide focus for that rapidly emerging field of study, and as the person present with most publishing contacts I was asked to find an outlet. The result was the *Journal of Child Language*, which I launched in 1975. A decade later, and a similar groundswell of interest in the clinical and remedial domain resulted in *Child Language Teaching and Therapy*; and the remarkable proliferation of linguistics subjects and journals during the 1970s and early 1980s led to the foundation of *Linguistics Abstracts*. Each of these journals I edited for a dozen years or so. I think it is bad for an Editor to stay with a journal for more than about a decade: journals need to be regularly refreshed from the top, if they are to avoid becoming too narrowly focused.

Although I kept my research interests in English grammar, intonation and stylistics alive during the 1970s, it is I think the growth of my clinical linguistic interests with which I would later come to be most associated. This was never premeditated. I was teaching the child language acquisition course at Reading, and had done some research in the development of infant vocalization and prosody, but the clinical dimension was not a major part of it. Then one day the phone rang and it was Kevin Murphy, from the Audiology Department of the Royal Berkshire Hospital, wondering if I would come and see a 3-year-old whom they were puzzled about. She wasn't deaf, and had no obvious physical problems, and yet she wasn't talking properly. This sounded interesting. I went down, sat in on some sessions, recorded a sample of speech, did a developmental analysis, and all kinds of interesting linguistic patterns emerged. In language acquisition terms, the child was delayed, but was obviously having particular difficulty with certain constructions. I wrote a report, sent it off, and thought no more about it. Then there was another phone call. Before long I found myself down at the hospital almost as much as I was in the department. It transpired that the kind of linguistically oriented report I had been writing was precisely the kind of orientation which the Department's speech therapists needed. On the other hand, there was a problem. Because I was using the terminology of linguistics, not everything was being understood. As I learned more about the profession, I discovered that although speech therapists had phonetics training, they had little or no background in linguistics.

The point had already been noticed higher up. A government report on Speech Therapy Services appeared in 1972, chaired as it happens by Randolph Quirk, and this recommended that linguistics should be a core discipline of that profession's expertise. But there were no course books integrating the two subjects, no in-service courses applying linguistics to the clinical domain, no diploma or degree courses in the subject with the requisite biases, and hardly any linguistically oriented research. The contrast with the established field of foreign language teaching was notable. During the mid-1970s, accordingly, I found myself increasingly involved in meeting these needs: the first thing was to develop the research foundation, to demonstrate that there was a systematically applicable connection between linguistics and the clinical domain – that is, between all areas of linguistics and all areas of speech therapy. It meant a lot of clinical observation, during those years, and a steep learning curve which took in such medical specialities as pediatrics, neurology, ENT and audiology, as well as the various relevant branches of psychology, education and social science. The result was a series of clinical linguistic assessment procedures and associated in-service training courses which kept me and my colleagues Paul Fletcher and Mike Garman heavily involved for a decade, and sparked off a series of research studies. It also resulted in the BA in Linguistics and Language Pathology, hosted by the Linguistics Department, and the arrival of an in-house observation and assessment clinic, and the appointment of full-time speech therapists within the Department. Later, I planned an analogous course for teachers, the Diploma in Remedial Language Studies. And, as it emerged that there was little written in these areas, I found myself writing again, in monograph and introductory publications, beginning with the write-up of our first clinical procedure, LARSP (Language Assessment, Remediation, and Screening Procedure), in *The Grammatical Analysis of Language Disability* (1976), then *Clinical Linguistics* (1981a) and *Introduction to Language Pathology* (1980a).

I had never expected the clinical domain to take over my life so much. But there were personal reasons as well as academic ones. My third child was born with a cleft lip and palate, and suddenly I found myself an anxious parent working with the same range of people who had previously been only colleagues. That gave me an empathy with the parents of language-disordered children, and indeed with the children themselves, which kept my linguistic feet firmly on the ground. Indeed, when it came to the kind of simplifications of complex linguistic positions which I found it necessary to introduce in order to make an applied linguistics model work in the clinical context, I often found myself in conflict with my theoretical linguistic colleagues in the Department. It was not all plain sailing, by any means. Then, in the mid-1970s, my link with the profession was consolidated once and for all, when I married a speech therapist.

The early 1980s were the beginning of the difficult times, for academics, especially for someone who had accreted as many editorial, authorial and extra-mural roles as I had. I had been spending a lot of time giving courses to teachers, in the wake of the Bullock Report (1975); I had been doing my bit on the ELT side abroad, with the Reading Department building up important teacher-training connections in several parts of the world; and the BBC had finally twigged that language issues were of general interest, which resulted in my devising several radio series. The new clinical courses were just taking off, new dimensions (such as sign language studies) were being added, and doctoral students were emerging. So when the first of the three, annual, 'Thatcher cuts' letters arrived in 1981, inviting me (and everyone else) to consider early retirement, I was not interested. I felt there was far too much going on in the department on the clinical and remedial side that I was personally responsible for. I had already turned down two professorial job offers at other places. I was going to stay at Reading for ever.

But by 1984 the situation had deteriorated: secretarial cuts and other constraints of a kind that today need no exposition were piling up. I had been commissioned by Cambridge University Press in 1980 to write a book (which eventually became the *Cambridge Encyclopedia of Language*), and had managed a few dozen pages only in three years. The day I decided to leave was when I had spent half a week working out whether it was cheaper to send my speech therapy students to their clinics by bus or by train. At the end of it, I had saved the university, I estimated, about £100. But nobody had entered my salary into the equation. Was this what a Professor of Linguistics should be doing? There was no likelihood of the situation getting any better. I went to the VC clutching my file of letters inviting me to retire early, said 'yes please', and was turned down flat. Apparently those letters were not really meant for members of successful (i.e. money-earning) departments, such as Linguistics. If I left, I would have to be replaced, and that would save no money. But by that time I had made up my mind, and I resigned anyway. (When I was replaced, it was at a junior level, which I have always felt was a bit of a dirty trick.)

The first year out, without a salary, was tough, but some part-time teaching and the availability I now had to write, edit and advise, as an 'independent scholar' (as the Japanese decided to call me, horrified at my self-description as a 'freelance linguist'), meant that we survived. Bangor offered me an honorary association, which kept me in touch with the profession. Then in 1986, I was asked to plan and edit the new *Cambridge Encyclopedia*, which, with its associated family of general encyclopedias, has been the half-time basis of my existence ever since. In the other 'half time', I try to do as much linguistics as I can. There seems to be no end to the number of subjects which need to be written about in the kind of introductory yet academically responsible way which I have tried to make my forte. I have a permanent obsession over terminology, which has led to various dictionary-type projects. I have aimed to maintain a writing schedule of one book a year. I miss some features of full-time academic life, such as doctoral supervisory work; on the other hand, I have visited so many departments and centres around the world in the past 15 years that I have never felt far away from the profession. None the less, I am aware that my self-removal from the orthodox academic world made me something of a maverick figure, in the eyes of some, and actually am somewhat surprised, although delighted, to be part of this volume!

Every subject needs its responsible popularizers, and I have aimed to fulfil that role for linguistics. I doubt whether, quantitatively, anyone could match the amount of time I have devoted to putting linguistics before general audiences or audiences of language professionals (such as teachers and speech therapists), in such varied contexts as literary festivals, sixth form conferences, and radio and television programmes (the latter still notoriously reluctant to give linguistics the profile it deserves), or writing articles for newspapers and general interest periodicals. Half my year is routinely spent away from home, engaging with audiences in this way. So I suppose this is where my main 'significance' lies. In terms of conventional research activities, I would like to think that I made a few small contributions to thinking in phonology, grammar and stylistics, chiefly in relation to English, and it seems I was in the right place at the right time in relation to clinical linguistics. I have never been much of a theoretical innovator, and look in awe at the achievements of my contemporaries in taking the subject forward in that way so significantly during the twentieth century. At the same time, I hope my efforts at communicating their thinking and findings to a larger professional and public world have been of value in their own right, and that I have done them no disservice. Lastly, I know from the letters I have received that many people have begun to study linguistics after reading one of my books (I have no data on how many were put off by the same experience), and it is through them that I hope I have been able to make some sort of long-term contribution to this remarkable subject.

REFERENCES

BLOOMFIELD, LEONARD, 1933. *Language*, New York: Holt, Rinehart & Winston.
BULLOCK REPORT, 1975. *A Language for Life*, London: HMSO.
CRYSTAL, DAVID, 1964. 'A perspective for paralanguage', *Le Maître Phonétique* 120, 25–9.
CRYSTAL, DAVID, 1965a. 'Review of D. Abercrombie, et al. (eds), *In Honour of Daniel Jones*', le *Maître Phonétique* 122, 26–7.

CRYSTAL, DAVID, 1965b. *Linguistics, Language and Religion*, London: Burns Oates, and New York: Hawthorn Books.

CRYSTAL, DAVID, 1968. *What is Linguistics?*, 4th ed. 1985, London: Edward Arnold.

CRYSTAL, DAVID, 1969. *Prosodic Systems and Intonation in English*, Cambridge: Cambridge University Press.

CRYSTAL, DAVID, 1971. *Linguistics*, 2nd ed. 1985, Harmondsworth: Penguin.

CRYSTAL, DAVID, 1976. *The Grammatical Analysis of Language Disability*, London: Arnold.

CRYSTAL, DAVID, 1980a. *Introduction to Language Pathology*, London: Arnold/Whurr.

CRYSTAL, DAVID, 1980b. *A Dictionary of Linguistics and Phonetics*, 5th ed. 2002, London: Deutsch, and Oxford: Blackwell.

CRYSTAL, DAVID, 1981a. *Clinical Linguistics,* Vienna: Springer, and London: Whurr.

CRYSTAL, DAVID, 1981b. *Directions in Applied Linguistics*, London: Academic Press.

CRYSTAL, DAVID, 1987. *The Cambridge Encyclopedia of Language*, 2nd ed. 1997, Cambridge: Cambridge University Press.

CRYSTAL, DAVID, (ed.) 1990. *The Cambridge Encyclopedia*, 4th ed. 2000, Cambridge: Cambridge University Press.

CRYSTAL, DAVID & BOLTON, W. F., (eds.) 1969. *The English Language: Essays by Linguists and Men of Letters, Vol. 2 1858–1964*, Cambridge: Cambridge University Press.

CRYSTAL, DAVID & DAVY, DEREK, 1969. *Investigating English Style*, London: Longman.

CRYSTAL, DAVID & QUIRK, RANDOLPH, 1964. *Systems of Prosodic and Paralinguistic Features in English*, The Hague: Mouton.

CRYSTAL, DAVID, FLETCHER, PAUL & GARMAN, MICHAEL, 1976. *The Grammatical Analysis of Language Disability*, 2nd ed. 1989, London: Edward Arnold.

OGDEN, C. K. & RICHARDS, I. A., 1923. *The Meaning of Meaning*, London: Routledge and Kegan Paul.

QUIRK, RANDOLPH, 1960. 'The Survey of English Usage', *TPhS*, 40–61.

QUIRK REPORT, 1972. *Speech Therapy Services*, London: HMSO.

SAUSSURE, FERDINAND DE, 1916. *Course in General Linguistics*, trans. Wade Baskin, New York: Philosophical Library.

GERALD GAZDAR

GAZDAR, Gerald James Michael, FBA 1988; Professor of Computational Linguistics, University of Sussex, since 1985; *b.* 1950. *Education:* Heath Mount; Bradfield College; University of East Anglia, BA in Philosophy with Economics; Reading University, MA in Linguistics, PhD; *Career:* Sussex University: Lecturer 1975–80, Reader 1980–5, Dean, School of Cognitive and Computer Sciences, 1988–93; Fellow, Center for Advanced Study in the Behavioral Sciences, Stanford University, 1984–5. *Major Publications: A Bibliography of Contemporary Linguistic Research* 1978 (with Klein, Pullum); *Pragmatics* 1979; *Order, Concord, and Constituency* 1983 (with Klein, Pullum); *Generalized Phrase Structure Grammar* 1985 (with Klein, Pullum, Sag); *New Horizons in Linguistics II* 1987 (with Coates, Deucher, Lyons); *Natural Language Processing the 1980s* 1987 (with Franz, Osborne, Evans); *Natural Language Processing in Prolog: An Introduction to Computational Linguistics* 1989 (with Mellish).

* * *

This chapter is the first 5,000 words of a transcript of an interview that Ted Briscoe conducted with Gerald Gazdar in Cambridge on 3 November 2000. The interview was recorded on minidisks and expertly transcribed by Tricia Roussel. The remaining 21,000 words of the interview, which includes sections dealing with pragmatics, GPSG, lexical knowledge representation, natural language processing and linguistics, can be found on the web at http://www.cogs.susx.ac.uk/lab/nlp/gazdar/briscoe/.

* * *

EJB The first thing that I noticed, especially after reading some of the other contributions, was that your background in terms of A-levels and undergraduate degree was really quite different from the second generation UK linguists, who nearly all have a languages background. You did physics, chemistry and maths at A-level and then philosophy and economics at UEA, so how did you get from that to linguistics?

GG Well, at that time UEA philosophy was very much ordinary language philosophy, so it isn't a huge jump from that to linguistics. I didn't want to continue in philosophy because I didn't think I was good enough at it. It seems to me that to contribute to philosophy you have to be very, very good at it. Other disciplines allow you to contribute without you needing to be very, very good. Also, I wanted to do something which had a kind of tangible subject matter, which philosophy doesn't really. I don't regret doing philosophy as my first degree. I think it was a useful thing to have done but I didn't want to continue with it.

EJB   And having a background in sciences at A-level is also unusual for a linguist. The jump from such A-levels to philosophy is also, I suppose, a non-standard one. I can see the link to economics via mathematics.

GG   My reasons for that jump were not really academic. My school took us on careers visits where we met old boys. I recall visiting an ICI factory. We were introduced to some old boy and told that he was the best chemist of his year. He was standing in a white coat next to a large vat of something unspeakable and I thought 'no, I am not going to do that.' So I looked for a degree that was maximally useless in terms of a subsequent career. Given that criterion, the choice of philosophy was an obvious one.

EJB   OK. So you had mathematics A-level, and you were interested enough in mathematics to include economics in your degree course. Do you think that affected your subsequent approach to research and to linguistics? Do you think that put you in a very different place from somebody who had come from modern languages or classics?

GG   I suppose it may have done, yes. I am not really conscious of it.

EJB   After UEA, you went to Reading. How did you come to choose Reading? Were there other possibilities?

GG   Yes, I went for an interview at Essex as well. I needed a conversion MA. I couldn't just start doing a PhD in linguistics and both Reading and Essex offered conversion MAs. I can't remember what else was available. I went for interview to both of them, and both offered me places. Reading seemed to me, at the time, to be the better one to do, so that is the one I did.

EJB   Was that because it was a bigger department with more people or because of the content of the course?

GG   I don't really remember that.

EJB   That presumably would have been a fairly standard route at the time into linguistics because there wouldn't have been too many undergraduate linguistics programmes.

GG   No, I don't think there were.

EJB   Right. So how was Reading when you got there? Did it live up to its promise and was linguistics what you had thought it was going to be, given that you arrived at it via an ordinary language philosophy route? Presumably you had come across Noam Chomsky's work in philosophy?

GG   Well, I did quite a bit of reading before I got there. I had read John Lyons's *Introduction to Theoretical Linguistics* (1969) from cover to cover and and I had read his *New Horizons in Linguistics* (1970) collection from cover to cover as well, so I didn't get any surprises. The Reading MA, at that time, was basically their undergraduate degree compressed into one year, so one found oneself in second and third year undergraduate classes. The difference was that the MA students had to work much harder than the undergraduates and every minute of our day was filled. I don't have any regrets – I think it was a good training. It exposed me to all kinds of bits of linguistics which I probably would not have come to terms with if I had had a free choice about what I studied. Parts of it were embarrassing, like phonetics: I just couldn't master any of the noises. Never have.

EJB Snap.

GG In fact, at my phonetics oral exam, the examiners burst out laughing, which was not very polite of them but I'm sure it was appropriate.

EJB And was any message conveyed to you about your suitability to be a professional linguist on the basis of this? I remember being reassured myself that not being able to say /oongar/ or something was actually not much of a barrier to being a philosophical linguist by the phonetician here, which was, I think, his attempt to reassure me.

GG No, I wasn't warned off. The fact that the examiners burst out laughing was indicative of the fact that they didn't think my performance was the end of the world – I'm sure a weaker student would have been treated more tactfully.

EJB Right. In terms of the staff at the time, was there anyone there who was particularly influential? Who directed what was going to happen next?

GG Well, I suppose, of the staff who were there, Peter Matthews had the biggest impact on me.

EJB And what was it about Peter's lecturing or the content of what he was doing that was . . .

GG Well, he was just a very skilled linguist and very careful and he really led by way of example.

EJB Somebody who really knew the history of the field very well and was careful not to reinvent the wheel and that kind of thing?

GG I did informant classes with him. We had classes where I guess a couple of us together with the tutor went through stuff with an informant. It was an aspect of linguistics that was not really of interest to me, but it was quite enlightening to see how one did it.

EJB Right, and you need somebody to show you that – you don't learn anything of that by reading.

GG No – and also he taught us what was then contemporary syntax, which I needed to know.

EJB And you stayed at Reading to do a PhD. Was that inertia or a positive decision to stay at Reading because there were things happening there that seemed interesting?

GG My memory is a bit vague. I think I stayed to do what must have been an MPhil. In other words, a year of research that would allow the MA to become an MPhil. Then I abandoned that project, perhaps because I had realized that MPhils were not worth having, or perhaps because I had gained the confidence to embark on a PhD. So then I switched to doing a PhD. I subsequently wanted to transfer my PhD registration from Reading, but the practicalities of that just proved impossible. In the event, Reading didn't supervise me for my PhD. All my supervision came from people outside Reading.

EJB Was that because by the time you had got into the PhD topic there was nobody at Reading who was in a position to supervise that topic?

GG That's right. Yes.

EJB Essentially, that was pretty much the point at which you moved to Cambridge?

GG Pretty much yes. I moved physically to Cambridge.

EJB And that was one of the high points of linguistics in Cambridge, as Ed Keenan was here and the King's College research was devoted to linguistics at that point.

GG Yes, it was certainly in that decade the most exciting place in linguistics to be in the UK.

EJB And was it Ed himself who was the attraction in terms of supervision?

GG Yes, very much so. It was he who had worked on presupposition and I had decided by then that presupposition was my core problem, although my thesis wasn't limited to that, but it was the nut that I most wanted to crack.

EJB And along the way you had to teach yourself model theoretic semantics, which I imagine there weren't too many people in the UK at the time who were in a position to help with.

GG No, I mean almost the first thing that Ed did was drop his favourite logic textbook (Thomason 1970) into my lap and say 'go away and work your way through this', which was extremely good for my soul.

EJB And were there other people around who were under the same influence?

GG It was just after the big formal semantics conference in April 1973 (Keenan 1975), which Ed had organized in Cambridge and which I had attended. That had opened my eyes to this whole world that I hadn't really been fully conscious of. Everybody who was anybody was there. It was a very exciting event and it was shortly after that that I moved to Cambridge.

EJB   So it was really Ed and the introduction to the Montague tradition and its linguistic reinterpretation that was the . . .

GG   Yes, but the Montague tradition hadn't really quite emerged in 1973. Montague had published those revolutionary papers but their importance wasn't recognized generally by linguists until after Barbara Partee did her PR job – I don't mean that in a pejorative sense – she did a very effective sales promotion on Montague's work to linguists. Her first paper in that genre (Partee 1973) didn't get published until 1973, for example, and the Thomason collection of Montague's papers only appeared the following year (Montague 1974).

EJB   It was absolutely critical at the time as everybody was doing TG. Even if you had the intellectual apparatus to understand Montague's papers, to make the kind of link to the kind of grammar that was being done was still a fairly large intellectual effort. That was, in some sense, what Partee and Thomason did. But you and presumably Ed were doing that independently . . . seeing that the stuff was relevant and was perfectly integratible with syntax.

GG   I wasn't thinking about syntax very much at that time.

EJB   But I assume Peter Matthews was teaching the current version of transformational grammar.

GG   Yes. But I didn't think about syntax until I had to teach it. I didn't think hard about it until I found myself teaching it to undergraduates. It was then that whatever faith I had in transformational grammar leaked away rather rapidly. In 1973, that was before that.

EJB   But it was clear that if you wanted to work on problems in pragmatics, the starting point was model theoretic semantics.

GG   Well, there wasn't any semantics in TG.

EJB   Absolutely. That again is, I would have thought, a fairly innovative position to adopt. There must have been other people around who were doing pragmatics, but I would have thought that none of them, certainly in the UK, were doing it in the context of model theoretic semantics.

GG   Well, pragmatics, I don't think really had a name at that stage: the notion that you could cut the field of meaning into semantics and pragmatics in the way that it was subsequently cut. I think that was still emerging.

EJB   But within five years, it was really a quite clearly identifiable assumption.

GG   By the late 1970s, yes. So pragmatics had become a legitimate sub-discipline in linguistics by the late 1970s, but it wasn't in the early 1970s. And, apart from lexical semantics, semantics wasn't really a component of linguistics in the early 1970s, either.

EJB   And so to what extent was your PhD influential in creating that kind of division and that kind of view of what pragmatics was?

GG   Well, there were a whole bunch of works at around that time of which my PhD was one, so I suppose they were jointly responsible.

EJB   And the rest were in the US?

GG   I suppose they would mostly be, though Kempson's (1975) and Wilson's (1975) theses were influential. Subsequently Steve Levinson's textbook (1983) defined the field if you like – but that was several years later. Geoff Leech published a textbook on pragmatics in that year also (1983).

EJB   Was Steve around in Cambridge at that time?

GG   Oh, yes. I'm not sure exactly when he came back to Cambridge, but he and I started a journal called *Pragmatics Microfiche*. I think we may have started that in 1974, so that would have been one of the beginnings of pragmatics, I suppose. I'm sure it wasn't a very influential journal, but it was probably a marker of the word 'pragmatics' coming into general currency.

EJB   Right. And what was the point you started to make contact with people like Geoff Pullum and Ewan Klein?

GG   Ewan did the MA at Reading the year after me. We became friends and he was instrumental in getting me to move to Cambridge. He started a PhD in Cambridge after he finished the Reading MA, and we shared a flat in Cherry Hinton. Geoff Pullum was also there in Cambridge because he was registered initially to do a Cambridge PhD – though he subsequently switched registration to London, when he moved there to take a teaching job at UCL. So all three of us were in Cambridge in 1973, and we all attended the weekly Universal Grammar seminar in King's College that Ed ran with Bernard Comrie. And Richard Coates, who subsequently became a colleague of mine at Sussex, he was also there part of that time. With hindsight, that seminar was quite remarkable because most of a doctoral generation of British linguists attended it: in addition to those I just mentioned, Jack Hawkins, John Payne, Andrew Radford and Nigel Vincent were regulars.

EJB   And Ewan and Geoff were registered to do PhDs in Linguistics?

GG   Ewan certainly wasn't. He was registered in Social and Political Sciences. Geoff was a research student in Linguistics attached to King's College at that time.

EJB   It is striking reading the earlier generation's stories how Cambridge was a nexus for nearly all of them. A lot of them did modern languages or classics at Cambridge but, in their day, there was no Linguistics Department. In 1973, there was a Linguistics Department?

GG   Yes. John Trim was its Head. He was extremely hospitable to me. I had no formal status in Cambridge at all, but he just treated me as if I was one of the graduate students in his department, with all the same sorts of privileges.

EJB   And, to some extent, he must have been influential in getting Ed to come over and in making possible the big conference that happened there?

GG   That, I don't know.

EJB   And you were in Cambridge, doing teaching and tutorial work?

GG   I did a bit of tutorial work.

EJB   But that was really just an excuse to be near Ed?

GG   I was just living in Cambridge in order to be supervised by Ed, and that lasted for a year, and then Ed went back to the States. I continued living in Cambridge as I had somewhere to live and there was no good reason to live anywhere else.

EJB   Which is an informal arrangement about how one does a PhD – to the point of neglect, perhaps, would be the one view. The other view would be that it was an extremely flexible set-up very different from the kind of thing that you would be able do in the US . . .

GG   Or even here now. I don't suppose Reading allows PhD students to disappear off into the sunset these days.

EJB   I think everywhere has some sort of residence requirements on full-time PhD students now. So, yes, the system has become less flexible. But, in your case, it seems that you were able to capitalize on that. The fact that Ed Keenen was around for a year was obviously an opportunity.

GG   Reading weren't in a position to offer supervision on what I wanted to do, and as I insisted on doing what I wanted to do and wouldn't hear of any alternatives, they were relaxed about my emigration.

EJB   Which is another big institutional difference between universities in the US and here. When I was at Penn I was astounded at the degree to which people were essentially told that if you want money then you do this. I think there still is a presumption in the UK that you have a lot of independence, perhaps more that you'll ever have again, when you do your PhD. It seems unlikely that you would have ended up writing a PhD on that particular topic if the system had been much tighter.

GG   Also, in those days, things were not so carefully costed. Ed was a freestanding research fellow and how he used his time was up to him, so perhaps that would not have changed. But, in the case of Hans Kamp, when I transferred to him he was a full-time teaching faculty member at another university, and he just took me on. There was nothing in it for him, it was not part of his official teaching load, and it is hard to see that happening these days. Maybe it was hard to see it happening in those days too, and it is just that that those issues weren't visible to me.

EJB   Your transfer to Hans was through Ed presumably. Hans knew Ed and . . .

GG   My memory of the story as it was passed to me, I think by Ed, was that he bumped into Hans at a conference and said 'I've got this guy in Cambridge whom I'm supervising and I'm going back to the US and he can't follow me and can I offload him on you?', and Hans said 'yes.'

EJB   And Hans was at that time at Essex?

GG   No, he was at Bedford College in London, in Regent's Park. I just commuted down every fortnight or so to see him.

EJB   There must have been someone at Reading who was the official supervisor?

GG   I was put down in Frank Palmer's name, as he was Head of Department and I had to be listed under somebody's name.

EJB   Did you go to the States before you finished your PhD?

GG   No.

EJB   But your PhD research was really being driven by American work?

GG   Yes, very much so. Karttunen is a Finn, of course, but he was working in the US.

EJB   In that sense, a number of the earlier people like Peter Matthews and John Lyons also have a sense of themselves as being people who imported Chomskian linguistics, or maybe generative linguistics, or whatever. I don't have much sense of to what extent, by the time you were doing your PhD, more or less everybody was looking to the US, and how much there was still an independent separate kind of tradition being pushed in British linguistics departments.

GG   It depended what you were working on. If you were interested in anything to do with syntax and above in the traditional layer-cake model, then you didn't have much choice about the nationality of the people you cited, because the US was where all the exciting work was being done.

EJB   And even before you finished you got a Lectureship at Sussex.

GG   I had pretty much finished. I hadn't written up but the components were all done. I pretty much had a set of chapters, and the implicature and presupposition stuff had all been distributed in June 1975. I had distributed three chapters privately. I had printed up about 50 copies and sent them to people like Karttunen, Stalnaker and Thomason. Really, it was just a tidying up task once I got to Sussex in October 1975.

I can remember being asked in the interview what I knew of AI. I think the reason I got the job was because the answer was that I knew rather a lot. I had read Charniak's thesis (1972). I had read Wilks's book (1972) and Winograd's book (1972). I had read the Rustin volume (1973). I had actually read a great deal of AI and natural language work for my own interest and because it connected with topics in my thesis. So, that from the interview panel's point of view, I was probably ideal, because there weren't many UK linguists round in 1975 who really knew anything much about AI.

EJB   So you arrived at Sussex and you had to start teaching?

GG   Yes.

EJB   Was there anybody else at Sussex doing linguistics at the time?

GG   There was no linguist by title. In the Arts Faculty, there were a couple of people who taught first year introductions to language and linguistics, and they knew a fair bit of linguistics. One was a psychologist, the other a lecturer in French. On the Science side, there was massive expertise in psycholinguistics and speech and language processing: Chris Darwin, Steve Isard, Phil Johnson-Laird, Christopher Longuet-Higgins, Richard Power, Mark Steedman and, a bit later, Anne Cutler and Donia Scott.

EJB   Was your appointment a conscious decision on the part of Sussex to try to build a department? Or was it simply 'we've got to have somebody to teach this kind of stuff who really wants to'?

GG   I think they made a conscious decision to build a department and they used John Lyons as their advisor, so he was on the committee that interviewed me. I was the first appointment.

EJB   When was the next appointment?

GG   John arrived as Chair the following year, and Richard Coates was appointed as the second lecturer the year after that.

EJB   That sounds like a rather happy series of events, because it would have been unfortunate to be the token linguist in Sussex, especially as a first appointment. For John Lyons to arrive there must essentially have made it a done deal that there was going to be quite a good department there.

GG   Well, that would be true in many other universities. Sussex was rather strange in that I was appointed to the Cognitive Studies Programme, as it was then. The plan was that the programme would have a significant linguistic component and that I would teach it. But the programme didn't really need more than one linguist, so the other linguists had to find other activities. There was an academic home ready for me when I arrived, and I remained very much in that home, I never strayed far outside it, so I wasn't ever really a central figure in the Linguistics Subject Group, because so much of what I did was tied up with the Cognitive Studies Programme. For example, I did other teaching for the programme that was not linguistics teaching: I taught logic, I taught programming – I taught POP-11 for a couple of years, I even taught AI vision.

EJB   This was quite early on?

GG   Yes, I taught a wide range of things which were all things which the

Cognitive Studies Programme did, and I rather enjoyed teaching those things. I didn't want to teach linguistics and nothing but linguistics.

EJB Why was that?

GG I think partly because I wasn't very confident about some areas of linguistics. With good reason – I couldn't have taught phonetics to save my life, and couldn't now. There were areas such as morphology and phonology which I could have boned up on, but I didn't really know very much, so it would have been more work. Whereas teaching logic, I could do quite easily. And, since I wanted to program anyway, teaching programming was a good way of learning. As for teaching vision, well, I wasn't particularly interested in vision but I co-taught a course that was half vision and half language with Max Clowes, and it was just convenient to be able to cover his teaching in the same way that he could cover mine, so that if he dropped out of a lecture or wasn't available for half a term I could just do it. So I taught line labelling, for example, and I think stereopsis too – God!

EJB But that's all a long time ago? You haven't done that kind of thing in recent years at all?

GG I suppose I've taught logic more recently – not very distinguishable from semantics at the early stages.

EJB So you said earlier on that you didn't think about syntax until you had to start teaching it, and presumably when you went to Sussex that would have been the thing that they primarily wanted you to do – to teach syntax, because that would have been the thing that was most associated with linguistics at that time.

GG Yes. I had to teach a two-term linguistics course to the cognitive studies students and at least half of it was devoted to syntax. That was my primary task, but there was other teaching as well.

EJB What was the background of the students? Most linguistics departments then and now are full of people who have done humanities A-levels. The challenge in teaching syntax is usually to cure a fear of notation and maybe teach a little of what it means to be formal about things. Were the cognitive studies students similar in that respect, or were they better trained in science and maths?

GG I don't know what their individual backgrounds, were, but they were students who had come to Sussex to do an AI-flavoured degree. They might be majoring in philosophy or psychology, say, but they had chosen to do a degree that included great slabs of AI and they had to program from day one. I got them in the second or third year, so they all knew how to program.

EJB So the whole flavour of that course was really quite different from elsewhere. The kinds of things that one thought about in teaching it and one's critical attitude to syntactic theory would thus also be rather different, I suspect. When you taught syntax to cognitive science students who had more of a mathematical and formal background than the average linguistics student, you were presumably teaching at least some kind of flavour of the generative grammar that was around at the time – generative semantics?

GG I taught them TG out of textbooks, as there were a huge number of TG textbooks.

EJB Which one did you use?

GG I can remember using Grinder & Elgin (1973), but I think I used a variety over the years. I think that the one I liked best in the end was the one that Keyser & Postal (1976) wrote – I think that was my favourite. But that wasn't around when I started teaching. Actually my teaching was critical – I hadn't really had illusions about TG but, to the extent that I had any, I discovered through teaching that it was worse than I thought.

EJB Presumably the students were also more critical because they had more of a background to actually question the real formality, precision and clarity of the TG of that era.

GG That's exactly what happened. We had rather good students at that time because the programme we were offering was very new – there wasn't anything else like it in the UK. And, as is the way with these things, good students self-select for things like that. So we mostly had very bright students who were also keen. I was teaching syntax for the first time. I had done a bit of tutorial work in Cambridge, but nothing that had stressed me and not with any great concentration on syntax, as I remember. So I was faced with teaching a whole term of syntax, and syntax wasn't my field. Although I knew about it, I was also learning it – at least for pedagogical purposes – learning it on the job. The students would ask me questions about things when I gave lectures and quite often I wasn't able to answer them, and this was acutely embarrassing, as I was meant to know the stuff. For example, they would ask me something about attachment conventions: you've got this transformation and it is notated this way and you've just shown on the blackboard that the constituent structure of the output of the transformation is this shape. Why is it that shape and not this other shape, given the nature of the attachment conventions? I would have to say 'don't know – tell you next lecture'. And, at the next lecture, I would have to respond. In fact, to a number of these questions, there simply weren't answers. It basically wasn't a formal system. It was being sold as a formal system, being marketed as a formal system, but it wasn't, and that struck me as a kind of con trick. Also deeply unsatisfactory – I no longer knew what it was.

EJB And, in particular, this was still supposed to be the great contribution of this field. The selling point of the whole thing. If it was flawed, this was unfortunate. So presumably one of the motivations for the work on GPSG was to try to get the details right, whatever flavour of syntax you came up with.

GG Yes, that was part of it.

REFERENCES

CHARNIAK, EUGENE, 1972. *Towards a Model of Children's Story Comprehension*, MIT AI Laboratory: Technical Report AI-TR266.

GRINDER, JOHN T. & ELGIN, SUZETTE H., 1973. *Guide to Transformational Grammar*, New York: Holt, Rinehart & Winston.

KEENAN, EDWARD L., (ed.) 1975. *Formal Semantics of Natural Language*, Cambridge: Cambridge University Press.

KEMPSON, RUTH, 1975. *Presupposition and the Delimitation of Semantics*, Cambridge: Cambridge University Press.

KEYSER, S. JAY & POSTAL, PAUL M., 1976. *Beginning English Grammar*, New York: Harper & Row.

LEECH, GEOFFREY, 1983. *Principles of Pragmatics*, Harlow: Longman.

LEVINSON, STEPHEN, 1983. *Pragmatics*, Cambridge: Cambridge University Press.

LYONS, JOHN, 1969. *Introduction to Theoretical Linguistics*, Cambridge: Cambridge University Press.

LYONS, JOHN, 1970. *New Horizons in Linguistics*, Harmondsworth: Penguin.

MONTAGUE, RICHARD, 1974. *Formal Philosophy*, New Haven: Yale University Press.

PARTEE, BARBARA H., 1973. 'Some transformational extensions of Montague Grammar', *Journal of Philosophical Logic* 2, 509–34.

RUSTIN, R., (ed.) 1973. *Natural Language Processing*, New York: Algorithmics Press.

THOMASON, RICHMOND H., 1970. *Symbolic Logic: An Introduction*, Toronto: Macmillan.

WILKS, YORICK, 1972. *Grammar, Meaning and the Machine Analysis of Language*, London: Academic Press.

WILSON, DEIRDRE, 1975. *Presupposition and Non-Truth-Conditional Semantics*, London: Academic Press.

WINOGRAD, TERENCE, 1972. *Understanding Natural Language*, New York: Academic Press.

M. A. K. HALLIDAY

HALLIDAY, Michael Alexander Kirkwood, FAHA 1979, Corresponding FBA 1989, Foreign Member Academia Europaea, 1994; Emeritus Professor of Linguistics in the University of Sydney since 1988; *b.* 1925; *Education:* Rugby School; University of London BA; MA, PhD, Cambridge. *Career:* Army, 1944–7; Assistant Lecturer in Chinese, Cambridge University, 1954–8; Lecturer in General Linguistics, Edinburgh University, 1958–60, Reader 1960–3; Director, Communication Research Centre, UCL, 1963–5; Linguistic Society of America Professor, Indiana University 1964; Professor of General Linguistics, UCL, 1965–71; Fellow, Center for Advanced Study in the Behavioral Sciences, Stanford, 1972–3; Professor of Linguistics, University of Illinois, 1973–4; Professor of Language and Linguistics, Essex University, 1974–5; Professor of Linguistics, University of Sydney, 1976–87; Visiting Professor of Linguistics: Yale 1967, Brown 1971, Nairobi 1972, National University of Singapore 1990–1, International Christian University Tokyo 1992, Lee Kuan Yew Distinguished Visitor, National University of Singapore, 1986; Honorary Senior Research Fellow, Birmingham University, 1991; Guest Professor, Peking University, 1995. Honorary Fellow, University of Wales, Cardiff, 1998; Dr *h.c.* Nancy 1968; Honorary DLitt: Birmingham 1987, York (Canada) 1988, Athens 1995, Macquarie 1996, Lingnan 1999. *Major Publications: The Language of the Chinese 'Secret History of the Mongols'* 1959; *The Linguistic Sciences and Language Teaching* 1964 (with A. McIntosh and P. Strevens); *Patterns of Language* 1966 (with A. McIntosh); *Intonation and Grammar in British English* 1967; *A Course in Spoken English: Intonation* 1970; *Explorations in the Functions of Language* 1973; *Learning How to Mean* 1975; *Cohesion in English* 1976 (with R. Hasan); *System and Function in Language* (ed. G. Kress) 1976; *Language as Social Semiotic* 1978; *An Introduction to Functional Grammar* 1985; *Spoken and Written Language* 1985; *Writing Science* 1993 (with J. Martin); *Construing Experience as Meaning* 1999 (with C. Matthiessen).

* * *

Memory, we know, cannot be relied on; it constructs its own recordings of past events. When written records turn up, in old box files and suitcases, they often surprise us. My own records are patchy; many were lost on one occasion when I moved. What I have written here is a blending of these two resources.

I was taught Chinese, wonderfully well, in the first of the wartime services courses, at SOAS in 1942–3. When I left the army, in 1947, I went to China to study further. It was there, after taking my BA in Chinese (a London external degree, the papers being administered to me by the British Council in Nanking), that I decided to continue studying – thanks to Professor Eve Edwards, I had been offered one of the 'Scarborough' scholarships for advanced study and research. I was very uncertain about this – I had already left Peking University and taken a job with the Chinese Industrial Co-operatives; but it seemed an opportunity for finding out more about language, the Chinese language in particular but also, I hoped, language in general.

I had always been fascinated by language. My father was an English teacher, with equal love for grammar and for Elizabethan drama, and also a dialectologist and dialect poet. At school I enjoyed the study of English literature; but I thought that what my teachers said about its language made no sense, and so I searched in the library, where I discovered a subject called 'linguistics' and a book about language by an American professor called Bloomfield, which of course I didn't much understand. But I hadn't been allowed to do modern languages at school, as I wanted, so when the chance came I volunteered for the armed services foreign language course. Those of us who applied, early in 1942, were brought to London and given wide-ranging aptitude tests, both for language learning in general and for the specific character of each of the four languages that had been picked out for the first intensive services course: Chinese, Japanese, Turkish and Persian. I was good at tones. I had my first lesson in Chinese, from Dr Walter Simon, shortly after my seventeenth birthday.

As a learner, I was often puzzled by the grammar of Chinese, and wanted explanations where no explanation was offered. How did you actually know what could (or could not) be said? But it was when, after serving a year in Chinese intelligence work overseas, I was sent back to England to be an instructor in the services language unit that I struggled hard to engage with the grammar of the language. I taught my first Chinese class on 13 May 1945, and continued teaching until the courses ended two years later; and in that time I tried to discover something about linguistics.

I didn't get very far. My real grounding in linguistics came from the two Chinese scholars under whom I studied in my last two years in China: Luo Changpei at Peking University, and Wang Li at Lingnan University in Canton. Returning to England in 1950, I was admitted as a PhD student at Cambridge, to be supervised by Professor Gustav Haloun. My chosen field of research, a grammatical study of dialects of the Pearl River Delta on which (under Wang Li's guidance) I had gathered a considerable amount of material, was rejected as inappropriate, and a grammar of early Mandarin based on a fourteenth-century written text was negotiated as an alternative topic. Professor Haloun died suddenly at the end of that year, and I was allowed to transfer to the supervision of Professor Firth, travelling regularly to SOAS for the purpose. As well as giving me time himself, Professor Firth arranged for Mr Robins to see me for tutorial sessions and assign me essays to write.

I attended lectures by both Firth and Robins, and also courses in phonology given by Eugénie Henderson and by Eileen Whitley. (A visiting Japanese scholar attending Firth's lectures was impressed to find himself in the same audience as Jones and Palmer. We had regretfully to explain to him that these were not, in fact, the Jones and Palmer that were well-known names in his country.) These teachers kept up and enhanced my enthusiasm for linguistics, already so richly nourished by my teachers in China.

I also attended lectures by visiting scholars whenever possible. I had missed André Martinet; but I heard a series of three lectures given by Louis Hjelmslev. He spoke on the semiotics of traffic lights. I was among a few privileged postgraduate students who were invited to afternoon tea in the Senior Common Room, and was introduced to Hjelmslev by Firth. Firth, said, 'The trouble with you, Louis, is that you are too stratospheric.' 'No, John', Hjelmslev replied. 'You are stratospheric. I have no ceiling.'

My time in China had been more or less evenly divided between two regimes, nationalist and Communist. I had been impressed by the achievements of the Chinese Communist Party, and I had studied a certain amount of Marxist theory. It seemed important to apply Marxist principles to the investigation of language. I joined the recently formed Linguistics Group of the British party, and met regularly with Jeffrey Ellis, Dennis Berg, Jean Ure, Trevor Hill, Peter Wexler and others to discuss Marxism and linguistics. We worked fairly hard on topics such as the emergence and development of national languages, the status of linguistic minorities, functional variation ('register') in language, unwritten languages and dialects, conceptual-functional grammar, and linguistic typology.

What might have been a major event for us, just at that time, was the crisis in Soviet linguistics (Ellis & Davies 1951). N. Y. Marr, who died in 1934, had claimed to be offering a distinctively Marxist interpretation of language; and after the war his successors pushed hard for this to be recognized as the official linguistic doctrine of the USSR. Marr's own work, which began with scholarly studies in the languages of the Caucasus and went on to raise serious questions about mainstream historical and typological theory, had degenerated in his later years into elaborate flights of fancy; and while his followers – notably Meščaninov – had discarded such embarrassing baggage from his heritage, they continued to promote 'Marr's teaching' as the uniquely Marxist approach to the study of language. They had a precedent on their side: the genetics controversy in 1948 had ended in a victory, for the time being at least, for 'Marxist genetics' as propounded by Lysenko. When *Pravda* launched its debate on 9 May 1950, the opposition were largely mainstream Indo-Europeanists; they managed to get Stalin on their side, and he put his name to a paper 'On Marxism in linguistics' (known later to have been written by Čikobava) which denounced the Marrists and reinstated comparative philology. As Stalin summed it up, 'A study of the linguistic affinity of these nations [sc. like the Slav nations] might be of great value to linguistics in the study of the laws of language development.' I still have the original nine weekly supplements of *Pravda* containing the articles that made up the two sides of the controversy.

It seemed to us, however, that this controversy, revealing as it was about the Soviet academic scene, had done little to illuminate the issue of Marxism and linguistics. Indeed Firth, who was at the other end of the political spectrum, once remarked to me that he didn't see anything in his own work which was contrary to Marxist principles; and I fully agreed with him. Firth's emphasis on the social nature of language, his central concern with meaning, his integration of the paradigmatic and syntagmatic modes of order, his sense of multiple patterning in language, his requirement of flexibility ('rigour' he parodied as rigor mortis), and his clear distinction between general (theoretical) and particular (descriptive) categories, as I gradually struggled towards an understanding of them, seemed to me to promote the kind of thinking about language that we were after. My own immediate problem, however, in coming to grips with the topic of my PhD thesis, was how to derive from Firth's writings, and those of his colleagues at SOAS, a model for describing the grammar of a medieval Chinese text.

I discussed the general problem with Firth himself; but he left it to me to translate his ideas into descriptive practice. Importantly, he advised me on what to read – he wanted his students to be broadly grounded in the branches and schools of linguistics. It is worth recalling, perhaps, that English was just one among numerous languages of scholarship, and in no way dominant on the international academic scene; readings might be prescribed in any language. I could read French with relative ease, and Russian and Italian with more effort but still with enjoyment; German, however, I avoided whenever possible, since I could understand it only with a vexing struggle and constant recourse to the dictionary. So when it came to Trubetzkoy, I read the *Principes* in Cantineau's French translation – and was sternly criticized for doing so. 'That's a bad translation', Firth said. 'You should read it in the original German.'

I was somewhat in awe of Firth, but on the whole I got on with him pleasingly well. Partly perhaps because I was always prepared to stand up for my own point of view; partly because we both came from Yorkshire. This last is not a sentimental attachment; it is simply that there is a greater degree of shared taken-for-grantedness in the discourse of people the Chinese call 'tóngxiāng' – fellow-countymen. In fact there were also family connections (never referred to, of course): my mother had known Firth (then known as Rupert) as a child – they were at the same elementary school, in Bramley, a suburb of Leeds. The principal, Miss Firth, was Rupert Firth's aunt. Rupert was five years older than my mother; Miss Firth sometimes asked him to help with teaching the younger children – he was very nice to them, my mother said. Later she often travelled on the same train with him when he was a student of history at Leeds; he used to quiz the high school girls on dates, she remembered.

I applied for a job in Firth's department, but didn't get it. That was probably in 1952. Had I got the job, I would have had closer contact with his colleagues, and been able to monitor whether my work on grammar was developing along 'Firthian' lines. As it was, I was left very much on my own, especially after being appointed (in 1954) as Assistant Lecturer in Chinese at Cambridge, with a teaching load of 12–14 hours a week; there was no longer time for such frequent visits to London. So when I finally produced my thesis, the grammatical framework had diverged somewhat from what was clearly recognizable as Firth's teaching. Firth himself acknowledged it as produced under his guidance, and later on supported its publication; he also agreed to let me dedicate it to him – rather to the surprise of the Series Editor, Professor W. S. Allen, who asked me to reassure him that I had consulted Firth about the dedication. I assured him I had done. But it was not unreasonable for Allen to query whether Firth approved of the way I had applied his precepts.

Several years later, in 1960, when I had written a longish article called 'Categories of the theory of grammar', I took a copy to show Firth before submitting it, hoping to be able to take account of his comments. I was going to give it to him, in person, on 14 December. There will be others who still remember that occasion: we had come to London, to a conference arranged by the British Council on English language teaching. Firth was to be the opening speaker. We had taken our places in the conference room and were waiting for Firth to appear, when the convenor came in and reported that he had died, suddenly, during the night. Forty years on, I would still have been glad to have known his views (for a study of the relationship of my own work to that of Firth, see Butt 2001).

I joined the Philological Society in 1951, and went regularly to its London and Cambridge meetings. I was invited to read a paper myself, in 1956; I spoke on Chinese grammar, in a talk that was far too long and far too dense, but was received with remarkable toleration by the audience (Halliday 1956). Professor Henderson commented that perhaps my analysis of Chinese grammar had been influenced by my recent experience in working on grammar for machine translation. I don't really think it had; I had been working on the grammar of Chinese for a much longer time, ever since I had begun teaching the language ten years earlier. The general interpretation had derived from my studies with Wang Li, and the theoretical framework was that developed for my PhD thesis. But Eugénie Henderson had a point; I had been taking part in the activities of the Cambridge Language Research Unit, and machine translation was the focus of the Unit's research.

The Cambridge Language Research Unit had been founded by the philosopher Margaret Masterman; the other founder members were Frederick Parker-Rhodes and R. H. Richens. We met for discussion once a fortnight, often with other scholars invited to take part – I particularly remember visits by Paul Garvin and by Willard V. Quine. Machine translation at the time was being pursued mainly by computer specialists, who saw it as essentially an engineering problem; the only linguistic component thought to be needed was a dictionary. The CLRU's approach was different; machine translation obviously depended on the machine, but it was no less centrally a linguistic problem, requiring powerful theoretical tools for analysing and synthesizing text, and this meant that it was also a field of research likely to enhance our understanding of the workings of language. We spent many interesting hours anatomizing a sentence about axillary buds, in English, Chinese and Italian; and at least as many arguing about principles for the representation of linguistic structure. It seemed to me that in order to relate target language to source language we had to be able to formalize paradigmatic as well as syntagmatic relations; but I wasn't convincing enough to persuade my colleagues of this notion. There were lots of ideas about, and Margaret rated exploring new ones more highly than pursuing those already on the agenda. Nevertheless by the time I left Cambridge, in 1958, the Unit had produced some useful research papers, and with new participants, including Karen Sparck-Jones, had become a presence in the arena that came later to be known as 'natural language processing' (Léon 1998).

Jeffrey Ellis became a lecturer in the German Department at Hull. He organized the Hull Linguistics Circle, bringing a number of linguists together for intensive weekend discussions once, or maybe twice, in a year. Those taking part had various affiliations and various angles on language; what they had in common was that they were linguists not employed in positions designated as linguistics. They also reached Hull from various directions; I remember one party from Manchester whose excuse for arriving late was that they had stopped for afternoon tea at a Chinese restaurant in Pontefract. I myself on one occasion took an overnight train journey from Cambridge, via – I think – March, Peterborough, Boston, Lincoln, Barnetby and New Holland Pier; you could still do that kind of thing in pre-Beeching days. Apart from my occasional attendance at the 'Junior Sinologues' these meetings were for me, and I suspect for quite a few others, the first encounter with the phenomenon of the academic conference, with people presenting papers and discussion following.

Thanks to Jeff Ellis's continuing initiative, and his own lively contributions (he was one of the underrated linguists of our generation), the Hull Linguistics Circle became popular, and evolved by stages into the Linguistics Association of Great Britain. This is a moment of history for which I needed documentation, and unfortunately the notes and correspondence I once had have all been lost. These would have helped me to recollect the steps along the way; as it is I feel too uncertain of the details. I hope there will be other folk who are able to tell the story (see Collinge, this volume).

At that time, linguistics was largely a London monopoly, with Daniel Jones's department at University College and Firth's at SOAS. As Firth himself wrote, 'The first Chair of General Linguistics in this country was established in the University of London in 1944, at the School of Oriental and African Studies' (Firth 1957). (It was not, I think, the first Chair of Linguistics; this had been created for Alan S. C. Ross at the University of Birmingham.) It was not until the mid-1950s that linguistics (as distinct from 'comparative philology') began to spread further afield. W. S. Allen was responsible for the appointment of John Trim to a Lectureship in Phonetics at Cambridge, where Allen himself had been appointed to the Chair of Comparative Philology, shortly after publishing a major article in which he challenged the entire foundations of the subject (Allen 1953). William Haas became Professor at Manchester in what I believe was the Montfollick Chair of Comparative Philology (founded to promote Montfollick's enthusiasm for spelling reform; 'Comparative Philology' was perhaps rather a misleading title).

But there was another flourishing centre of linguistics studies, namely Edinburgh, which had the Department of Phonetics under David Abercrombie and the Department of English Language headed by Angus McIntosh. Then in 1957 the university opened the School of Applied Linguistics, with the support of the British Council, who needed a postgraduate programme in this field, both for their own staff and for their scholarship holders from overseas. The Director was J. C. Catford. Firth had just retired from SOAS, and Ian Catford invited him to lecture at the School for the first year of its operation. I moved to Edinburgh in 1958, as Lecturer in General Linguistics in a new position created in Angus McIntosh's department, which now became the Department of English Language and General Linguistics.

For me this was a big change: after having taught Chinese for most of the past 15 years, I now had to learn how to teach linguistics. I gave undergraduate courses in introductory linguistics and in stylistics, and lectured on English grammar for the applied linguistics programme; then David Abercrombie got me to teach intonation on his Summer School in English Phonetics. In my second year we started our own Postgraduate Diploma in General Linguistics. We needed an external examiner for this diploma, and I invited Sidney Allen to act for us.

There were (as I remember it) no obvious models for such a course, and one issue had to be faced right at the start. Should one organize the course as a survey of branches and schools of linguistics, or should one begin with a detailed exposition of one particular approach? Allen tended towards the former view. I felt that, while an aspiring academic linguist ought certainly to be informed about all contemporary theories, the primary task of a course at this stage was to teach the students how to engage with language – in other words, that they should learn about language before learning about linguistics. (This has since become a familiar issue in the social sciences. I have known history students complain that they now study historiography without ever learning any history.) They would be given a summary survey-type course – one in which different schools were presented positively and with understanding, not the kind of tokenistic survey in which all theories other than the lecturer's own were triumphantly demolished; but the main burden would be a broad system-structure framework for representing phonology and grammar.

And here I recall one of those customized little ironies that sometimes distract us in life. Allen kindly sent me an offprint of his most recent publication – an article on ancient Greek prosody; accompanied by the comment 'You will see that I have returned to my first love.' Now, my key resource for system-structure grammar had been Allen's own work: I had started with his studies of Hindi (from which I took the term 'group', as in 'nominal group'), but the pièce de résistance was his 'Structure and system in the Abaza verbal complex' (Allen 1956), which I thought was unequalled as a model of grammatical description. Not that I undervalued the study of Greek prosody. But what I was really hoping for were some further rich insights into grammar.

What made Edinburgh such a memorable intellectual environment was, of course, the people who were taking part. Heads of Department, senior and junior staff, students from home and overseas all seemed to interact with openness and a sense of going somewhere. A special feature – though one I simply took for granted at the time – was the way phonetics, general linguistics and applied linguistics interpenetrated at every level. The fact that they were three different departments was beside the point – since that time there have been various marriages and divorces – and irrelevant to the genuine intellectual wellbeing of the collective. The academic culture that I found there was one of inclusion.

It was in Edinburgh that I began collaborating regularly with teachers in schools. It seemed evident to me that as linguists working at tertiary level we had both much to offer to and much to learn from our secondary and primary level colleagues. Four of us held Saturday morning sessions each with a group of teachers in Edinburgh or Glasgow. I liked Glasgow – it reminded me of Leeds – so I joined the group at Jordanhill. It was always a very stimulating encounter; and the College grounds grew the finest raspberries I have tasted before or since.

Then in 1963 I moved back to London, as Director of the Communication Research Centre that had been set up at University College by A. H. Smith and Randolph Quirk. I approached the Nuffield Foundation with a project for working on the grammar of English from an educational standpoint, with a view to curriculum development at primary and/or secondary level.

My idea had been to bring together a small research team for one or two years, and then to start collaborating with teachers – I thought we needed to put our grammar in order first; but the Foundation, backed up by the Inspectorate at the Department of Education, persuaded me (rightly!) to involve the teachers from the start. So we set up the Nuffield (later Schools Council) Programme in Linguistics and English Teaching, with a project team composed of primary school, secondary school and university teachers working in collaboration.

This was the 1960s: rich in ideas, rich in research funds, rich in initiatives for reshaping the social order – and in the disputes such initiatives inevitably provoked. Our efforts were opposed not so much by conservatives (the so-called 'authoritarian classroom' had already largely disappeared) as by the new romantics, who disliked any form of structure either in language or in learning; to them 'educating' meant cultivating each learner's individual life flame, or else simply removing obstacles so that learning would take place by itself (the latter approach I christened 'benevolent inertia'). In our view learning was an interactive, social process and the teacher, whether tertiary, secondary or primary, had to provide knowledge, structure and informed guidance. The materials developed by the teachers in our project – *Breakthrough to Literacy*, *Language in Use* and, indirectly, *Language and Communication* – were, I thought, a monument to linguistics as a democratic force, a theoretically informed activity being put to community service and itself being notably enriched as a result (Pearce et al. 1989).

The 1960s was also the time when the new Labour government discovered a massive hole in Treasury funds and began culling the universities to make it good; the first axe fell just two weeks after UCL had created the Department of General Linguistics. Hugh Smith's plan for a staff of five, soon to advance to seven, melted into air; I was allotted one Lectureship. It was a mistake, as it turned out, to agree to being a separate department; but I had wanted to develop linguistics as an undergraduate subject, appropriate for a first degree. Thanks to generous co-operation from the Department at SOAS, we put the regulations in place; and thanks to the participation of researchers from the two Communication Research Centre projects, the PLET and the 'Linguistic Properties of Scientific English' funded by OSTI, we were able to play our part in teaching the course. But I had no skills as an entrepreneur, and by the end of the decade I was tired of always pushing up hill.

Times had changed in other ways as well. Linguistics had become a battleground, with a new dynasty in power, although still presenting itself as a beleaguered minority while it moved to take over the world. I worked hard on the new theories, trying to find them of use; but they seemed to me to provide answers only to questions they themselves had construed. I was concerned with questions posed by other people, coming from outside linguistics rather than from within; notably at that time from Basil Bernstein, whose research into cultural transmissions – how the social order was reproduced, and potentially transformed, through language – demanded a theory of semantics that was still some way beyond our powers.

It was this kind of challenge, from educators, sociologists, computer scientists and others to whom language mattered, that impelled the continued study of language as text, at a time when linguists who paid attention to real-life discourse were being dismissed as 'data-oriented' (or 'taxonemic' [sic], as one MIT graduate labelled me) and language as social process was merely 'performance' and hence of no serious interest. Many linguists escaped into sociolinguistics, or applied linguistics, or pragmatics, which were no longer seen as part of linguistics but separately packaged as independent disciplines. What was being imposed was a restricted perception of language in which theorizing was replaced by formalizing and 'common-sense' descriptive categories – those of 'the linguist on the Clapham omnibus' – left unquestioningly in place (Matthews 1966). Linguistics had become increasingly precious, and departments had few to defend them when economy-conscious deans sought to close them down.

I resigned from UCL, with regret, 30 years ago and, apart from a year at Essex in the mid-1970s, have lived away from Britain ever since. The context of academic linguistics is different now. The downside is, of course, the ideology-driven onslaught on universities; in Australia we face this in its extreme anti-intellectual form, but it is a general feature of this phase of corporate capitalism. It will take time to repair the damage now being done. On the positive side, linguistics is at last moving beyond its pre-scientific stage: for the first time, thanks to the computer's ability to store and manage information, linguists have adequate data, in the corpus and all the research tools that now go with it. They can undertake large-scale quantitative studies in grammar and, in time, semantics which will sort out the relationship between observation and theory and clarify the problematic nature of a semiotic system. Studies of other semiotic systems in terms derived from theory of language (e.g. O'Toole 1994), as well as wider applications of linguistics especially in the critical field of language disorders, are part of the changing context of linguistic research; among other news from outside, that from neuroscience – the amazing new insights into the nature, development and evolution of the brain (Deacon 1997) – is perhaps the most significant, making sense of our observations of child language, of speech, writing, sign and other modalities, and of our attempts at modelling the multi-dimensional character of language. With the current restructuring of knowledge in transdisciplinary terms, so that language can be viewed in differing interpretative perspectives – of systems thinking, complexity theory, ecosocial dynamics and the like – perhaps our understanding of processes of meaning may finally begin to match our understanding of the processes of matter. It promises to be an interesting time.

REFERENCES

ALLEN, W. S., 1953. 'Relationship in comparative linguistics', *TPhS* 52–108.
ALLEN, W. S., 1956. 'Structure and system in the Abaza verbal complex', *TPhS* 127–76.
BUTT, DAVID G., 2001. 'Firth, Halliday and the development of systemic functional theory', in Konrad Koerner et al. (eds.), *History of the Language Sciences Vol. 2*, Berlin/New York: Walter de Gruyter.
DEACON, TERRENCE, 1997. *The Symbolic Species: The Co-evolution of Language and the Human Brain*, London: Allen Lane (Penguin Press).
ELLIS, JEFFREY & DAVIES, ROBERT W., 1951. 'The crisis in Soviet linguistics', *Soviet Studies 2* 209–64.
FIRTH, J. R., 1957. Preface to *Papers in Linguistics 1934–1951*, London: Oxford University Press.
HALLIDAY, M. A. K., 1956. 'Grammatical categories in Modern Chinese', *TPhS* 177–224.
LÉON, JACQUELINE, 1998. 'LANGUES AUXILIARES, TRADUCTIONS ET MODÈLES DE TRADUCTION AUTOMATIQUE (1950–1970)', LEUVEN: *XI International Colloquium of the Studienkreis der Geschichte der Sprachwissenschaft*.
MATTHEWS, P. H., 1966. 'The concept of rank in "Neo-Firthian" grammar', *Journal of Linguistics 2*, 101–10.
O'TOOLE, L. M., 1994. *The Language of Displayed Art*. London: Leicester University Press/Pinter Publishers.
PEARCE, JOHN, THORNTON, GEOFFREY & MACKAY, DAVID, 1989. 'The programme in linguistics and English teaching, University College, London, 1964–1971', in Ruqaiya Hasan & J. R. Martin (eds.), *Language Development: Learning Language and Learning Culture. (Advances in Discourse Processes XXVII)*, Norwood, NJ: Ablex, 329–68.

RICHARD HUDSON

HUDSON, Richard Anthony, FBA 1992; Professor of Linguistics, University College London, since 1989; *b.* 1939; *m.* 1970, Gaynor Evans, 2 d; *Education:* Loughborough Grammar School; Corpus Christi College, Cambridge, BA; School of Oriental and African Studies, London, PhD; *Career:* University College London: Research Assistant, Linguistics, 1964–70; Lecturer 1970, Reader 1980, Dept of Phonetics and Linguistics. President Linguistics Association of Great Britain 1997–2000. *Major Publications: English Complex Sentences: An Introduction to Systemic Grammar* 1971; *Arguments for a Non-Transformational Grammar* 1976; *Sociolinguistics* 1980 [2nd ed. 1996]; *Word Grammar* 1984; *An Invitation to Linguistics* 1984; *English Word Grammar* 1990; *Teaching Grammar: A Guide for the National Curriculum* 1992; *Word Meaning* 1995; *English Grammar* 1998.

* * *

At one level the story of my academic life is a very simple one: I have studied nothing but languages since the age of 16, and I have worked at UCL since I got my PhD at the age of 24. After engaging with French and German up to BA level (at Cambridge), I flirted with a Cushitic language at PhD level, but since then I have not worked seriously on any language but English. During my PhD years I developed a taste for grammatical theory which is still with me; and, just as in the early days, I still find myself swimming against the tide of the mainstream Chomskian view of language. The story becomes slightly more complicated when I include three further strands of interest which intertwine with each other and with grammatical theory: educational linguistics, sociolinguistics and cognitive linguistics, which evolved in that order. However diverse this list may look to others, it feels completely natural and coherent to me, with each of the four strands contributing to each of the others; so the whole enterprise could be summarized as the study of language structure in relation to its cultural context. The institutional links among the four strands are not strong – indeed some of them barely exist at all – so I have had to build bridges. I have also tried hard to do the same in my work on grammatical theory, so it is as a bridge-builder that I should like to be remembered.

Like other contributors I first became fascinated by languages in early secondary school, thanks to a series of excellent teachers who took grammar seriously across the various languages I studied, including English. Admittedly it was traditional grammar, but it was sensible and helpful; I don't remember anyone talking about ablatives, genitives or datives in English (which is more than one can say of some current theories), and I don't think it was drummed into us as pure dogma (any more than was the case for, say, physics or geography).

At about the same time I also developed a rather abortive interest in Ancient Egyptian, which my father encouraged by buying me a book about the language; unfortunately the foreword to the book recommended first learning Coptic, which (it turned out) one could not do properly except via German (which at that time I had not yet started). I gave up, but in later life I was rather pleased to learn that the language of my PhD research (Beja) was related to Ancient Egyptian.

In short, I believe my career as a linguist started at about the age of 11. No wonder that I yielded to the temptation of specializing entirely in languages in the sixth form (i.e. at age 16), with awful consequences for other subjects; I especially regret having dropped maths so young. It was equally obvious that languages would be my choice at university, so I took the quaintly labelled 'Modern and Mediaeval Languages Tripos' at Cambridge, stuffing into it as much language and as little literature as I could get away with. Much of the linguistics was comparative and historical, which I found difficult because of the heavy factual content; but I still enjoyed my tutorials with Rebecca Posner, who managed not to be as frighteningly erudite as another linguist, who (literally) read us the chapters of his forthcoming book in lieu of lectures. This experience confirmed what I had suspected for some time: that I was better at comparing facts than at remembering them. In contrast, Sidney Allen's lectures and John Trim's tutorials (which I shared with Neil Smith) were on exactly the right wavelength.

Not surprisingly an academic career beckoned (and always had done, since my father was an academic too – a scientist, whose work I found intriguing). The next step was a PhD (for which grants were relatively generous and easy to come by in those days). By chance my father was working at the University of Khartoum at the time, so I spent my last summer vacation with him and met an anthropologist who persuaded me to work on the language of 'his' tribe, the Beja. Sidney Allen and John Lyons (newly arrived in Cambridge from London) advised me to do the PhD at SOAS, which was an excellent choice. When I arrived in 1961, Firth had left (and had just died) but was still very influential; I particularly enjoyed the systematic presentation of English phonology by Eileen Whitley (Eileen Evans) – my first experience of an analysis for an entire language system. My second year was spent collecting data in Port Sudan – a wildly exciting intellectual experience, though I turned out again to be better at analysing languages than at learning them. The final year brought me into contact with the most important influence on my intellectual development, Michael Halliday, who had just joined UCL.

I should mention that Neil Smith and I not only shared tutorials at

Cambridge, but both ended up doing PhDs in London, at UCL and at SOAS respectively. In fact our lives were so intertwined that we travelled out to Africa together as far as Khartoum, where I settled in Port Sudan while he roughed it across the Sahara to Nigeria (and Nupe country). On our return we both took time from writing up our theses to attend the same two courses of lectures: David Reibel on Chomsky's theory, and Michael Halliday on his own. Why we made opposite choices at that time I cannot say. The better I came to understand Chomsky's views, the less convincing they seemed – and still seem. I decided that I could contribute more by developing alternative theories than by joining what was even in those days clearly the mainstream. This, then, was the start of my work on grammatical theory.

What I liked about Halliday's grammatical system was that it integrated a lot of disparate facts and clearly 'worked', in the sense that it could easily be applied to any language, though at that time it was only described in the barest outline in one journal article (Halliday 1961). I used it as the framework for my thesis (a descriptive study of Beja grammar) and found only a handful of problems; and Halliday himself was brought in as a third examiner alongside Frank Palmer (who impressed me greatly by spotting a typo in a Beja example) and my SOAS supervisor, Charles Bazell (who claimed not to understand a word of Halliday's theory). In those halcyon days universities were expanding and Halliday, recently arrived at UCL, had landed two research grants which, by modern standards, were simply colossal: one which funded four people for three years and another which funded about ten people for six years! Not surprisingly, given the paucity of linguistics PhDs, he had a vacancy for me on one of these, so my career as a linguist started in the way it continued: in a job that I owed to Michael Halliday.

The next three years (1964–7) were spent in the company of Rodney Huddleston, whom I had first met at Cambridge. The research project was a grammatical analysis of scientific English, which involved detailed analysis of a corpus – a wonderful experience for any novice linguist. Huddleston taught me almost as much as Halliday, although he was only a year older than me; from him I learned the pleasure and pain of developing a grammatical analysis that works when applied to texts, and the importance of attending to detail. We also had a great deal of contact with Halliday at a time when his theory was developing fast, which was a great opportunity for an enthusiastic young theory-builder. We both appreciated the broad vision and deep insights that Halliday brought to bear (Halliday 1967a; 1967b; 1968), but we also appreciated the clarity of Chomsky's generative approach and tried to move Halliday's theory in that direction. The inevitable happened; as Huddleston and I tinkered with the theory, changing a detail here and another there, we found that some of the main pillars were disintegrating in our hands. He moved out of 'high theory' altogether, while I persisted for a few more years and wrote the first generative systemic grammar (Hudson 1971) before accepting that what I was developing was no longer a version of systemic grammar, but a new theory (which I called daughter dependency grammar – Hudson 1976).

Meanwhile, however, I was learning about another important aspect of Halliday's work, which he had been developing even longer than his grammatical theory (Halliday, McIntosh & Strevens 1964): educational linguistics. When the first research project expired I simply transferred to the other, whose aim was to apply linguistics to the teaching of English as a native language throughout the school system, from initial literacy to the end of secondary school. Part of the project's remit was to give linguistics training to schoolteachers, so it funded a diploma in Linguistics and the Teaching of English, which was taught jointly by Halliday's team at UCL and by the English Department at the nearby Institute of Education. My job was to teach grammar to the 20 schoolteachers who were seconded for a year to this course (halcyon days again!); this course ran three times, from 1967 to 1970, before the funding ran out. As far as the teaching profession was concerned the training we provided was just a tiny drop in the ocean of need, and it happened at a particularly bad moment in English educational history when the world was reacting hard against the supposed 'grammar grind'. In retrospect it is easy to see why the course (and the whole project) did little to stop the drift in our schools away from explicit teaching about language. However, I'm sure that the experience of this close interaction with school-teachers had a major impact on my thinking. I was impressed by the quality of the teachers, as well as by many of the things that Halliday offered them.

At the end of this contract in 1970, Halliday again came to my rescue with my third job, this time a permanent one: replacing Bob Dixon as a lecturer in his department. A year later Halliday himself had followed both Dixon and Huddleston on the way to Australia, and since then our paths have rarely crossed; but by that time he had once more influenced my destiny by detailing me to teach a course in sociolinguistics. This was a subject that I had never had any particular interest in and knew little about, but as I read myself into the literature I could see why it really mattered for anyone interested (as I was) in language structure. Not surprisingly, perhaps, I was particularly excited by Labov's work, which was most obviously relevant (e.g. Labov 1969a; 1972). In spite of my primitive mathematics I enjoyed the rigour of his evidence, which linked well with the statistical analyses that I had done during the project on scientific English. I was also surprised and disappointed by the complete lack of interest in this work that I found among Chomskian linguists. I admired Labov for the professional way in which he built his bridges to Chomskian linguistics and felt he deserved to be taken much more seriously. For some years I taught a joint course in sociolinguistics with Bill Downes at the LSE (one of our star pupils was Jenny Cheshire, who then went on to do a PhD with Peter Trudgill in Reading). I think we can claim the credit for having organized (in about

1975) the first ever conference on sociolinguistics in the UK, a one-day meeting at the LSE where the participants divided cleanly into those who were really interested in pragmatics (including Steve Levinson, Penny Brown and Gerald Gazdar) and those who were really historical linguists and/or dialectologists (e.g. Peter Trudgill). Such was the uncertainty in those days about what sociolinguistics was.

One of the attractions of sociolinguistics was the links that it provided between language structure and education. One link is the question of the nature of linguistic differences between social groups: are they profound enough to explain the well-documented educational differences between these groups? One sociolinguist, Basil Bernstein, was claiming that they were – that some groups might have 'more language' (in some rather hard-to-grasp sense) than others, who had just 'restricted code' (Bernstein 1973); while another, no less than Labov himself, was denying it (Labov 1969b). Whoever was right, it was clearly an important question where sociolinguists needed to talk seriously about language structure – the range of structures and vocabulary available to different children. Oddly enough the question has never been satisfactorily answered; like so many other issues it has just drifted out of the limelight.

Another link to education lies in the study of language attitudes, where the work of Howard Giles had a major impact during the 1970s (Giles & Powesland 2000). This produced objective evidence for what we all knew to be true: that we judge people differently according to how they speak, and that this prejudice applies even – perhaps especially – in education. Socio-linguists (and linguists in general) are united in proclaiming the equality of accents and dialects, but in the 1970s most teachers and legislators still held the prescriptive views that we decried. This was a campaign issue that united everyone who had any interest in such things, so a group of us met twice in early 1980 to discuss this and similar issues. The meetings were convened by John Rudd, a teacher-trainer who worked at the college in Bromsgrove where the meetings took place. The immediate outcome of these meetings was the Committee for Linguistics in Education (CLIE), which was sponsored jointly by the LAGB and BAAL and which is still active. As the only founding member still involved in the committee I feel proud of the role it plays as a vital (and unique) conduit of information about language education. During the first few years of CLIE's existence I think I was one of the most active; for example, I edited a series of working papers, I helped to organize a number of section meetings at the LAGB, and I compiled a list of 83 'issues' on which I found linguists could agree (Hudson 1981). More recently, I rejoined CLIE *ex officio* as President of the LAGB, and now I am once again an ordinary committee member.

On the important question of language prejudice I am happy to report that the battle has been won, at least in terms of official attitudes and documentation. For example, the current (1999) National Curriculum for

English in England (DfEE 1999) recognizes the existence of non-standard varieties of English, calls them 'non-standard' rather than 'wrong', accepts that non-standard speakers cannot use standard forms without learning them (so it is no longer a moral issue), and requires standard forms only in formal contexts. This is light years from the confused and prejudiced statements that controlled teaching in the 1980s, and I have no doubt that the change is partly due to pressure from linguists, in particular Peter Trudgill, David Crystal and Jean Aitchison (Aitchison 1981; Crystal 1984; Trudgill 1975). As a member of CLIE I helped to present the linguists' case to the world of education (for example, a group of us gave evidence to the Kingman commission), and my 1980 textbook on sociolinguistics (Hudson 1980) seems to have presented it to a surprisingly large number of students (to judge by the sales figures); so I suppose I can claim a small part of the credit for this victory.

Meanwhile a number of other small groups were working on the educational links. For some years I represented the LAGB on the National Council for Languages in Education, a body whose status I never fully understood and whose main achievement may have been to have brought together a group of people with a shared interest in language education. However, one of the main themes of these meetings was the benefit of 'language awareness' – the idea that schools ought to teach children about language (Hawkins 1987; 1999). One argument for such teaching is that it is part of a liberal education to know such things as the history of one's language or how human and animal communication differ; another is that it helps children to learn foreign languages. One of the roots of this idea was Halliday's work in secondary schools (Doughty, Pearce & Thornton 1971), but it was basically a 'grass-roots' development in schools by teachers with an interest in language. The number of schools offering LA work has always been quite small, but its existence may well have eased the acceptance of more formal work on language by teachers in the late 1990s, to which I turn below. Another development which played an important part in preparing schools for the study of language was the introduction of A-level English language, which has been a runaway success by any standards: about 20,000 candidates per year. I have always taken an interest in these exciting changes in the educational system and have done whatever I could to bring them to the notice of my colleagues in linguistics (e.g. by helping to organize themed sessions on 'Linguistics at School' at the LAGB).

Another aspect of linguistic education in which I have taken an interest is the teaching of introductory linguistics, where I was struck by the tendency in university-level teaching to launch straight into high-level theory. This would probably be appropriate if all incoming students already had a solid basis in description and analysis of language structure, but the fact is that very few of them do have this kind of preparation. These foundations need to be laid first, so that students can easily recognize (say) a subject and a preposition before they learn about alternative theories about subjects and prepositions. This ability to analyse is valuable in itself and may be the end of the training, rather than serving as the foundation for more theoretical work; and without the basic training in analysis, theory is meaningless and pointless. This principle may seem obvious, but it was not reflected in publishers' lists, so I persuaded Routledge to launch their Language Workbooks, which now include a dozen titles of which (as Series Editor) I feel proud.

All this discussion of education may seem out of place in the history of an academic linguist, but I see it as an important unifying thread in my work. It was through education that I first became a 'linguist' (in the dual senses of being interested in language and of studying it); it was through education that I studied linguistics formally; it is through my teaching that I try to pass my enthusiasms and knowledge on to the next generation of adults; but so long as schools refused to teach about language (as they did until recently) our academic linguistics could never reach the people to whom it is most relevant: schoolchildren. I am happy to see that 'educational linguistics' is now officially recognized as a branch of linguistics (for example, it is one of the major divisions of the Pergamon *Encyclopedia of Language and Linguistics* [Asher 1994]); but those of us who are committed to it have the uphill task of bringing together two groups which have historically tended to assume they have nothing to say to each other: academic linguists and schoolteachers. Most academic linguists see this kind of discussion as very marginal to their interests, and schoolteachers see linguistics as a technical, forbidding and largely irrelevant discipline. I see the fundamental gulf between academic linguistics and school-level work as one of the failures of the twentieth century and hope to see a healthy bridge grow between the two during the twenty-first.

During all this activity in education, however, the more 'academic' side of my work continued. Without the educational and sociolinguistic interests I could easily be accused of monomania and obsession with grammatical theory as the author of not one but two different theories: as well as the daughter dependency grammar which I developed in the 1970s, I am responsible for word grammar (Hudson 1984; 1990). The first, which represented my final break with Halliday's systemic grammar, shows the influence of John Anderson, who first introduced me to dependency grammar (Anderson 1977; 1971). The most obvious attraction of dependency grammar is in the treatment of valency, so I simply added it to systemic grammar to give a mixture of constituent structure and dependency. It took several more years to realize that the constituent structure was not only redundant, but even got in the way.

Meanwhile I had also learned a little about work in artificial intelligence, thanks in part to contact with Terry Winograd during a study year that he spent with Halliday in UCL during the late 1960s (Winograd 1972). AI generally assigns a lot of work to the mechanism of default inheritance, but linguists have tended to take it less seriously. It is implicit, of course, in any analysis which recognizes generalizations that have exceptions, so this neglect may be a case of familiarity breeding contempt; but I found that default inheritance could be extended to areas of language structure where it had not previously been applied, such as word order. A theory of grammar which incorporates default inheritance can capture most of the generalizations that other theories express in terms of 'underlying' patterns, markedness and transformations. I am pleased to see that Ivan Sag and Carl Pollard have recently incorporated default inheritance into their theory, head-driven phrase structure grammar (Pollard & Sag 1994; Sag 1997), but default inheritance seems to me to have immense potential which has still hardly been exploited in linguistics (Hudson 2000).

Word grammar combines pure dependency structure with default inheritance in a way that seems to work rather well. I have been working on this theory since the early 1980s, and am still making more or less major improvements. Many of these improvements use ideas from other theories, which brings me to another of my bridge-building activities. One of the many things that I admired in Michael Halliday's teaching was the emphasis he laid on cross-theory work. His postgraduate course in linguistics centred on a weekly seminar in which students learned about alternative theories by reading the originals. This struck me as an excellent training precisely because it was often such hard work. There is no doubt that it is hard to understand alternative frameworks, and the temptation to specialize in one framework is strong; but the danger of wasting one's life by rediscovering the wheel (or worse, by failing to discover the wheel) is even greater. I have always tried to understand other theories (at least in outline) and to take them seriously on the principle that for all I knew they might be better than my own. However, it struck me in the 1980s that this process was made harder than it needed to be by the lack of suitable introductory reading aimed at people like me (as opposed to novices in linguistics). I tried to bridge this gap by initiating and editing a series of books called the Routledge Linguistic Theory Guides. This series is now closed, but it covers most of the competing theories of the past two decades and I think it made a small contribution to the state of the art.

Returning to my own theory, word grammar, it has three main controversial components, of which I have already discussed two: dependency and default inheritance. The third is networks – the idea that language is a cognitive network (i.e. a network of linguistic concepts such as phonemes, meanings, word-classes, grammatical relations and so on). This has been central since the early days of word grammar (Hudson 1984), and is worth mentioning here because it links my work on grammatical theory to the other strands of my work. If language is indeed a network in this sense, then it must be part of a much larger cognitive network which includes the whole of (conceptual) knowledge. In brief, it is *not* a module, *pace* Fodor, Chomsky and the mainstream (Chomsky 1986; Fodor 1983), and most of it is learned rather than inherited genetically. In short, word grammar is an example of cognitive linguistics. This movement, which is unified by the belief that language is part of general cognition rather than a distinct module, has grown around the work of Ronald Langacker, Charles Fillmore and George Lakoff, all in California, all of whom in different ways have influenced my work (Fillmore, Kay & O'Connor 1988; Lakoff 1987; Langacker 1987). Internationally, cognitive linguistics is growing fast (e.g. 700 participants attended the international CL conference in Stockholm in 1999), but it has taken longer to attract serious support in the UK. I shall feel some personal satisfaction if it grows here as it deserves to.

The idea of non-modular cognitive networks is important for me because, as I have said, it provides the main link between grammatical theory and the other strands of my work. First, as far as sociolinguistics is concerned it opens up the possibility of integrating social categories with linguistic ones because no boundary is assumed between the two. We can show that the word *bonny* is (typically) used by a Scot, that *attempt* is typically used in formal situations, and that *shit* is rude, without worrying about whether these facts are 'really linguistic'. I have the impression that sociolinguists and psycholinguists are in general not well informed about each other's work, or even interested in it, so there does not seem to be much interest in the question of how sociolinguistic findings might be modelled cognitively. However, I have tried to suggest ways in which this kind of research programme might be implemented (Hudson 1996; 1997), though I have not been able to develop the ideas as thoroughly as I should have liked.

I end, as I began, with education. Suppose that language is indeed part of general cognition, as I believe; and suppose, in particular, that it is learned from experience, that it influences other parts of cognition and that other parts of cognition influence it. All these assumptions highlight the import-ance of language education. If it is learned we cannot simply rely on our genes to get it right, nor can we assume that ordinary experience is enough – in both cases contrary to the accepted wisdom of introductory linguistics textbooks. Some parts of language do need to be taught. If it influences other parts of cognition, language training may need to be clearly planned and structured so that children's minds grow as they should; and if other parts of cognition influence language the converse is also true. These possibilities are all critical not only for education but also for linguistics because they presuppose solid research which only linguists can do: what effect does literacy have on language structure? How does school-age language develop? How do the more literary constructions develop? My impression is that linguists have not been active in such areas, and that this is partly to do with the mainstream view in linguistics that language is an 'organ' that grows unaided. As a result, very little of the research that we do bears directly on educational issues.

However, the last few years have seen the beginnings of a revolution in the UK's schools, thanks to the National Literacy Strategy (http:// www.standards.dfee.gov.uk/literacy). This already requires all primary schools (at least in England) to teach grammar, and lays out in great detail both what should be taught and how it should be taught; and during the next few years it is to be extended to the first three years of secondary education. The basic ideas of the Strategy strike me as very sensible and compatible with modern linguistics; for example, the aim is to help children to explore (and become aware of) grammatical structures in their own speech or writing, the approach is wholeheartedly descriptive, and 'grammar' is taken very broadly to include discourse structures. However, the NLS team turned out to be desperately short of skill when it came to the details – not surprisingly, perhaps, since they had all come through a school system which was virtually grammar free. By a combination of sticks and carrots a small group of linguists – David Denison, Catherine Walter, Katherine Perera and myself – persuaded the NLS team to let us help with what we called the 'technicalities' of grammar.

The result is that we have at last achieved the goal of the various pressure groups I described earlier: at least some of those who control our education system have accepted the need for academic linguists to contribute to school education. Our influence has extended beyond mere technicalities (such as the introduction of the term 'determiner') now that we have built a relation of mutual trust with a number of civil servants in the Teacher Training Agency, the Standards and Effectiveness Unit and the Qualifications and Curriculum Authority. For example, I have been commissioned to write training material for both primary and secondary teachers (who of course know little or no grammar) (DfEE 2000). The result in schools is by no means perfect – for example, at present the focus on literacy leaves no time for the more general work of 'language awareness' mentioned earlier. However, the pendulum is clearly swinging towards more emphasis on explicit study of language; and recently this has even become evident in the teaching of foreign languages. I believe this has to be good for the pupils and good for linguistics; those who suffer (and need whatever support we can offer) are the teachers.

The Literacy Strategy itself is distantly related to a scheme developed in Australia under the influence of Michael Halliday, so ultimately we may owe this revolution to him; perhaps we can see it as a delayed outcome from his UCL project. In the lean years in between the flag was flown energetically by linguists who communicated well with teachers, especially Katharine Perera and Ron Carter (Carter 1990; Perera 1984); these people built quite explicitly on Halliday's work and developed a body of professional opinion that was receptive to the ideas of the Strategy. More immediately, though, I should like to claim some credit for the new bridge between academic linguistics and schools, which was so disastrously missing throughout the last century. If this bridge survives and grows as I hope it will, I believe it will change the dynamics of our subject as schools become a major 'stakeholder' in linguistics. Seen from this perspective it is perhaps less strange that Lucien Tesnière, the father of dependency grammar, wrote his magnum opus (Tesnière 1959) in order to improve the teaching of grammar in schools!

REFERENCES

AITCHISON, J., 1981. *Language Change: Progress or Decay?*, London: Fontana.
ANDERSON, J. M., 1971. *The Grammar of Case: Towards a Localistic Theory*, Cambridge: Cambridge University Press.
ANDERSON, J. M, 1977. *On Case Grammar: Prolegomena to a Theory of Grammatical Relations*, London: Croom Helm.
ASHER, R. E., (ed.) 1994. *The Encyclopedia of Language and Linguistics*, 10 vols., Oxford / New York / Seoul / Tokyo: Pergamon Press.
BERNSTEIN, B., 1973. *Class, Codes and Control, vol. 2: Empirical Studies*, London: Routledge and Kegan Paul.
CARTER, R., 1990. *Knowledge about Language and the Curriculum: The LINC Reader*, London: Hodder and Stoughton.
CHOMSKY, N., 1986. *Knowledge of Language. Its Nature, Origin and Use*, New York: Praeger.
CRYSTAL, D., 1984. *Who Cares about English Usage?*, London: Penguin.
DFEE, 1999. *English. The National Curriculum for England*, London: Department for Education and Employment; Qualifications and Curriculum Authority.
DFEE, 2000. *Grammar for Writing*, London: Department for Education and Employment.
DOUGHTY, P., PEARCE, J. & THORNTON, G., 1971. *Language in Use*, London: Arnold.
FILLMORE, C., KAY, P. & O'CONNOR, M. 1988. 'Regularity and idiomaticity in grammatical constructions: the case of *let alone*', *Language* 64, 501–38.
FODOR, J., 1983. *The Modularity of Mind*, Cambridge, MA: MIT Press.
GILES, H. & POWESLAND, P., 2000. *Speech Style and Social Evaluation*, London: Academic Press.
HALLIDAY, M. A. K., 1961. 'Categories of the theory of grammar', *Word* 17, 241–92.
HALLIDAY, M. A. K., 1967a. 'Notes on transitivity and theme in English. Part 1', *Journal of Linguistics* 3, 37–82.
HALLIDAY, M. A. K., 1967b. 'Notes on transitivity and theme. Part 2', *Journal of Linguistics* 3, 199–244.
HALLIDAY, M. A. K., 1968. 'Notes on transitivity and theme. Part 3', *Journal of Linguistics* 4, 179–216.
HALLIDAY, M., MCINTOSH, A. & STREVENS, P., 1964. *The Linguistic Sciences and Language Teaching*, London: Longman.
HAWKINS, E., 1987. *Awareness of Language: An Introduction*, Cambridge: Cambridge University Press.
HAWKINS, E., 1999. 'Foreign language study and language awareness', *Language Awareness* 8, 124–62.
HUDSON, R., 1971. *English Complex Sentences: An Introduction to Systemic Grammar*, Amsterdam: North-Holland.
HUDSON, R., 1976. *Arguments for a Non-Transformational Grammar*, Chicago: University of Chicago Press.
HUDSON, R., 1980. *Sociolinguistics*, 2nd ed. 1996, Cambridge: Cambridge University Press.
HUDSON, R., 1981. 'Some issues on which linguists can agree', *Journal of Linguistics* 17, 333–44.
HUDSON, R., 1984. *Word Grammar*, Oxford: Blackwell.
HUDSON, R., 1990. *English Word Grammar*, Oxford: Blackwell.
HUDSON, R., 1996. See Hudson 1980.
HUDSON, R., 1997. 'Inherent variability and linguistic theory', *Cognitive Linguistics* 8, 73–108.

HUDSON, R., 2000. '*I amn't', *Language* 76, 297–323.

LABOV, W., 1969a. 'Contraction, deletion and inherent variability of the English copula', *Language* 45, 715–62.

LABOV, W., 1969b. 'The logic of non-standard English', *Georgetown Monographs in Language and Linguistics* 22, 1–31.

LABOV, W., 1972. 'Negative contraction and negative concord in English grammar', *Language* 48, 773–818.

LAKOFF, G., 1987. *Women, Fire and Dangerous Things*, Chicago: University of Chicago Press.

LANGACKER, R., 1987. *Foundations of Cognitive Grammar I: Theoretical Prerequisites*, Stanford: Stanford University Press.

PERERA, K., 1984. *Children's Writing and Reading. Analysing Classroom Language*, Oxford: Blackwell.

POLLARD, C. & SAG, I., 1994. *Head-Driven Phrase Structure Grammar*, Chicago: Chicago University Press.

SAG, I., 1997. 'English relative clause constructions', *Journal of Linguistics* 33, 431–83.

TESNIÈRE, L., 1959. *Eléments de syntaxe structurale,* Paris: Klincksieck.

TRUDGILL, P., 1975. *Accent, Dialect and the School*, London: Arnold.

WINOGRAD, T., 1972. *Understanding Natural Language*, New York: Academic Press.

JOHN LAVER

LAVER, John David Michael Henry, CBE 1999, FBA 1990; Research Professor of Speech Sciences, Queen Margaret University College, Edinburgh, since January 2001; *b.* 1938; *m.* (i) 1961 Avril Morna Anel Macqueen Gibson, 2s 1d; (ii) 1974 Sandra Traill, 1 s; *Education:* Churcher's College, Petersfield; Royal Air Force College, Cranwell; University of Edinburgh MA Hons 1962, Postgraduate Diploma in Phonetics, 1963, PhD, DLitt; *Career:* Assistant Lecturer and Lecturer in Phonetics, University of Ibadan, 1963–6; University of Edinburgh: Lecturer, Senior Lecturer, Reader in Phonetics 1966–85, Professor of Phonetics 1985–2000; Director 1984–9, Chairman 1989–94, Centre for Speech Technology Research; Associate Dean, Faculty of Arts, 1989–92, Vice-Principal 1994–7; Hon. Visiting Professor, University of York, 2000–3; President International Phonetic Association 1991–5 (Member of Council 1986–); Member: Board, European Speech Communication Association, 1988–92; Council, Philological Society, 1994–8; Council, British Academy, 1998–2001 (Chairman, Humanities Research Board, 1994–8, Chairman, Linguistics and Philology Section, 1998–2001); FRSA 1995; FRSE 1994 (Council, Royal Society of Edinburgh, 1996–2002, Vice-President 1996–9, Fellowship Secretary 1999–2002); Fellow, Institute of Acoustics, 1988–2001; Hon. DLitt, Sheffield, De Montfort. *Major Publications: Communication in Face-to-Face Interaction* 1972; *Phonetics in Linguistics* 1973; *The Phonetic Description of Voice Quality* 1980; *The Cognitive Representation of Speech* 1981; *Aspects of Speech Technology* 1988; *The Gift of Speech* 1991; *Principles of Phonetics* 1994; *The Handbook of Phonetic Sciences* 1997.

* * *

Most phoneticians think of phonetics as the study of spoken language. All would agree on this as the heartland of the modern subject. But I have always been more attracted by a wider vision of phonetics, as the study of all aspects of speech. In such a view, phonetics and linguistics together make up the linguistic sciences, overlapping in the study of phonology, but each with legitimate interests outside the scope of the other.

The core of my work as a phonetician has been general phonetic theory, and within this the study of speech production. But I have also frequently pursued research into areas that more traditional phoneticians might say were peripheral to the study of spoken language – voice quality and speaker characterization, speech pathology, speech errors and neuromuscular control, communication in face-to-face interaction, and speech technology.

I would concede that such research, often in collaboration with colleagues from other disciplines, lay at the frontiers of the subject. But if phonetics can legitimately be viewed as the study of all aspects of speech, then I would claim that any success in this research extended the frontiers of phonetics as an inherently interdisciplinary subject, rather than crossed a border into territory alien to phonetics (Laver 2001).

Like many of my generation, I grew up largely unaware of the subjects of phonetics and linguistics, although I was exposed to many languages from my earliest days. A child of empire, I was born in the Northwest Frontier Province of what was then India, near Peshawar, and became bilingual in Hindustani (Urdu) and English. My father was in the Indian and later the British Army, and we moved at least every year to a new posting, sometimes every six months. After six years in India, and up to the age of 10, I lived in Egypt (twice), Libya, Kenya and Cyprus, where I learned smatterings of Arabic, Italian, Swahili, Turkish and Greek. In Nairobi, I recall learning Swahili partly from a grammar (which turned out not to accord very closely with local linguistic patterns).

Moving so often as a child, I became psychologically and socially very dependent on books, and the habit of wide-ranging reading has stayed with me ever since my dazzled discovery of the riches of the Carnegie Public Library in Nairobi. My mother, who was a French teacher, nurtured this interest. I remember in particular a birthday present from her of Margaret Mead's *Coming of Age in Samoa* (1928). I now recognize Mead's book as imposing an inappropriate framework on the realities of Samoan culture, but it opened for me an early vista of understanding of social behaviour as rule-based rather than solely instinctive, to which I was later to return in some work on sociolinguistic aspects of communication. Coming to England at the age of 10, initially to Sheffield, I had the run of my grandfather's library and avidly consumed his encyclopedias and other works of reference. Perhaps it is fanciful to think so, but my career-long interest in a multi-disciplinary perspective may have had some roots in this early literary freedom.

After boarding school in Hampshire, I went to the Royal Air Force College at Cranwell, to pursue a military career as a pilot (misguidedly, as it turned out). One bonus for my future training in experimental phonetics, however, was the very well-taught introduction I received there to aspects of subjects such as aerodynamics and engineering. Turning away from the Royal Air Force, I applied to the University of Edinburgh, where in 1958 I began a degree in French language and literature, graduating in 1962 in the standard Scottish tradition of four-year honours degrees. Unknown to me before arriving at Edinburgh was the requirement of the French degree that the so-called Ordinary Course in Phonetics should be followed in the first year as a secondary, one-year subject. That was my introduction to the extraordinary Department of Phonetics at Edinburgh, and to David

Abercrombie, son of the poet Lascelles Abercrombie and father of a lineage of phoneticians that includes three Presidents of the International Phonetic Association and many others who have populated departments of phonetics and linguistics around the world. Peter Ladefoged was in charge of the Experimental Phonetics Laboratory in the department, Ian Catford was the Director of the nearby School of Applied Linguistics in the university, and Angus McIntosh the Head of the Department of English Language and General Linguistics. Also nearby was the Linguistic Survey of Scotland, with its Scots and Gaelic sections, the first associated with Jim Mather and the second with Kenneth Jackson. As part of my undergraduate degree, I also followed a course in psychology in James Drever's Department of Psychology. I believe this had some influence in an orientation to a cognitive perspective in much of the research I was later to undertake.

On graduation, I had little clear idea about what I wanted to do. I had an interview arranged with the McCann-Erickson advertising agency in London, and I had been accepted by Oxford for teacher-training, with a place at St Edmund Hall. But then Abercrombie generously offered me one of two Ford Foundation Scholarships in his gift to pursue a Postgraduate Diploma in Phonetics in his department. There followed a year (1962–3) of training in practical, theoretical and experimental phonetics whose depth, range and relevance I find I only really appreciate at this distance in time. One always tends to think of the days of one's apprenticeship as a golden era, but I know of no other course, then or since, with quite the richness of preparation for a life as a professional phonetician.

Teachers on the Edinburgh Diploma course, besides Abercrombie, included Betsy Uldall, Bill Jones, Laurie Iles, Ken Albrow, Lindsay Criper, John Kelly and Klaus Kohler. An important figure outside the department was Michael Halliday, then developing his categorial grammar and his elegant work on a phonological approach to the intonation of English (Halliday 1963). Techniques in the Phonetics Laboratory included a sound spectrograph, a speech synthesizer (PAT, of which more below), direct palatography and a classical Rousselot-style kymograph.

The Diploma syllabus included the work of figures such as Sweet, de Courtenay, Saussure, Trubetzkoy, Jespersen, Scripture, Stetson, Pike, Sapir, Bloomfield, Chao, Twaddell, Trager, Joos, Jakobson, Martinet, Hjelmslev, Hockett, Lehiste, Harris, Chomsky, Fant, Daniel Jones, Gimson, Ladefoged and Catford, and particularly of J. R. Firth and the prosodic school, notably Henderson, Robins and Scott. Abercrombie's style of teaching frequently used the tactic of mentioning other authors in passing, with the unspoken implication that no phonetician worth the name would want to remain ignorant of the work of such masters. In this way I became familiar with two American writers who have been a foundational influence for me, the nineteenth-century pragmaticist philosopher and semiotician Charles Saunders Peirce, and the modern sociologist Erving Goffman.

Politically, Abercrombie was left-wing. Socially, he was liberal, urbane, patrician, paternalistic and closely interested in the mental and personal life of each of his postgraduate students. A fundamental if tacit attitude he held about these students was that all his geese were swans. Outside academic life, his expertise on wine as a Chevalier du Tastevin was an especially enriching and civilizing influence on all who enjoyed the hospitality that he and his wife Mary dispensed generously and often. His friends were drawn from a very broad range of interests. For instance, he had worked in Greece and Egypt during the war and knew Lawrence Durrell. Some say Abercrombie was a model for one of Durrell's leading characters in his Alexandria Quartet. Peter Ladefoged has written an excellent appreciation of Abercrombie's life and contribution for the British Academy, of which Abercrombie was a Senior Fellow (Ladefoged 1996), and another assessing the changing nature of phonetics through Abercrombie's career (Ladefoged 1997).

Foremost in my own memory of Abercrombie's professional attributes are the breadth of his appreciation of all aspects of speech; his orderly and principled interest in general phonetic theory; his cogent and original marshalling of the principles underlying writing systems and phonetic transcription; the depth of his sympathetic knowledge of the history of phonetics; and the remarkable quality of his personal abilities in both the performance and perception of speech patterns in the languages of the world. His five books all show the depth of original thinking and clarity of expression that made him to my mind the greatest phonetician of the twentieth century (Abercrombie 1956; 1964; 1965; 1967; 1991). His *Elements of General Phonetics* (1967) is still widely read, and deservedly so. But I think his best work was published in two early articles on the history of phonetics and writing theory, on 'Forgotten phoneticians' (1948), which was a strong influence on one of my own historical articles (Laver 1981a), and 'What is a "letter"?' (1949), respectively. Like Peter Ladefoged, I owe a pervasive debt to Abercrombie's thinking about phonetics. My other two formative influences were the psychologist Donald Boomer and Peter Ladefoged himself.

On graduating with the Diploma in Phonetics in 1963, I was invited by Abercrombie to work on a short-term basis as a Research Assistant in the Phonetics Laboratory, on a project funded by the then Ministry of Aviation, using PAT (Parametric Artificial Talker), one of the earliest speech synthesizers, designed in the early 1950s by Walter Lawrence. Abercrombie would soon after be able to persuade Lawrence, everybody's idea of a dedicated but absent-minded inventor, to join the staff of the department after a long career as a government scientist in the Signals Research and Development Establishment at Christchurch.

Up to that point, PAT had been used chiefly to generate passages of connected speech to consolidate the technique of synthesis as such. Betsy

Uldall, aided technically by Tony Anthony, had synthesized what was regarded internationally at that time as the most intelligible continuous text in synthetic research, in her work on the story of the North Wind and the Sun. As my contribution to the PAT project, with the technical help of David Cruickshank, I chose to explore speaker-differences, drawing on proposals by Ian Catford that he later published in 1964. My method involved synthesizing a sentence of another text as a base (the Rainbow Passage; Fairbanks 1960), and then varying the laryngeal parameters to produce a number of different phonation types as variations of voice quality. These simulations of phonation types were acoustically crude but phonetically recognizable, and formed the basis of my first paper to an International Congress of Phonetic Sciences, in Prague in 1967 (Laver 1970). Abercrombie seldom indulged in attendance at Congresses, but I was treated there with the greatest kindness by Gimson, Daniel Jones's successor as Professor of Phonetics at University College London, who introduced me, as a novice phonetician, to the leading international figures in the subject.

After the brief work on PAT in 1963, I was still uncertain what professional path to follow. Seymour Chatman kindly suggested that I should apply to his Department of English at the University of California at Berkeley. Bob Cochrane encouraged me to take up a position in linguistics at Brisbane. But Abercrombie was once more instrumental in my choice. Peter Ladefoged had recently moved to UCLA after a year in the Department of Linguistics and Nigerian Languages at Ibadan. A vacancy as an Assistant Lecturer to take up his previous responsibilities in running the Phonetics Laboratory at Ibadan was advertised by the Inter-University Council, and the appointment was subject to interview in London by Gimson and Abercrombie. Gimson ran the interview, and asked me only two questions: what practical phonetics would I teach, and could I perform a voiced bilabial implosive. I said I would teach the Edinburgh Ordinary Course syllabus, and my performance of the implosive was apparently to his satisfaction. The rest of the interview consisted of conversation about claret, chiefly between Gimson and Abercrombie.

Formally, my post in Ibadan lasted three years (1963–6), but in the second year I returned to Edinburgh on exchange for one year with John Kelly. In the two separate years I spent in Ibadan, I mostly did research on Etsako, one of the Edo languages of the Niger–Benue confluence. The sound patterns of Etsako can be analysed as showing a quite unusual consonant harmony system, with greater and less degrees of muscle tension (correlated as well with relative duration and some differences of phonation type) as a distinctive phonological feature (Laver 1967; 1969; 1971). Colleagues at Ibadan included the Africanist Carl Hoffmann from Hamburg, working on Margi and other languages of northern Nigeria, Kay Williamson, whose PhD was from Yale, working on the languages of the Niger delta, and Elisabeth Dunstan, working on Ngwe, a language of Cameroon. Together with my contact with Etsako, this was for me the beginning of a first-hand appreciation of the real diversity of the phonetic repertoire of the languages of the world.

In 1966, I returned to take up a permanent post in the Department of Phonetics at Edinburgh, where I was to remain until 2000. I registered as a part-time PhD candidate to continue studying voice quality while working as a member of staff. Abercrombie was officially my supervisor. I would prefer to believe that it was a mark of his all-encompassing influence on my own thinking that we only had one formal supervisory session in the whole 10-year period of my candidature. But perhaps Gill Brown (this volume) is right to suggest that the real reason was that he had a dismissive opinion of the value of PhD degrees. Gimson was my external examiner, but my oral examination was waived, so my dissertation remained essentially undiscussed. It did, however, form the basis of my monograph on the anatomy, physiology, acoustics, phonetics and semiotics of voice quality published by Cambridge University Press in 1980. A central concept was the idea of an articulatory setting as a tendency of the vocal organs to constrain segmental performance in an individual's speech (or in that of a sociolinguistic speech community) towards particular long-term articulatory or phonatory values (Honikman 1964; Abercrombie 1967; Laver 1968). I was able to show that a given voice could usefully be described as a joint product of an individual's organic endowment and phonetic habit, and as a composite, phonetically, of multiple settings of different parts of the vocal apparatus.

My 1980 book was in turn the platform for a broad strand of phonetic, sociolinguistic and clinical research into voice quality and speaker characterization which continues today, especially in my collaboration with Janet Mackenzie Beck, who combines expertise in genetics, speech pathology and phonetics. A chapter summarizing our Medical Research Council-funded work on the application of vocal profile analysis (VPA) of individual speakers in speech pathology clinics and elsewhere is Laver, Wirz, Mackenzie & Hiller (1991).

The VPA project provided valuable information about voice quality characteristics of subjects with a range of speech disorders, including cleft palate, cerebral palsy and Parkinson's disease. Of particular interest was a group of subjects with trisomy-21 (Down syndrome), where the contribution of atypical physical characteristics to voice quality was particularly striking. The perceived voice quality of a speaker with trisomy-21 would normally be descriptively characterized as showing a palatalized setting – in other words a long-term tendency for the tongue apparently to constrict the vocal tract near the hard palate. But the genetic effects of trisomy-21 often have the anatomical consequence of underdevelopment of the mid-face, so that the tendency towards a habitual palatal constriction during speech would have in these voices in fact an organic rather than a phonetic explanation. Such cases led us to propose the principle of configurational equivalence between organic and phonetic contributions to voice quality.

Findings like these raise interesting questions about the impact such organically determined voice characteristics might have on social inter-action. Insights gained from such work have implications for a wide range of disciplines, including not only phonetics and speech pathology but also sociolinguistics, psychology, medicine and genetics. Other collaborations in research on voice quality are reported in Laver & Trudgill (1979) and Laver & Hanson (1981), and these and other relevant papers were reproduced in Laver (1991). Recent developments are described in Laver (2000). Voice quality is probably the area of research for which I am most widely known and most often cited, though I would want to say that it is one strand amongst several in which I take a research interest.

A seminal development for me happened in 1967, when Donald Boomer came for a year to the Department of Phonetics on sabbatical leave from the National Institutes of Mental Health in Bethesda, Maryland. A pre-war farm-boy from Kansas with few prospects, he joined the US Air Force as a gunner, and had been shot down over Germany early in the Second World War. He made several ultimately unsuccessful escapes from prison camp. After the war he took advantage of the GI Bill to go to the University of California at Berkeley, and graduated with a doctorate in clinical psychology.

Boomer's previous research on spontaneous speech had used data on hesitations to model the brain's encoding processes for producing utter-ances. Looking now at other dysfluencies in conversational speech, he had become interested in (non-Freudian) slips of the tongue, and brought with him a corpus of about 100 tape-recorded (English) slips he had collected. He asked me to help him in analysing these phonetically. Nothing in my experience of research had prepared me for the nature of the intensive, demanding and rewarding collaboration with Donald Boomer that ensued. Sardonic, intuitive and ruthlessly attached to truth, his tenacity in establish-ing the links in the chain of argument linking a hypothesis to a conclusion from relevant data, and his persistence in seeking to establish the further implications, were little short of ferocious. He was the ideal mentor to sharpen the scientific edge of one's thinking about cognitive processes.

We collected a supplementary corpus of another 100 or so slips of the tongue from conversations, seminar presentations and broadcasts, and analysed their segmental, rhythmic and intonational characteristics. Our approach was to treat them as transient malfunctions of the normal speech production process, whose analysis might illuminate the otherwise largely opaque neurolinguistic processes of the brain in generating and monitoring speech. It rapidly became clear that making involuntary speech errors and correcting them was a process that very often happened outside the conscious awareness of both the speaker and the listener. Recurrent, subtle, structured patterns emerged from the data. We were able to present a set of eight statistical laws characterizing such slips. Most slips obeyed most of the laws, and no slip obeyed none of them.

The most important conclusion was that an utterance in English (of the size of intonational phrases typically of seven to eight syllables) is neurolinguistically planned as a unitary behavioural act in advance of articulation, stored in short-term memory and only then executed neuromuscularly. The neurolinguistic plan was proposed to assemble the neural correlates of the separate elements, thus partially activating them ('priming' them) before the audible utterance began. The storage in short-term memory maximized the opportunity for interaction between the elements of the planned performance. A given slip of the tongue was then seen as an interaction between an intended articulation (the target) and an interfering source (the origin). We showed that target and origin were usually contained in the plan for the same intonational phrase; that the tonic word (the word showing the most salient intonational and rhythmic prominence in the intonational phrase) was the predominant location of either the origin or the target; and that sharing the same place in the structure of their respective syllables was an attribute that predisposed target and origin to interaction.

When we started the research on slips, we were able to find only 10 publications on the topic, including Freud's *Psychopathology of Everyday Life* (1901). Only three had been published since 1950. I think it is not unfair to say that the summary of our work (Boomer and Laver 1968) was one of the definitive publications that then helped to accelerate an international wave of research over the next 25 years or so into neurolinguistic strategies of speech production. Many of the consequent publications were published in two books edited by Vicki Fromkin of UCLA (1973, 1980).

Collaborating with Boomer was the stimulus for me to continue with neurolinguistic research. My own view is that of the 100 or so publications I have written to date, the chapter I wrote in the early 1970s on monitoring systems in the neurolinguistic control of spontaneous speech production (published in Fromkin 1980 and reprinted in Laver 1991) is the best and the most sustained piece of logical thinking that I have been able to do. I tried to pose the question 'What linguistic or motor information does the brain need, at a given stage in the construction of its plans for producing a particular act of speaking, in order to translate a given idea into an audible, well-formed utterance?' The chapter offered a cybernetic model, based on propositional logic, of the brain's decision processes and the prerequisite conditions necessary for formulating, executing, monitoring and correcting the neurolinguistic and neuromuscular programs for the production of an utterance.

The model used networks of the Boolean relations of conjunction, and inclusive and exclusive disjunction. Black boxes of unknown internal process modelled the actual constructional tactics. Feed-forward links and feedback loops were an integral part of the model representing the flow of information from one such constructional process to another, through logic gates borrowed as concepts from electronic networks. These gates specified the set of conditions which together constituted the informational prerequisites for the action of each of the chain of black boxes. Six major stages were proposed: ideation; abstract linguistic programming; abstract motor programming; conversion of abstract motor programs to neuromuscular commands; pre-articulation monitoring (between all the above stages) for covert error; articulation; and post-articulation monitoring for overt error. Overt speech errors were thus treated as a translation mismatch arising at some level between the conversion of a plan at one level and its execution at the next, logically associated with a failure of covert monitoring to detect and correct the mismatch before public utterance.

The publication of the chapter in 1980 coincided with the growth in popularity of spreading activation models of neurolinguistic action in linguistic performance, and the chapter didn't receive much critical attention. In the last decade, however, Blackmer and Mitton (1991), Postma (2000), Oomen (2001) and Oomen & Postma (2001a; 2001b) have explored the model's implications for neurolinguistic and neuromotor processes of construction, execution and covert and overt monitoring against the partly different implications of Levelt's (1989) model of the brain's performance in controlling speaking. Some of my specific proposals for the way that individual modules work, especially in their implications for the timing of repairs to detected covert and overt errors, have been shown by these researchers to be problematic. But the model retains sufficient overall plausibility for me to continue to believe that this work is my best.

A key development for me was a six-month period I spent in 1971 as a visiting Assistant Professor in Peter Ladefoged's Phonetics Laboratory in the UCLA Department of Linguistics. I learned important lessons from him and his wife Jenny about the resolution and stamina needed to reach one's academic and personal goals in times of adversity as well as in more sanguine periods. Peter Ladefoged's thinking, then and now, strongly reinforced my interest in the diversity of the phonetic repertoire of languages of the world, and in the need for a general phonetic theory able to account systematically for all such differences. I find it hard to believe that anyone would dissent from my opinion that he is today and has been for many years the world's leading phonetician.

During the 1970s in Edinburgh I continued to work on speech production and experimental phonetics. I was put in charge of the Phonetics Laboratory, and managed to replace the old KDF-9 computer, programmed by punched paper tape, by first a DEC PDP-9 and latterly a DEC VAX computer. The classical kymograph was relegated to a museum, and airflow was instead measured by an electroaerometer coupled to a mingograph. The system of direct palatography gave way to electropalatography, using an artificial palate with embedded sensors for registering tongue–palate contact. My first doctoral student, William Hardcastle, graduated in 1971 with a dissertation developing this new technique of electropalatography, and his world-pioneering role over 30 years in making this into a now very well-established practical technique for experimental and clinical purposes is internationally recognized.

My own thesis on voice quality was submitted in 1975. In the 1970s I also began to publish in the broad area of sociolinguistics, beginning with a book edited with my colleague Sandy Hutcheson, soon to be my wife, on linguistic and paralinguistic communication in face-to-face interaction (Laver & Hutcheson 1972). Chapters followed on Malinowski's concept of phatic communion (Laver 1975), non-verbal interaction (Laver 1976), and negotiations of social status and solidarity in the use of terms of address (Laver 1981b), appealing to Goffman's concept of face (1955) and Brown & Levinson's ideas (1978) about the functions of polite routines in conversation. Cheepen was later to publish a book (1988) on the predictability of informal conversation, where she tested the proposals in my paper on phatic communion against recorded conversational data. Once again, some proposals were found to be unsupported by her data, but many were confirmed as applicable. See also many of the contributions to Coupland (2000).

The Department of Phonetics had amalgamated in 1967 with the Department of General Linguistics, and then in 1970 with the School of Applied Linguistics, to form the Department of Linguistics. David Abercrombie retired in 1980. The two professorial Heads of Subjects for applied linguistics and general linguistics, against my emphatic advice, took the position that filling Abercrombie's established Chair of Phonetics was not a priority for the amalgamated Department, in which vacancies left by staff in phonetics had frequently been converted to posts in other areas. This was perhaps consistent with a view of phonetics as merely one constituent of an overall subject of linguistics, but as I have explained, this was not my view of the relationship between the two relatively autonomous subjects of phonetics and linguistics. As Head of Subject for phonetics and Director of the Experimental Phonetics Laboratory, and with the close support and advice of Ron Asher, I decided that the best way to nurture the survival of phonetics as a viable subject in these circumstances might be to pursue a programme of enhanced research activity.

In 1984, just before the launch of the UK Government's Alvey Programme on Information Technology, and with the very helpful support of the Principal, John Burnett (soon to be knighted), Ron Asher and I set up the Centre for Speech Technology Research (CSTR) as a multi-departmental collaboration between the Departments of Linguistics, Artificial Intelligence and Electrical Engineering. By any standards, during the 10-year period in which I was Director then Chairman of CSTR (1984–94), the academic staff collaborating in the Centre were outstandingly successful in gaining grants and contracts in speech technology research and development, securing more than £11m. Industrial collaborators included NEC, the De La Rue Company, Digital Equipment Corporation, Olivetti, Apple Incorporated, the Rowntree Company, and Chambers Dictionaries.

Research funding also came from the European Commission, the Medical Research Council, the Science and Engineering Research Council, and the Cancer Research Campaign.

The largest of the contracts was for an industrial collaboration, initially with the Plessey Company, and later with GEC Marconi, for the Alvey Large-Scale Demonstrator project to build an advanced speech recognition and synthesis capability. The principal investigators on this project (1984–91), funded at over £5m overall and the largest in the history of the Scottish universities at that date, included two from Artificial Intelligence (Henry Thompson and Peter Jackson), one from Electrical Engineering (Mervyn Jack), and five from Linguistics (Jim Hurford, Ellen Bard, Steve Isard and Jim Miller, with myself as Director of the Edinburgh effort). The Universities of Loughborough, Oxford, Leeds and Dundee also collaborated.

We learned a great deal about industrial collaboration, commercial politics and intellectual property in this project. We succeeded in reaching our technical goals on time, in competition with American laboratories working in the context of the US Strategic Computing Initiative. I personally learned many lessons, both positive and negative, about strategic administration. Eventually, however, tensions between an engineering philosophy of directing one's efforts to meeting limited commercial objectives within specification and on time, versus a more traditional academic interest in continuing to pursue research objectives wherever data revealed promising paths, diluted the collaborative spirit of the Centre. Most researchers including myself eventually turned to different enterprises, though CSTR itself survives.

Hopeful though the launch of CSTR had been as a means of strengthening the future of phonetics as a subject, and successful though the projects conducted within the Centre had certainly been, I have to say with the benefit of reflection that the effect on the survival of phonetics in the University of Edinburgh of trying to set up a large research institute was not ultimately as beneficial as I had hoped. It removed key figures from day-to-day involvement in their parent departments, especially in teaching; it distracted them from attending to the endless administrative skirmishes in the wider university that progressively affect the life of departments; and perhaps most damaging, because CSTR was engaged largely in applied (albeit ambitious) research, significant advances in the fundamental theoretical understanding of the collaborating subjects were less often achieved. A perhaps obvious conclusion is that, if choice is unavoidable, the longevity of a subject is better secured by student interest than by the transitory stimulus of a surge of external research funding.

I had only limited contact with students during my 10 years in CSTR, apart from supervising a number of doctoral dissertations (Steve Hiller 1985, Fouzia Bukshaisha 1985, Sheila Wirz 1987, Janet Mackenzie Beck 1988, Gerard Docherty 1989, Helen Fraser 1989, and Eddie Rooney 1990). In addition, CSTR's research in speech technology was specialized in a relatively small sector of phonetics. My way of staying in touch with general phonetic theory throughout this period was therefore to work on writing a large-scale reference textbook, which I hoped would give a view of the whole reach of a descriptive theory for phonetic aspects of spoken language. *Principles of Phonetics* was published by Cambridge University Press in 1994. I was privileged to have had Eugénie Henderson appointed by the Press as an advisor in its earlier years. I very much regret that her death in 1989 meant that she never saw the outcome of her scholarly and thoughtful advice. I had earlier edited a book with Bill Jones on the British School of phonetics in which her work figured prominently amongst the contributions of the prosodic analysts (Jones & Laver 1973).

When I eventually sent the manuscript of *Principles of Phonetics* off to Cambridge, I felt I had written it at the pitch of my ability. Of course, I now see many options for expressing ideas slightly differently. But the book meant much to me then and still does. It was my proxy for all the contact with students I had missed, and was my intimate conversation with the students of the future. It made no assumptions about prior knowledge, and was designed to equip the reader with a foundation for graduate-level work. I tried hard to achieve maximum clarity while avoiding patronizing the reader, and to offer a detailed understanding of phonetics as a subject worthy of standing beside all other university-level subjects. I sought to cover all known phonological features and their phonetic realizations. Linguistic diversity was illustrated by transcribed examples from over 500 languages from all the inhabited continents, drawn from the published research of a wide range of phoneticians and phonologists as well as from my own experience. I also paid particular attention to offering clear and realistic articulatory diagrams, having a low opinion of the accuracy of those in most phonetics textbooks. I hope that this book will be the most enduring of my contributions to phonetics.

In 1994 I left CSTR to become Vice-Principal for Research in the University (1994–7), and was attached to the University's Institute for Advanced Studies in the Humanities. I was also appointed as the founding Chairman of the British Academy's Humanities Research Board (1994–8), spending half my time in London and visiting many different universities and professional associations every year. In addition, I was appointed to a number of other committees concerned with the national support of research. These various strategic appointments, rewarding though I found them, had the combined effect of putting a five-year hiatus into personal research. I published mainly synoptic and editorial work in this period (for instance, Hardcastle & Laver 1997), apart from publications about the work of the humanities in general, and arguing the case (for example, as the humanities advisor to the research committee of the Dearing Inquiry) for a Humanities Research Council. The successor to the Humanities Research

Board, the Arts and Humanities Research Board, has achieved more than three times the funding, is widely admired for the way that it has stimulated and enabled excellent research in all subjects in the arts and humanities, and is now in all but name generally regarded as having equivalent standing to a Research Council. I hope that its formal recognition as a Research Council will now not be long delayed.

I had been elected a Fellow of the British Academy in 1990, just after Peter Trudgill. I was chairman of the Linguistics and Philology section 1998–2001, following John Lyons, Peter Matthews and Anna Morpurgo Davies as my immediate predecessors. It has been particularly pleasing, from the point of view of phonetics and phonology, that John Wells, Neil Smith and David Crystal have recently been elected. Peter Ladefoged and Eli Fischer Jørgensen are Corresponding Fellows. In 1994 I was elected a Fellow of the Royal Society of Edinburgh, Scotland's national academy of sciences and letters, where I am presently the Fellowship Secretary.

In 2000, the Departments of Linguistics and Applied Linguistics, which had earlier separated, reamalgamated to form the Department of Theoretical and Applied Linguistics. The new Department kindly invited me to join its staff, which I much appreciated. By this stage, however, the Department had a very much reduced complement of staff with phonetic interests. By contrast, Queen Margaret University College (QMUC), also in Edinburgh, had a large and very well-equipped Department of Speech and Language Sciences, with a significant number of expert phoneticians. William Hardcastle was a Professor of Speech Sciences there as well as being Dean of Research for the institution, and Janet Mackenzie Beck was also on the staff. I was therefore very pleased to be able to join the QMUC Faculty of Health Sciences as a Research Professor of Speech Sciences on 1 January 2001, and am very grateful for the warm welcome I have received. It was also a particular pleasure to be appointed recently as an Honorary Visiting Professor at the University of York for three years, where John Local leads a very active phonetics and phonology group specializing in conversational analysis, prosodic analysis and laboratory phonology. We are planning to collaborate on the paralinguistic analysis of tone of voice in conversation.

Janet Mackenzie Beck and I are currently collaborating in QMUC on two projects. One is the exploration of an integrated theory of non-verbal communication, and the second is the development of better techniques for analysing voice quality. In these and in many other ways, I look forward to contributing to QMUC's active and important research in experimental and clinical phonetics, and to continuing there the tradition of work on the broadly based study of speech begun by David Abercrombie in the University of Edinburgh more than 50 years ago.

A continuing collaboration with Ron Asher, now an emeritus member of the Edinburgh University Department, is writing an encyclopedic dictionary of speech, covering speech-relevant aspects of the vocabulary of all disciplines with a professional interest in speech, for Blackwell. With some 4,000 out of 10,000 planned entries now written, about 40 different sectors have emerged in the broad definition of phonetics that I have been describing here. They are: acoustics; aerodynamics; anatomy; anthropology and anthropological linguistics; artificial intelligence; audiology; computing; conversational analysis; dentistry; discourse; experimental phonetics; forensic phonetics; historical phonetics; historical phonology; human–computer interaction; languages and language classification; language learning; linguistics; neurology; non-verbal communication; paralinguistics; phonetics; phoniatrics; phonology; physiology; poetics; pragmatics; psychology and psycholinguistics; semiotics; signal processing; singing; sociology and sociolinguistics; speech pathology and therapy; speech science; speech technology and natural language processing; transcription and writing systems. The range and variety of the disciplines listed, with their evident intersection in the study of speech, surely assert the nature of phonetics as an interdisciplinary subject par excellence (Laver 2001).

To conclude, I confess to a passionate, career-long engagement with phonetics. But deep though such feelings may be, one needs to remember that there are more important objects of affection in life even than one's intellectual pursuits. Phonetics lost a more able phonetician than I am when my wife Sandy Hutcheson decided in 1990 to turn to directing the university's schools and colleges liaison service. She has given me unswerving support through every moment of an academic career where the flow has not always been untroubled. She, our son, my three other children and our three grandchildren are what really matter.

REFERENCES

ABERCROMBIE, DAVID, 1948. 'Forgotten phoneticians', *TPhS* 47, 1–34.
ABERCROMBIE, DAVID, 1949. 'What is a "letter"?', *Lingua* 2, 54–62.
ABERCROMBIE, DAVID, 1956. *Problems and Principles*, London: Longman.
ABERCROMBIE, DAVID, 1964. *English Phonetic Texts*, London: Faber & Faber.
ABERCROMBIE, DAVID, 1965. *Studies in Phonetics and Linguistics*, Oxford: Oxford University Press.
ABERCROMBIE, DAVID, 1967. *Elements of General Phonetics*, Edinburgh: Edinburgh University Press.
ABERCROMBIE, DAVID, 1991. *Fifty Years in Phonetics*, Edinburgh: Edinburgh University Press.
BLACKMER, ELIZABETH R. & MITTON, JANET L., 1991. 'Theories of monitoring and the timing of repairs in spontaneous speech', *Cognition* 39, 173–94.
BOOMER, DONALD S., 1965. 'Hesitation and grammatical encoding', *Language and Speech* 8, 148–58.
BOOMER, DONALD S. & LAVER, JOHN, 1968. 'Slips of the tongue', *British Journal of Disorders of Communication* 3, 2–11, repr. in V. Fromkin (ed.), *Speech Errors as Linguistic Evidence*, The Hague: Mouton (1973), 120–31.
BROWN, PENNY & LEVINSON, STEVEN C., 1978. 'Politeness: some universals in language usage', in E. N. Goody (ed.), *Questions and Politeness: Strategies in Social Interaction*, Cambridge:

Cambridge University Press, 56–310. Rev. and pub. as an independent vol. by P. Brown & S. C. Levinson, *Politeness: Some Universals in Language Usage*, Cambridge: Cambridge University Press (1987).

BUKSHAISHA, FOUZIA A. M., 1985. *An Experimental Phonetic Study of Some Aspects of Qatari Arabic*. PhD dissertation, University of Edinburgh.

CATFORD, J. C., 1964. 'Phonation types', in D. Abercrombie, D. B. Fry, P. A. D. MacCarthy, N. C. Scott & J. L. M. Trim (eds.), *In Honour of Daniel Jones*, London: Longman, Green, 26–37.

CHEEPEN, CHRISTINE, 1988. *The Predictability of Informal Conversation*, London: Pinter.

COUPLAND, JUSTINE, 2000. *Small Talk*, Harlow: Pearson Education.

DOCHERTY, GERARD, 1989. *An Experimental Study of Obstruents in English*. PhD dissertation, University of Edinburgh.

FAIRBANKS, GRANT, 1960. *Voice and Articulation Drillbook*, New York: Harper & Row.

FRASER, HELEN B., 1989. *The Subject of Speech Perception: An Analysis of the Philosophical Foundations of the Information-Processing Model*. PhD dissertation, University of Edinburgh.

FREUD, SIGMUND, 1901. *Zur Psychopathologie des Alltagslebens*, trans. A. Tyson, ed. J. Strachey, as *Psychopathology of Everyday Life*, London: Benn (1966).

FROMKIN, VICTORIA, (ed.) 1973. *Speech Errors as Linguistic Evidence*, The Hague: Mouton.

FROMKIN, VICTORIA, (ed.) 1980. *Errors of Linguistic Performance*, New York: Academic Press.

GOFFMAN, ERVING, 1955. 'On face work', *Psychiatry* 18, 213–31.

HALLIDAY, M. A. K., 1963. 'The tones of English', *Archivum Linguisticum* 15, 1–28.

HARDCASTLE, WILLIAM J., 1971. *Electropalatography in the Investigation of Some Physiological Aspects of Speech Production*. PhD dissertation, University of Edinburgh.

HARDCASTLE, WILLIAM, J. & LAVER, JOHN, (eds.) 1997. *The Blackwell Handbook of Phonetic Sciences*, Oxford: Blackwell.

HILLER, STEVEN M., 1985. *Automatic Acoustic Analysis of Waveform Perturbations*. PhD dissertation, University of Edinburgh.

HONIKMAN, BEATRICE, 1964. 'Articulatory settings', in D. Abercrombie, D. B. Fry, P. A. D. MacCarthy, N. C. Scott & J. L. M. Trim (eds.), *In Honour of Daniel Jones*, London: Longman, Green, 73–84.

JONES, WILLIAM E. & LAVER, JOHN, (eds.) 1973. *Phonetics in Linguistics*, London: Longman.

LADEFOGED, PETER, 1996. 'David Abercrombie 1909–1992', *Proceedings of the British Academy* 90, London: British Academy, 239–48.

LADEFOGED, PETER, 1997. 'David Abercrombie and the changing field of phonetics', *Journal of Phonetics* 25, 85–92.

LAVER, JOHN, 1967. 'A preliminary phonology of the Aywele dialect of Etsako', *Journal of West African Languages* 4, 53–6.

LAVER, JOHN, 1968. 'Voice quality and indexical information', *British Journal of Disorders of Communication* 3, 43–54.

LAVER, JOHN, 1969. 'Etsako', in E. Dunstan (ed.), *Twelve Nigerian Languages*, London: Longman, Green, 47–56.

LAVER, JOHN, 1970. 'Synthesis of components in voice quality', in B. Hála, M. Romportl & P. Janota (eds.), *Proceedings of the Sixth International Congress of Phonetic Sciences* (1967), Prague: Czechoslovak Academy of Sciences, 523–5.

LAVER, JOHN, 1971. 'Etsako in the Polyglotta Africana', *African Language Review* 257–62.

LAVER, JOHN, 1975. 'Communicative functions of phatic communion', in A. Kendon, R. M. Harris & M. R. Key (eds.), *The Organization of Behavior in Face to Face Interaction*, The Hague: Mouton, 215–38.

LAVER, JOHN, 1976. 'Language and nonverbal communication', in E. C. Carterette and M. P. Friedman (eds.), *Language and Speech*, vol. 7 of *Handbook of Perception*, New York: Academic Press, 345–63.

LAVER, JOHN, 1979. 'Monitoring systems in the neurolinguistic control of speech production', in V. Fromkin (ed.), *Errors of Linguistic Performance*, New York: Academic Press, 287–305.

LAVER, JOHN, 1980. *The Phonetic Description of Voice Quality*, Linguistics Monographs Series, Cambridge: Cambridge University Press.

LAVER, JOHN, 1981a.'The analysis of vocal quality: from the classical period to the twentieth century', in R. E. Asher & E. J. A. Henderson (eds.), *Towards a History of Phonetics*, Edinburgh: Edinburgh University Press, 79–99.

LAVER, JOHN, 1981b. 'Linguistic routines and politeness in greeting and parting', in F. Coulmas (ed.), *Conversational Routines*, The Hague: Mouton, 289–304 .

LAVER, JOHN, 1991. *The Gift of Speech: Papers in the Analysis of Speech and Voice*, Edinburgh: Edinburgh University Press.

LAVER, JOHN, 1994. *Principles of Phonetics*, Cambridge Textbooks in Linguistics Series, Cambridge: Cambridge University Press.

LAVER, JOHN, 2000. 'Phonetic evaluation of voice quality', in R. D. Kent & M. J. Ball (eds.), *The Handbook of Voice Quality Measurement*, San Diego: Singular Publications.

LAVER, JOHN, 2001. 'The nature of phonetics', *Journal of the International Phonetic Association* 30, 31–8.

LAVER, JOHN & HANSON, ROBERT J., 1981. 'Describing the normal voice', in J. Darby (ed.), *Speech Evaluation in Psychiatry*, New York: Grune and Stratton, 57–78 .

LAVER, JOHN & HUTCHESON, SANDY, (eds.) 1972. *Communication in Face-to-Face Interaction*, Harmondsworth: Penguin.

LAVER, JOHN & TRUDGILL, PETER, 1979. 'Phonetic and linguistic markers in speech', in K. R. Scherer and H. Giles (eds.), *Social Markers in Speech*, Cambridge: Cambridge University Press, 1–32.

LAVER, JOHN, WIRZ, SHEILA, MACKENIZIE, JANET & HILLER, STEVEN M., 1991. 'A perceptual protocol for the analysis of vocal profiles', in J. Laver, *The Gift of Speech: Papers in the Analysis of Speech and Voice*, Edinburgh: Edinburgh University Press, 265–80.

LEVELT, WILLEM J. M., 1989. *Speaking: From Intention to Articulation*, Cambridge, MA: MIT Press.

MACKENZIE BECK, JANET, 1988. *Organic Variation and Voice Quality*. PhD dissertation, University of Edinburgh.

MEAD, MARGARET, 1928. *Coming of Age in Samoa: A Psychological Study of Primitive Youth for Western Civilisation*, New York: W. Morrow.

OOMEN, CLAUDY C. E., 2001. *Self-Monitoring in Normal and Aphasic Speech*. PhD dissertation, University of Utrecht.

OOMEN, CLAUDY C. E. & POSTMA, ALBERT, 2001a. 'Effects of time pressure on mechanisms of speech production and self-monitoring', *Journal of Psycholinguistic Research* (in press).

OOMEN, CLAUDY C. E. & POSTMA, ALBERT, 2001b. 'Resource limitations and speech monitoring', *Language and Cognitive Processes* (in press).

POSTMA, ALBERT, 2000. 'Detection of errors during speech production: a review of speech monitoring models', *Cognition* 77, 97–131.

ROONEY, EDMUND J., 1990. *Nasality in Automatic Speaker Verification*. PhD dissertation, University of Edinburgh.

WIRZ, SHEILA, 1987. *Voice Quality Assessment in the Speech of Profoundly Deaf Speakers*. PhD dissertation, University of Edinburgh.

GEOFFREY LEECH

LEECH, Geoffrey Neil, FBA 1987; Research Professor of English Linguistics, University of Lancaster, since 1996; *b.* 1936; *m.* 1961 Frances Anne Berman 1 s, 1 d; *Education:* Tewkesbury Grammar School; University College, London, BA 1959, MA 1963, PhD 1968; *Career:* Assistant Lecturer, UCL, 1962–4; Harkness Fellow, MIT, 1964–5; Lecturer, UCL, 1965–9; University of Lancaster: Reader 1969–74; Professor of Linguistics and Modern English Language 1974–96; Visiting Professor: Brown University 1972; Kobe University 1984; Kyoto University 1991; Hon Fil Dr Lund 1987. *Major Publications: English in Advertising* 1966; *A Linguistic Guide to English Poetry* 1969; *Towards a Semantic Description of English* 1969; *Meaning and the English Verb* 1971 [2nd ed. 1987]; *A Grammar of Contemporary English* (with R. Quirk, S. Greenbaum and J. Svartvik) 1972; *Semantics* 1974 [2nd ed. 1981]; *A Communicative Grammar of English* 1975 (with J. Svartvik) [2nd ed. 1994]; *Explorations in Semantics and Pragmatics* 1980; *Studies in English Linguistics: For Randolph Quirk* 1980 (ed. with S. Greenbaum and J. Svartvik); *Style in Fiction*, 1981 (with M. Short); *English Grammar for Today* 1982 (with R. Hoogenraad and M. Deuchar); *Principles of Pragmatics* 1983; *A Comprehensive Grammar of the English Language* 1985 (with R. Quirk, S. Greenbaum and J. Svartvik); *Computers in English Language Teaching and Research* 1986 (ed. with C. N. Candlin); *The Computational Analysis of English: A Corpus-Based Approach* 1987 (ed. with R. Garside and G. Sampson); *An A–Z of English Grammar and Usage* 1989; *Introducing English Grammar* 1992; *Statistically-Driven Computer Grammars of English* 1993 (ed. with E. Black and R. Garside); *Spoken English on Computer* 1995 (ed. with G. Myers and J. Thomas); *Corpus Annotation: Linguistic Information from Computer Text Corpora* 1997 (edited with R. Garside and T. McEnery); *Longman Grammar of Spoken and Written English* 1999 (jointly); *Word Frequencies in Written and Spoken English: Based on the British National Corpus* 2001 (with P. Rayson and A. Wilson).

* * *

1 A FORTUNATE ACCIDENT

I regard it as the most fortunate accident of my career that when I went to study English at University College, I chanced upon a magic circle of leading scholars in the study of language. During my undergraduate years (1956–9), I became particularly interested in the linguistic part of the syllabus, and had opted for what was then called 'Syllabus B' – a set of courses which contained a large component of language work, more historical than contemporary. For example, in Syllabus B, we had to study the *whole* of *Beowulf*, in the original, not just a part of it. Among the courses I took were Old English, Middle English, Old Norse, English philology and phonetics. This last course was taught by A. C. Gimson and J. D. O'Connor, world names in English phonetics.

Thinking of famous teachers, I should mention that as a freshman undergraduate I was fortunate enough to attend a series of lectures by J. R. Firth, the first Professor of Linguistics, and in many ways the founder of linguistics as a discipline in the UK. He gave a series of intercollegiate lectures at the University of London during my first year, and the polemic glint in his eye left an indelible impression on me. At that time, I could scarcely understand his message, although I remember that the term 'context of situation' figured prominently in it. Another great man whose lecture I was privileged to attend was Daniel Jones, the first Professor of Phonetics in the UK, and the father of the British school of phonetics. He was nearing 80 when I attended a lecture of his on – predictably enough – 'the phoneme'.

2 AN MA STUDENT: 1959–62

After graduation, I wanted to continue my studies as a research student at UCL. By this time I was becoming interested in modern linguistic research, but knew very little about it. Linguistics had so far made little impact in the UK, and no teacher in our department could adequately supervise in that area. However, at that time (c.1955–60) there was an initiative at UCL to promote the study of communication. An interdisciplinary conference on communication was held, and a new Communication Research Centre (CRC) was inaugurated. But there were two severe handicaps on the work of this Centre: first, the Centre had no funds or research staff; and second, scholars could not agree on what 'communication' was, or how it might be studied. Everyone agreed that 'communication' was important – but different disciplines had different insights into it.

As a modest start to the work of the CRC, three postgraduates in the English Department at UCL began to study the use of language in public communication. One student took as his province the study of public information documents, another began to study the language of press advertisements, and a third – myself – began to study the language of television commercials, then a relatively new medium in the UK.

I had been granted a state studentship enabling me to study for an MA (then a research degree at London University). However, we three students made little progress, since none of us knew what techniques would be appropriate. I grew disheartened with the work, left the university, and began teaching at a secondary school. I continued schoolteaching for about 18 months, keeping my MA studies going as well as I could in my spare time.

On 1 January 1962, I was fortunate enough to be granted a research studentship at UCL: this was a meagre sum of £750 per year (slightly less even than I had been earning as a very junior teacher), but I was overjoyed to have the opportunity to abandon schoolteaching and take up full-time research. I owed this 'break' to a commercial television company, ATV. How fortunate I was that some television magnate happened to donate to UCL a moderate sum for research on the language of advertising, at that time!

But we still had the problem of a lack of research tools. At that time, Randolph Quirk, who had been both student and teacher in my department at UCL, had accepted a Chair there. He was about to return to his old department once again, after spending a number of years at the University of Durham. He suggested to our supervisor that we should read the new linguistics at that time coming out of the USA, in order to arrive at the best analytic categories for describing the language of advertising. 'New linguistics', for us, included books now largely forgotten: books on English syntax by Paul Roberts, W. Nelson Francis, A. A. Hill and James Sledd. These works showed the influence of American structuralism: we had yet to catch up with the new generative grammar of Noam Chomsky.

3 TEACHING AT UNIVERSITY COLLEGE, LONDON: 1962–9

In the summer of 1962, I had another piece of good fortune, when an Assistant Lecturer's post became available in the English Department at UCL. My head of department, A. H. Smith, was prepared to appoint me, but before the decision was made, he offered his new professorial colleague, Randolph Quirk, the opportunity to vet me, and decide my fate. This interview was my first meeting with Quirk, who was to become my mentor in my developing career. At the interview, I was overawed, but his manner was so cordial that he soon put me at my ease. It seems that he was satisfied with my performance as an interviewee, for I was offered the post, much to my surprise and delight.

My most important task as a novice Lecturer was to plan and deliver a series of lectures on 'rhetoric' for first-year students. Previously, this lecture series had been on the history of rhetoric from classical times, and was by repute the dullest course offered by the Department. I was given carte blanche to redesign the course, and chose to treat literary language (especially the language of poetry) from the modern linguistic point of view, rather than from that of rhetorical tradition.

In 1963 I finished my MA thesis on *The Language of Commercial Television Advertising*. I had studied commercials ad nauseam. I should have been more grateful to my ATV sponsors: without them I could scarcely have put a foot on the academic ladder. At least I was grateful enough to send them a copy of my thesis, but there was no evidence that they read it or found it useful.

However, Professor Quirk invited me to embark on a book, to be based in part on my MA thesis, but extending to a more general treatment of the language of advertising. It was eventually published under the title of *English in Advertising: A Linguistic Study of Advertising in Great Britain* (1966).

After working on my new 'rhetoric' course, however, my favourite subject had become the language of literature, on which I published two papers in 1965 and 1966. This was a time when, for the first time, modern linguistics was being applied to the study of literary language. Often, I felt, this approach led to misunderstanding and even animosity between literary and linguistic scholars. However, I had been much influenced, as an undergraduate, by the lectures of the textually oriented literary critic Winifred Nowottny (especially Nowottny 1962), now a senior colleague in my own department. I felt a rapprochement could be achieved between these two approaches – the linguistic and the literary. This thinking eventually became the leitmotiv of my book *A Linguistic Guide to English Poetry* (1969a), again written with editorial encouragement from Randolph Quirk.

My period teaching in the Department of English Language and Literature at University College, London, lasted from 1962 to 1969. I have mentioned two strands of my academic development in that period – the study of register (particularly advertising) and the study of literary style. I will now backtrack to introduce a third strand – semantics.

In 1963 M. A. K. Halliday was appointed the first full-time Director of the Communication Research Centre, and under his influence the whole direction and thrust of the CRC underwent a transformation. Soon after, indeed, Michael Halliday became the first Professor of Linguistics at UCL. As he was a charismatic teacher and delightfully approachable colleague, I benefited greatly from close contact with him in 1963–4, when he was Director of the CRC, and I was Assistant Director. I understood that the UCL powers that be were reluctant to establish a Department of Linguistics, although linguistics was then becoming a popular and 'fashionable' new subject in the UK. Hence the CRC, of which I was a caretaker at that time, conveniently became an incipient Linguistics Department, which could safely be launched after Halliday was installed. It was considered a great coup that UCL had managed to entice him down to London, from Edinburgh where he had made his reputation. After he had been at UCL for a few months, the CRC faded into the background, and the Linguistics Department came into its own. At that time I was greatly influenced, as were many in the country, by Halliday's linguistic theory, then called 'scale and category grammar' (Halliday 1961), later renamed 'systemic linguistics' or 'systemic functional grammar'. I was interested in exploring Halliday's concepts of system and structure in new directions, and asked his advice about which branch of linguistics I should tackle – morphology or semantics – as neither of these had so far been sufficiently investigated within this model. He advised me to take up semantics, and indeed I did, soon finding myself teaching a new course on the subject to postgraduate students. However, my ideas on semantics, which veered towards the integration of componential analysis and logical relations, were rather different from those of Halliday, for whom the notions of 'context' and 'situation' (related to his teacher J. R. Firth's concept of 'context *of* situation') were paramount for the study of meaning.

While I was trying to develop my 'Hallidayan' semantics, I sought the opportunity to spend a year in the USA as a Harkness Fellow (1964–5). At the interview for this fellowship, I was confronted by a 10-man panel of 'the great and the good' of the academic world, of which one, Sir Isaiah Berlin, had the task of interrogating me about my research programme. I can only assume that his bark was worse than his bite, as I was granted the Fellowship, which by my standards was amazingly generous. It gave me the opportunity to study my chosen subject at the American university of my choice: so (who would not at that time?) I decided to study linguistics at MIT. Ironically, Chomsky was not there at the time, and I found to my chagrin that he was on leave in London! However, he returned to the USA later during my stay, and I had the opportunity to meet him and attend one or two of his lectures. I was struck by the contrast between Chomsky's public persona and his private personality. In lectures, as in his writings, he was tough and uncompromising in defending his own ideas and dismissing those of others. As a private man, he was mild, almost diffident, and easy to chat to.

Although MIT taught me a great deal, particularly about the habit of rigorous thought and application of theory, the MIT approach to linguistics was too constraining for my taste. Perhaps I was not caught young enough to imbibe the powerful drink of transformational grammar uncritically. Nevertheless I got to know many of the budding linguists of my generation: (Haj) Ross, Perlmutter, McCawley, George Lakoff and other notables all passed through the MIT portals at that time. Barbara Hall (later Barbara Partee) taught an excellent course on the mathematics and logic of linguistics, which I found the most valuable of my MIT courses.

The MIT graduate programme taught me a great deal about many areas of linguistics. Nothing like it existed in the UK. But one of the things easily learned at MIT at that time was a sense of conviction – that Chomskian linguistics led the world (as indeed it did), and alternative viewpoints could be summarily dismissed. Although I remained something of an outsider at MIT, I suppose I must have carried something of an MIT-bred arrogance back to the UK with me. However, any sense of superiority was soon punctured when I gave a paper on semantics at the Philological Society, where my nascent semantic theory met with scepticism. Later, I sent my work to John Lyons at Cambridge, to see if he would publish it in the newly founded *Journal of Linguistics*, but he was similarly unimpressed. It was evident that my ideas on semantics needed more careful exploration, so I developed my theory further into a monograph. Even then, I could not get it published – but fortunately it was accepted in my department that I could use this material as the basis for a PhD thesis. From 1965 and 1969, after my return to UCL from MIT, I rethought and developed my work on semantics until it became a PhD thesis with the title *An Approach to the Semantics of Place, Time and Modality in Modern English*. Finally, I revised the material yet again, and it was published in 1969 as a book entitled *Towards a Semantic Description of English*. The book was out of print in a very few years, and is not read today. But – perhaps because McCawley recommended its publication in the USA – this did more to advance my reputation in linguistics than any other volume.

This was a period when work in semantics as a sub-field of linguistics was developing extremely quickly. In the USA, it was the era of the dispute between generative semantics and interpretative semantics. My thinking was more attuned to the generative semantics school, but at the same time I tried to developed my own theory, based on autonomous semantic and syntactic representations, linked by mapping rules.

Another important facet of my academic career in 1962–9 was a close association with the Survey of English Usage: a research centre founded by Randolph Quirk in 1959, and attached to my department at UCL. The most important part of the Survey's work was the compilation of a large corpus of modern English texts, both spoken and written. Three of Quirk's leading researchers in the early years of the Survey were David Crystal, Jan Svartvik and Sidney Greenbaum. Svartvik and Greenbaum later collaborated with Quirk and me as co-authors of *A Grammar of Contemporary English* (*GCE*), a detailed descriptive grammar of the language (Quirk et al. 1972).

The grammar was a large enterprise, drawing on the accumulating work of the Survey of English Usage. We felt at that time that there was a big gap between the type of academic, theory-driven grammar that was studied in linguistics departments, and the type of grammar which was needed for the English language classroom. In the study of English grammar, there was a consequent need for mediation between theory and pedagogy. It was this reconciliation that *GCE* tried to achieve.

4 ESTABLISHING A NEW DEPARTMENT AT LANCASTER UNIVERSITY: 1969–74

In 1969, I applied for the post of Senior Lecturer at the new University of Lancaster. After my appointment to this post, Lancaster became my permanent 'academic home' and even today (2001), it remains the university which pays my salary as a part-time research professor.

During my early years at Lancaster, much of my research time was spent on the collaboration with Quirk, Greenbaum and Svartvik on *GCE*. However, I also found time to continue my work on semantics, with the publication of *Meaning and the English Verb* (1971) and *Semantics* (1974) – both books that have subsequently been published in a second, revised edition.

After *GCE* was published in 1972, the four authors decided, with the agreement of the publishers, to write two advanced students' grammars based on the approach of the larger work. One of them, written by Quirk and Greenbaum, was in effect a shorter version of *GCE*, entitled *A University Grammar of English* (1973). The other, written by Svartvik and me, was *A Communicative Grammar of English* (1975). In this book we tried to develop a somewhat fresh approach to English grammar, based on the idea that grammar, to be useful to the learner, should be 'communicative' in the sense of relating the forms and structures of language to their meaning and use. This became a popular book, and has since also been published in a revised edition (1994).

Lancaster University had been founded in 1964, and during my early years there the university was growing at a rapid rate. New buildings were being erected, new departments founded, new disciplines established. Student numbers rose, and this gave us the opportunity to develop the study of linguistics almost by stealth, within the English Department. I was head of the 'Linguistics Section', as we called ourselves, and in 1974 this became the Department of Linguistics and Modern English Language, one of the three constituent departments of a new entity called the School of English. With the new Department established, I was promoted to the post of Professor of Linguistics and Modern English Language. At about that time, also, we began to offer linguistics as a major undergraduate subject: Lancaster was one of the first British universities (*the* first?) to offer a BA in linguistics.

5 THE BEGINNINGS OF COMPUTER CORPUS LINGUISTICS: 1970–8

As early as 1970, before linguistics became a separate department, the small group of young linguists at Lancaster got together round a table, and considered how Lancaster could make its mark in the world as a new centre for research. I suggested we should develop a computer corpus of British English, one which would match in every possible respect the Brown University Corpus of American English, which had recently been completed and distributed: the first computer corpus of modern English. Like the Brown Corpus, the 'Lancaster Corpus' would consist of 1,000,000 words of various registers of written (printed) English. As its director, I found this project frustrating and time-consuming. Our computing facilities were primitive. We received some financial help from Longman and later from the British Academy, but the money was soon used up. There were also great and apparently insuperable problems of copyright. In 1976 I was about to abandon the whole project, but a former student of Jan Svartvik, Stig Johansson, offered to take the project to Norway (where he had recently obtained a post), to complete the corpus there. At last, in 1978, this corpus of written British English was completed, through the combined efforts of three universities: Lancaster, Oslo and Bergen. The Lancaster–Oslo–Bergen Corpus (or the LOB Corpus, as it soon became) has since been widely used throughout the world, alongside the Brown Corpus.

In the previous year, 1977, a group of English language specialists including Randolph Quirk, Jan Svartvik, Stig Johansson and myself met in Oslo and founded the International Computer Archive of Modern English (ICAME), an organization to develop and promote the use of computer corpora in English language research. Curiously enough, the original impetus for this initiative was the need to achieve copyright clearance for the LOB Corpus. To persuade the London publishers and other copyright holders to grant free copyright permission (which was all we could afford), it helped to have an address in Norway rather than provincial Lancaster, and to write as 'Secretary General of the International Computer Archive of English Texts'. This gambit succeeded, and more importantly, ICAME (now re-entitled the International Computer Archive of Modern *and Medieval* English Texts) has continued to flourish, as an organ for the promotion of corpus-based research. It has an annual conference, a journal (*ICAME Journal*) and a dissemination service, based in Bergen. During its lifetime, the use of computer corpora, from being a fringe activity, has become a mainstream methodology, both in computational linguistics and in English language research. Only in theoretical linguistics has the use of a computer corpus remained suspect.

6 OTHER ACTIVITIES AND PUBLICATIONS: 1976–87

In 1977 I finished my three-year stint as the first Head of the Department of Linguistics and Modern English Language (a post I have managed to evade since that time).

One new research interest had already been developing in the mid-1970s from my earlier work in semantics. This was the study of pragmatics, then a fast-growing and new area of research in linguistics, enlivened by the controversies about meaning which had dominated linguistics around 1970, as well as by the work of philosophers such as J. L. Austin and H. P. Grice.

In 1976 and 1977 I published a number of papers on the border between pragmatics and semantics – indeed, a recurrent theme of these papers was that there *was* necessarily such a borderline. These I eventually revised to make a book *Explorations in Semantics and Pragmatics* (1980). Dealing with themes such as metalanguage, performatives and politeness, the book was transitional and inconclusive: it showed a train of thought beginning in semantics and ending in pragmatics. As work progressed, I felt that pragmatics needed tackling by a separate, full-scale study. This was finally published as *Principles of Pragmatics* (1983). Perhaps the best-known part of this book is that where I develop a theory of politeness, a theme which had begun earlier in a paper, *Language and Tact* (1977). This was also the theme which Brown and Levinson were developing at that time, in a more universal way, through their theory of politeness, which has since been the most influential model in the field (1978, revised 1987).

At the same time, I worked with a Lancaster colleague, Mick Short, on a book dealing with literary stylistics: *Style in Fiction* (Leech & Short 1981). This was a return to an area that had stimulated my earlier book *A Linguistic Guide to English Poetry*, and in fact we began by thinking of the two books as companion volumes. Like the earlier book, *Style in Fiction* was intended to be a course book for students, but it was also an attempt to develop a theory of prose style. It grew out of the teaching of stylistics to undergraduates, which Mick Short and I had shared for several years.

Soon after this I was writing, again in collaboration with departmental colleagues, a book entitled *English Grammar for Today: A New Introduction* (Leech et al. 1982). The book was actually commissioned by the English Association, a national body which at that time was concerned about a decline in the study of grammar in British schools. However, the book succeeded more in other parts of the world than in Great Britain. It seems that the British educational world, or at least students, were not yet entirely ready for the notion that grammar was worth studying. (This sentence would remain true if changed into the present tense.)

I was getting used to co-authorship. My experience has always been that a co-authored book is more difficult to write (because of difficulties of negotiating with co-authors), but is more satisfactory in the end. *English Grammar for Today* was the third book I had co-written on English grammar. Then, in 1985, came yet another co-authored grammar – much larger even than *GCE*. From about 1978, the 'gang of four' (as the Quirk et al. team was familiarly called) began work on a second edition of *GCE*. Since *GCE* had been published in 1972, ideas on grammar, and knowledge of English grammar, had moved forward considerably. Moreover, *GCE* had received many reviews, which detailed both its strengths and weaknesses. We authors felt ready, then, to embark an updated edition of the grammar. When we started work on it, however, we found ourselves rewriting the whole book, changing its organization, and introducing much additional material based on the Survey of English Usage experience. The second edition of *GCE* evolved into a new grammar, more grandly named *A Comprehensive Grammar of the English Language* (*CGEL*) (Quirk et al. 1985).

In the initial stages of working on this new grammar, three of the 'gang of four' were secretly producing a Festschrift honouring its leading member, Randolph Quirk. The book was published (Greenbaum et al. 1980), with contributions from distinguished linguists and English language scholars in various parts of the world. Unfortunately we failed to keep the secret until the day of publication: the sharp observation of Randolph sensed that 'something was up' a few months before the book was due to be published.

Perhaps my part in *CGEL* may be deemed to be the summit of my career. The book made a big impact, and began to be treated as 'the authority' on English grammar.

7 LATER CORPUS RESEARCH: 1978–2001

Let me return to the computational work in which I had been engaged on and off since 1970. In the late 1970s, the computational analysis and annotation of computer corpora of English became my main research preoccupation. This has continued ever since: we still have at Lancaster a small team of researchers, working in, or linked to, a research centre entitled UCREL. My chief collaborator in this research has been Roger Garside, of the Computing Department at Lancaster.

After the completion in 1978 of the computer corpus of British English, the LOB Corpus, we were lucky enough to win a research grant from the Social Science Research Council (now the ESRC) to undertake an *automatic grammatical tagging* of the corpus. That is, every word in the million-word corpus was to be assigned a tag indicating its grammatical category, and complex computer programs had to be written for this purpose. We completed the task in 1983, with the collaboration of Stig Johansson and his team based in Oslo, Norway. The software then developed – the tagger CLAWS1 – was the first tagger to employ a statistical algorithm, similar to that of a Hidden Markov Model. This has now become a commonplace method of grammatical tagging; but at the time it was discovered (by one of our researchers, Ian Marshall) we felt that a sudden breakthrough had been achieved. Success in automatic tagging leaped from *c.*77 per cent to *c.*96 per cent. We were able to achieve this by using the Brown Corpus (which had been previously tagged by Greene & Rubin 1971) as a *training corpus* – that is, CLAWS learned its frequencies from the Brown Corpus, and then applied them to the LOB Corpus, which in current parlance would now be called the *test corpus*. This was another important advance of a kind: as far as I know, we were the first team to employ (without knowing it) the distinction between a 'training corpus' and a 'test corpus', now another commonplace of corpus-based natural language processing methodology.

During the 1970s and 1980s, the use of computer corpora for linguistic research was becoming accepted by a small group of researchers in the UK, and the research councils were beginning to respond to the need for funding to support programmers and other research staff.

Our next piece of good fortune (in 1983–6) was a grant from the Science and Engineering Research Council (now the EPSRC), with which we tackled the more complex task of *automatically parsing* a corpus. In this case we had no training corpus – the Brown Corpus had not been parsed – so we had to create our own training corpus by hand. A senior colleague at Lancaster at that time, Geoffrey Sampson, had become fascinated by corpus research, and was the first person to build a *treebank* – that is, a corpus, or part of a corpus, annotated for sentence structure. (Soon afterwards, Sampson left Lancaster for Leeds and then Sussex, where he developed his own treebanking research.) The term 'treebank' – which I believe I invented – has since become established in computational linguistics. However, the automatic parsing task proved to be more difficult than we had imagined, and by 1990, only 13 per cent of the LOB Corpus had been accurately parsed, using statistical methods. To do this more successfully, we would have needed a much bigger treebank, a better model of syntax, and more powerful computing facilities.

The task of automatic parsing of unrestricted text data – which is, generally, what the syntactic annotation of a corpus amounts to – was a tough nut to crack, and indeed even now, in the year 2001, the problems of automatic corpus parsing (or 'robust parsing') have not been solved. There was obviously a need for larger teams to tackle this important area of computational research, and in 1987 we were approached by a group led by Fred Jelinek, at the IBM Thomas J. Watson Research Centre, Yorktown Heights, New York, to engage in collaborative research funded by IBM. The IBM team was at that time leading the way in developing new technology for speech recognizers, and was also blazing a trail in new and highly sophisticated statistical methods, making use of enormous electronic text collections of 300 million words or more. Lancaster was the first to develop, during this collaboration, large-scale treebanks of three or four million words, from which more adequate statistics, and hence more accurate parsing results, could be obtained. However, our work was superseded, in the 1990s, by more advanced work by Mitchell Marcus's group at the University of Pennsylvania, and the term 'treebank' nowadays is more associated with the 'Penn Treebank' created by Marcus and his team in the 1990s (Marcus et al. 1993) than with the IBM/Lancaster treebank created in the late 1980s. However, one book on statistical parsing did come out of our collaboration with IBM: Black, Garside & Leech (1993).

During the 1990s UCREL continued to win grants for research projects.

This was a time when, it seemed to me, the opportunities of corpus-oriented research were opening up left, right and centre. After word tagging and parsing, other areas such as semantic tagging, anaphoric annotation and parallel corpus alignment were ripe for exploitation. Although our work with Yorktown Heights ceased in 1991, other projects continued: with a market research firm, with a telecommunications institute (ATR Kyoto), with the publishers Longman and Oxford University Press. In some ways it was refreshing to work with private enterprise, sidestepping the intense competition for public research council grants. But industrial and commercial collaboration brought severe pressures and constraints of their own, particularly the need to 'deliver on time' according to contract, whatever problems might have been turned up by our research.

The largest project in which I was involved during this period was the British National Corpus (1991–5), a collaborative project between three publishers (Oxford University Press, Longman and Chambers), two universities (Oxford and Lancaster) and one national institution, the British Library. Here, again, the pressures of tackling something previously unattempted were very considerable, and the result was a 100-million-word corpus of spoken and written British English, completed 12 months later than scheduled, and in far from perfect condition. Nevertheless, the BNC was an important national achievement, and the British lead has since been followed by other countries. Only now is an American National Corpus being planned (on similar lines to the BNC, but predictably, bigger and better).

Also during the 1990s my colleagues Garside and McEnery were engaged, with me, in research sponsored by the European Union. This was a time when the 'corpus revolution' had taken off internationally, and there was a big push to capture and annotate the data of other languages, apart from English, in computer corpora. We were involved, with continental partners, with the development of parallel (i.e. mutual translation) corpora of English, French and Spanish. Also, as a participant in the EAGLES initiative, I took a co-ordinating role (e.g. in Grice et al. 2000) in proposing guidelines for corpus annotation for European languages. Between 1993 and 1999, we engaged in three different assignments of this kind, concerned respectively with word-class tagging, syntactic annotation, and dialogue representation and annotation.

8 THE CONTINUING IMPACT OF CORPUS LINGUISTICS ON MY OWN
  CAREER: 1986–99

It will be clear that by this stage I had become deeply engaged in computer corpus work, which has a tendency to monopolize the research time of anyone who becomes seriously involved in it. This work is very satisfying from some points of view: collaborating in a team of like-minded researchers is something which is normal for scientists, but both novel and stimulating for scholars trained in arts or social sciences. The excitement of blazing a trail in a new and fast-developing area of research has been a second benefit. Another has been that corpus research has enabled UCREL to build a network of international links with scholars and computer scientists with similar interests. The corpus linguistics world now forms a well-established research community, with links to many parts of the world.

On the other hand, corpus work has disadvantages: a considerably amount of it is painstaking 'donkey work', rather than challenging investigation. The labour-intensive nature of this work has meant that I have had to put on the shelf some of the research interests I used to be involved in – notably stylistics and pragmatics. Much time is also spent seeking funds from research sponsors, so that research staff can remain in post. Moreover, because of the team-built nature of corpus research, there is less room for individual research initiative. Research tends to be steadily incremental, in contrast to the breakthroughs of the early days of corpus research. The pioneering days are over, and as resources and software become more generally available, we appear to be overtaken by the 'big battalions' – departments and teams, whether in the USA, the UK or elsewhere, better endowed in terms of funding, equipment and staff. In the computational world, we are now a relatively small fish in a big pond.

In terms of publications, four edited collections on computational linguistic topics were the most visible fruit of UCREL research in the period 1986 to 1997: Leech & Candlin (1986), Garside, Leech & Sampson (1987), Leech, Myers & Thomas (1995), and Garside, Leech & McEnery (1997).

As I move on into my mid-sixties, I have been extricating myself gently from the pressures of running large-scale research projects and large-scale research teams. At the moment, I am involved in two relatively small but new kinds of corpus projects. One project, supported by the EPSRC, is a pragmatic annotation (on the level of speech acts) of a corpus of dialogues. The other is a comparison of two corpora (the LOB and FLOB [Freiburg–Lancaster–Oslo–Bergen] corpora) representing written English in 1961 and 1991, enabling us to trace diachrony in English grammar over the intervening 30-year period. The project, supported by the Arts and Humanities Research Board (AHRB), enables me to do what I think I do best – which is descriptive study of the English language, rather than leading-edge language technology.

My latest major collaborative publication (Biber et al. 1999) has capitalized on both this descriptive research background, and my growing experience of quantitative methods in the study of language: it is another large-scale English grammar, based on corpus research in a much more thorough way than the previous co-authored grammars GCE and CGEL, and focusing on the quantitative comparison of contrasting varieties of spoken and written English.

Recently I have become 'typecast' as a computational grammarian. But I still hope that, in my remaining years at Lancaster, I will have the opportunity to return to stylistics and pragmatics – two other areas of research I have found to be both challenging and fulfilling.

REFERENCES

BIBER, DOUGLAS, JOHANSSON, STIG, LEECH, GEOFFREY, CONRAD, SUSAN & FINEGAN, EDWARD, 1999. *Longman Grammar of Spoken and Written English*, London: Longman.
BLACK, EZRA, GARSIDE, ROGER & LEECH, GEOFFREY, (eds.) 1993. *Statistically-Driven Computer Grammars of English: The IBM/Lancaster Approach*, Amsterdam: Rodopi.
BROWN, PENNY & LEVINSON, STEVEN C., 1978. 'Politeness: some universals in language usage', in E. N. Goody (ed.), *Questions and Politeness: Strategies in Social Interaction*, Cambridge: Cambridge University Press, 56–310. Rev. and pub. as an independent vol. by P. Brown & S. C. Levinson, *Politeness: Some Universals in Language Usage*, Cambridge: Cambridge University Press.
GARSIDE, ROGER, LEECH, GEOFFREY & McENERY, ANTHONY, (eds.) 1997. *Corpus Annotation: Linguistic Information from Computer Text Corpora*, London: Longman.
GARSIDE, ROGER, LEECH, GEOFFREY & SAMPSON, GEOFFREY, 1987. *The Computational Analysis of English: A Corpus-Based Approach*, London: Longman.
GREENBAUM, SIDNEY, LEECH, GEOFFREY & SVARTVIK, JAN, (eds.) 1980. *Studies in English Linguistics: For Randolph Quirk*, London: Longman.
GREENE, B. & RUBIN, G., 1971. *Automatic Grammatical Tagging of English*, Providence, RI: Brown University, Linguistics Department.
GRICE, MARTINE, LEECH, GEOFFREY, WEISSER, MARTIN & WILSON, ANDREW. 2000. 'Representation and annotation of dialogue', in Dafydd Gibbon, Inge Mertins & Roger K. Moore (eds.), *Handbook of Multimodal and Spoken Dialogue Systems: Resources, Terminology and Product Evaluation*, Boston: Kluwer, 1–101.
HALLIDAY, M. A. K., 1961. 'Categories of the theory of grammar', *Word* 17.3, 241–92.
LEECH, GEOFFREY, 1966. *English in Advertising: A Linguistic Study of Advertising in Great Britain*, London: Longman.
LEECH, GEOFFREY, 1969a. *A Linguistic Guide to English Poetry*, London: Longman.
LEECH, GEOFFREY, 1969b. *Towards a Semantic Description of English*, London: Longman.
LEECH, GEOFFREY, 1971. *Meaning and the English Verb*, 2nd ed. 1987, London: Longman.
LEECH, GEOFFREY, 1974. *Semantics*, 2nd ed. 1981, Harmondsworth: Penguin.
LEECH, GEOFFREY, 1977. *Language and Tact*, Series A, Paper No. 46, Trier: Linguistic Agency University of Trier.
LEECH, GEOFFREY, 1980. *Explorations in Semantics and Pragmatics*, Amsterdam: John Benjamins.
LEECH, GEOFFREY, 1983. *Principles of Pragmatics*, London: Longman.
LEECH, GEOFFREY & CANDLIN, CHRISTOPHER, (eds.) 1986. *Computers in English Language Teaching and Research*, London: Longman.
LEECH, GEOFFREY & SHORT, MICHAEL, 1981. *Style in Fiction: A Linguistic Introduction to English Fictional Prose*, London: Longman.
LEECH, GEOFFREY & SVARTVIK, JAN, 1975. *A Communicative Grammar of English*, 2nd ed. 1994, London: Longman.
LEECH, GEOFFREY, HOOGENRAAD, ROBERT & DEUCHAR, MARGARET, 1982. *English Grammar for Today: A New Introduction*, London: Macmillan.
LEECH, GEOFFREY, MYERS, GREG, & THOMAS, JENNY, (eds.) 1995. *Spoken English on Computer: Transcription, Mark-up and Application*, London: Longman.
MARCUS, M., SANTORINI, B. & MARCINKIEWICZ, M., 1993. 'Building a large annotated corpus of English: the Penn Treebank', *Computational Linguistics* 19.2, 313–30.

NOWOTTNY, WINIFRED, 1962. *The Language Poets Use*, London: Athlone Press.

QUIRK, RANDOLPH & GREENBAUM, SIDNEY, 1973. *A University Grammar of English*, London: Longman.

QUIRK, RANDOLPH, GREENBAUM, SIDNEY, LEECH, GEOFFREY & SVARTVIK, JAN, 1972. *A Grammar of Contemporary English*, London: Longman.

QUIRK, RANDOLPH, GREENBAUM, SIDNEY, LEECH, GEOFFREY & SVARTVIK, JAN, 1985. *A Comprehensive Grammar of the English Language*, London: Longman.

JOHN LYONS

LYONS, John, Kt 1987, FBA 1973; *b.* 1932; *m.* 1959, Danielle J. Simonet, 2 d; *Education:* St Bede's College, Manchester; Christ's College, Cambridge; MA, PhD 1961, LittD 1988; *Career:* Lecturer in Comparative Linguistics, SOAS, 1957–61; Lecturer in General Linguistics, University of Cambridge, 1961–4; Professor of General Linguistics, Edinburgh University, 1964–76; Sussex University: Professor of Linguistics 1976–84, Pro-Vice-Chancellor 1981–4, Master of Trinity Hall, Cambridge, 1984–2000; DèsL *h.c.* University Catholique de Louvain, 1980; Hon. LittD: Reading 1986; Edinburgh 1988; Sussex 1990; Antwerp 1992. *Major Publications: Structural Semantics* 1964; *Introduction to Theoretical Linguistics* 1968; *New Horizons in Linguistics* 1970; *Chomsky* 1970 [3rd ed. 1991]; *Semantics, Volumes 1 and 2* 1977; *Language and Linguistics* 1981; *Language, Meaning and Context* 1981; *Natural Language and Universal Grammar* 1991; *Linguistic Semantics* 1995.

* * *

1

It is an honour and a privilege to have been invited to contribute to this volume of 'personal histories'. I must confess immediately, however, that I was initially very reluctant to participate in the venture. Principal among the reasons for my reluctance was the feeling that there was little that I could say that I have not said elsewhere over the years: in the prefaces to several of my books; in the updated notes to the republished articles in volume 1 of my *Essays in Linguistic Theory* (1991b); in my contribution to the symposium celebrating the 150th anniversary of the foundation of the Philological Society (published in *Transactions 1999*); and in the chapter I wrote for the Festschrift in my honour published by Cambridge University Press in 1991 (Palmer 1991).

It so happens that, when the time for preparing this particular 'personal history' arrived, I was about to retire from my post as Master of Trinity Hall, which I had held for 16 years, and from Cambridge. Having been heavily involved in college affairs throughout this period, in the last few years I had given up teaching and had published nothing. I was all too conscious of how out of touch I had become with what was going on in linguistics. This was brought home to me with special vividness in my final year at Cambridge. This was the year in which Trinity Hall celebrated the 650th anniversary of its foundation and, as part of the programme of events celebrating this 'milestone' in its history, the college organized a series of 'Milestones Lectures' on a range of subjects in both the arts and the sciences. It fell to me, ex officio, to deliver the first of these. The title I gave it was, unsurprisingly, 'Milestones in language and milestones in linguistics'. As I remarked at the time, it was the last formal lecture that I would give before retirement and thus marked officially, for me at least, the end of my academic career. Both the topic and the occasion inevitably encouraged, and indeed obliged, me to adopt, throughout the lecture, but especially at the beginning and at the end, a retrospective stance. Retrospection promoted introspection; and introspection, as always perhaps, but more particularly at this point in my life, induced a feeling of dissatisfaction and of personal inadequacy. Why had I not been able to continue to contribute as actively to the development of my subject, in teaching and publication, towards the end of my career as I was widely acknowledged to have done in an earlier period? The question was one that troubled me at the time; and it still troubles me, even more perhaps, as I set out to write the present 'personal history'. It is a question that I will not seek to answer directly, but some of what I have to say below will be relevant to the answer.

2

Like many of those of my generation, I came into what we now think of as linguistics – the scientific study of language – via classics, including for some of us, classical philology: i.e. the comparative and historical study of Greek and Latin. At school, where I had a very traditional grammar school education (on the 'classical' rather than the 'modern' side), I had studied not only Greek and Latin, but also (though not to the same standard) French and German. I was well taught and had always been interested in grammar and what was often referred to as the mechanics of language.

I went up to Cambridge as an undergraduate in 1950 to read classics. When it came to choosing my special subject for Part II of the degree in my third year, it was almost inevitably the philology option – 'Group E' – that I chose. This was never one of the most popular options, and there were only six of us who took it in my year. We also continued with our study of Greek and Latin literature, the history of Greece and Rome and (ancient) philosophy, which, together with translation into and out of the classical languages, were the subjects we had studied for the preceding two years for Part I. The fact that my education, at school and university, was so thoroughly – and so narrowly – classical conditioned much of my subsequent intellectual development and, in due course, my attitude towards particular issues in linguistic theory.

But let me say a little more about my undergraduate training in comparative philology. More important perhaps than the content of the courses was the fact that our teachers were so enthusiastic about their subject and, whether they deliberately sought this effect or not, communicated this enthusiasm to us. Since there were so few of us, the classes were more like seminars than lectures. I should add in passing that in addition to the six 'normal' undergraduates, there was also a graduate student in the group – technically an 'affiliated student' – from New Zealand, who unlike the rest of us already had some background in classical philology. His presence and his ability to ask informed questions undoubtedly encouraged the adoption of what I have called a seminar format, from which we all benefited. This was the late Robert G. G. ('Bob') Coleman, who subsequently made his own scholarly contribution to the field and in due course was appointed to the Chair of Comparative Philology in Cambridge.

The Professor of Comparative Philology at the time – N. B. Jopson – was very different. I think it is fair to say that 'Joppy' (as he was known) was no longer actively involved in research and had long abandoned any attempt to keep up with developments in either general linguistics (for which he was also responsible) or classical philology. But he was lively, amusing and inspirational. By contrast, our other two principal teachers, as well as being equally inspirational, were very much involved in their own fields of research. Sir Harold Bailey (as he later became), who taught us Sanskrit, was by then acknowledged to be one of the world's leading authorities in Indo-Iranian. I did not know this, of course, until later. His erudition was, I think, evident to all of us, though he never paraded this or revealed it gratuitously. What impressed me as an undergraduate was, on the one hand, his kindness and gentleness of manner and, on the other, his total commitment to a life of scholarship.

The other person that we were privileged to have as one of our 'Group E' teachers was John Chadwick. It was he who conducted the classes in Ancient Greek dialects (from a historical and comparative point of view). He had been collaborating with Michael Ventris on the decipherment of Linear B; and he introduced into his lectures a brief non-technical account of the nature of the Minoan syllabary and of the implications of the decipherment for the history of Early Greek. Unless I am mistaken, this was just before or just after Easter in 1953 and preceded the first public announcement of the decipherment. Needless to say, we were all thrilled to be privy to what was, even to neophytes like us, such an outstanding and revolutionary scientific achievement.

3

So much for my formal induction into linguistics – as an Indo-Europeanist, specializing in the history of Greek and Latin, with a smattering of Sanskrit, and just a little knowledge of (largely outdated) general linguistic theory.

I had always intended to go into schoolteaching and in the following year I took the postgraduate Diploma in Education. As part of the course, I did one term of teaching practice, which I very much enjoyed, but during that term I decided that I was more interested in teaching at university level. At the end of the year, encouraged and supported by my Tutor, at Christ's College, the late Sir John Plumb, I applied to the Ministry of Education for the extension of my state scholarship and to the Classical Faculty in Cambridge for admission as a PhD student. But before returning to Cambridge, I had to do two years of military service. Given that I had a first class degree in what was judged to be a relevant field of study, like many others with a similar educational background, I was accepted by the Navy for training as a Russian interpreter. This meant that I spent 20 of the 24 months learning Russian intensively (and less than three weeks on board ship!) and at the end of my period of 'active' service, like my peers, had a very good knowledge of the language.

I had given some thought to a possible topic of research and done some preliminary reading before I went into the Navy. As an undergraduate, I had been enamoured of Plato: this is one way of putting it; perhaps I should say that I had been enchanted or bewitched by Plato, especially as he appears in the early Socratic dialogues. I had also been well taught, as far as Greek philosophy is concerned, by my college supervisor, the late Arthur Peck, well known to classicists for his editions of Aristotle's biological works. He too was a committed and inspirational teacher – and delightfully eccentric – and should certainly be mentioned in this context. I do not now remember how exactly I came to choose what eventually became the subject of my PhD research: the vocabulary of knowledge and understanding in the works of Plato. If there had not been any interval between my undergraduate and my post-graduate career, it would have been natural for me to choose a topic in the field of comparative philology. But this interval, as it turned out, was of crucial importance.

Professor Jopson retired in 1954 and was succeeded by W. Sidney Allen. It was therefore the latter whom I consulted in the year before I came back to Cambridge. When I went to see him for the first time, I told him that I was thinking of working on the meaning of certain words in Plato, but from a linguistic rather than a philosophical point of view. He asked me what I meant by 'meaning'. It soon became clear that I did not even know that the very concept of meaning in language was theoretically or methodologically problematical. He then gave me what was, I suppose, my first lesson in structural linguistics. It included an introduction to the ideas of Saussure, on the one hand, and to J. R. Firth's notions of čollocation and context of situation, on the other. I think he also mentioned Zellig Harris's *Methods in Structural Linguistics* and his papers on discourse analysis and distributional structure, but this may have been at a later meeting. However that may be, by the time I returned to Cambridge as a PhD student in October 1956, he had agreed to act as my supervisor and, under his guidance, I had done enough background reading for me to get started, more or less straightaway, on my research.

Sidney Allen was the ideal supervisor: patient and encouraging; always ready to see me and read my drafts at short notice; constructively critical; drawing my attention to books and articles that he thought would be helpful. It was he who first mentioned to me Chomsky's *Syntactic Structures* in the early summer of 1957. This proved to be a turning point. It provided me with the theoretical justification for abandoning my methodological commitment to the 'discovery procedures' with which I had been operating: these had been yielding intuitively suggestive, but frustratingly inconclusive and only partial, results. It also provided me with the technical apparatus of Chomsky's version of transformational-generative grammar, to which I could appeal in the formulation of the structural relations of meaning among the words in which I was interested. At the time, this was the principal reason why Chomsky's work was important to me: it helped me to resolve the theoretical and methodological problems I was having with my research. At a later stage of my career, I developed a broader interest in generative grammar.

4

At the end of my first year as a research student, I had the good fortune to be appointed to a Lectureship at the School of Oriental and African Studies in London. Had this not happened, I would have gone to the United States to take up the one-year Rockefeller Fellowship which I had been awarded, tenable in my case at the University of Yale. But university posts in linguistics were few and far between in Britain in the mid-to-late 1950s. I could not take the risk of not seizing the opportunity that was offered.

By going to SOAS (in October 1957) I had secured my future as a university teacher. Given that this was so, I was tempted to discontinue my PhD research. In those days, a PhD was by no means a *sine qua non* either of one's first appointment to a tenured post or of subsequent promotion. My research topic was totally unconnected with the subject for which I now had responsibility as a teacher. From the point of view of career advancement, it might have seemed more sensible therefore to concentrate on comparative linguistics. Be that as it may, I decided to continue with my Cambridge PhD. Since I was no longer resident in Cambridge and I was required to have a local supervisor, R. H. Robins took over from Sidney Allen in this role. They had been colleagues for several years in the same department at SOAS. Indeed, Sidney Allen had previously held the Lectureship to which I had just been appointed. 'Bobby'

Robins, as I learned to call him much later, was also a superbly conscientious and helpful supervisor. As I said in the preface to the published version of my dissertation (*Structural Semantics*, 1963): 'It was Professor Allen who first kindled my interest in linguistics and directed my attention to much of the fundamental literature in the subject in the year in which I was working under his supervision in Cambridge. Mr. Robins supervised my research in London for nearly three years and upon him fell the main burden of reading and criticizing my work in its various stages of completion.'

Actually, 'completion' was not really the right word. My research was never completed (is any PhD research project ever completed?); nor even was the writing up of the results of the research that I had done. It was abruptly terminated and brought to a pseudo-conclusion, because it had to be submitted, typed and bound, by 30 September 1960 under pain of rejection, or so I thought at the time. The fact that the writing up of my dissertation was not concluded, but merely terminated, is self-evident, though not explicitly mentioned, even in the ('slightly revised') published version: the final section (7.3), devoted to the meaning of '*sophos*' and '*sophia*', is only one-and-a-half pages long! Ever since terminating my research on the vocabulary of Plato, I have cherished the nostalgic ambition of continuing from the point at which I left off. So far, with other demands and pressures, in my later career, this has not proved possible.

I had been greatly relieved when my thesis had been accepted for my Cambridge PhD and enormously encouraged (and surprised) that it had been so highly commended by my examiners, the late Professors Stephen Ullmann and John Brough, to whom I here record my gratitude: both of them were tolerant as examiners and very kind and supportive in my later career. The thesis was published by the Philological Society as one of the occasional Special Publications associated with *Transactions* and I was surprised, but delighted, that what proved to be my first book was so well received. It was quite widely reviewed by representatives of several disciplines, including philosophy and anthropology, as well as classics and linguistics.

5

But let me now return to my time at SOAS. What effect did my experience there have on my views on linguistics and on my later career? There is no need to emphasize that the Department of Phonetics and Linguistics at SOAS, built up by Professor J. R. Firth, was, by then, without question, the best department of linguistics in Britain. Firth himself had just retired from the Chair, but the ethos was still, both doctrinally and in its *modus operandi*, distinctively 'Firthian'.

Firth's successor in the Chair, Charles E. Bazell, was just about as different from Firth as it was possible to be and, as far as I know, made no attempt to introduce any organizational changes in the Department. He gave the weekly professorial intercollegiate lecture on Wednesdays at 11 a.m., as Firth had done for many years, and he participated in the weekly staff seminars on Friday at the same hour. But, I think it is fair to say, this was about the extent of his active involvement. He had none the less a very great influence on me, as I have acknowledged on many occasions, in print and orally

Apart from me (the most junior), Bazell (officially and by title the most senior) was the only member of staff who had not been a colleague of Firth's and in most cases appointed and trained by him: we were both, in this sense, outsiders – and conscious of it. It so happened also that, when I went to SOAS in October 1957, not only had Bazell already read *Syntactic Structures*, but he had been for some considerable time engaged in correspondence about it with Chomsky. By then, as I have explained, I was, for my own research purposes, a Chomskian. This meant that Bazell and I spent a lot of time discussing Chomsky's theory of syntax. Almost immediately, he asked me to review *Syntactic Structures* for *Litera*, a journal that he had founded during the many years he had spent in Istanbul and which he continued to edit. I should perhaps add for the record that this review of *Syntactic Structures* was my first publication and, to the best of my knowledge, was the first review of the book to be published in any of the linguistics journals, even though it was published in a journal that most linguists had never even heard of and was almost inaccessible!

I learned a lot from Bazell, both from his lectures and in conversation. He was one of the most knowledgeable and one of the cleverest linguists I have ever met. He was also widely read in the linguistically relevant branches of logic and the philosophy of language. To be in his company, for someone in my position, was an educational experience. I have elsewhere attributed to Bazell's instruction (formal and informal) such understanding of glossematics and (perhaps to a smaller degree) of Prague School structuralism as I have. But there is much else that I learned from him. As I (and others) have often said, it is sad that he did not publish more and that what he did publish was not more readily comprehensible, especially to those who had not had the benefit of personal acquaintance with him.

My formal induction, as a new staff member, into the Department of Phonetics and Linguistics at SOAS was not limited to attendance at the weekly staff seminars and Bazell's lectures. Until then I had had no systematic and comprehensive training in general and descriptive linguistics (to use the terms that were current at the time). What we were taught as undergraduates by 'Joppy' was ancillary to Indo-European and classical philology and, in many respects, out of date. During my year as a postgraduate student at Cambridge, I went to some of Sidney Allen's lectures on general linguistics (and, as I have recorded elsewhere, I was greatly influenced by his inaugural lecture, which shocked so many of the traditionalists). But my knowledge of modern linguistics when I went to SOAS was sketchy: it was also unbalanced, in the sense that it was biased towards its relevance or applicability to my research. It was one of the requirements of my appointment that I should attend the courses that were being given for postgraduate students: in particular, the lectures on general linguistics by Robins and the lectures (and practicals) given by N. C. Scott on phonetics. It soon turned out that, unlike everyone else in the Department (with the possible exception of my fellow maverick, Bazell), I had little aptitude for phonetics. This, if anything, increased my respect and admiration for those who had; and I did learn enough, on the theoretical level at least, to be able to acquire some understanding of 'prosodic analysis' and to follow the presentations given in the staff seminars.

The lectures given by Robins were more relevant to my interests. Although very much a 'Firthian', he took a broader view of linguistics than most of the other senior members of the Department, many of whom (or so it seemed to me) shared Firth's theoretical prejudices. Some idea of the content of his lectures, as I remember them, can be got from the textbook he published a few years later (*General Linguistics*, 1964). At the time, they provided me with my first systematic and comprehensive introduction to modern linguistics and helped me to put my own ideas into a broader context. A few years later, when I was appointed to my first post in general linguistics (at Cambridge), they served as a model, in outline and outlook if not in detail, for my own lectures.

6

In the late summer of 1960, I went to the United States to take day-to-day charge, for a year, of a machine translation project at Indiana University. I had been invited by Fred W. Householder, the 'Chief Investigator'. I had met him in London, but his invitation came out of the blue and at short notice. I assume that Bazell had recommended me to Householder and had told him that I had already had some relevant experience. I had worked for part of the summer of 1959 as a consultant on a machine translation project at the National Physical Laboratory in Teddington. This latter project, unlike Householder's, was concerned directly and specifically with the translation of Russian into English. I had been recruited because of my expertise in both Russian and linguistics, which was lacking in the group of full-time researchers: they were all electronic engineers.

My year at Indiana proved to be an ideal complement to the preceding three years at SOAS and equally formative as far as my induction into linguistics is concerned. Most of the working day was spent on the supervision of the research project for which I had been engaged. There was a certain amount of rather tiresome administration, including the writing of quarterly reports for our paymasters, the US Air Force, and the preparation of an application for a renewal of the contract. One of the consequences of this part of the work was that for the rest of my career I did my best (with a certain amount of success) to avoid making grant applications for team research which would involve me thereafter in presenting, periodically, the required 'results'. But I did acquire some knowledge of computational linguistics (of a rather rudimentary kind) at a time when few linguists, even in America, had such knowledge.

This was one of the benefits of the time I spent in the United States, first of all, in 1960/1 and then for a further period of six months, which I will come to presently, in 1963. The principal benefit, however, as far as my future career is concerned, was being in one of the major American centres, not only of linguistics, but also of anthropology and semiotics. These latter two disciplines were closely associated with linguistics and were represented, most notably, by Carl Voegelin and Thomas A. Sebeok, respectively.

Householder was not only my day-to-day 'boss' (a very benign boss). Of the three professors I have mentioned by name, he was also the one whose interests in linguistics were closest to mine: I learned a lot from him, as I had done from Bazell at SOAS. But I also learned much from Voegelin and Sebeok, and indeed from many others who were at Indiana University at that time.

The actual teaching of linguistics at Indiana University in my time, by Householder and his colleagues, was very definitely 'post-Bloomfieldian'. While I was there, I too had some experience of teaching linguistics (more particularly phonology and morphology) in this paradigm. These were the first courses in general linguistics that I ever gave; and I learned on the job, endeavouring to keep one step ahead of my students. The assigned textbooks were (the first edition of) Gleason's *Introduction* (1955) – and the associated workbook – for one of the courses and Nida's *Morphology* (1949) for the other. (The fact that it was the earlier, strictly post-Bloomfieldian, edition of Gleason's textbook is important: the second edition, 1961, was influenced by, and to some degree expounded, Chomsky's earliest version of transformational grammar.) I followed the two textbooks fairly closely and, like the students, worked through all the problems in terms of the prescribed 'discovery procedures'. It was useful experience and, apart from anything else, taught me a lot, in a general way, about the phonological and morphological structure of a large number of typologically different languages.

One feature of the departmental programme was the series of weekly 'ethnolinguistics seminars'. These, in their very title, overtly acknowledged the close links between anthropology and linguistics, if not semiotics. For me personally, like the staff seminars at SOAS, they contributed to my training in linguistics. I myself gave a talk entitled 'Phonemic and non-phonemic phonology', which was subsequently published in *IJAL*. It is the only paper I have ever published in phonology. I have explained in some detail, in the epilogue and notes specially written for the version reprinted in my *Natural Language and Universal Grammar* (1991b) many years later, why I gave the original talk and how it came to be published. As my SOAS colleagues would certainly have agreed, it is ironical that the paper in question should have come to be regarded later as an authoritative exposition of the principles of prosodic analysis. Many of my SOAS colleagues thought that my views on linguistics were characteristically 'American'.

7

In the normal course of events, I should have returned to SOAS in October 1961. In the meantime, however, I had been appointed to the newly established Lectureship in General Linguistics at Cambridge. I also held the Rouse Fellowship in Classics at Christ's College (where I had been both an undergraduate and a research student.) For the next three years, therefore, I had a double range of teaching duties: I supervised for Part I classics at Christ's (where I also did some Part I supervision in Russian translation) and, more widely in the university, both lectured and supervised in linguistics. But most of my time was devoted to general linguistics. Although I had no formal qualifications in most branches of the subject, I like to think that the apprenticeship I had served at SOAS and at Indiana University, together with the supplementary reading programme upon which I now embarked, had prepared me well enough for my new post. The rest of my career as a university teacher was in general linguistics exclusively.

   John Trim was already well established in Cambridge as the University Lecturer in Phonetics when I arrived and we divided the lecturing between us. He took responsibility for phonetics and phonology, and I for (synchronic) morphology, syntax and semantics. There was as yet no Department of Linguistics, and John Trim and I were based in two different faculties: he (as a Germanist) in Modern Languages and I in Classics. He was of course very much the senior member of the team and handled such administration as there was. I look back on this freedom from administrative responsibility (either in the university or in college) as one of the most pleasurable aspects of being back in Cambridge in my new role.

   I was to be there for only three years. And I spent the third term (and the long vacation) of my third year back in the United States. When I had left in the autumn of 1961, James Peter Thorne had replaced me for a year. I had been charged with the task of finding a successor, and 'Jimmy' Thorne had been recommended to me by Michael Halliday, whose advice I sought. It was agreed that Jimmy and I between us would cover the period from April to September 1963, and that Peter Matthews, whom I had also recruited on Householder's behalf, would take over for a year in October. We had not known one another before, and it was this 'Indiana connection' which brought us together. It also so happened that the three of us were interested in generative grammar before we went to the United States or had met one another: we had acquired this interest independently and had come to it from different directions. As far as I know, this was not a prerequisite of the job, but it may have been relevant in Householder's mind. In any event, the three of us came back to our several positions in Britain with practical experience in computational linguistics at Indiana University which was not easy to acquire in Britain in the early 1960s. We were on campus together, all three of us, for about a month or so, the handover period, at the end of the summer of 1963. Although we went our separate ways academically in the years that followed and adopted in various degrees a more critical stance, in the Britain of the mid-1960s we were widely thought of, not without reason I think, as proselytizing 'Chomskians'.

I duly returned to Cambridge in October 1963, but a few months later I was appointed to the new Chair of General Linguistics in Edinburgh, with effect from October 1964, and to the Headship of the new Department of General Linguistics, established at the same time. I had served as external examiner for the Diploma in General Linguistics two years before, but otherwise had had no previous connection with the University of Edinburgh. I was to spend the next 12 years there.

8

Until 1964 Angus McIntosh had been Professor of both English Language and General Linguistics, and he had been the Head of the similarly titled Department of English Language and General Linguistics. The funds for the new Chair (as I learned later) were provided, in part, by the Ford Foundation. So too were the funds for one or two posts in the by then well-established and independent School of Applied Linguistics (which, with the appointment of S. Pit Corder as Head in 1964, became the Department of Applied Linguistics) and the Department of Phonetics, headed by David Abercrombie. The other three members of the new Department of General Linguistics, apart from me, were Jeffrey Ellis, John Sinclair and Rodney Huddleston, who had transferred from Angus McIntosh's Department, which now became officially the Department of English Language. But many of those who did not transfer to the new Department, like Angus McIntosh himself, maintained their interest in linguistics and, indeed, continued to incorporate a considerable amount of linguistics in their courses. One of these (whom I had met in Indiana and who was by now a close friend) was Jimmy Thorne.

My inaugural lecture was published by the University of Edinburgh in 1965. When I reprinted it myself as an appendix in *Natural Language and Universal Grammar* (1991b), I was 'at first tempted to remove some of the more local and ephemeral comments and allusions', but, on reflection felt that 'it would be more valuable to present-day and future historians of linguistics in Great Britain in the 1960s if I reprinted the lecture in full without any kind of revision [but with updated (though fewer and shorter) notes]'. One thing I made very clear in the lecture was that 'I [did] not claim to be bringing linguistics to Edinburgh' and that 'to make any such claim would be as absurd as it would be ungracious'. I paid tribute to the work that Angus McIntosh and David Abercrombie, in particular, had done in their respective areas of responsibility. I also said something about the relations, as I saw them, between the new Department of General Linguistics, on the one hand, and the Departments of English Language, Phonetics and Applied Linguistics, on the other.

Initially, the Department of General Linguistics (unlike the Departments of English Language and Phonetics) was not involved in undergraduate teaching. It ran a Postgraduate Diploma (which, in effect, had been very much the responsibility of Michael Halliday, before he had moved to London) and had a few research students. In this respect it was like the Department of Applied Linguistics, which was, however, rather larger in numbers both of staff and of students.

As it happens, the other three original members of staff in the Department of General Linguistics all took up posts elsewhere at the end of my first year. They were replaced by: Ronald Asher, who had been a colleague of mine at SOAS (though not in the Department of Phonetics and Linguistics) and became, in effect if not by title, the Deputy Head of Department; Erik Fudge, who had been my first PhD student and had also worked on the Indiana machine translation project; and Keith Brown, who had been one of our postgraduate students at the time the Department was created and was also one of my PhD students.

9

In the meantime, other organizational changes relating to linguistics had taken place. First of all, in 1967 the Department of Phonetics and the Department of General Linguistics had amalgamated, by mutual agreement, as the Department of Phonetics and Linguistics. Then, in 1970 this new Department and the Department of Applied Linguistics were amalgamated as the Department of Linguistics. It was agreed that the Headship of

Department should 'rotate' among the Professors for periods of three years; and it fell to me to be the first Head of Department on the occasion of both amalgamations. It was also agreed (as I have explained in the notes appended to the republished version of my inaugural lecture) that academic responsibility would be kept separate from administrative responsibility and that, regardless of who was Head of Department at the time, the three Professors – David Abercrombie, Pit Corder and I – should continue to be the Heads of our particular subject (Phonetics, Applied Linguistics and General Linguistics, respectively), no distinction being drawn from this point of view between established and personal chairs. David Abercrombie had held a Personal Chair in Phonetics for some years and Pit Corder was awarded a Personal Chair in Applied Linguistics at the time of the second amalgamation. I was very pleased to have been instrumental, with the support of the Dean and some of the other professors in the Faculty of Arts, in having the Chair of Phonetics established shortly after the amalgamation. This was something that was very important to David Abercrombie as a mark of the academic status of the subject, and I accepted his view. I should add that after the amalgamations Ron Asher continued to be my deputy in terms of academic responsibility both during and after my term as Head of Department and that (given my own lack of competence in this specialized area) I appointed John Laver as the administrative head of the Phonetics Laboratory. Both of them were supremely efficient and reliable and very helpful to me personally all the time I was in Edinburgh. Some little time after my departure the second of the two amalgamations was reversed and the Department of Applied Linguistics once again became independent. I was sorry about this, but I suppose it is true to say that applied linguistics (as a wholly postgraduate subject) was never as fully integrated within the single Department, either administratively or academically, as phonetics and the other branches of linguistics were.

I have never enjoyed administration and, given the size of the Department, I found this side of the work onerous. But I was well served by other senior members of staff, to whom I was able to delegate many of the chores. I think I can say that both amalgamations were successful in that they enabled us to make a better use of our resources and (as I remember things) we all got on well together with remarkably few disagreements of principle or personal conflicts. When I did leave Edinburgh in 1976, one of my reasons for leaving was that my second term as Head of Department was imminent and I did not wish to find myself heavily involved, once again, in administration.

Applied linguistics continued to be taught solely at a postgraduate level after the amalgamation. But one of the more immediate consequences of the formation of the enlarged and integrated Department of Linguistics was the creation of a whole range of new undergraduate degrees, in which linguistics could be combined, for a 'joint honours' four-year MA, with English language, psychology, social anthropology, French, German and Russian. Partly comparable 'joint honours' degrees had been or were being set up in other British universities in the 1960s. But most, if not all, of them were different in two important respects.

In Edinburgh, as in the other ancient Scottish universities, the whole structure of undergraduate courses was different from what was normal elsewhere in Great Britain. The 'MA Ordinary' was a broadly based three-year degree (at that time there was no BA) and did not include any 'honours level' courses: the curriculum was made up wholly of 'ordinary' (i.e. non-honours) courses. The 'MA Honours' was a four-year degree: the curriculum for the first two years was made up of ordinary courses, in a variety of possible combinations, and for the third and fourth years of honours courses. For several years, there had been a one-year Ordinary Course in Phonetics. We now incorporated the content of this within the new 'First Ordinary' and 'Second Ordinary' Courses in Linguistics and Phonetics, the former of which could be taken without the latter (but not conversely) for the MA (Ordinary) degree, both of which, however, were required for the newly established 'joint honours' degrees. I have always thought that the traditional Scottish pattern of undergraduate teaching (which in its breadth and the range of options that it permits bears some resemblance to the American) is better for most students than what is, or used to be, the normal pattern elsewhere in Great Britain. As far as linguistics (including phonetics) at Edinburgh from the late 1960s is concerned, it meant that a relatively large number of undergraduates – of the order of 150 per year – did the one-year First Ordinary course and about half of these went on to do the Second Ordinary course. A much smaller number took the third-year and fourth-year Linguistics 'honours' courses.

As to the new 'joint honours' degrees at Edinburgh (and this is the second difference from what was normal elsewhere), there was, in all cases, at least one obligatory paper specially designed for the joint degree in question and taught jointly by members of the two Departments that shared responsibility for the degree.

I am of course prejudiced, but I think that the undergraduate courses in linguistics set up at that time in Edinburgh were the best to be found anywhere in Britain. In saying this, I am aware that linguistics (in the broadest sense) was, at that time, more generously funded there than it was in any other British university. (The cuts came later.) We had the resources within the Department, not only to provide 'joint' specialized teaching for each of the Honours degrees, but also for small-group seminar back-up, geared to the lectures, for all students taking the First and Second Ordinary Courses.

It is also true to say, I think, that Edinburgh was soon widely recognized as one of the best centres in Britain (and internationally) for the study of general linguistics, phonetics and applied linguistics at the postgraduate level. But this was already coming to be the case before the expansion of the mid-1960s. The number of those who had the whole or part of their training in linguistics (once again, in the broadest sense) at Edinburgh and went on to posts in other universities is too large for me to list them all here. Many of them have been actively involved in the further promotion of linguistics either in Britain or in other countries and are well known as international authorities in their chosen fields of research. I am privileged to have taught several of them and, in some cases, to have supervised their PhD research. The relevant chapters of my *Introduction to Theoretical Linguistics* (1968) were based on the lectures I gave to our Diploma students in my first two years in Edinburgh. Most of the first volume of *Semantics* (1977) also derives partly from the courses I taught at Edinburgh in the late 1960s and early 1970s. The content of both volumes of this latter work was further influenced by my experience as a PhD supervisor at Edinburgh; from the courses I taught at several American universities (for the annual LSA Summer Institutes) during this period or at the University of Paris (where I twice held a visiting Associate Professorship in the 1970s); or from the occasional lectures I had been invited to give at other universities in Britain or abroad. As I have said on many occasions, I have learned a good deal of my linguistics from my students.

10

At Edinburgh, then and now, interest in linguistics was by no means confined to the Department (or at different times Departments) which included the name in its (or their) title. I have already mentioned the Department of English Language (which continued to be a major centre of teaching and research in the subject and has also produced many of those who are now in prominent positions in linguistics in Britain) and the Departments with which we collaborated for the teaching of the shared undergraduate degrees.

As to the latter, special mention should be made of the Department of Psychology and more particularly of John Marshall and Roger Wales, who played a leading role in the development of psycholinguistics in Britain in that period. Both of them were there when I arrived in 1964 and were already teaching a good deal of the relevant parts of linguistics in their courses on the psychology of language. An important international (mainly Anglo-American) conference on psycholinguistics took place in 1965: I had no part in organizing it (indeed I knew almost nothing of psycholinguistics before I went to Edinburgh). But I chaired the opening session (to demonstrate the new Department's and my own willingness to collaborate in this field) and with Roger Wales co-edited the Proceedings (*Psycholinguistic Papers*, 1966). I was subsequently the titular 'Principal Investigator' in charge of a research project on child language acquisition, sponsored by the Social Sciences

Research Council (as it was then called). Several of those who worked on this project (and did the day-to-day research) took their PhDs in the Department of Linguistics and, in due course, moved into university posts. When the joint degree in Psychology and Linguistics was established, Roger Wales and I taught the special paper and, throughout the course, sat in on one another's lectures.

Another area of research strongly represented at Edinburgh, related to both linguistics and psychology (and their intersection), was what has come to be called cognitive science. For reasons that are of no concern in the present context, this was institutionalized in Edinburgh in the School of Epistemics. Three of the leading figures in this emergent discipline, who were all together for a while at Edinburgh and can be described as the founding fathers of the School, were Richard Gregory, H. Christopher Longuet-Higgins and Donald Mickie, each of whom had a solidly based international reputation in another (or more than one) well-established and more traditional discipline.

Christopher Longuet-Higgins, who was the first Chairman of the School of Epistemics (Jimmy Thorne, incidentally, whilst still a member of the Department of English Language, was the Secretary), had previously held a Chair in Theoretical Chemistry in London, a Chair in Theoretical Physics at Cambridge and now had a Royal Society Research Professorship, which allowed him considerable freedom in the determination of his particular field of research and where he would be based. There is no doubt that his prestige in more established fields of scientific research helped the new discipline of cognitive science to acquire academic respectability in the late 1960s and early 1970s, not only at Edinburgh, but also more widely in Britain. He, together with (the late) Donald E. Broadbent (who was also very supportive of linguistics) and me, organized an international two-day symposium on 'The Psychological Mechanisms of Language' under the joint auspices of the Royal Society and the British Academy at the premises of the Royal Society in London, in March 1981. (My colleagues acted on behalf of the Royal Society and I acted on behalf of the British Academy.) The symposium was attended by more than 400 linguists, psychologists, cognitive scientists (as they were now being called) and others, many of whom (as I have said elsewhere) 'took an active part in the discussion'. The Proceedings were published, both in the Royal Society's *Transactions* (see Longuet-Higgins et al. 1981) and separately and no doubt gave a further impetus to the study of linguistics within the framework of cognitive science. By this time, however, both Christopher Longuet-Higgins and I had moved to Sussex (independently, and he a few years before me), where cognitive science (though not yet linguistics as such) was already established.

11

Many of my friends and colleagues, in Edinburgh and elsewhere, were surprised by my move to the University of Sussex in 1976. One of my principal reasons I have already given: I wished to be as free as possible of administrative responsibilities. Another was, quite simply, that I felt that it was probably not a good thing either for me personally or for the Department that I should stay there until my retirement. I was one of the youngest professors in the University (aged 32) when I took up my appointment and under the old statutes had unrestricted tenure for the following 38 years. Looking forward in the mid-1970s, the year 2002 seemed a long way off. (*Eheu fugaces* . . .*!*) I was even then aware (and am more conscious of this now) that, intellectually, I had probably 'peaked' and needed a change of professional environment and perhaps also of direction. Everything that was of concern to me and in which I had been involved in Edinburgh appeared to be in good shape, and I could leave with a good conscience.

When I was offered the new Chair of Linguistics at Sussex, I had been told that there were no departments (or faculties) as such and that professors were not expected to get involved in administration. On the Arts and Social Sciences side, most of the recognized 'subject groups' were based in two or more Schools; and these were the major administrative units. Gerald Gazdar, who had already been appointed as the first Lecturer in Linguistics, was a member of the School of Social Sciences (which was where the 'Cognitive Sciences Programme' had its administrative home). I opted to be a member of the same School, though, given my other interests (apart from psycholinguistics and sociolinguistics), I might equally well have chosen the School of European Studies. Linguistics was taught in both of these Schools, as also in the School of English and American Studies and the School of Cultural and Community Studies. Initially, Gerald Gazdar and I were the only two linguists by title. Soon two further appointments were made, Richard Coates and Margaret Deuchar. We were then able to launch a set of undergraduate degrees in linguistics: i.e. degrees which, in the Sussex context, allowed for the possibility of taking linguistics as a 'major'.

From 1976 until 1980, I was indeed, as I had hoped to be, relatively (and blissfully) free of administrative responsibilities at Sussex. But things changed, as university funding became increasingly tight and the more junior members of staff became correspondingly less willing to take on the administrative chores. Such things as 'research assessment exercises' were still far off in the future. But 'publish or perish!' – a slogan I first heard in the United States – was perceived, with some justification, as coming to be relevant in British universities.

12

I was elected as Dean of the School of Social Sciences in 1980, but held this post for only one year, having been appointed during that year as Pro-Vice-Chancellor. Being the Dean of the School of Social Sciences was not excessively onerous or disagreeable. I was still based in the same building as previously and working, for the most part, with colleagues I knew well and whose academic interests I shared. The Pro-Vice-Chancellorship was very different. Officially, I continued to be in the linguistics subject group for one-third of my time (this was at my own request) and I did indeed continue with some teaching and PhD supervision. But for the greater, and an increasing, part of my time I became part of the 'central administration'. I occupied the office next to the Vice-Chancellor, Sir Denys Wilkinson, and worked closely with him (as his deputy in his absence, but also with my own regularly delegated areas of responsibility) and with the Registrar and Secretary, the Finance Officer and other senior, non-academic, full-time 'administrators'.

In addition to membership of all the major university committees, my regular responsibilities as Pro-Vice-Chancellor included being the chairman of the major committees dealing with matters relating to the non-academic parts of the university and the person at whose desk, in these matters (employment issues, promotions, complaints, etc.), 'the buck (usually) stopped'. The Pro-Vice-Chancellor also had delegated responsibility for the several research institutes on campus (many of which were world-famous) and was the final, or pre-final, 'court of appeal' on student admissions, and a variety of other things.

I learned a lot that I did not know previously about the way a university is run. I also learned a lot about my own limitations and – I record this without going into details – how unreasonable in their demands and behaviour many of those who are professionally committed to the pursuit of rationality can be at times. (I am not implying that I myself am in any way different from my fellow academics in this respect!) I conceived an admiration for those of my other senior academic colleagues involved in administration at various levels who were able to come out of a sometimes contentious committee meeting or negotiating session with one of the four unions on campus (the most unreasonable of which, in my experience, being the AUT: if I dare say this in print) and, if they had a little time before the next such administrative chore, carry on immediately with their research or their preparation for a seminar or class. I was temperamentally unable to 'switch off' in this way.

Within a day or two of my taking up office as Pro-Vice-Chancellor, as expected, the letter from the University Grants Committee (UGC), arrived, informing us of the amount that Sussex would be receiving for the next funding period. There was already in existence a small *ad hoc* committee that had started to formulate a draft plan for the implementation (within three years) of the anticipated reduction in the annual grant, which, in the event, for Sussex (which was treated more severely than most universities) turned out to be of the order of 18 per cent. The nucleus of the committee in question was composed of the Chairman and Vice-Chairman of Council (a partly lay 'watchdog' body), together with the Vice-Chancellor and Pro-Vice-Chancellor: the 'Gang of Four', as we soon came to be known, perhaps inevitably. I took over from my predecessor on 1 August, and for the next two months we worked on the draft of a detailed plan for the whole of the university, specifying for each unit, down to the level of individual subject groups, what would be its future complement of staff. The draft plan was published on the first day of term and then (Sussex being a notoriously democratic university) presented, a few days later, for comment and discussion by the 'Gang of Four' at a general assembly to which all members of staff, academic and non-academic, and student representatives were invited. Several hundred attended. It was my baptism of fire.

One of the principles underlying the draft plan was that the implementation of the inevitable reductions could not be left to the chance of so-called 'natural wastage'. Another was that, as far as the academic staff were concerned, the reductions would not necessarily be spread equally and proportionately across all categories and all subject groups, but selectively. Some of the numerically smaller subjects would be eliminated; others would be 'protected' at what was judged to be their level of viability. These two principles were, of course, highly contentious, as was the deliberate refusal to subscribe to an undertaking that there would be no 'compulsory redundancies' and the explicit rejection of the policy of 'last in, first out'. The logical consequence of the two underlying principles was that, if one subject fell below its 'quota' whilst others were still above theirs, the subject below 'quota' would be able to recruit immediately. It is not surprising that the publication of the draft plan (as a preliminary discussion document at this stage) was greeted with consternation and anger. The meeting at which it was presented was for me without question, in the whole of my career, the most unpleasant that I have ever been involved in. The behaviour of many of those who attended – including that of several quite senior academics – was nothing short of disgraceful. My fellow members of the 'Gang of Four' were made of tougher stuff than I was and had had more experience of what one might refer to, euphemistically, as the rough and tumble of full participatory democracy. But even they may have been taken aback, I think, by some of the vituperative and personally defamatory interventions.

However that may be, the meeting in question was the prelude to what proved to be for me, from a professional point of view, the most stressful period of my life. There is, however, a less self-indulgently personal reason for mentioning it and, for the record, going into some detail about it in the present context. My position, as it turned out, was especially sensitive. So too, in consequence, was that of linguistics: it was one of the smallest subject groups, whose members, as it happened, had all been more recently appointed than many members of staff in other equally small subjects. I had of course inherited my role as one of the proponents of the draft plan that was published at the beginning of October (the main outlines of which had been drawn up before I arrived on the scene). But I participated fully in its finalization. It had already been decided before I joined the group that linguistics would be recommended for 'protection' with its complement of four members of staff (or more precisely their 'full-time equivalents'). It was hardly surprising that when this was revealed in the draft plan there should have been angry talk of 'the Lyons' share' (if that is the way to spell a phrase that I never saw in print but heard several times during the period that I am chronicling here).

In the course of the next few months, the draft plan, amended and re-amended on the way, went through two cycles of committee meetings at every relevant level, until it was approved in its final form, at the end of the second term of 1981/2, as the University Plan. Most of the amendments, in the event, were relatively minor. As far as linguistics is concerned, I was only too happy to propose a reduction from four to three-and-a-half posts. Two-thirds of me (for the time being at least) counted logistically in the central administration's quota and part of Gerald Gazdar could be included, legitimately given both his research interests and his teaching, in computer studies.

The reason why I have gone into this amount of detail, in the context of the history of linguistics in Great Britain in the late twentieth century, is now clear. At the time of the 1980s 'cuts' in university funding many small linguistics departments in Britain were eliminated or absorbed into other departments. That this did not happen at Sussex is due to the support that was given to the subject, not only by the Vice-Chancellor, the two academic Pro-Vice-Chancellors (who, unlike me, were not part of the 'central administration') and the Deans of the relevant Schools, but also by influential representatives of allied disciplines who did not necessarily have posts of administrative responsibility.

I will say no more about my time as Pro-Vice-Chancellor. In October 1984, I expected to revert to being a full-time professor. Some months earlier, however, I had been approached in confidence (as of course had been many others) about being considered for the Mastership of Trinity Hall, Cambridge. When it eventually appeared probable that I would be offered the post, I obtained from the Vice-Chancellor and other senior colleagues the assurance that they would do what they could, personally and *ex officio*, to ensure that the Chair of Linguistics would be filled if I did resign in order to go to Trinity Hall. (Without this assurance I would have found it very difficult, and perhaps impossible, to leave.) I record this as further evidence of the support that linguistics had received, and continued to receive, at Sussex, in financially difficult circumstances.

After my departure, Gerald Gazdar was appointed to the Chair, which was renamed to reflect his interests. During my term as Pro-Vice-Chancellor, he, together with Richard Coates and Margaret Deuchar, had taken on my share of the running the linguistics subject group. Various organizational developments relating to linguistics took place after I had left (some of which were already in prospect at that time). But these are not part of my 'personal history'.

13

I should now say something about my editorship of the *Journal of Linguistics* (in the 1960s) and about my involvement in various national and international bodies during my career, in so far as this is relevant to the development of linguistics in this country. For reasons which I will explain presently, most of my involvement in this came to an end abruptly not long after I took up my post as Master of Trinity Hall. For the same reasons, I did not play as active a role in linguistics in Cambridge (or indeed more widely in the university) in the period 1985–2000 as might have been expected. This seems to be, therefore, the best point for me to deal with some, if not all, of the activities that I was involved in relating to linguistics to which I have just referred in the preceding 20 years or so. I will start with my editorship of the *Journal of Linguistics*.

I had not played any part at all in the Linguistics Association of Great Britain (LAGB) until I was asked to edit the new *Journal of Linguistics* (*JL*) in late 1962 or early 1963. The fact that I was at Cambridge at the time and Cambridge University Press (CUP) was to publish the *Journal* on behalf of the Association may have been one of the factors which influenced the Committee's choice of Editor: I do not know. Anyway, I accepted the invitation, a Board of Consultant Editors was appointed, and I got to work, soliciting articles for the first issue (scheduled for Spring 1965), writing to publishers for review copies of books in the field, and so on.

While I was in the United States in the summer of 1963, I took the opportunity of asking several well-known American linguists to contribute. Fred Householder, who by then of course was a good friend of mine, agreed to publish in *JL* an article that he was writing highly critical of aspects of what was to become, in due course, the epoch-making Chomsky-and-Halle theory of generative phonology. When I invited them to do so, Chomsky and Halle were only too pleased to reply in the second issue: it gave them a chance of presenting their current views in advance of the publication of *The Sound Pattern of English* (1968), upon which they were working at the time. The appearance of these two articles, and especially the one by Chomsky and Halle, in Volume 1 of the *Journal* meant that it was now well and truly launched on the international, or at least Anglo-American, scene.

It continued to be, and still is, the journal of the LAGB, but, unlike many other journals associated with national organizations or particular 'schools' of linguistics, it has never been, in its editorial policy, parochial or partisan. By the time the first issue appeared, I was in Edinburgh. This had the advantage that, as a professor, I had secretarial assistance (which was not the case in Cambridge). But more and more articles were being submitted and more and more books were being sent for review. Also, my own responsibilities, in Edinburgh and elsewhere, were steadily increasing. I therefore handed over to my appointed successors, Frank Palmer and Peter Matthews, then based at the University of Reading, who jointly edited Volume 6 (1970) and subsequent volumes of the *Journal* (more professionally and less idiosyncratically perhaps than I had done), until they in turn handed over to Nigel Vincent a decade later.

There was no formal connection between the *Journal of Linguistics* and the monograph series Cambridge Studies in Linguistics (CSL). But they were both published by CUP. It was perhaps natural, therefore, that, as the editor of the *Journal*, I should have been invited to be a member of the Editorial Board of CSL, chaired by Sidney Allen, when this series was launched in the late 1960s. It rapidly established itself internationally, as the *Journal* had done. In due course, two additional series (with the same Editorial Board) were established, Cambridge Textbooks in Linguistics (CTL) and Cambridge Language Surveys. All three series were very successful, and I am pleased to have been on the Editorial Board and for many years actively involved, as most of the members were, in reading manuscripts, encouraging authors to submit their proposals and, in many cases, giving detailed editorial advice. I am especially pleased to have been associated in this way with the publication of several of the Textbooks on topics that were close to my own interests.

I took over the Chairmanship when Sidney Allen retired and continued in that role until I myself was approaching retirement in the mid-1990s. I have to confess, however, that I was less and less actively involved in the later period.

14

I should now turn to the support given to linguistics by the British Academy, in so far as I have been involved in this. I was elected as a Fellow in 1973. At that time, there was no Linguistics Section, but many of the Fellows who were based in one or more of the other sections (including several of the philologists, philosophers and social anthropologists) were sympathetic to the subject. Given my own academic interests (and those of existing Fellows who sponsored my election or voted for me), I became a member of four sections: African and Oriental Studies, Classics, Philosophy, and Social and Political Sciences.

Among those who were sympathetic to linguistics was Sir Isaiah Berlin (whom I had known personally since I gave one of the public lectures on structuralism in Oxford in 1972). He was the President in 1974–8, and he asked me to serve as one of the Vice-Presidents for 1977–9. In this capacity I became a member of Council and several of the Academy's committees. One of these was the small committee which dealt with joint ventures with the Royal Society. (I have already mentioned one such venture relevant to the development of linguistics: the 1981 symposium on 'The Psychological Mechanisms of Language'.) I was also one of those who represented the Academy in *ad hoc* discussions with the Social Sciences Research Council.

Many changes have taken place in the British Academy in the last 20 years or so, in respect of its internal organization and of its responsibility for the funding of scholarship and research. Some of these, directly or indirectly, are of relevance to our present theme: the development of linguistics in Great Britain and its establishment as a recognized academic discipline. One of these in which I played my part at a fairly early stage of the process (as the Chairman of the Section for Social and Political Sciences) is that the social sciences are now better represented: there are currently six sections, including one for Psychology, which at one time was completely unrepresented. Another change is that the Academy has taken on many of the functions of the non-existent Humanities Research Council. These two changes have gone a fair way towards correcting what many saw earlier as outdated anomalies. One of the consequences of the Academy's increased responsibility for funding is that in recent years it has become more important than was previously the case to see that (ideally) all branches of particular disciplines are represented and that in the relevant sections there should be Fellows who can properly assess applications for research in a variety of specialized areas.

The most important change in the organization of the British Academy during my time, as far as linguistics is concerned, was of course the establishment of a separate section for the subject in the 1970s. As I have already explained, there were many existing Fellows with an interest in modern linguistics when I was elected; and their support was of course essential. When the new section was formed, it was agreed that Fellows who wished to do so might join it whilst retaining their existing membership of one or more other sections. It was also agreed as a matter of policy that (1) the term 'linguistics' would be construed broadly and would, in particular, include philology but (2) for some time at least the new section (of which Frank Palmer became the first Chairman) would propose for election as Fellows those whose primary interest was in modern general or theoretical linguistics (though they might also be eligible for membership of other sections – as many have been). Both parts of this policy have been maintained. Currently, the Section in question (H4) is officially entitled 'Linguistics and Philology' and, I think it is fair to say, has for some time now been satisfactorily representative of the subject in all its major branches (with the possible exception of applied linguistics). Members of the Section have also served on Council and on many of the major committees. All this is very gratifying.

15

Another of the national bodies with which I was involved for some years, as a representative of linguistics, was the Social Sciences Research Council. The SSRC had already been supporting a certain amount of research in sociolinguistics and psycholinguistics (such as the Edinburgh project on child language acquisition with which I was associated in the mid-1970s). Several members of the Council, including the Chairman, Professor Robin (C. O.) Matthews, were well disposed towards linguistics. But it could not be classified as one of the social sciences and given the same degree of representation, under the SSRC Charter, as, say, sociology or psychology. (When the British Academy reorganized its Section structure in 1999, two Groups were established 'mainly for electoral purposes, but also to conduct other business falling within their disciplinary coverage': the Humanities Group and the Social Sciences Group. The Linguistics and Philology Section is the only one to belong to both Groups. This classificatory problem has been with us for a long time.)

For the practical purpose of assessing applications that were more linguistic than, say, sociological or psychological (but were none the less judged to be methodologically and otherwise within the SSRC remit) and making recommendations for support, a small 'Linguistics Panel' was established, which, for several years, was successful in obtaining support for many projects in linguistics that would otherwise have been unfunded. The Panel survived the politically motivated transformation of the SSRC into the Economic and Social Research Council (ESRC) in 1985.

Michael Posner, who succeeded Robin Matthews as Chairman of the SSRC (and had the difficult task of managing its transformation into the ESRC without having to concede more of its ability to sponsor genuinely academic research than was absolutely necessary), was equally well disposed to linguistics. The subject owes a lot to his personal support.

I have gone into some detail about the role played by the British Academy and the SSRC/ESRC as two of the major national bodies (with different but overlapping aims) in what may be called the establishment of linguistics in Britain as a 'normal' academic discipline and giving it in their different ways, so to speak, their seal of approval. These are the two such bodies with which I myself have been associated. Some branches of linguistics, of course, link it more closely with the physical or biological sciences. A full account of its establishment and institutionalization in this country (differently in different universities and research institutes) in the second half of the twentieth century and of the support given to it by other national bodies such as the Medical Research Council (MRC) or the Science and Engineering Research Council (SERC) would need to deal with these. But I have had no personal involvement with them (except, of course, for supplying the occasional reference or assessment).

16

I should close this part of my 'personal history' by mentioning the one international body on which I served, for several years, as a representative of British linguistics: the European Science Foundation (ESF), based in Strasbourg. Actually, I represented, not linguistics as such, but (primarily) the British Academy and (secondarily) the SSRC. The Academy appointed a delegate to the ESF Humanities Committee and the SSRC (jointly perhaps with the Academy: I am not sure of this) to its Social Sciences Committee. Since linguistics fell within the joint remit of the two ESF Committees, it was administratively convenient, I suppose, for me to be a member of both Committees. The Chairman of the SSRC at the time of my appointment to the two ESF Committees was Michael Posner (to whom I have already referred). As it happened, he later became Chairman of the ESF Social Sciences Committee and subsequently, at the end of his term as Chairman of (what was by then) the ESRC, moved to Strasbourg as Secretary General of the ESF. He continued to be, in Strasbourg as in London, very supportive of linguistics; and I very much enjoyed working with him.

The most ambitious linguistic research project supported by the ESF in my time was devoted to the study of adult language acquisition in a social (and interethnic) context: more particularly the acquisition of five different 'target languages' by groups of immigrant workers in five different countries: Britain, France, Germany, Holland and Sweden. Its official title was 'Second Language Acquisition by Adult Immigrants' (SLAAI). This project, which ran for a good part of the 1980s, involved six teams of researchers in the five 'host countries'. (The British group was based at what was then the Ealing College of Higher Education.) It derived from an application to the ESF by Professor W. ('Pim') Levelt. (He was also the prime mover in the establishment of the now world-famous Max-Planck-Institut für Psycholinguistik in Nijmegen, where many British linguists have held research posts for longer or shorter periods and which for some years has had a Section for Anthropological Linguistics, directed by Stephen Levinson.)

I was closely associated with the SLAAI project from the outset and, on behalf of the ESF, served as Chairman of its Steering Committee from 1981 until 1985. Apart from me, all the other members of the Steering Committee were experts in the relevant branches of applied (or applicable) socio-linguistics and psycholinguistics. I very much enjoyed my association with the Project and benefited from it. In particular, I enjoyed the opportunity of meeting and getting to know those members of the Steering Committee and of the research teams (especially the team leaders) in the several countries whom I did not already know in other capacities. Also, as an ivory-tower linguist and armchair researcher myself, I learned a lot about the problems of the particularly difficult empirical research – methodologically difficult and politically sensitive – in which those working on the SLAAI Project were engaged. (For a full account of the aims, research design and organization of the SLAAI Project and of its results, see Perdue 1993.)

17

I had been very much looking forward to returning to Cambridge, where I had spent so many of my educationally formative years and where I had a large number of friends and colleagues in linguistics and related subjects, and of course at my *alma mater*, Christ's College. Among these, in the Department of Linguistics itself, there were, most notably, Peter Matthews, the Professor of General Linguistics, and Terence Moore, the next most senior member of staff. I had known both of them for some 30 years and had collaborated with Peter Matthews on all sorts of projects. He had assured me that, although I had no university teaching post, I would be welcomed as a potential MPhil and PhD supervisor and be able to do some teaching for the Department. As far as research was concerned, there was the prospect of being within easy walking distance of the University Library and other libraries in Cambridge, with their readily accessible specialized books of reference and runs of journals. From this point of view, both Sussex and Edinburgh were of course well resourced by comparison with many British universities. But Cambridge, especially with its personal associations, was *prima inter impares*! There was therefore much to make the prospect of returning to Cambridge academically attractive, and Trinity Hall had made it clear that I was expected to pursue my academic career and play my part on the university scene.

It was an added bonus that two of the Fellows of Trinity Hall were themselves linguists by title and known to me personally: Dr Joseph A. Cremona and Dr (now Professor) Nigel Vincent. There were others, as I discovered later, with an interest in linguistics. One of these whom I should certainly mention is the late Frank Fallside. As the Professor of Information Engineering, he was in the process of establishing, in the Engineering

Department itself, what has since become one of the major British centres of multidisciplinary research and teaching in the computational analysis of speech and language. Joe Cremona was both Vice-Master and Acting Master when I was first contacted by the college about the Mastership (my predecessor had died, suddenly, in post) and, *ex officio*, had chaired the 'search committee' and the Governing Body for the period leading up to my election. He remained in office as Vice-Master for a further two years; and in that role and more generally – as I take the opportunity of recording publicly here – was immensely supportive and helpful. (It is good to see that he is contributing to the present series of 'personal histories'. Through him Trinity Hall has produced for linguistics a succession of good scholars.)

18

Most of my activities in linguistics were terminated, unexpectedly, shortly after I took up my post as Master of Trinity Hall. I had been appointed to a Visiting Professorship at Sussex, and it had been agreed with the college that I would continue with some of my teaching during the first term of 1984/5 (returning from Cambridge for one day a week for the purpose) and possibly give occasional lectures for a little time after that. About half-way through the term (after I had indeed given some classes at Sussex), I was diagnosed as having a lymphoma. An intensive six-months' course of chemotherapy was scheduled, starting in January. Meanwhile, I had withdrawn from all non-college commitments, including not only my Sussex teaching, but also membership of all the national and international committees with which I was involved. I had to cut down on my workload and felt that Trinity Hall had first call on such time and energy as I had during this period. My hope, naturally, was that the first and most intensive course of treatment would be effective. That was not so. There were several further courses of chemo-therapy and radiotherapy over the next eight or nine years. These took their toll. Apart from being unpleasant and disruptive at the time and physically debilitating thereafter, they were also psychologically demotivating as far as undertaking any long-term projects was concerned. Needless to say, if my illness had been diagnosed even a few months earlier I would not have come back to Cambridge, where, I have to say gratefully, I received superb treatment and from many of my new colleagues in college, medical and non-medical, much-needed and much-appreciated support.

As things turned out, college affairs took up more of my time than I had anticipated – an increasing amount of time as the years passed. This was partly a matter of choice. I have mentioned the academic attractions of Cambridge and (for me though not for my wife) its nostalgic associations as factors in my decision to accept the Mastership of Trinity Hall. Another important factor was that it provided an opportunity for my wife and me to operate jointly in something we judged to be worthwhile and potentially satisfying for both of us. Such administration and committee work as came my way – and I had been assured that this would not be excessive – was a price that seemed to be worth paying.

In an earlier period, this might have been the case. Anyone who was in post in a British university, at whatever level and in whatever role, from the late 1980s and throughout the 1990s will know that administrative demands have become continuously more onerous: committees have multiplied; additional, extraordinary or emergency, meetings of existing committees have become the order of the day; and paperwork has increased. Oxford and Cambridge colleges, as well as university faculties, departments, schools of study, research institutes, etc., have also felt the effect of this, both directly and indirectly.

Oxford and Cambridge, like all British universities, have had to adjust to a lower level of public funding (and, as far as the Oxbridge colleges are concerned, to new and more complex administrative arrangements). Fund-raising is now very definitely part of the job description for most, if not all, Heads of Houses (to use the generic term for the different titles). If this had been so for the Mastership of Trinity Hall in 1984, I would not have been interested in taking the post. Once I was in office, of course, and when the college launched its major five-year fund-raising appeal in 1995 (which involved two years of detailed preparation), I accepted that playing a major role in this was part of my job.

One way and another, then, my college duties were more time-consuming than I had expected. In saying this, however, I am aware of two things. One is that it was a matter of choice to involve myself to the degree that I did, together with my wife, on the one hand, with the students, the staff and the alumni and, on the other, with such things as the state of our buildings and gardens. But I have no regrets here. This has brought both of us, at the time and now in retrospect, a good deal of satisfaction. The second thing of which I am aware – I mentioned it earlier in connection with my experience as Pro-Vice-Chancellor at Sussex – is that, unlike many of the colleagues I have known in positions of authority and administrative responsibility, I am temperamentally unable to switch readily between administration and academic work or, I have to admit, to cope with the pressures of recurrent crises.

It is perhaps idle to speculate how my career in linguistics might have developed if it had not been for the recurrent problems of ill-health in the later period or, alternatively, if I had not come back to Cambridge in 1984. I might have written other books (including two that I started before I came back to Cambridge). I would presumably have continued to go to conferences and to attend meetings of the professional bodies with which I was associated in my earlier career, especially the Philological Society and the LAGB. Who knows? Counterfactual conditionals are notoriously difficult either to prove or disprove – or even, for a semanticist, to explicate. Whether they make sense or not, semanticists, like ordinary folk, need to subscribe to them in their daily life for their comfort if not for their survival.

However that may be, I was not as active in linguistics, even locally, in recent years as I expected to be. I did a certain amount of undergraduate and postgraduate teaching, for the Department of Linguistics and for other departments, and also a limited amount of college undergraduate supervision and MPhil and PhD supervision. This, as always, I enjoyed. But I wish it could have been more.

On the administrative side, as far as linguistics is concerned, my contribution to the development and welfare of the subject was more limited than, ideally or in another counterfactually possible world, it might have been. One thing that I am especially pleased to have been involved in, originally in an advisory capacity, was the establishment of the Chair of English as an International Language and the foundation of what, under the first holder of the Chair, Gillian Brown (an erstwhile Edinburgh colleague), has become the Research Centre for English and Applied Linguistics: I am pleased too that, over the years since the establishment of the Centre until my retirement, I served as the Chairman of the Management Committee – one of the most pleasurable and least onerous of such administrative roles I have had to play, in Cambridge or elsewhere.

19

I began this 'personal history' of what linguistics has meant to me and of the role I have played in the development of linguistics in Britain by saying that I had been very reluctant to write that kind (or any kind!) of autobiography. The reasons for this initial reluctance are now clear. In the event, I am pleased to have done it: it has helped me to put some of the professional frustrations and disappointments of the linguistics part of my later career into perspective. It has also renewed for me many pleasurable memories associated with particular occasions and particular friends and colleagues (only a very small number of whom, regrettably, I have been able to mention here). I should, in conclusion, make reference to my knighthood, since this is clearly relevant in the present context. It is perhaps not as widely known as I should like it to be that when I was knighted (in 1987) the citation was 'for services to linguistics'. This pleased me for two reasons. I was, of course, pleased (and proud) that my own academic work should have been given this kind of public or 'official' recognition. But I was also pleased that, at the same time, the subject itself – linguistics – was, as it were, receiving the accolade.

REFERENCES

ALLEN, SIDNEY, 1957 'On the linguistic study of languages', in P. D. Strevens (ed.), *Five Inaugural Lectures*, Oxford: Oxford University Press (1966).

CHOMSKY, NOAM, 1957. *Syntactic Structures*, The Hague: Mouton.

CHOMSKY, NOAM & HALLE, MORRIS, 1965. 'Some controversial questions in phonological theory', *Journal of Linguistics* 1 97–138.

CHOMSKY, NOAM & HALLE, MORRIS, 1968. *The Sound Pattern of English*, New York: Harper & Row.

GLEASON, H. A. JR., 1955. *An Introduction to Descriptive Linguistics*, New York: Holt, Rinehart & Winston.

HARRIS, ZELLIG S., 1947. *Methods in Structural Linguistics*, Chicago: University of Chicago Press.

HOUSEHOLDER, F. W. JR., 1965. 'On some recent claims in phonological theory', *Journal of Linguistics* 1 13–34.

LONGUET-HIGGINS, H. C., LYONS J. & BROADBENT, D. E., 1981. *The Psychological Mechanisms of Language*, Philosophical Transactions of the Royal Society, London B295, London: Royal Society and British Academy.

LYONS, JOHN, 1958. 'Review of Chomsky 1957', *Litera* (Istanbul) 5, 109–15.

LYONS, JOHN, 1962. 'Phonemic and non-phonemic phonology', *International Journal of American Linguistics* 29, 127–33. Repr. in John Lyons, *Natural Language and Universal Grammar: Essays in Linguistic Theory, Vol. 1*, Cambridge: Cambridge University Press, 96–109.

LYONS, JOHN, 1963. *Structural Semantics*, Publications of the Philological Society 20, Oxford: Blackwell.

LYONS, JOHN, 1965. *The Scientific Study of Language*, Edinburgh: Edinburgh University Press. Repr., with extensive notes, in John Lyons, *Natural Language and Universal Grammar: Essays in Linguistic Theory, Vol. 1*, Cambridge: Cambridge University Press, 179–201.

LYONS, JOHN, 1968. *Introduction to Theoretical Linguistics*, Cambridge: Cambridge University Press.

LYONS, JOHN, 1977. *Semantics*, 2 vols., Cambridge: Cambridge University Press.

LYONS, JOHN, 1991a. 'Grammar and meaning', in Frank Palmer (ed.), *Grammar and Meaning*, Cambridge: Cambridge University Press, 221–49.

LYONS, JOHN, 1991b. *Natural Language and Universal Grammar: Essays in Linguistic Theory, Vol. 1*, Cambridge: Cambridge University Press.

LYONS, JOHN, 1999. 'Diachrony and synchrony in twentieth century lexical semantics: old wine in new bottles', *TPhS* 97, 287–330.

LYONS, JOHN & WALES, ROGER, (eds.) 1966. *Psycholinguistic Papers: The Proceedings of the 1966 Edinburgh Conference*, Edinburgh: Edinburgh University Press.

NIDA, EUGENE ALBERT, 1949. *Morphology: The Descriptive Analysis of Words*, 2nd ed., Ann Arbor, MI: University of Michigan Press.

PALMER, FRANK, (ed.) 1991. *Grammar and Meaning*, Cambridge: Cambridge University Press.

PERDUE, CLIVE, (ed.) 1993. *Adult Language Acquisition: Cross-linguistic Perspectives*, 2 vols., Cambridge: Cambridge University Press.

ROBINS, R. H., 1964. *General Linguistics*, London: Longman.

PETER MATTHEWS

MATTHEWS, Peter Hugoe, FBA 1985; *b.* 1934; *m.* 1984 Lucienne Marie Jeanne Schleich; *Education:* Montpellier School, Paignton; Clifton College; St John's College, Cambridge, BA 1957, MA 1960, LittD 1988; *Career:* Lecturer, University College of North Wales, 1961–5; Lecturer, University of Reading 1965–9, Reader 1969–75, Professor 1975–80; Professor of Linguistics, University of Cambridge, 1980–2001 (Head of Department 1980–96); President of the Philological Society 1992–6; Assistant, later Joint, Editor *Journal of Linguistics* 1970–9; Member Editorial Board Cambridge Studies in Linguistics, etc., since 1980; Hon. Member Linguistic Society of America since 1994. *Major Publications: Inflectional Morphology* 1972; *Morphology* 1974 [2nd ed. 1991]; *Generative Grammar and Linguistic Competence* 1979; *Syntax* 1981; *Grammatical Theory in the United States from Bloomfield to Chomsky* 1993; *The Concise Oxford Dictionary of Linguistics* 1997; *A Short History of Structural Linguistics* 2001.

* * *

As a schoolboy I was hopeless with figures, a disability that I retain; but good at Ancient Greek and Latin. My main interests were in literature, and I came to Cambridge in 1954, after the then obligatory national service, intending to read classics for the first two years and English in my last. If I had followed that plan I might have ended up as a traditional literary scholar, grumbling, as I retired as early as possible, about the latest fashionable obfuscation from Paris or elsewhere.

Two things saved me. One was the character, as it then was, of the Cambridge English Faculty. Its dominant member was a critic, F. R. Leavis, whose biases of taste were decisive and off-putting. The other was the election of Sidney Allen to the Professorship of Comparative Philology. I attended his course on general linguistics in my second year, out of pure curiosity. In those days it was considered beneath the dignity of the more intelligent students in arts subjects to be seen too frequently at lectures that related to the examinations they were taking. Therefore there was ample leisure to explore ideas beyond them. I recall no more than passing details of what Allen said. But I do remember that I was fascinated, and had to learn more.

I will not pretend that, before then, I had shown much interest in language as such. I was bowled over by the language of Greek literature, Homer and the tragedians especially. Another reason for spurning the English Faculty was the confidence with which its students spouted rubbish about plays that they knew only in translations by Gilbert Murray. I have also kept an essay on formal patterning in Virgil's *Eclogues*, which I would have liked to rework later in a Festschrift for Roman Jakobson, who once found time to talk to me, as a research student, when he could easily have pleaded more important engagements. But my wider interests were in poetry in other languages, especially in Italian. I frankly do not know why, in my final year, I decided to do nothing but linguistics. Caution, and my tutor, counselled choosing philological options in the Classical Faculty, which would have obliged me to take further papers in philosophy, literature and history. But I found that, in the Faculty of Modern and Medieval Languages, I could do exactly what I wanted. This was to follow Latin and Italian right through, from the beginning to the modern period, in relation first to Indo-European and then to the other Romance languages. I did not understand at first how good a general introduction to philology that would be. But everything was there, from speculative reconstruction to close study of texts. I remember that the works that most excited me were ones that dealt in elegant abstractions: Benveniste on roots and suffixes in Indo-European (1935), or Martinet on change in phonological systems (especially Martinet 1951–2). I also took a paper on general linguistics, for which no supervision on the Cambridge pattern could be organized. I believe it pulled me down badly.

I was not then attracted by a career in universities. I therefore worked for two years for an insurance company, before deciding that, since I was doing so much academic reading in my spare time, it would make sense to come back to Cambridge as a research student. As an undergraduate I had been guided in Romance philology by Joe Cremona, and the proposal I put to him was to investigate the dating of Greek loan words into Latin and Romance, in relation to changes in the phonology of both languages. But he referred me to Allen, sensing doubtless that, despite my leanings as an undergraduate, I might do better as a general linguist. I have rarely received advice so crucial and perceptive. I would not have shone as a specialist in Romance philology, and I can only hope that, when I have myself guided students, I have occasionally shown a similar insight into their prospects.

Allen's advice was that I should get a copy of Chomsky's *Syntactic Structures* (1957), published two years earlier. As an undergraduate I had read Saussure's *Cours*, Bloomfield's *Language* and the French translation of Trubetzkoy's *Grundzüge*. That was most of what I knew about linguistics in general; and, in particular, I read nothing by Bloomfield's followers until, in the next phase of my education, I made a detailed study, lasting, as I recall, a week in which I did very little else, of Harris's *Methods* (1951). I therefore came to *Syntactic Structures* quite cold. It was an eye-opener, and, for a reader who responded to it before 1960, to precisely the things that later commentaries, including Chomsky's own, have tended to downplay. The excitement lay in the conception of a grammar as a formal system, in which the sentences of a given language, in a sense of 'sentence' and 'language' that went back to antiquity, were defined precisely, for the first time, by a set of rules that were as revealing as they were simple. Of the nature or development of what was later called a speaker's 'competence' there was less, at that time, than could be found in passing remarks by Harris or Hockett. I have since been accused of failing to see in *Syntactic Structures* things that many readers have convinced themselves are there. But they have been told what to look for; and tend to overlook what was actually said.

My PhD was never finished; and, although I have not consciously thrown away drafts, I no longer seem to have them. It would have dealt with prepositions in Italian, in a transformational framework that perhaps owed more to Harris (1957) than to Chomsky's theory as it was in fact unfolding. The method was to uncover patterns in the distribution of lexical items, in Harris's term of 'co-occurrence', which explicated differences of meaning; and that, basically, was as far as I remember getting. I do not think, for example, that I would have explored ideas like those of Fillmore in the later 1960s; though I did feel, after reading his first paper on this topic (1966), that he might be pulling what were once my chestnuts out of the fire. But I pulled none out myself, then or later. In 1961 I had my first job, as a Lecturer in a new department headed by Frank Palmer, at the University College of North Wales. At that time I knew no phonetics, and for my first term I was generously seconded to the School of Oriental and African Studies, for this ignorance to be remedied. That interrupted my research completely; and, when I returned to it, I realized that I would not want to publish my thesis. When I sought advice I was told, correctly in the circumstances of the early 1960s, that the doctorate itself was not essential. I therefore left it and pursued another current interest, in the inflectional morphology of Latin. This had started when, by chance, I had acquired the first three volumes of the *Grammatici Latini*. I remember sitting in the garden, idly leafing though Charisius, and suddenly imagining how a generativist might do it better.

These interests are reflected later in my first substantial group of publications, in 1965–6. Meanwhile, however, I had a brief flirtation with phonetics, through my term in SOAS, and another, in a year spent in America in 1963–4, with computational linguistics. By 1965 I had turned 30, and it was not until then that I began to settle down.

The first flirtation could easily have gone further. In SOAS at least, phonetics in Britain was by then emerging from what may, without disparagement, be called its Daniel Jones phase. Its instruments were mostly primitive; but, with a face mask and a larynx microphone, it was easy to see, for instance, that the consonants in English that were called 'voiced' often had no voicing whatever. Wave forms were at that time registered with a kymograph, with all the mess of smoke and varnish. But, in its own room well away from the pollution, the School also had an early Sonagraph. I was introduced to it by Jack Carnochan, and I have always suspected that we alone were using it. I remember few instruments from which so much could be learned so quickly. I was not destined, however, to work seriously in instrumental phonetics. A short while afterwards I read Fant's *Acoustic Theory of Speech Production* (1960), and felt strongly that this was the way the subject should be going. But, alas, the maths was quite beyond me.

To loosen my vocal organs, I was sent to classes on the phonetics of a variety of languages: Hausa, with Carnochan; Egyptian Arabic, with Terry Mitchell; Cambodian, with Eugénie Henderson; Malayalam, with Elizabeth Whitley. 'Phonetics' naturally embraced phonology, and I learned from their example not to make dogmatic divisions in this field. I was also given conventional training in the cardinal vowels and such-like, in the Jones tradition. But I was no good at it. At the end of the term N. C. Scott, who had struggled to teach me, wrote to Palmer saying that, though I tried hard, I would never make a phonetician. This letter later fell into my hands and was useful to me. Thirty or more years ago, most phoneticians used to insist on students of linguistics spending unbelievable hours in practical classes, for production and ear-training, in small groups. That was how they had themselves been taught, on diploma courses in, for example, Jones's old department at University College London. They were eventually forced to be more reasonable. But while that restrictive practice lasted any competent colleague, on the principle of equality of teaching hours, might be pressed to help them. I was very grateful for such clear assurance that I was not competent.

My second flirtation began at the RAND Corporation in Santa Monica, on a summer course attended by a number of linguists more distinguished than me, organized by David Hays. From there I went to Indiana University, as an Assistant to Fred Householder on a project funded for general information retrieval. Most readers of these reminiscences will not have seen computers of the 1960s, or set programmers to work in an assembly language or worse. But the dreams of early computational linguists were defeated, above all, by the limitations of technology. I think I realized this in Bloomington. I also realized that I would learn little about language by continuing in this field. Many people in the 1960s were seduced by the original fallacy of artificial intelligence: that, in programming a computer to do something, we would gain an insight into how our own brains handled similar problems. But if I ever thought this I was quickly disillusioned. For the systems then envisaged were constrained both by the difficulty of locating faults in programs, and by the limits of our hardware: in particular, the capacity of central processing units. To work efficiently a system had to be articulated as a sequence of sub-systems: first, for example, parse the syntax of a sentence; then 'parse' its 'semantics'. At each stage, rules for a specific language were one thing; general operating programs, to which such rules were input, were another. That way of thinking somehow, alas, passed into psycholinguistics. But there was no reason to suppose that human minds are similar.

From Bloomington, then, I returned to syntax and morphology. I also returned to teaching, which was definitely not my strong point. At Bangor I was let loose mainly on postgraduate students. But in 1965 Palmer was appointed to a new Professorship at Reading, and three lecturers, including me, moved with him. These were the years that followed the report of the Robbins committee (1963), when the university system was expanding rapidly. It was therefore possible for whole departments to be set up instantly in that way. Our brief at Reading was to develop linguistics in joint honours courses: with French, with German, with English literature, and so on. But we saw that, with little further effort, we could also offer single honours. This option proved more popular; and we were soon teaching both undergraduate and MA courses full time.

Moving to Reading, with Frank Palmer, was a vital stroke of good luck. When I was appointed three candidates were applying for two Lectureships; but, after the interviews, there were posts for all of us. I was told that the Vice-Chancellor had said of me, in particular, that I was a luxury the university ought to be able to afford. I hope that, in time, I was something more than that. But the faith that others had in me was still supported by little visible achievement.

I do not remember very much about the meetings at which we planned either of our courses. Both at Reading and in earlier years at Bangor our postgraduate class included many people who taught English as a foreign language; often, in the beginning, from South America. They were delightful students, and the British Council, who were funding most of them, did not waste their money. But I tried, for a while, to follow ideas in 'applied linguistics' and did not think they were a credit to our discipline. Too often in the 1960s, its practitioners seemed to believe that they could 'apply', quite literally, whatever linguistic theory was in fashion, and good practical results would follow. My conclusion was that I should simply teach linguistics, and leave the teachers themselves to find the 'applications', if there were any. But, although my memory of these developments is dim, I think my conscience did rest easier when, within a few years of our arrival in Reading, the Department had the resources to run separate courses for such students.

We were on safer ground with undergraduates, though, looking back, it is remarkable how few textbooks were available. As a student I had rarely opened such things; it was something else, like reading poetry in translation or attending bread-and-butter lectures, that was not done. But I seem to have accepted readily that our pupils could learn from them, and that the ones which were available in the 1960s, which at first were mostly American, covered the right topics either in the right way or in ways that were at least a suitable foundation for our own lectures. In our own country there was Robins's *Introductory Survey* (1964), which we must have recommended as a starter; and, within a few years, we all worked successfully with Lyons's *Introduction to Theoretical Linguistics* (1968). Both were international in their outlook, and fitted admirably with our own view of the subject. In particular, we were determined not to teach it in a form that was nationalistically 'British'. Unlike so many of our colleagues in France, having lost hegemony to linguists in the United States, we did not turn parochial.

This is a delicate matter, and I trust that there are contributors to this volume who can represent the opposite view. But there were those who gave the impression, at least, that they regarded 'British linguistics' as distinctive and superior; and we did well, I believe, to resist them.

Firth, it will be recalled, had died in 1960. I did not meet him; though I had a keen sense, when I was attached to his department in the following autumn, that his ghost still ruled it. Certainly Bazell, who had succeeded him, and was an inspiration to anyone whose mind was up to it, was not the kind of scholar who aspires to found schools or lead those among us who do not themselves know where they are going. Into that role as putative leader stepped, or tried to step, Michael Halliday. His theories were described as 'Neo-Firthian', and were represented, rightly or wrongly, as developing ideas of which Firth would have approved. As such they were promoted vigorously, not least, early in the 1960s, through the new Linguistics Association of Great Britain. I knew little of the beginnings of the Association; there were rumours that it was at first more like a cell of the Communist Party than a normal learned society. But when I attended my first meeting, in London in 1961, it seemed riddled with Halliday's followers and sympathizers. In the middle of the decade, he gave at least one lecture abroad in which he seemed to be suggesting that his own views were the dominant tendency in British linguistics. This naturally annoyed some other British linguists. In America I had come to know John Lyons and Jimmy Thorne, both near contemporaries; and, on returning to this country, two of us at least believed that we were a triumvirate whose mission was to open colleagues' minds to new, especially to Chomsky's early, ideas. My first reaction at this point was to concoct a polemic for the second volume of the *Journal of Linguistics* (1966), to advertise, as plainly as I could, that Neo-Firthianism did not reign unchallenged. Its topic was less important, my main purpose being to object to, in the wording of a passage I was persuaded to delete, 'the large "made in Britain" label'.

I do not think that I accomplished that much by this exercise. It was certainly far less serious, and far less significant in my own intellectual history, than a long and critical review of Chomsky's *Aspects of the Theory of Syntax* (1965) which I contributed to the next volume (1967). This took me two months, and my trust in Chomsky's methods of academic (and, for that matter, political) argument has never been restored. But the skirmish with Halliday was one incident in an academic battle that, like other battles, might have gone the other way. That it did not was due much more to John Lyons. I hesitate to describe him as the Augustus of our triumvirate, since his methods were not Octavian's. But he played a central role as Editor, for its first five years, of the *Journal of Linguistics*. This was established while I was out of the country, and I know little of the details of what went on. But it seemed miraculous that a journal that was to be published for the Linguistics Association, whose direction I had earlier so much distrusted, should be edited independently by someone who I so much admired. It was certainly the very best thing for the future of the subject. There was no whiff of parochialism, and no doctrinal bias either, in a periodical whose circulation shot up rapidly.

It was also a miracle for me personally, since, at the very beginning, I was one of its main contributors. I was then still pretty well unknown, having published only a review article (1961), which Allen had encouraged me, as a research student, to send to *Archivum Linguisticum*. But in 1964 I finally began to scribble to some purpose, and I do not know how else my work could have appeared, or have been noticed, so fast.

By then the Linguistics Association had itself evolved; and, for some years, it was very useful to me both to attend its meetings and to read papers to them. Most sessions were then plenary, and one could easily speak for 40 or 50 minutes. It was therefore possible to address the Association on broad issues; not on clitic movement in Ruritanian, or the theoretical implications of consonant harmony in Glubbdubdrib. From 1967 onwards there are records of its meetings on the inside cover of the *Journal of Linguistics*; and they are, to me, a sad reminder of how much the nature of such conferences has changed. The last time I seem to have spoken was in the autumn of 1972, on the topic of 'How seriously has transformational grammar failed in its objectives?' I am not sure when I last attended a meeting; but I remember clearly one in the later 1970s, when the officers, in pushing through a new system for selecting speakers, also deigned to explain to us the kind of paper they preferred. Glubbdubdrib would have been perfect; and, since such things are better read than heard, I have had little to do with the Association since. But I look back on the meetings I attended with true pleasure. I suppose we are all seduced by rosy memories. But mine is of a discipline that was still unified, in which everyone of consequence was interested in what everyone else was doing, and discussed it freely. That is also how I remember meetings of the Linguistic Association of America, also plenary, when I was based in Bloomington. The controversies were the liveliest I have ever heard, but on matters that everyone agreed were vital.

By the mid-1970s specialists were laying proprietary hands on more and more of the subject. I remember, for example, a discussion in the old style in our department at Reading, when we all pitched into Roger Brown's interpretation of children's language (Brown 1973). I reviewed his book in the *Journal of Linguistics* (1975), of which I was then an editor, as an important contribution to our subject in general. It did not occur to me that, since I was not a professional 'developmental psycholinguist', I might be incompetent. But a colleague's intervention was rejected by the board of editors of a specialist journal, with the comment that the author was not in the field. I believe I was right to be shocked. But the evaluation of such books is now routinely the prerogative of other 'experts', who do not usually have the gift to see their field as those outside might see it.

I was at Reading until 1980, when I returned to Cambridge as the university's first Professor of Linguistics. Before then I had never run a department, and, apart from meetings about teaching and eventual service on the Council of the Philological Society, I had spent perhaps, on average, one hour a year on committees. Reading promoted me to a Readership and, in 1975, to a personal Professorship. But, even before then, I was determined not to seek an established chair until I was ready for it. I could admittedly afford this attitude: I was as yet unmarried, and often far too busy to spend what I earned. But in the 1960s the establishment in many subjects had expanded too fast. Good people were being scattered across universities too thinly, and too many promoted beyond their ability or experience. It was important, I thought, that linguistics should not follow that example. In 1976 a new Chair was established in Oxford, and was the first I considered seriously. Unfortunately, for the first time in my career, a book I was engaged to write was causing me real difficulty. It was finally published five years later (1981). But for the moment I had lost my confidence; and, recollecting in tranquillity, I think that I was not emotionally in a state to take on what would certainly have been a hard task. The next year I was invited by Bob Uhlenbeck to spend a year at NIAS, the research institute in Holland for whose foundation he had been mainly responsible. While I was there I got my book straight; and, when the Chair in Cambridge was proposed, I was very happy for my name to be considered. I had been away for two decades, apart from one year when, in another interval of unpaid leave, King's College had most generously elected me to a Fellowship. There were now two decades more before I retired.

The University of Cambridge is one that new professors come to love gradually. Their power is formally minimal, and power in general is not concentrated in a single hierarchy. Changes can take time, especially if the interests of colleges are affected. A Professor will also have a college Fellowship, and this helps one to understand the way the collegiate structure works in practice. I have never regretted, in particular, the four years that I spent in the early 1980s on the council of my own college. But one can easily get impatient.

One crucial factor is that colleges are responsible for admitting undergraduates. At Reading, there had been a quota for linguistics, as for other honours courses, and we met it as we saw fit. But in Cambridge applications are to individual colleges, and their quotas relate to broader faculties. Since the Department of Linguistics is part of the Faculty of Modern and Medieval Languages, any college might admit sixth-formers interested in the subject under that head. But whether any do so will be up to them entirely. New undergraduates are then faced with options that include, for example, excellent courses on the 'structure and varieties' of French, German and other languages. In later years, they can choose freely among papers on the histories of these languages, on comparative Romance, Germanic or Slavonic, and in branches of general linguistics. But they will be advised, again in colleges, by Directors of Studies who may not be friendly to such subjects. A few try very hard to force their pupils to take literary papers, sometimes, in the first year, by concealing from them that alternatives exist. This is, alas, the flip-side of a system that has many educational advantages. But, despite it, there have been years when, for example, the paper on Dante has had fewer takers than our option in Phonetics. Much as I love *The Divine Comedy*, I note this with satisfaction.

At the end of the 1970s the Department of Linguistics had three lecturers, and included another member of staff, a technical officer and three technicians, responsible for what is now the university's Language Centre. Palmer had had a 'language laboratory' in his first department at Bangor, and in the 1960s, when the one in Cambridge was planned, this arrangement may have seemed to make administrative sense. But by 1980 it did not and, though it was to take the best part of 10 years to hive off the centre, it was one thing I was set on doing. Beyond that, I had no ambition other than to foster the development of linguistics in the best way that I could. I was aware that I should not consider 'linguistics' as established only in my Department. Within that I could have immediate influence. But in Cambridge the majority of linguists are outside it. Some are in institutions, like the Computing Laboratory, quite beyond my orbit. Others are in a range of language faculties. I have been able to meddle in these at best indirectly.

The Department itself soon had three further teaching officers, and by stages has come to offer undergraduates more than twice as many options as it used to. But the expansion had to be, in part, opportunistic. In the beginning the university gave us one more Lectureship, which I was keen to fill with someone who could teach historical linguistics. We then got two more posts through special schemes that ran in the early 1980s. One in the history of grammar was a so-called 'New Blood' Lectureship, which I proposed in the knowledge that Vivien Law would be a candidate. I had inherited a paper in this field with no one there to teach it; and, although I coped at first as well as I was able, I would have suppressed it if, Heaven help me, I had had to lecture seriously on the Middle Ages. A little later, Francis Nolan put up a proposal under a scheme for 'Information Technology', which expanded our coverage of phonetics. I cannot say that, on a rational calculation of new needs, either a second phonetician or a historian of linguistics might have been our first priority. But universities were entering on a period of cut-backs, the ebb in part of the tide that had carried my generation forward, and if we had not seized opportunities like these we would without doubt have got nothing. Elsewhere in the faculty lectureships were already being lost.

The rest is a chronicle of this development and that development, and I think posterity should be spared it. But, in general, I have had two main anxieties. One was simply that I should have a successor. My Professorship was originally for one tenure, and the bitterest failure would have been if, when I retired, the university had let it go. I am therefore delighted that, despite continued tightening of belts, it is now established, with my Faculty's enthusiastic backing, like any other.

Another concern was that the university should not lose posts in the linguistics of individual languages. This has now become so easy: so-and-so retires and, since belts do have to be tightened, what is simpler than to drop a subject which perhaps, through so-and-so's own policy, has never had that many students? Some literary posts are similarly vulnerable. Why keep one in medieval Latin when more undergraduates are interested in film studies or French literature since 1900? So much depends on the people who now teach such subjects, and I am very glad that our philological establishment, for which, of course, I have never been directly responsible, is in general sounder than it was two decades ago. The Oriental Faculty went through a period in which it seemed to be attempting suicide by a thousand cuts. It was at that time that we lost, in particular, the Chair in Sanskrit. But the Classics Faculty retained one that is now effectively in Greek and Latin linguistics, although, when Allen retired in the early 1980s, we had to resist an argument that my own had made it redundant. Under its wing the study of Indo-European flourishes. In my own faculty, Romance linguistics has always done so; and, after interregna whose varied causes I will not go into, I also have good colleagues in Germanic and Slavonic.

The exception is the English Faculty. It has within it a Department of Anglo-Saxon, Norse and Celtic, which has never been a cause of despair. But when I arrived the English Tripos had a paper in the History of the English Language, which, for reasons I again prefer to forget, no prudent candidate would take. This was later taught by Sylvia Adamson and, since she taught well, it became so popular that two lecturers were soon needed. But she left for Manchester in 1999 and, as I write, the subject has been put to sleep. It is to me quite scandalous that the history of our language can no longer be studied in a leading institution. But in the English Faculty, as in mine, there are people who think that only the study of literature is central. In mine they are most easily found by turning over stones in colleges. There they are more prominent, and this does not seem to be scandalous at all.

In the 1990s I was to serve for four years as the President of the Philological Society, and for three I also chaired what is now the Linguistics and Philology Section of the British Academy. I remember writing at least two separate letters of protest, under these hats, when the director of SOAS proposed that their Department of Phonetics and Linguistics, which I had known in its great days, should disappear. It was a comfort to reflect that that at least could never have happened in Cambridge in that way. When I retired from these roles I was also resolved that someone else should head my own Department. I had done it, leave apart, for 16 years; and, in the beginning, with such friendly and co-operative colleagues in my faculty, that job and a Professor's were compatible. But by the end of the 1980s governments, through their cat's-paws, were increasingly messing up the work of universities. This is a broader story, and someone some day may be able to tell it without bitterness. But one form of interference even affected my development as a scholar. I had decided that it did not matter, from now on, how many publications were on my c.v. What other post, for example, was I likely to apply for? I therefore started to explore a long-term project, for an encyclopedic study of grammatical categories. But, by the time I was ready to commit myself, our universities were about to fall foul of short-term 'research assessments'. It seemed that, if my department was not to suffer, I would need a regular supply of '['riːsəːtʃ]' to submit. I therefore cast around for other topics, and, although it is still 30 years since I submitted papers blind to refereed journals, my publications have been bittier and more varied than I had hoped. I was determined not to write in fields in which my contributions might seem negative: my inaugural lecture (1982) should, I decided, be my last piece in that vein. As regards the theory of syntax, in particular, I have therefore found peace in internal exile. I had meanwhile promised Giulio Lepschy, an old colleague in the Italian department at Reading, to contribute on the history of linguistics in the Greek and Roman periods, for the survey he was editing. This was finished, in its English version, in 1986 and, by the time it was published (1990), I had also been persuaded to do a new edition of my introductory *Morphology* (1991). Such things were perfectly respectable; but it was only at that point that I once more focused on new projects of my own. My wife, in particular, was then rightly pressing me to do so.

My underlying difficulty, for many years, has been in trying to keep up with my subject. By 'my subject' I mean simply linguistics; and in the 1960s I read critically, in detail, most of what appeared. But by the early 1970s matters were beginning to get out of hand. The photocopier was a fairly new invention, and was widely abused, much as the internet can be abused now, as a means of putting trivial or half-baked papers into circulation. This did not affect my own work in morphology, since the culprits were not in that field. But I still had to decide if their stuff was worth following. I thought not; and, before long, most of it was seen to have got nowhere. Since then I have become increasingly suspicious of whatever work is most in fashion. Too much of what is published is by pseudo-theorists chasing their own tails, and overshadows what is of true value. I suppose that all scholars have their own solution to this problem. Mine has been, in part, to do my own work in fields that are not fashionable. In the past 10 years, for example, I have written two books on the history of ideas in twentieth-century linguistics, which does not attract researchers in droves. An earlier exception was my work on syntax, and I found it simpler, in that case, to develop my own answers to the problems, and review what others had written afterwards. When I was younger, at least, such methods ensured that I did not get bogged down in my speciality, with no leisure to study and think beyond it.

My larger strategy has simply been to read, for preference, the things that others might be tempted to neglect. I used when young to follow a pack of beagles in South Devon, and one day, in talking to the kennelman, my brother and I asked him why he often set out at an angle of 90 degrees from the rest of us. He explained that hares run in circles. If he walked off to the left and the hare turned to the right, no one would notice he was not around. But if it bore to the left, as he no doubt thought it would, people like us would be amazed how well he understood the lay of the country. I like to suppose that when I worked on morphology I was subconsciously following that lesson. When I began some people even doubted that there was such a topic; but, in the end, a sufficient hue and cry overtook me. I have also followed it consciously in branches of linguistics on which I have never written. Sometimes I have, indeed, appeared to some of my friends to understand the country better than I do. At other times I have instead gone left when the field has gone right. But academic work is definitely more fun if one does not run with the hounds.

Was that not, in brief, why many of us came into linguistics anyway?

REFERENCES

BENVENISTE, EMILE, 1935. *Origines de la formation des noms en indo-européen*, Paris: Maisonneuve.
BROWN, ROGER, 1973. *A First Language: The Early Stages*, Cambridge, MA: Harvard University Press.
CHOMSKY, NOAM, 1957. *Syntactic Structures*, The Hague: Mouton.
CHOMSKY, NOAM, 1965. *Aspects of the Theory of Syntax*, Cambridge, MA: MIT Press.
FANT, GUNNAR, 1960. *Acoustic Theory of Speech Production*, The Hague: Mouton.
FILLMORE, CHARLES J., 1966. 'A proposal concerning English prepositions', in Francis P. Dinneen (ed.), *Report of the Seventeenth Annual Round Table Meeting on Linguistics and Language Studies*, Washington, DC: Georgetown University Press, 19–33.
HARRIS, ZELLIG S., 1951. *Methods in Structural Linguistics*, Chicago: University of Chicago Press.
HARRIS, ZELLIG S., 1957. 'Co-occurrence and transformation in linguistic structure', *Language* 33, 283–340.
LYONS, JOHN, 1968. *Introduction to Theoretical Linguistics*, Cambridge: Cambridge University Press.
MARTINET, ANDRÉ, 1951–2. 'The unvoicing of Old Spanish sibilants', *Romance Philology* 5, 133–56.
MATTHEWS, PETER, 1961. 'Transformational grammar', *Archivum Linguisticum* 13, 196–209.

MATTHEWS, PETER, 1966. 'The concept of rank in Neo-Firthian grammar', *Journal of Linguistics* 2, 101–10.

MATTHEWS, PETER, 1967. 'Review of Chomsky, 1965', *Journal of Linguistics* 3, 119–52.

MATTHEWS, PETER, 1975. 'Review of Brown, 1973', *Journal of Linguistics* 11, 322–43.

MATTHEWS, PETER, 1981. *Syntax*, Cambridge: Cambridge University Press.

MATTHEWS, PETER, 1982. *Do Languages Obey General Laws?*, inaugural lecture, Cambridge: Cambridge University Press.

MATTHEWS, PETER, 1990. 'La linguistica greco-latina', in Giulio Lepschy (ed.), *Storia della linguistica*, vol. 1, Bologna: Il Mulino, 187–310.

MATTHEWS, PETER, 1991. *Morphology*, 2nd ed., Cambridge: Cambridge University Press.

ROBBINS ET AL., 1963. *Higher Education: Report of the Committee appointed by the Prime Minister under the Chairmanship of Lord Robbins*, London: HMSO.

ROBINS, R. H., 1964. *General Linguistics: An Introductory Survey*, London: Longman.

ANNA MORPURGO DAVIES

MORPURGO DAVIES, Anna, Hon. DBE 2000, FBA 1985; Professor of Comparative Philology, and Fellow of Somerville College, University of Oxford, since 1971; *b*. 1937; *m. J.* K. Davies 1962 (marriage dissolved 1978); *Education:* Liceo-Ginnasio Classico Giulio Cesare, Rome; University of Rome Dott. Lettere 1959, Libera Docenza 1963; University of Oxford MA 1964; *Career:* Assistente, University of Rome, 1959–61; Junior Fellow, Center for Hellenic Studies, Washington, DC, 1961–2; Lecturer in Classical Philology, University of Oxford, 1964–71; Fellow of St Hilda's College, Oxford, 1966–71 (Hon. Fellow 1972–); Visiting Professor: University of Pennsylvania 1971; Yale University 1977; University of California at Berkeley 2000; Collitz Professor of the Linguistic Society of America 1975. Hon DLitt, University of St Andrews, 1981; Hon. Member American Academy of Arts and Sciences 1986–; Foreign Member American Philosophical Society 1991–; Corr. Member Oesterreichische Akademie der Wissenschaften 1988–, Institut de France (Académie des Inscriptions et Belles-Lettres) 1992–, Bayerische Akademie der Wissenschaften 1998–; Member of the Academia Europaea 1989–; Hon. Member Linguistic Society of America 1993–; Premio Linceo per la linguistica 1996; President Philological Society 1976–80, Hon. Vice-President 1980–; President Henry Sweet Society 1991–3, Vice-President 1993–; Delegate Oxford University Press 1992–; Co-Editor *Untersuchungen zur indogermanischen Sprach- und Kulturwissenschaft* 1985–2000; Member Editorial Board *Kadmos* 1989–, *Rivista di Linguistica* 1989–98, *Seminari Romani di cultura greca* 1999–, *Writing and Literacy* 1998–. *Major Publications: Mycenaeae Graecitatis Lexicon* 1963; *Studies in Greek, Italic and Indo-European Linguistics offered to L. R. Palmer* 1976 (ed. with W. Meid); *Linear B: A 1984 Survey* 1985, reprinted 1988 (ed. with Y. Duhoux); *La linguistica dell'Ottocento* 1996; *Nineteenth Century Linguistics* 1998.

* * *

My interest in historical linguistics arose relatively late. During most of my school years I was convinced that I was going to become a mathematician. I liked the subject and my grandfather, Guido Castelnuovo, whom I much admired, was a Professor of Mathematics. Only in the last year or so of school did I decide that I was not good enough and I would do better to turn to a literary subject. I went to the University of Rome as a matter of course since I was living in Rome and I decided to study 'lettere antiche', a broad course which included a great deal of Greek and Latin. In my penultimate year of school a good teacher, Mario Bonardi, who tragically died soon afterwards, had made classics alive for me; Greek was no longer epitomized by the irregular verbs which I had been relentlessly taught, but by the poems of Sappho and Alcaeus. It is only much later that the verbs became as important.

I had no intention of becoming a linguist – I was more interested in history of religion or, failing that, in straight classics. Yet I remember going out of curiosity to a lecture on Sanskrit because I had heard that Sanskrit was the mother of all languages. In his first sentence the Professor said that this was an old and wrong belief and I walked out. But I had to follow a course with the unexciting title of 'Grammatica greca e latina', which turned out to be an introduction to the recently deciphered Linear B script of Ancient Greece. Carlo Gallavotti was perhaps the first to lecture on the subject in Italy, was enormously excited and succeeded in exciting some of his students, me included – the most ancient form of Greek written at least five centuries before Homer; a newly deciphered script, a series of second-millennium-BC texts which had never been interpreted, a field in which everything had to be done and even an undergraduate could contribute something. It was irresistible. I felt that to work on Linear B required omniscience: history, archaeology, technology, economics were all necessary to interpret the texts, but at that point in time the correct interpretation depended above all on a correct linguistic analysis. The script rendered Greek only imperfectly. It was necessary to have a clear view of how the Greek language had developed and to know what was possible at the relevant period (1400–1200 BC). Linguists had reconstructed the Indo-European parent language and attributed it to a much earlier period than our first documents; Greek was known from c. 800 or 700 BC. The Mycenaean language was somewhere in the middle but one needed the correct methodology to find out what the possibilities were. I was now pushed in a certain direction and I returned to the Sanskrit course, this time knowing why I was doing it. There followed a number of related courses and while Linear B provided the immediate focus, historical and comparative linguistics became my main interest. I shall always be grateful for the very flexible university system which allowed me to choose subjects which originally I had not intended to specialize in. One of the things I remember from those years is the surprising discovery that I could not any longer be bored – not even when waiting for a bus or listening to a bad lecture. There was always a difficult Linear B word whose meaning needed to be puzzled out. I also remember the mistakes due to self-instruction. I spent ages reading a late Byzantine compilation, the *Etymologicum Magnum*, in the mistaken persuasion that I could use it as a modern etymological dictionary – nobody had pointed me in the direction of the real etymological dictionaries. Similarly I read more than once the whole of Homer to find the attestations of a particular word: I did not know that indexes and concordances existed.

In practice I was given a very traditional training à la neogrammarian (though the word neogrammarian was practically an insult in my faculty): sound change, morphological change, little or no mention of syntax; I tried to learn some more ancient languages. I painfully struggled with German in order to read secondary literature but the basic textbooks I used were in French: Meillet (1937) for Indo-European, Lejeune (1955), Chantraine (1947) and Humbert (1954) for Greek, Niedermann (1953), Ernout (1953) and Ernout & Thomas (1953) for Latin. As for theory, I was never clear what if anything I was taught in the official courses. There was a great deal of *Crocianesimo* in the air but it did not particularly impinge on what I was doing (I heard little or nothing about Vossler); there were some survivals of *neolinguistica* but in Rome this was not much mentioned. I heard some interesting general lectures by Antonino Pagliaro, the Professor of *Glottologia*, but I often found them obscure and I was incapable of seeing their relevance to what I wanted to do. Things changed in the last part of my undergraduate course and in the two years which followed when I became an assistant to Professor Gallavotti. Tullio de Mauro, a somewhat older contemporary, told me to read Saussure's *Cours* and then patiently explained to me its importance; later he introduced me to European and American structuralism. I remember some early morning sessions when he and I and one or two others read together the French translation of Troubetzkoy's *Grundzüge* (1957) and with even greater excitement Zellig Harris's *Structural Linguistics* (1960). It was a new world – one of which we did not speak to our teachers because we felt, rightly or wrongly, that they would have been indifferent or hostile – and also because there was not much communication between the great professors and the humble students or assistants. We had, however, the constant help of Mario Lucidi, a senior assistant of Pagliaro, almost blind, who had one of the sharpest and most original minds that I have ever encountered. He and de Mauro persuaded me that even the most factual statements presupposed a series of theoretical assumptions. Lucidi's death in 1961 when he was 47 was shattering. By that time I had taken my first degree, with an undergraduate dissertation on the morphology of Mycenaean, had had my first experiences of teaching as Gallavotti's *assistente straordinaria* (there were no graduate courses), had written two or three articles on Mycenaean and on classical philology, and had practically completed a Mycenaean lexicon, which was eventually published in 1963. Thanks to Mycenaean I had also met two scholars whom I greatly admired, John Chadwick and Michel Lejeune. But my interests had partially shifted. I was still fascinated by the Greek language, I still saw myself as a historical linguist interested in *Laut- und Formenlehre*, but now I wanted to use for Ancient Greek the rudimental structuralistic principles I had learned; above all I wanted to study a Greek dialect combining a synchronic approach with a history of its development (cf. Morpurgo Davies 1960). In 1961 and in Italy I was blissfully unaware of the fact that in the States linguistics was moving on; I felt modern because I simply wanted to introduce the concepts of synchrony and diachrony, of phoneme and morpheme, into Greek historical grammar.

For 1961/2 I was granted a Junior Fellowship at the Center for Hellenic Studies founded by Harvard in Washington, DC. It was a purely classical institution and 1961/2 was its first year, but I was allowed and even encouraged to follow my linguistic interests. I took a trip to Philadelphia because I had a letter of introduction to Zellig Harris, one of my heroes. He was very kind to me but pointed out that, given my interests, the person that I should meet was his colleague, Henry Hoenigswald. Hoenigswald's *Language Change and Linguistic Reconstruction* had appeared in 1960, but I did not know about it. Even a brief meeting made me realize that serious work in structural historical linguistics was going on. At the LSA convention in Chicago I first came across Chomsky's name. *Syntactic Structures* (1957) was a hot topic for young linguists, but I did not understand how important it would become and a few years passed before I read it. I found it more exciting to see the great names of structuralism: Bloomfield and Sapir were dead, but Hill and Joos were there and I had met Harris. In Mycenaean studies I felt at home, but that year made me realize how ignorant I was in anything linguistic and that linguistics really existed as a self-standing discipline. I could not follow most theoretical discussions and even in Indo-European studies I had immense gaps. Hoenigswald gave me a copy of the preliminary version of *Evidence for Laryngeals* (Winter 1960). I read it but I had not been taught about laryngeals and understood little or nothing. A week spent at Harvard did not increase my linguistic knowledge (I just met Whatmough briefly and Watkins was away) but gave me my first experience of a really good library; to see Widener was a revelation. The other revelation concerned academic life: it did not need to be as hierarchical as it was in Italy.

One year later I was married to J. K. Davies, an Oxford graduate student in ancient history met at the Center for Hellenic Studies, and I was in Oxford struggling to get a job, any sort of academic job, doing some teaching and translations for a living, coming to terms with the English tongue and with the coldest winter for some 60 years. Here too the linguistic scene was different. In Italy *glottologia*, which at the time often meant Indo-European studies, was present in all universities and compulsory for all undergraduates in literary subjects; almost all of them of course had gone through a *liceo classico* and had learned or pretended to learn some Greek and Latin. Theoretical linguistics, if it was not taught under the aegis of *glottologia* (and mostly it was not) or perhaps more frequently under that of Romance philology, did not exist at all. I did not belong to any linguistic society or circle because in Rome there was none. In the States there was Indo-European and/or historical linguistics in a few universities, but linguistics was present in most large universities and even some smaller ones. The

LSA's convention had seemed to me the sign of an established discipline. In Britain there was a Chair of Comparative Philology, which roughly meant Indo-European with a strong Greek and Latin bias, in three universities (Cambridge, Oxford and London), in each case tied to classics. There was a tradition of work in phonetics, but only a few universities had institutionalized linguistics. I was advised by Giulio Lepschy, who had come to England shortly before me, to join the old and respected Philological Society (founded in 1842), which mainly heard papers on historical and philological subjects but also some theoretical papers; Giulio also mentioned that there was a small new society, the LAGB (founded in 1959), which one could join. I did so and was left with very different impressions from the first meetings I attended. At the Philological Society I heard a paper about Old and Middle Iranian by Dr Gershevitch, very scholarly and traditional in its approach. I did not understand all of it because I was too ignorant of Iranian but I had no difficulties in following the type of argumentation. The LAGB meetings discussed theory and description rather than history and comparison. I remember an almost obsessive period when everyone tried to make descriptive sense of e.e. cummings: 'Anyone lived in a pretty how town' or 'he sang his didn't he danced his did'. In spite of my interests, my conversion to structuralism, etc., I remained substantially ignorant and felt out of place in many theoretical discussions. I persevered with the Philological Society partly because I made friends, partly because the papers given were closer to my (historical) interests, partly because its meetings were less expensive in time and money.

My other links outside Oxford were in the world of Mycenologists. There was a regular Mycenaean seminar in the Institute of Classical Studies, which I often attended and which I was invited to address; there was John Chadwick in Cambridge, who, after the death of Michael Ventris, stood for Mycenaean studies everywhere and had welcomed me with open arms.

In Oxford there was a very good tradition of work in historical linguistics – above all in the English school. I just met J. R. R. Tolkien and C. L. Wrenn, but Alistair Campbell, Norman Davis, and Eric Dobson were visible and very prominent, and so was the younger Bruce Mitchell. T. B. Reid, Professor of the Romance Languages, was a medievalist but also a historical linguist with general interests and a very sharp mind; T. Burrow, the professor of Sanskrit, was a distinguished Indo-Europeanist and a Dravidologist. Two successive Professors of Comparative Slavonic Philology (Boris Unbegaun and Robert Auty) contributed, together with Idris Foster (Celtic) and Charles Dowsett (Armenian), to the general preeminence of historical linguistics and philology. The Professor of Comparative Philology, Leonard Palmer, was a brilliant, if occasionally perverse, historical and comparative linguist who had been trained in Vienna with Kretschmer, had worked on post-*koiné* Greek, and had written not only a standard textbook on the external and internal history of Latin but also an introduction to linguistics, published in the 1930s, which introduced into historical linguistics a number of structuralist concepts à la Prague School; at the time he was working mostly on Mycenaean and above all on Mycenaean archaeology. There were no general courses on linguistics nor were there general undergraduate or postgraduate lectures in historical linguistics. Indeed there was no common forum where these experts could meet. Most undergraduate schools in language-based subjects had very austere and technical philological options (often on the history of the language or historical grammar, as well as on palaeography, textual criticism, etc.); principles of Indo-European reconstruction were taught as a minority option within classics and were somehow absorbed, though not explicitly taught, within English. For postgraduates, at a time when the doctorate was still not compulsory (though it was beginning to be so), there was the so-called Diploma in Comparative Philology – a two-year post-graduate course founded in 1928 on the initiative of the then Professor of Comparative Philology, Gustav Braunholtz; C. E. Bazell and Angus McIntosh had been among the first students. In addition to more technical Indo-European papers, the Diploma also required an examination on 'the principles and history of Comparative Philology with special reference to the Indo-European languages'. The candidates (one or two a year as a maximum, though frequently there were years with no candidates) had a very few individual tutorials on the subject from Palmer.[1] The Committee for Comparative Philology, which administered the Diploma, was indeed the one body where some at least of the philologists, who belonged to different faculties, came across each other. The committee's meetings were formal, at stated times, with the proctors present, but were not frequent. The Secretary was the Professor of Comparative Philology, who kept handwritten minutes.

With hindsight it is clear that the philological talent available in the university at the time was impressive, but it was not co-ordinated and a number of opportunities were lost. Things began to change in 1964 when an ex-Diploma student, C. J. E. Ball, came back from SOAS, where he had been a Lecturer in Comparative Linguistics for three years, to take up a Fellowship in English at Lincoln College. That was also the year when, after two years in which I had done odd bits of lecturing for Palmer and the Committee for Comparative Philology, at the normal rate of £24 per term, I was suddenly offered a University Lectureship in Classical Philology. The job, I believe, had become available in the period of university expansion two or three years earlier and had been advertised, but the Selection Committee had not agreed on the appointment. On my arrival I was told that such a position existed, but clearly I was too much of an unknown quantity. After two years, prompted by Palmer's request for a year's sabbatical leave, a decision was taken – I do not know by whom or how. I was simply asked to submit a curriculum to Palmer: no advertisement, no proper application, no references. There followed a letter informing me that I had been appointed: no interview was required. My task was to teach first and second year classicists the special subject in comparative philology and to help the Professor to look after the rare graduates who took the Diploma. I had done most of it on a temporary basis but I still had problems with English and the responsibility was frightening – though I discovered that my undergraduate lectures became much better when I acquired enough self-confidence. Even more frightening was to become Temporary Secretary of the Committee for Comparative Philology during Palmer's leave. I had never sat on a committee in my life and never written minutes; my English was clearly inadequate. I eventually resolved never to use a sentence which had not been used before in a similar context. I succeeded and by the end of the year I had almost learned by heart all the previous minutes, a useful training in bureaucratic English.

Chris Ball's arrival from SOAS, where he had been the colleague of Robins and Bazell and had been breathing a very Firthian atmosphere, brought linguistics to Oxford. He founded the Oxford Linguistic Circle, of which he became the Secretary and I the Treasurer. We had papers of a more general nature by invited speakers (paying their expenses was a problem) and also had a small group which met to read more advanced monographs. Most of the philology professors joined (Palmer gave us some money to help us along) and others took part: Jonathan Cohen, the philosopher, Freddie Beeston, the Arabist, Roy Harris, who taught romance linguistics, the much younger John Marshall, and then Geoffrey Sampson, who had a Research Fellowship. Initially the excitement was great and we even attracted people from outside the university: Mr Eckersley, who had just founded the Eckersley School of English, was one of them. At some stage Ian Mulder, who was the librarian of the Oriental Institute, a devoted follower of Martinet, became a prevailing voice and tried to instruct us all in a form of functional linguistics. Meanwhile I was teaching the basic historical grammar of Greek and Latin, Greek dialects, etc., to students who probably knew more Greek and Latin than I did but to whom 'philology', i.e. historical and comparative grammar, was entirely new. I was offered a Supernumerary Fellowship at St Hilda, and that carried a new task (I became College Lecturer in Classics) but also some benefits; to my surprise I found college life quite congenial and very much liked St Hilda's.

I was working hard but there was time to learn and take part in other activities – there was little or no administration. I learned Old English and some Old Norse from Celia Sisam, a fellow of St Hilda's; Oliver Gurney, then Shillito Reader in Assyriology, taught me Hittite, and I took part in a seminar started by Palmer about Hieroglyphic Luwian; we did not get very far until David Hawkins joined us from SOAS in 1965. Obviously I kept up with classics. A strong influence was that of Eduard Fraenkel, who had retired from the Corpus Chair of Latin in 1953 but kept his seminar going and effectively taught us how a real classicist reads a text. I was bowled over by his learning and his intelligence but also by his deep earnestness, his sense of tradition and his devotion to scholarship. At the same time I came to know and admire Arnaldo Momigliano, the ancient historian, who was based in London but came frequently to Oxford. Fraenkel and Momigliano were very different (not only in age), but both combined seriousness and immense warmth; it was impossible not to respond. I felt I was growing up: previously I had frequently yielded to the hero-worship typical of non-British students, but for Fraenkel and Momigliano I managed to feel deep devotion and affection while retaining some at least of my critical faculties.

In 1970 Palmer announced that he would retire in September 1971; the Chair was readvertised and I waited with some anxiety to see who the new Professor would be. To my surprise I was offered the Chair, though I had not applied; I accepted it, still not understanding what had happened. Hugh Lloyd Jones, Regius Professor of Greek, had hinted that that was a possibility, but I had not taken him seriously. Much earlier, I had accepted an invitation to teach for the first semester of 1971/2 at the University of Pennsylvania, replacing Hoenigswald; I could not back out, and I went. The experience was exhilarating: a real department, some very good students, including Ivan Sag and George Dunkel, frequent contacts with Hoenigswald who was on leave and ready to discuss everything, further contacts with Indo-Europeanists at Harvard (Calvert Watkins) and Yale (Warren Cowgill, Stanley Insler). I felt happy in the States and felt that I had friends there. When I came back things were different. I had to change college. The Chair was attached to Worcester, which was a men-only college; the rule was that women's colleges would take it in turn to have the rare women Professors: Helen Gardner, Merton Professor of English, had gone to Lady Margaret Hall (also from St Hilda's) and I, who came second, went to Somerville, which was somewhat shaken by the amount of book space I needed. I found myself doing the job of two people in two terms instead of three – and this at a time when we had doubled the syllabus because we promised to offer classes for all four years of the classical undergraduate course. It was a very hard year, but after the appointment of John Penney to my previous Lectureship life became much easier.

The 30 years between 1971 and 2001 disappear in a blur; I find it difficult to know retrospectively how much of what happened was planned and how much was due to chance, though I suspect that the latter played a considerable role. Time passed very fast, though a constant feature was the brightness of undergraduates; now they know far less in the way of Greek and Latin than in the 1960s but the ability of some of them is still impressive in the extreme.

Institutionally I felt, I do not know how consciously, that something needed to be done on two fronts. First, subjects like historical linguistics or comparative philology or Indo-European were at risk, since the detailed knowledge of languages, and particularly ancient languages, which they required was disappearing. In the previous century Berthold Delbrück

(1875: 3f) had given as example of how useful and exciting Indo-European studies could be the fact that they allowed teachers to explain to their students why a word like Greek *menos* was a neuter though it ended in -*s*. In the second part of the twentieth century this argument did not seem very appealing, but it still seemed possible to show to classicists and others the importance of a method which identified genetically related languages and contrasted them with languages joined by chance similarities. The same method could lead to the reconstruction of the earlier stages of an ancient language and lengthen its history. Clearly the comparative and historical study of related languages has a great deal to offer, but labour-intensive teaching has now to be done at all levels, undergraduate and graduate. So much was always clear, but I had moments of worry. My colleague John Penney, who has a far more balanced attitude than I do, calmed me down: 'This is a good subject; if they forget it they will have to reinvent it.' I found, and find, the thought singularly comforting.

Second, it seemed clear to me, after my American experiences, that it was time that linguistics got established in British universities in general and in Oxford in particular, and that comparative philology could not dispense with linguistics. Yet that required in each university a group of academics prepared to act as a pressure group. In Oxford a few enthusiastic dons worked far harder than anyone could have expected them to:[2] linguistics has had its ups and downs but now exists as a relatively independent discipline with a few posts reserved for it (previously there were none), a phonetic lab and a graduate centre. Any creation due to pressure from lower down rather than diktat from higher up necessarily leads to less consistent structures, but the gain is a wider range of activities and a broader outlook than would have been possible otherwise. Serendipity plays a role: it is our good and unexpected luck that currently the Khalid bin Abdullah Al Saud Professor for the Study of the Modern Arabic World, Clive Holes, is a distinguished sociolinguist. Other faculties selected linguists for their posts: witness the English Chairs held by Jean Aitchison and Suzanne Romaine. I have now shared a number of administrative tasks with three successive Professors of General Linguistics (Roy Harris, James Higginbotham, Stephen Pulman), and we have seen that the system may work.

My own work developed along different lines. A Professorship involves graduate supervision, and I was exceedingly lucky in the first four students I supervised: John Penney, Kim McCone, Elizabeth Tucker and Katrina (Mickey) Hayward. They required little or no help but worked in different fields: Indo-European, Celtic, Greek morphology, Greek dialectology – I felt very stretched but learned a great deal.[3] Later on I was again out of my depth when David Langslow, who also became a colleague, started working on technical languages and Latin medical terminology; I was more confident when I followed Ivo Zucha's study of Hittite word formation.

Ancient Greek was my main interest and still is. In the history of Greek or indeed of any language, I never cease to be amazed and fascinated by the interaction between sociolinguistic and/or historical development and the repercussion on the language's structure, the contrast between systemic changes and arbitrary new developments. As an undergraduate my main ambition was to introduce or correct one or two points of detail in the great edifice of Greek historical grammar, to be responsible for the addition of one or two footnotes in one of the great *Handbücher*. I still feel exactly the same way, though I now know that this panders to a concept of progress which most people would label antiquated and positivistic. On the other hand the old view that in every subject there are a number of problems to be solved, of fields to explore, is unlikely to disappear. I am immensely impressed by the work done on Greek by my graduate students; some of it ought to rate more than a footnote. Problems of morphology have been studied by Elizabeth Tucker (contract verbs), Torsten Meißner (*s*-stems), Jason Zerdin (*skelo*-verbs) and in a different framework Philomen Probert (accentuation); those of linguistic variety by Katrina Hayward (verse inscriptions), Rudolf Wachter (vase inscriptions), Stephen Colvin and Andreas Willi (both Aristophanes); those of morphosyntax, syntax, semantics and pragmatics by Eleanor Dickey (forms of address), Pietro Bortone (prepositions), Maria Karali (word order) and again Jason Zerdin. The extraordinary thing is how they all start with the feeling that the secondary literature is overpowering and everything has been done before. Yet by the time they write their conclusions they all state – and believe – that an enormous amount remains to be done and that the most elementary questions have not been asked or answered. I am much older, but every time I embark on a new project I go through the same mental reactions. However, I do envy the recent graduates; they have received that formal training in linguistic theory which I never had and are capable of using in their historical work what they learned.

Mycenaean work brought me to the regular Mycenaean colloquia every five years, and there too after the first enthusiasm I normally went with the feeling that lots had been done and little was new; every time I came away excited and in a sense refreshed. They were and are good venues to meet colleagues or teachers whom I admire or admired. Some have disappeared, and I still miss them: Oswald Szemerényi, Ernst Risch, Michel Lejeune, John Chadwick, Olivier Masson; others closer to me in age or sometimes much younger have become good friends. It is extraordinary how much Mycenaean has done to create good international relationships. I also owe to Mycenaean my most recent interest, that in the observation of onomastic development. I always thought that the study of personal names was meritorious but unexciting, until I discovered how interesting it is to compare and contrast the patterns of phonological and morphological development in the standard lexicon of a language (Greek in my case) with that in the onomastic system of the same language: classical Greek does not have a special feminine form for *hippos* 'horse or mare', but the sequence *hippē* appears in feminine names like *Xanthippē*, where pragmatic reasons dictate that the feminine is morphologically marked. Currently the diachrony of names contrasted with the diachrony of nouns seems to me a very fruitful field for analysis; in both cases there is continuity, but pragmatic causes determine different forms of continuity. To observe this type of phenomenon horizontally across the Greek dialects and vertically from Mycenaean to later Greek is extraordinarily valuable (Morpurgo Davies 1999; 2000).

In the late 1960s I was invited by Arnaldo Momigliano to give a paper on one of the great linguists of the nineteenth century at the seminar which he and Sally Humphreys run at the Warburg Institute. I have never been good at saying no and I agreed, under protest, since I felt, and was, ignorant in the subject. I ended up working on Karl Brugmann and the history of the neogrammarians' controversy in the 1870s. The story had a gossipy, malicious side which was naturally appealing, but for me the important discovery was that most of what I had absorbed from textbooks or from my teachers about our predecessors was quite simply wrong. I had a vision of boring old scholars, Teutonic in appearance and mentality, conservative and dull; I discovered a set of arrogant, irritating and self-confessedly revolutionary youngsters. I had thought that most of what I knew about Indo-European had been established at the beginning of the century, but reading the periodicals of the late nineteenth century I found myself in the midst of a subject in complete flux. Everything was under discussion and everything was reconsidered to a point which I had never experienced. New questions were asked but solutions were not always forthcoming. At the time the excitement must have been overpowering, and I began to understand what vibrant scholarship meant. At the same time I acquired a new understanding of what I thought I knew; I now saw how it had been reached, and that opened new vistas about certainties and above all uncertainties. In a way I was relearning my subject, making it mine in a way which I had not previously experienced. I did not like my Brugmann paper and only returned to it some 15 years later, but in the late 1960s I felt flattered and pleased when Tom Sebeok wrote to ask me whether I would contribute the chapter on the historiography of language classification to volume 13 of *Current Trends in Linguistics*. It was very hard work, partly because I had a great deal to learn from the primary sources, partly because I had to read an immense amount of secondary literature. At the end, however, I had the feeling that I was beginning to understand what the linguistics of the nineteenth-century was all about; this induced me years later to accept Giulio Lepschy's invitation to contribute the nineteenth century chapter to the volumes he was editing for Il Mulino and Longman about the history of linguistics. That too turned out to be an exciting but almost impossible task – I had little time (my administrative tasks were increasing daily) and I kept missing all the deadlines. Time was also wasted in trying to settle on a language, until I found out that I had greater difficulties in writing in Italian than in English. Since I still make mistakes in English the conclusion – not very cheerful – was that I did not have any longer a language in which I felt entirely confident. The Lepschy chapter grew until in a later version it became a book (Morpurgo Davies 1998). In writing it I felt again, as I had when I first worked on Mycenaean, that I needed to be omniscient. There was a difference: in my early days I had simply wished for all-encompassing erudition; now I also realized that I did not know enough about historical method or philosophical theory. At times I felt very despondent. I was cheered up by a few friends – Giulio Lepschy, Bobby Robins, Peter Matthews – though when I compared my difficulties with the apparent ease with which they worked I became even more despondent. Compared with other authors, my one advantage was that I knew, and cared for, what nineteenth-century scholars were doing. Historians of ideas had a much better understanding than I did of the general intellectual atmosphere, but I could see what developments were prompted by the internal economy of the subject. In the end I took comfort in Hoenigswald's dictum that in the history of nineteenth-century linguistics what really matters is what linguists did, not what they thought they did.

My third line of research is largely due to serendipity. The Hieroglyphic Hittite seminars started by Palmer continued for a while but in the late 1960s/ early 1970s, things were changing. Hawkins had begun to look at the actual inscriptions and realized that past editions were inadequate; he used his outstanding draughtsmanship to produce new drawings and naturally new interpretations. The two of us continued to meet because we wanted to make sense of the texts; I was also eager to make sense of the language in comparative terms. How could an Indo-European language have a word like *atimaī* meaning 'name'? The discovery of two words written in the Hieroglyphs and identified with two measures which we knew from cuneiform script texts led to a new reading of four signs; no longer ⟨i, ī, a, ā⟩ as previously believed, but ⟨zi, za, i, a⟩. The consequences were dramatic because the signs in question were used mainly in the inflectional endings; suddenly the grammar changed and the so-called Hieroglyphic Hittite was proved to be Hieroglyphic Luwian. We reported, with considerable trepidation, our theories at the Symposium on the Undeciphered Languages organized by the Royal Asiatic Society in 1973 to celebrate its sesquicentenary. A few experts were there; one of them, Günther Neumann from Würzburg, agreed with us but persuaded us that the reading ⟨a⟩ was wrong and should be ⟨ia⟩. We ended with a joint publication (Hawkins, Morpurgo Davies & Neumann 1973). The word for 'name' now turned out to be *adaman-za*. Shortly afterwards Hawkins demonstrated that some signs which had been taken as indicating relative pronouns were in fact negative particles. This time what changed was not the grammar but the meaning of the texts. Later discoveries (including some digraphic seals) have shown that the new readings were correct. Hawkins and I wrote and are still writing a number of joint articles, and though my task was mostly that of understanding the linguistic consequences of his interpretations, we found it useful to discuss with each other every part of the work – few things have been more satisfactory in my life than the discovery that it is possible to work on a regular basis with a colleague who is also a friend. The culmination is of course Hawkins's monumental corpus of Hieroglyphic Luwian inscriptions, which appeared in 2000, some 35 years after his work first started. The historical consequences of the understanding of these texts are very great; the linguistic consequences are also important. Equally interesting is the fact that the script is a rare and perhaps unique example of a script developed in the first instance for an Indo-European language. Now that Hawkins's *Corpus* has appeared, we must plan for a systematic account of the linguistic facts.

Historians of linguistics know that the institutionalization of of linguistics has made it impossible to concentrate exclusively on the views of outstanding linguists. 'Normal' practitioners are also influential, because they decide on the composition and direction of departments and on the subjects to be taught. In the nineteenth century it was natural to link the history of linguistics with that of the universities because most contacts depended on the university to which one belonged or from where one originated. Nowadays, with increased mobility, we must also think in terms of scholarly networks – once again noting that recognized geniuses are laws to themselves. On the assumption that this account is meant to provide some down-to-earth material for future historians, I note that my own 'network' – a word which I do not like – has been changing over the years. It never was a purely Italian one, because Mycenaean, with which I started, was such an international subject, but initially it was largely limited to classicists, historical linguists and Indo-Europeanists in continental Europe. These contacts and friendships remain, of course, and in recent years my links with Italy have increased. Yet in the last decades I have also had frequent and close personal and scholarly contacts with American Indo-Europeanists: Hoenigswald, of course, who has been a mentor and a friend all along, but also Warren Cowgill before his premature death, Stanley Insler, Calvert Watkins, Jay Jasanoff, Alan Nussbaum, Andrew Garrett, Craig Melchert, Don Ringe and of course others. I was lucky to meet J. Schindler in Harvard, and the friendship continued when he returned to Vienna.

As Lejeune once noticed, conferences are 'bons instruments de voyage'; yet real progress is made in specialized colloquia. I have gained a great deal from the quinquennial Mycenaean Colloquia, which were started by Lejeune in 1956 (before my time), and from the Greek Dialectology Colloquia started by Claude Brixhe in 1986. In the States, Warren Cowgill and Stanley Insler founded in 1982 a yearly series of East Coast Indo-European Conferences (ECIEC), which offer a chance to discuss Indo-European problems informally. I have had to miss most of them, but those I could attend and the odd weeks or months or semesters which I spent at the Universities of Pennsylvania, Yale, Harvard and Berkeley have been among my most important experiences. I keep asking myself whether the strength of my link with American universities and American scholars depends on linguistic factors (I feel more at home in English than in French or German) or on some other form of natural affinity, but I do not seem to be able to reach an answer. I can simply note, for the future historian, that this variety of contacts is probably more typical of the twentieth than of the nineteenth century. I have been lucky in having the chance, but I know that the real luck consists in having found a subject which allows endless possibilities and whose interest never diminishes.

I have occasionally tried to describe academic work to an outsider: teaching is easy, administration is not very different from what is done elsewhere, research is much more difficult to explain. 'Do you like doing it?' I am asked. 'What is it like?' I have learned not to give an honest reply; if I did I would probably say that it is a great deal of drudgery alternating with brief moments of excitement so overpowering that it is impossible to keep still, and with other moments when one's head seems about to explode because it is required to absorb too many things at once. All of this is in various ways painful – and yet I doubt that we do it only to keep the RAE happy.

NOTES

1 In my first two years in Oxford I gave tutorials in Greek philology to two graduates, Michael Mann and David Ferris, who were specializing in Greek and Slavic and Greek and Sanskrit respectively. We were pretty close in age and I found the experience immensely rewarding. After the end of the Diploma Michael Mann was offered a position in SOAS and became a specialist in Bemba; David Ferris obtained a Lectureship in General Linguistics at the University of Exeter. In both cases they had to learn their new job more or less from scratch.
2 Most of them are still there and working towards the same aim; others were mentioned before in the list of the first members of the Linguistic Circle; yet others resigned or retired, like C. J. E. Ball, Cathy Slater and Rebecca Posner; the list could be much longer. Sadly a few died prematurely: Stephen Ullmann (d. 1976), Ann Pennington (d. 1981), Leslie Seiffert (d. 1990); it is impossible to forget them.
3 Few things are more painful than to see one's students disappearing before oneself. The recent (2001) death of Katrina Hayward at the age of 49 is difficult to bear.

REFERENCES

CHANTRAINE, P., 1947. *Morphologie historique du grec*, Paris: Klincksieck.
CHOMSKY, NOAM, 1957. *Syntactic Structures* (Janua Linguanum, No. IV), The Hague: Mouton.
DELBRÜCK, B., 1875. *Das Sprachstudium auf den deutschen Universitäten*, Jena: Dufft.
ERNOUT, A., 1953. *Morphologie historique du latin*, 3rd ed., Paris: Klincksieck.
ERNOUT, A. & THOMAS, F., 1953. *Syntaxe latine*, 2nd ed., Paris: Klincksieck.
HARRIS, Z. S., 1960. *Structural Linguistics*, Chicago: University of Chicago Press. 1st ed. as *Methods in Structural Linguistics*, 1947.

HAWKINS, J. D., 2000. *Corpus of Hieroglyphic Luwian Inscriptions.* Vol. I *Inscriptions of the Iron Age,* 3 parts, Berlin: de Gruyter.

HAWKINS, J. D., MORPURGO DAVIES, A. & NEUMANN, G., 1973. 'Hittite hieroglyphs and Luwian: new evidence for the connection', *Nachrichten der Akademie der Wissenschaften in Göttingen,* Phil.-hist. Kl. 6.

HOENIGSWALD, H. M., 1960. *Language Change and Linguistic Reconstruction,* Chicago: University of Chicago Press.

HUMBERT, J., 1954. *Syntaxe grecque,* 2nd ed., Paris: Klincksieck.

LEJEUNE, M., 1955. *Traité de phonétique grecque,* 2nd ed., Paris: Klincksieck.

MEILLET, A., 1937. *Introduction à l'étude comparative des langues indo-européennes,* 8th ed., Paris: Hachette.

MORPURGO DAVIES, A., 1960. 'Review of Thumb-Scherer, *Handbuch der griechischen Dialekte*', *Parola del Passato* (*PdP*), 458–70.

MORPURGO DAVIES, A., 1975. 'Language classification in the nineteenth century', in T. Sebeok (ed.), *Current Trends in Linguistics* 13, The Hague: Mouton, 607–716.

MORPURGO DAVIES, A., 1998. *Nineteenth Century Linguistics,* vol. IV of G. Lepschy (ed.), *History of Linguistics,* London: Longman.

MORPURGO DAVIES, A., 1999. 'The morphology of personal names in Mycenaean and Greek: some observations', in S. Deger-Jalkotzy, S. Hiller & O. Panagl (eds.), *Floreant studia mycenaea,* Vienna: Oesterreichische Akademie, 389–405.

MORPURGO DAVIES, A., 2000. 'Greek personal names and linguistic continuity', in S. Hornblower & E. Matthews (eds.), *Greek Personal Names: Their Value as Evidence,* Oxford: British Academy and Oxford University Press, 15–39.

NIEDERMANN, M., 1953. *Phonétique historique du latin,* 3rd ed., Paris: Klincksieck.

TROUBETZKOY, N. S., 1957. *Principes de phonologie,* trans. J. Cantineau, Paris: Klincksieck.

WINTER, W., (ed.) 1960. *Evidence for Laryngeals: Work Papers of a Conference in Indo-European Linguistics,* Austin: University of Texas. Rev. ed. 1965, The Hague: Mouton.

FRANK PALMER

PALMER, Frank Robert, FBA 1975, MAE 1993; Professor Emeritus, University of Reading, since 1987; *b.* 1922; *m.* 1948 Jean Elisabeth Moore; *Education:* Bristol Grammar School; New College Oxford, Merton College Oxford, MA 1947. *Career:* Lecturer, School of Oriental and African Studies, University of London, 1950–60; Professor, University College of North Wales, Bangor, 1960–5 (Head of Department of Linguistics 1960–5); Professor, University of Reading, 1965–87 (Head of Department of Linguistic Science 1965–87, Dean of the Faculty of Letters and Social Science 1969–72). Hon. D Litt, University of Reading, 1996; Chairman Linguistics Association of Great Britain 1965–8; Vice-President Philological Society 1992–; Editor *Journal of Linguistics* 1969–79. *Major Publications: The Morphology of the Tigre Noun* 1962; *A Linguistic Study of the English Verb* 1965; *Selected Papers of J. R. Firth 1952–59* 1968 (ed.); *Prosodic analysis* 1970 (ed.); *Grammar* 1971 [2nd ed. 1984]; *The English Verb* 1974 [2nd ed. 1987]; *Semantics* 1976 [2nd ed. 1981]; *Modality and the English Modals* 1979 [2nd ed. 1990]; *Mood and Modality* 1986 [2nd ed. 2001]; *Studies in the History of Western Linguistics* 1986 (joint ed.); *Grammatical Roles and Relations* 1994; *Grammar and Meaning* 1995 (ed.).

* * *

My career has been determined, far more than that of most other people, 'by a set of curious chances'. If it had followed the most natural line, I would have been a mathematician (as two of my children and two of my grand-children are). I was once tempted by the idea of studying medicine (and two of my children have followed that career). I seemed destined at one time for a teaching post in the classics, first in Greek and then in ancient history. I was offered, accepted and then declined a post in Chinanja at SOAS, but ended up, somewhat unexpectedly, in linguistics.

Naturally, the first influence on my life was that of my father. He was Headmaster of one of the best elementary schools in Gloucestershire, and I was taught there from the age of four. He persuaded the Headmaster of Bristol Grammar School to offer me a free place (a 'Governors' scholarship') when I was 10 and a half, (although then, as now, the normal age for entering a grammar school was 11). I went into 'Shell', which was the third form for boys who had not been to the preparatory school – they went into 3A, 3B and 3C. Curiously, Shell was the only form at the school in which I was expected to learn to speak a foreign language, for the form master and

French teacher was 'Pish' Guerra, a Frenchman. For the rest of my time at school, French was, like Latin and Greek, a purely written language – and yet I managed to pass School Certificate French with Distinction, even though there was an oral examination!

It was here that the system managed to persuade me to study classics, even though mathematics was by far my best subject. At the end of the first year we were given the choice of 'Classical' and 'Modern', 4A being Classical and the remaining forms Modern, and I chose Classical. It was understood that those in 4A could choose, at the end of the year, to carry on with classics in 5A or to go into Modern 5B. We had begun Latin in Shell, but were introduced to Greek in 4A, by a most wonderful form master, Caudwell, who gave us all nicknames, many of which stuck for years, and who used to read from P. G. Wodehouse for the last 10 minutes of his Greek lessons. About half of the form made the choice to switch to Modern 5B, and I thought about changing too. But I was persuaded that I could carry on in the classical side for another two years (until School Certificate), since mathematics was still taught in the classical forms, and Caudwell had instilled in me a love of Greek.

During this time our study of Greek and Latin consisted of reading classical texts and translating them orally in class, translation of English texts into verse and prose, mostly as homework, and rote learning of declensions, conjugations and the 'gender rhymes' in Kennedy's *Revised Latin Primer* (Kennedy 1933).

After School Certificate, I was persuaded, yet again, by the form master of the classical lower sixth, Langford, to continue with classics in the sixth form. His argument was that I could still study maths as a hobby, and he even visited my parents and suggested to them that all the best jobs went to classical scholars (which was probably still true at the time). On reflection, I know that it was wrong of Langford to put pressure on me and my parents in this way, when it was so obvious that mathematics was my best subject. I was always top of the form in that subject, but in that subject alone, being usually fifth overall. Yet I have to be grateful to him for all his help over the next few years, when I was in the classical sixth form, although he was not the form master of the classical sixth. He coached me, in his own time, not only in the classics, but also in essay writing, which was an important part of the Oxford Scholarship examinations.

I spent over four years in the sixth form, most of the last two years spent in private study of the classical texts. I believe that I read more of them than is required today for degrees in classics in some universities. I won a state scholarship and the Ella Stephens Scholarship for Greek at New College, and went to Oxford in January 1941, requesting to be allowed to start my course immediately because that would allow me to take Hon. Mods, the first part of the Classics syllabus. Otherwise, I would have been called up into the armed forces, for the War Office allowed call-up to be delayed if we joined the Volunteer Reserve and carried out military training towards what was known as 'Cert. B'. As a result, I spent four terms rather than the normal five for Honour Mods and was obliged to spend a day and a half on military training. In addition, there were fire-fighting duties, so that, on the whole, I did not really enjoy these four terms, for they lacked the more relaxed nature of life at a university. I will add one thing only – I am sure that the discipline of studying Latin and Greek texts fitted me well for my encounter with languages during my wartime service and for my move into linguistics.

It was here at New College that I first met R. H. ('Bobby') Robins, whose experience of life in college (as described in his paper in this volume) reflects my own. I will not, therefore duplicate what he has said.

I was called up in May 1942, and commissioned into the Royal Artillery in September 1943, only to be transferred, after a very brief (six-week) and quite unsatisfactory course, to the Somerset Light Infantry in April 1944. As it turned out, the battalion to which I was posted was one of those that landed on the beaches of Normandy on the first day of the invasion. However, the War Office, showing uncharacteristic sense, decided at the last moment not to send the troops into battle with a new and only half-trained officer. So in early May 1944 I found myself on a troopship to East Africa instead and heard of the invasion on D-day during our three-week voyage.

It was in East Africa that I developed my interest in languages. I went first on a six-week course in Swahili and took every advantage to learn the language – spending evenings in optional conversational classes rather than drinking in the mess, as almost everyone else did. Even though I had had no phonetic training, I soon noticed that our Swahili teacher (an English captain) failed to pronounce initial velar nasals, using palatal nasals instead – and yet he had been appointed to his teaching post. I became quite fluent in those six weeks and, in the final examination, I came second. The man who came first was a missionary who had been given permission to join the course – but he had spent 20 years in Kenya and spoke fluent Kikuyu! Not surprising (for it was so typical of the army), I was then sent to a Somali battalion where no Swahili was spoken, but that gave me the opportunity of learning Somali as well, for the troops did not speak either Swahili or English. Even so, a year later I managed to pass the Civil Service Junior examination in Swahili, for which there was an award of £10.

I returned to New College in January 1946, thanks to a special release scheme for arts students, to read 'Greats'. Unfortunately for me, the Greats syllabus did not then have a classical literature component, but consisted of philosophy and ancient history. However, my military career had taught me how to discipline myself and organize my work. I had no difficulty with working twice as hard as I had worked before, though I also made many friends and enjoyed college life.

The philosophy I found rather boring, though it proved relevant to my later career. My philosophical views were greatly influenced by Isaiah Berlin, who developed in me a sceptical, if not cynical, attitude towards much of philosophical thought (and later towards much of linguistic speculation). My views have remained highly empirical, in the traditional understanding of that term, so that I have never accepted the idea that linguistics is concerned with the mind or any kind of mental system.

I quite enjoyed ancient history, although it had been my worst subject at school and my teacher had described me as 'the world's worst historian', for, at least I was able to read the prose of Herodotus and Thucydides. My hard work won me two postgraduate awards that appeared to be setting me on a course to spend my career as a historian – the Craven Fellowship and a Post-mastership at Merton College. But this was the worst period of my life – my research topic was on early Roman foreign policy and this entailed reading vast amounts of the works of the incredibly boring Livy. After just over a year, I realized that I had no hopes of attaining a DPhil – and in any case would need a further year's financing to do so, for both awards were for two years only. By November 1949, in the second year of my research, I was in despair. I had a wife and son and no future prospects. I had been virtually promised a Fellowship at one of the colleges, even reaching the stage when the retiring Fellow had discussed with me the students that I should be teaching. Yet I was not appointed when it was discovered that I was married, for what was wanted was a Fellow who would live in college.

The only bright part about this time was that I spent six months in Italy and learnt to speak Italian in a very short time. I found this easy, not only because of my knowledge of Latin, but also because I was able to apply the knowledge that I gained from reading traditional grammars of Italian (contrary to what some language teachers would believe).

It was then that my life was directed to linguistics – thanks to Robins, who now appeared in the role of a fairy godmother. Although I had known him in 1941, it was only in 1945–8 that we became close friends. (His sudden death in April 2000 was a very sad event for me, though I was happy to write two obituaries and to give the eulogy at his funeral.) He went to SOAS when I remained in Oxford, but would visit us occasionally. I knew about the work at SOAS, because I myself could also have been there in the Africa Department, for I had been offered a Lectureship in Chinanja by the famed Professor Ida Ward, but had declined it when I won the postgraduate awards for ancient history.

One day Robins visited us and seeing our difficulties said to me that there was a Lectureship in Phonetics (salary the princely sum of £500 a year) in the Department of Phonetics and Linguistics. My reaction was 'What's phonetics?', but he persuaded me to come to London and meet the great man, J. R. Firth. For, since linguistics was unknown in the universities except at SOAS, Firth was willing to appoint good scholars with no

knowledge of the subject. I came to London and was first interviewed by
Jack Carnochan and Eileen Evans (later Mrs Whitley), who asked me to
imitate some curious sounds (including implosives, I remember, and some of
the consonants of Malayalam). I was then interviewed by Firth, who said I
would never make a phonetician – and then offered me a Lectureship in
Linguistics! So I accepted the offer and joined the Department in January
1950. On reflection, I am glad that I was not appointed to a phonetics post.
Yet Firth was wrong to say that I would never make a phonetician, for,
apart from my earlier success with Swahili, Somali (with some very 'difficult'
sounds) and Italian, I later succeeded in the detailed study of the phonetics
of five Ethiopian languages. I am sure that I (or anyone else who is ready to
practise and to shed inhibitions) can learn to become proficient in phonetics,
just as people without perfect pitch can become great musicians.

I will not say a great deal about Firth or the Department – for I do not
want to repeat what Robins has said in his paper. I must, however, say that I
got on well with Firth and that we remained on very friendly terms right up
to his death in 1960. Yet I admit that he was brusque, often to the point of
rudeness, and autocratic – especially in his demand that nothing should be
offered for publication without being read and approved by him. Even I
suffered from that when he returned a paper on grammar with the comment
'There's a lot of junk there, Palmer', because he did not like its essentially
notionally semantic basis, and such semantics was not part of his 'linguistic
meaning'. I did not have it published until I had left the Department and
Firth had died (Palmer 1960). (Firth, of course, talked about 'meaning' and
'semantics', but this included all levels of linguistic analysis, even phonetics,
except, paradoxically, what is generally understood by the terms!)

My respect for Firth, and, I think, his respect for me were established in
the first few weeks of my being in the Department. At one of the weekly
Friday morning seminars, I had disagreed with him and his rather rude reply
annoyed me so that my response was, to put it mildly, very forceful. N. C.
Scott, then Reader in the Department, commented to me afterwards that it
was 'a bit of a fracas'. Early that afternoon, I sat in my room very depressed,
convinced that I would have to resign and find another post. There was a
knock on the door, Firth came in, put his hand out and said 'I'm sorry,
Palmer.' He had realized that it was impossible for me to apologize without
feeling crushed, and was generous enough to make the apology himself. We
never had another cross word, although I heard that he referred to me as
being 'prickly Palmer'.

My main interest at SOAS and the topic of most of my publications was
Firth's 'prosodies' (see articles in Palmer 1970). This was, in my view, the
most important of Firth's contributions. It was a topic that had its origins in
Firth's publications in the 1930s (see articles in Firth 1957), but has seldom
been fully appreciated. There is a certain irony in the utter incomprehension
of prosodic analysis by one of Chomsky's disciples, who attempted to

reanalyse a set of prosodic articles in terms of distinctive features (Langendoen 1968). For Firth's views on phonology reflected his rejection of the American structuralist phonemics, morphemics and morphophonemics, and, while Chomsky too claimed to be rejecting structuralism, his distinctive feature analysis was based on phonemic structure, while prosodic analysis utterly rejected it. Perhaps Firth is best known for his 'context of situation', but this was never more than an expression of a theoretical stance and had virtually no practical application. It was believed that Firth was preparing a book on linguistics and, just before he died, he suggested that I should join him in writing a book on English. However, when I edited his unpublished papers (Palmer 1968), there was no sign of any work on either subject, apart from what was contained in copies of lectures to various bodies. His greatest claim to fame lies in the enthusiasm that he inspired in others, especially those in the Department, many of whom were, like me, later to become Heads of new departments of linguistics.

Almost all of my work during the 10 years that I spent at SOAS concerned the five Ethiopian languages Tigrinya, Tigre, Amharic, Bilin and Agau. One great benefit of being at SOAS was that we were allowed study leave (for a year) and that native speakers were brought to London (again for a year) to act as 'informants'. So I worked with a native speaker of Tigrinya (Ethiopian Semitic) for a year and then went to Eritrea with him for the next year (together with my wife and three very small children). Here I not only improved my knowledge of Tigrinya (and became fairly fluent in it), but also worked with speakers of the 'sister' language Tigre and the Cushitic languages Bilin and Agau. I later worked in London with a native speaker of Amharic. I wrote articles (14 in all) on these languages and published a book on Tigre (Palmer 1962).

I was particularly pleased that I found no real difficulty in reproducing the laryngeal and ejective consonants of the Semitic languages and that I could describe Cushitic Agau as a tone language (Palmer 1959) – thus belying Firth's remarks about me as a phonetician. Some years later I was to show that the Nubian language Dongola was also a tone language (Palmer 1978), although the author of a major work on it had quite specifically denied this. I also learnt from working with my Agau assistant in Eritrea, a man who was illiterate but intelligent, that native speakers can easily acquire an objective view of the structure of their languages, for he would happily supply me with full verbal paradigms of Agau without any prompting. These years of studying these languages, combined with my background in Latin and Greek, were, I am sure, an excellent training for linguistics and they confirm my faith in linguistic description as an essential part of linguistics. I regret that so many scholars in the subject today have little familiarity with actual spoken languages.

Firth suggested to me that I should take an interest in computing. I am rather glad that I did not, for in 1963 I went on a computing course in the

Rand Corporation in Santa Monica, California, and it proved a complete waste of time. The highly complicated instructions that we were taught to write (for a computer of immense size) were soon made totally unnecessary with the appearance of more user-friendly computer programs. Robins was encouraged, with much more success, to take an interest in the history of linguistics, and this had one sad result for me. I read the proofs of his first book (Robins 1951) and he thanked me in the preface. One reviewer suggested that there was a misprint – 'F. R. Palmer' should read 'L. R. Palmer' (the Professor of Comparative Philology at Oxford). This was a great disappointment to me, as this was the first time my name had appeared in print!

A major development in 1960 was the establishment of a Department of Linguistics at the University College of North Wales, Bangor. I was appointed to the Chair, and I have no doubt that, to some degree, I owed this appointment to a very favourable reference from Firth, who was, naturally, delighted that a second Chair of Linguistics had now been created. (Firth died at the end of that year.) Bangor had three reasons for this – the Department of Welsh wanted linguistic research into the dialects of Modern Welsh, the German Department wanted help with the teaching of English to its exchange students, and the English Department wanted linguistics as a subject in its syllabus.

It was at this time that I began to take an interest in English grammar and the teaching of English. I had previously taken part in summer schools for foreign students in London and, at the invitation of the British Council, in Austria and in Poland in 1958 and 1959. In 1961 I was invited to go to Indonesia, and in January 1963 to a summer school in Argentina, where I gave a set of lectures on English grammar that were the basis of my book *A Linguistic Study of the English Verb* (Palmer 1965.) (I later went to a similar course in Uruguay – in 1965). There was great interest at that time in the development of teaching of English as a second or foreign language (TESL and TEFL), but very few scholars in the subject. In 1963 joint action by the UGC and the Ford Foundation provided the means to appoint several more lecturers to the staff at Bangor. The UGC provided ear-marked grants for five years and the Ford Foundation a lump sum for the first year, which, for some unknown reason, it did not repeat, as had been virtually promised.

It was in 1959 that the Linguistics Association was formed. This followed from a series of meetings arranged by the Hull Linguistic Society, which had demonstrated that there was interest in having extended meetings lasting over several days. It has always seemed to me that this was an initiative that should have been taken by the Philological Society, which would then have held the same position in Britain as that of the LSA in the USA. Possibly, it was too early, since at that time there were still so few scholars in linguistics (although there were small units in Hull and other places), but the

Philological Society had the resources and could have acted, without losing its individual lectures in London, Oxford and Cambridge. Five years later, in 1965, the Association began the publication of the *Journal of Linguistics*, with John Lyons as editor. I was its Editor from 1969 to 1979, with David Crystal and Peter Matthews as Associate Editors at first and later with Peter Matthews as Joint Editor.

While at Bangor, I was visited by a delegation from Reading University headed by Professor Gordon, the professor of English, that was interested in establishing linguistics there too. Nothing happened for two years, until, in late 1964, Reading advertised the post of Professor. I did not apply for this but was invited to come to Reading and offered the post. At first, I declined, partly because I was happy in Bangor, both professionally and personally, and because, with much higher house prices in Reading, I should not be able to live in a house as fine as the one we had in Penmaenmawr. But while I was on the course in Uruguay (January 1965) I changed my mind, because Reading offered much better schools for my children than north Wales did and because, at the same time, Professor Gordon wrote to me again and offered a university house. This time I accepted.

Reading at first offered two Lectureships, but increased it to three. I brought with me Peter Barnes, David Crystal and Peter Matthews. As a result we were able to offer undergraduate courses in linguistics in the very first year. We offered linguistics as a course in the first year three-subject course, and then combined courses with other departments, mainly those of English, French, German and Italian, plus a single linguistics course. The single linguistics course still had a modern European language component, taught by one of the other departments, but concerned solely with the spoken language. These were, I believe, the first linguistics courses to be taught at undergraduate level.

The Department was advertised as the 'Department of Linguistic Science', a name suggested, I believe by Michael Halliday. I thought about changing it to simply 'Department of Linguistics', but there was no enthusiasm for the change among the members of staff, and so the name remained.

With my experience at SOAS, I insisted that a significant part of the course should be the study of actual spoken languages, in addition to that provided by the other departments. Students taking the combined courses with foreign languages were already required to spend their third year in a relevant country, and this year abroad was made compulsory for the single linguistics students too. These single linguistic students, however, were allowed to spend half of this in any country that they chose (provided that they could pay the fares and their LEA, which financed their grants, did not object), the other half being spent in a country where 'their' European language was spoken. In addition, all students in the department attended weekly 'language tutorials', where they worked with native speakers of various, often 'exotic', languages, under the supervision of a member of staff. For the 22 years that I spent in Reading, all but two members of staff had no hesitation in taking such classes.

There was one incident that I found most pleasing. The German Department reported that it had given a mark of 100 per cent for proficiency in the spoken language to one student, something it had never done before. The student was taking single linguistics (with just the one paper on German), and had elected to spend the whole of the year abroad in Germany, but had begun her interest in German only after her A-levels.

There were several linguistic theories current in the 1960s, notably Chomsky's transformation grammar (as it was then called), Lamb's stratificational grammar, Pike's tagmemics and Halliday's systemic grammar, though none of them seems to have been applied extensively in descriptive grammars, except for tagmemics by scholars trained by the Summer Institute of Linguistics. I found none of them had much to offer me, mainly because they seemed difficult to use in language description, except, to some degree, TG as presented in *Aspects of the Theory of Syntax* (Chomsky 1965). For this seemed, for the first time, to offer a way of incorporating such categories as the passive and subordination into a theoretically based grammar. The only theory that was taught in any detail at Bangor or Reading was TG, but there was no departmental theory or doctrine.

My main publications at the time were either on English grammar or on general linguistics. *A Linguistic Study of the English Verb*, published in 1965, was followed by a second edition entitled *The English Verb* (Palmer 1974), for the earlier title was foisted upon me by the publishers, because Martin Joos had just published his *The English Verb* (Joos 1964). *Semantics* (Palmer 1976) and *Grammar* (1971) were both intended to be introductions to the subjects for students or others that were interested, for there were few introductory books available. Both were successful, particularly *Semantics*, which has been translated into German, Japanese, Italian, Spanish, Portuguese and Bahasa Malaysia, with several special English editions for use abroad. Later books on grammatical typology – *Mood and Modality* (1986) and *Grammatical Roles and Relations* (1994) – reflect my lasting interest in the grammars of actual languages.

By 1975, ten years after its formation, the Department had a very high reputation. There were three Professors – myself, David Crystal and Peter Matthews – and the Department had grown considerably, thanks to generous grants to the universities from the government in the so-called 'Robbins era'. (I was Dean in 1971 – see below – and found myself in the position of being told, on a Thursday, to recommend, by the following Monday, the Departments in the Faculty that should be awarded no fewer than 15 posts!) We had also established MA courses in Linguistics and in Applied Linguistics and an undergraduate course in Language Pathology which provided an officially recognized qualification in speech therapy. A financially independent Centre for Applied Language Studies was established (officially within the Department), with David Wilkins (later to become Professor of Applied Linguistics) as its Director.

I was elected a Fellow of the British Academy in 1975. A few years later, it was suggested that there should be a Section for Linguistics. I was asked to chair a working party, and when it was agreed that the Section should be established, I became its first Chairman. At this stage, I felt linguistics had fully 'grown up' as an academic discipline.

I should like to add that from 1969 to 1972, I was Dean of Letters and Social Sciences. This was at the time of student protest and there were several sit-ins in the administration building (and the university was run from the telephone in the Dean's office). There was, undoubtedly, some inconvenience, but the whole affair was treated with good humour, and I do not share the hostility, anger or contempt that are felt by some. Indeed, I almost prefer the lively students of that time to the more apathetic students of today.

I have been asked to assess my contribution to linguistics. I will not be falsely modest, for I think I can probably claim to have been highly influential in its development. I would cite the establishment of the departments in Bangor and Reading, my being the first Chairman of both the Linguistics Association and the Linguistics Section of the British Academy, and my being Editor of the *Journal of Linguistics* (together with Crystal and Matthews) from 1969 to 1979. I have done more than my share of being external examiner and sitting on selection committees, as well as producing considerable publications. Three of those publications have been particularly useful to students of English or linguistics – *The English Verb*, *Grammar* and *Semantics.*

I hope I have not made many enemies. I know I have given offence on several occasions at conferences – but I have never intended to do so. David Wilkins told me, with some amusement, that he was advised against applying for the post in Reading, because I was such a difficult person. Yet when a new Vice-Chancellor at Reading visited all the departments and spoke to all the staff, he told me that the Department of Linguistic Science was quite unique in the University, in that everyone seemed happy and no one had any complaint to make. I should like, in this respect, to quote from a card sent to me by a now distinguished ex-colleague on the occasion of my being awarded an honorary DLitt by Reading University in 1996:

David Wilkins said most of what needed to be said. But one additional, and rather unusual, achievement is the way you were able to help so many people at the beginnings of their careers, like me, like . . ., like . . ., without forcing or encouraging them to fit your own mould. The rest of us can't do this, as you did it. We either form schools, so that the people we try to help too literally become what we make them, or leave them far too much to their own devices. Thinking of the diversity of the people there, I don't know how you did it. We are all very grateful.

As I said at the beginning, I entered the subject almost by accident, and I wonder whether I would have chosen the same path if I had my time again. If I had still chosen linguistics, I should have preferred to devote much more of my time to the languages of East Africa. I ought to have been a mathematician, but I confess my first choice would have been the literature, especially the drama, of classical Greek.

REFERENCES

CHOMSKY, NOAM, 1965. *Aspects of the Theory of Syntax*, Cambridge MA: MIT Press.

FIRTH, J. R., 1957. *Papers in Linguistics 1934–1951*, London: Oxford University Press.

JOOS, MARTIN, 1964. *The English Verb: Form and Meaning*, Madison: University of Wisconsin Press.

KENNEDY, BENJAMIN H. (rev. J. F. MOUNTFORD), 1933. *The Revised Latin Primer*, London: Longman Green.

LANGENDOEN, D. TERENCE, 1968. *The London School of Linguistics: A Study of the Linguistic Theories of B. Malinowski and J. R. Firth*, Cambridge, MA: MIT Press.

PALMER, FRANK R., 1959. 'The verb classes of Agau (Awiya)', *Mitteilungen des Institut für Orientforschung* 7, 270–97.

PALMER, FRANK R., 1960. 'The "derived forms" of the Tigrinya verb', *African Language Studies* 1, 109–16.

PALMER, FRANK R., 1962. *The Morphology of the Tigre Noun*, London: Oxford University Press.

PALMER, FRANK R., 1965. *A Linguistic Study of the English Verb*, London: Longman.

PALMER, FRANK R., (ed.) 1968. *Selected Papers of J. R. Firth*, London: Longman; Bloomington / London: Indiana University Press.

PALMER, FRANK R., 1970. *Prosodic Analysis*, London: Oxford University Press.

PALMER, FRANK R., 1971. *Grammar*, 2nd ed. 1984, Harmondsworth: Penguin.

PALMER, FRANK R., 1974. *The English Verb*, 2nd ed. 1987, London: Longman.

PALMER, FRANK R., 1976. *Semantics*, 2nd ed. 1981, Cambridge: Cambridge University Press.

PALMER, FRANK R., 1978. 'Possessive pronouns in Dongola', *BSOAS* 41, 362–4.

PALMER, FRANK R., 1986. *Mood and Modality*, 2nd ed. 2001, Cambridge: Cambridge University Press.

PALMER, FRANK R., 1994. *Grammatical Roles and Relations*, Cambridge: Cambridge University Press.

ROBINS, ROBERT H., 1951. *Ancient and Mediaeval Theory in Europe with Particular Reference to Modern Linguistic Doctrine*, London: Bell.

RANDOLPH QUIRK

QUIRK, Randolph, FBA 1975, CBE 1976, Kt 1985, cr. Baron (Life Peer) 1994; *b.* 1920; *m.* (i) Jean 1946, 2 s, (ii) Gabriele 1984; *Education:* Cronk y Voddy School and Douglas High School, Isle of Man; University College London 1939–40, 1945–7, MA, PhD, DLit; Commonwealth Fund (now Harkness) Fellow, Yale and Michigan, 1951–2; *Career:* Lecturer in English, UCL, 1947–54; Reader, University of Durham, 1954–8, Professor 1958–60; Professor, UCL, 1960–8, Quain Professor 1968–81; Vice-Chancellor, University of London, 1981–85; President, British Academy, 1985–9; Director, Survey of English Usage, 1959–83; Senate, University of London, 1970–85, Court 1972–85; Governor, Guisborough Grammar School, Cleveland, 1957–60; Chairman, Inquiry into Speech Therapy Services, 1969–72; BBC Archives Committee 1975–81; Governor, British Institute of Recorded Sound, 1976–80; Chairman, A. S. Hornby Educational Trust, 1979–93; Governor, Richmond College, since 1981; Governor, English-Speaking Union, 1980–5; President, Institute of Linguists, 1982–5; Vice-Chairman, English Language Council, E-SU, since 1985; Board of the British Council 1983–91; Chairman, British Library Advisory Committee, 1984–97; Chairman, Anglo-Spanish Foundation, 1983–5; Council of RADA since 1985; Trustee, City Technology Colleges, 1986–98; Vice-President, Foundation for Science and Technology, 1986–90; President, College of Speech Therapists, 1987–91; Trustee, Wolfson Foundation, since 1987; Governor, American School in London, 1987–9; Royal Commissioner, 1851 Exhibition, 1987–95; President, North of England Education Conference, 1989; House of Lords Select Committee on Science and Technology since 1998. Hon. Bencher, Gray's Inn; Hon. FCST; Hon. FIL; Fellow UCL, KCL, QMW, Goldsmiths', Royal Holloway, Imperial. Hon. doctorates: Aston, Bar Ilan, Bath, Brunel, Copenhagen, Durham, Essex, Glasgow, Helsinki, Leicester, Liège, London, Lund, Newcastle-upon-Tyne, Nijmegen, Open, Paris, Poznan, Prague, Reading, Richmond, Salford, Sheffield, Southern California, Uppsala, Westminster; Member of Academia Europaea, Royal Belgian Academy of Sciences, Royal Swedish Academy, Finnish Academy of Sciences, American Academy of Arts and Sciences. *Major Publications: The Concessive Relation in Old English Poetry* 1954; *Studies in Communication* 1955 (with A. J. Ayer and others); *An Old English Grammar* 1955 (with C. L. Wrenn) [enlarged ed. 1994 with S. E. Deskis]; *Charles Dickens and Appropriate Language* 1959; *The Teaching of English* 1959 (with A. H. Smith) [rev. ed. 1964]; *The Study of the Mother Tongue*

1961; *The Use of English* 1962 (with supplements by A. C. Gimson and J. Warburg) [enlarged ed. 1968]; *Systems of Prosodic and Paralinguistic Features in English* 1964 (with D. Crystal); *A Common Language* 1964 (with A. H. Marckwardt); *Investigating Linguistic Acceptability* 1966 (with J. Svartvik); *Essays on the English Language: Medieval and Modern* 1968; *Elicitation Experiments in English* 1970 (with S. Greenbaum); *A Grammar of Contemporary English* 1972 (with S. Greenbaum, G. Leech and J. Svartvik); *The English Language and Images of Matter* 1972; *A University Grammar of English* 1973 (with S. Greenbaum); *The Linguist and the English Language* 1974; *Old English Literature: A Practical Introduction* 1975 (with V. Adams and D. Davy); *A Corpus of English Conversation* 1980 (with J. Svartvik); *Style and Communication in the English Language* 1982; *A Comprehensive Grammar of the English Language* 1985 (with S. Greenbaum, G. Leech and J. Svartvik); *English in the World* 1985 (with H. Widdowson); *Words at Work: Lectures on Textual Structure* 1986; *English in Use* 1990 (with G. Stein); *A Student's Grammar of the English Language* 1990 (with S. Greenbaum); *An Introduction to Standard English* 1993 (with G. Stein); *Grammatical and Lexical Variance in English* 1995.

* * *

This chapter is based on an interview with Keith Brown in February 2001.

* * *

Like everyone else, I suppose, I'm very much a product of my background and childhood, the child being father of the man, as Wordsworth said. I was brought up in a farming family to be obsessively enamoured of hard work and to be just as obsessively sceptical about orthodoxies, religious or political. So in retrospect it's easy for me to see why I became such a restless, free-ranging eclectic as I have been.

You see, my family was a mixture of Catholic and Protestant, of Anglican and Methodist, in an island community where self-consciously Manx values cohabited uneasily with increasingly dominant English values. Indeed, if I'm an eclectic pluralist, it may simply be that the Manx in general are. Although we tend to be a bit equivocal and semi-detached about national identity, we're very conscious of our Celtic roots: we share St Patrick with Ireland and we have the remnants of a Celtic language that is close to being intercomprehensible with Irish. I say 'remnants' because, although the rudiments are now taught in school, when I was a child there were already very few fully competent Manx speakers, and most of us (though living in Manx-named Ballabrooie or Cronk y Voddy) only used Manx for the odd greeting or proverb or our very own euphemism for 'loo', *tthai beg* 'little house'. But we were conscious too of Scandinavian roots. We sang of King Orry and bowed to St Olave; we proudly gawped at our quite splendid

Viking-Age crosses with their runic inscriptions – some of the best in Kirk Michael, only a couple of miles from our family farm, which itself bears a Scandinavian name, Lambfell. The Manx Parliament has retained its Scandinavian name for a thousand years: Tynwald, cognate in form and function with Iceland's Thingvoll. In the Middle Ages, our bishop was appointed from Trondheim and his title still recalls that his domain once included 'Sodor', which derives from the Scandinavian name for the Hebrides.

You may well be wondering, but are too courteous to ask: what has all this to do with my academic career? Well, in addition to underlining this nonconforming eclecticism of mine, it may help to explain my interest in language, history and language history. So when I had reluctantly abandoned school science for the 'arts', I came to UCL, eventually settling for the subject 'English' because of the historical and linguistic bias in the curriculum: Gothic, some Old Saxon and Old High German, a lot of Old Norse, and even more Anglo-Saxon: Germanic philology, history of language and the *writing* of language: palaeography from runes to court hand.

Not that the course of my true love for this English degree ran smoothly to begin with. I diverted some of my energies into the lively politics of the time, and a lot into music – especially into playing in a dance band, not least to fund nights out with girls. The war had made my bit of UCL relocate in Aberystwyth and I was further diverted into dabbling in the Welsh spoken around me, tickled that Cronk y Voddy's *tthai beg* was Aber's *tŷ bach.* I still love singing those minor-key Welsh hymns – in Welsh. But most seriously I was diverted from the English degree by five years in RAF's bomber command, where I became so deeply interested in explosives that I started to do an external degree in *chemistry* through evening classes at what is now the University of Hull.

But with demobilization in 1945 I suddenly felt middle-aged and so I soberly resumed my UCL degree with unexpected dedication, enlivened by new excitements. With the college back in Bloomsbury, I discovered I could tap into phonetics with Daniel Jones and (just down the road at SOAS) into a subject then just daring to speak its name ('linguistics') with J. R. Firth. By the time I'd got my BA, I was hooked on the idea of research. Ah, but in what? It's hard now to explain to young graduates how *lucky* we were in austerity England, bombarded with tempting career offers. I was invited to take up a research fellowship in Cambridge to work on Old Norse (and in fact I did subsequently do some bits of work on *Hrafnkelssaga* and a student edition of *Gunnlaugssaga* with P. G. Foote in 1957). But I was counterattracted by the offer (*offer*: no ad, no application, no referees) of a Junior Lectureship at UCL itself. Without so much as an *hour's* teacher training, I happily charged into undergraduate classes on medieval literature, history of the language, OE, Old Norse, and anything else the powers thought I had more time to do than they. And then there was the exciting challenge of embarking on research – a matter far more important in the eyes of the said powers.

At that time, there was much controversy over a now yawn-inducing issue in old Germanic philology: what Grimm had called *Brechung*. Were the vowels in OE words like *heard* 'hard' or *feoh* 'cattle' really diphthongs or just simple vowels plus diacritics indicating consonant 'colour'? With great gusto, I took on Fernand Mossé of Paris and Marjorie Daunt of Birkbeck, with the enthusiastic approval of my supervisor, A. H. Smith. Supervision was often rather nominal in those days, and so it was with Hugh Smith, but it was always a privilege to have ready access to such an extraordinary polymath: big in toponymics, of course, but big also in ultra-violet photography, horology and typography, to name just a few of his interests. My research involved learning some Old Irish where the vowel graphemics showed apparent similarities (and where the stories from the *Táin* held – like the Norse sagas – a literary interest for me as well). My work also involved learning some Danish and Swedish for a lot of the relevant published research. So it was that I came to sit at the feet of Elias Bredsdorff, the Hans Andersen scholar, then Lektor in Danish at UCL, who could sometimes be coaxed into telling of his exploits in wartime Denmark when he was prominent on the SS wanted list. Despite such temptations to dawdle and dabble, the thesis got finished but (astonishingly as it may now seem) the controversy rumbled on, joined by up-and-coming Bob Stockwell on the one side and Sherman Kuhn, stoutly joining forces with me, on the other.

Meanwhile, teaching students OE was bringing home to me how little Germanic philology helped them and how much syntax and lexicology would. So for my PhD, I switched to syntax, incurring some displeasure among the powers for whom sticking to one's scholarly last was a prime virtue, and my field was phonology, was it not? But in one quarter the switch was welcomed. A book based on my thesis was published by Yale University Press in 1954 (*The Concessive Relation in Old English Poetry*) just when C. L. Wrenn at Pembroke, Oxford, was planning to write an OE grammar. Because such grammars traditionally covered only phonology and morphology, he roped me in to help write a different kind of text book, replete with a fairly full treatment of syntax as well as word-formation. *An Old English Grammar* was duly published by Methuen in 1955.

But I'm getting ahead of myself. Before that collaboration with Wrenn, I had another life-changing stroke of luck. In 1951, I was awarded what is now called a Harkness Fellowship that took me to Bernard Bloch, Helge Kökeritz and Yale. I rejoiced in attending Bloch's classes as a 'post-doc' but revelled also in the proximity (given a splendid car and the Merritt Parkway) of Columbia and Cabell Greet to the south and of Brown (Freeman Twaddell) and Harvard (F. P. Magoun, Joshua Watmough, et many al., but especially Roman Jakobson) to the north. I was made to feel very welcome, and Bloch in particular (in Bloomfield's old chair) tried to recruit me into Bloch–Trager structuralism and teased me about Firth – though I told him *he* hadn't recruited me either. Now, actually, the powers-that-were at UCL 'sent' me (as they saw it) to America so that I could work lexicologically upon the great UCL *Piers Plowman* project that had been begun decades earlier by the then Quain Professor, R. W. Chambers. So, after a semester at Yale, I dutifully repaired to Ann Arbor, where I was generously given a desk in the great Michigan project, the *Middle English Dictionary*, headed by Hans Kurath and Sherman Kuhn.

I enjoyed trawling through the *MED*'s voluminous files and managed to do a few things related to my Langland mission. I was also briefly tempted back into OE phonology to do a couple of papers with Kuhn (1953; 1955). But of far greater long-term importance for me was the close contact I came to have with the stars of Ann Arbor linguistics: Charles Fries, Albert Marckwardt, Ken Pike, Herbert Penzl and Raven McDavid, for example. I became more acquainted with the historical and contemporary relations between American and British English and (especially through seminars hospitably organized *chez* Fries) with modes of working empirically on the syntax of spoken language. Fries had of course already done innovative work on unedited manuscript English (soldiers' letters, for example). But now the new electronic recording had enabled him to do even more innovative work on unedited *spoken* English, and whatever its obvious deficiencies his book on *The Structure of English* (1952) gave me a huge buzz. From then on, I've never been without a tape-recorder – and never above using a hidden mike.

By travelling round the US, I was able to establish working friendships with many other scholars, such as Jim Sledd and Archie Hill. But I was also able to witness the darker side of academia: LSA meetings reduced to chaos, as (surely pre-planned) vilification was hurled at senior figures like Adelaide Hahn by gangs of Young Turks peddling their current brand of structuralism against those they saw as stuck in the mind set of the *Junggrammatiker*. Not a few of these same Young Turks were within a couple of years to desert Trager and Hill to become just as fanatical about TG, and in 1962 I was dismayed to see just such fascistic intolerance at the International Congress in Cambridge, Massachusetts, when it was scholars like Bloch who were disgracefully shouted down.

Not long after my return from the US in 1952, I moved to Durham, in no small part to get away from an increasingly bibulous departmental culture which I was not alone in finding a bit oppressive. The Durham department, headed by the critic Clifford Leech, was excellent but small, and everyone was expected to teach more or less everything. There weren't many linguists around, but there were a few very active ones such as Neville Collinge in classics, while over in Newcastle there was my close friend, Barbara Strang. The tiny 'language side' that I was appointed to take over in Durham had been eminent in the cultural and textual history of Anglo-Saxon England, but while doing my amateurish best to keep this tradition alive I devoted myself more to convincing students and colleagues that a linguistic approach could contribute valuable insights to the study of Shakespeare, Swift, Wordsworth, Dickens, and all stations to T. S. Eliot and beyond. And I started seriously examining the grammar of present-day and especially *spoken* English. That included the speech of my children. One of them regularly (in more senses than one) spoke of 'a-r-apple', rightly divining that sandhi [r] was of greater phonotactic currency than sandhi [n] (though he didn't actually say so); and both lads contributed mightily to the series of broadcast lectures that eventually grew into *The Use of English* (1962). I made frequent weekend trips to London, where the BBC had kindly given me not just a desk but free access to all their tapes and transcriptions of the spontaneous speech in numerous discussion programmes. I had ideas for harnessing the then vast and clumsy computer in the task of sorting out the conditions under which linguistic variants occurred, and I took a programming course with Ewan Page (later Vice-Chancellor of Reading) in his Newcastle department. The University of Durham provided modest seed money for such things as primitive recording and analysis facilities, and I was soon well on the way to devising a long-term project for the description of English syntax ('The Survey of English Usage', described in Quirk 1960). This had already received some welcome funding from a Danish publisher, from Cambridge University Press, from Oxford University Press, and above all from Longman by the time I moved back to UCL in 1960, bringing with me the infant Survey and a research assistant.

The infant thrived and many, many people contributed to its nurture. I got unstinting support from UCL itself, the department and successive Provosts (Ifor Evans, Noel Annan and James Lighthill); from the British Council, who funded postgraduate and more senior scholars to work with me over the years (Florent Aarts, Wolf-Dietrich Bald and Jan Firbas, for example); from the Ford Foundation, who brought to UCL such scholars as Jim Sledd and Nelson Francis; from the research councils and the great charities like Leverhulme (during one of the Survey's financial crises, Keith Murray responded to a weekend call with what amounted to a year's bailout); and from Longman (thanks especially to John Chapple and subsequently Tim Rix, the latter setting up a generous Longman Fellowship that funded post-docs from the third world so they could use the Survey materials in the production of English teaching materials back home).

Among the researchers thus funded, several were key to the day-to-day development of the project. These have been recorded in annual reports and in prefaces to Survey publications (full lists available from UCL), but one or two should be recalled here. Jan Rusiecki (and later Robert Ilson) took prime responsibility for what we called the 'Work-book', specifying the criteria for every single linguistic and taxonomic decision as the corpus was analysed. David Crystal became the lead partner in devising the scheme by which the multiple systems of prosodic and paralinguistic features of speech were recognized, categorized, and transcribed by experts such as Janet Whitcut. Jan Svartvik and Henry Carvell led the way in computational analyses, with many nocturnal hours on off-peak access to the vast Atlas machine in Gordon Square. Geoffrey Leech's leadership was crucial in shaping *A Grammar of Contemporary English* (Quirk et al. 1972), as also its successor of 1985 – another of the many works in which I have indulged my enjoyment of collaborative writing. Sidney Greenbaum and Ruth Kempson devoted a good deal of time and ingenuity to psycholinguistic techniques of elicitation (e.g. Quirk and Greenbaum 1970; Quirk and Kempson 1971) – an aspect of the Survey that I have always (and already in the Philological Society paper of 1960) seen as constituting an at least equal partnership with corpus analysis.

All this has been acknowledged before and is, so to say, in the public domain. Less well known has been my dependence for day-to-day spade work on a host of devoted volunteers led by René Quinault (ex-BBC) and comprising such loyal friends as Oonagh Sayce, Grace Stewart (wife of the University Principal), Jocelyn Goodman, Audrey Morris and many many others. It was in no small part through their efforts that the Survey rapidly became (and increasingly continues to be) a valued resource for researchers from near (e.g. Frank Palmer) or far (e.g. Yoshihiko Ikegami), and the list of Survey-dependent publications grows more impressive by the year.

And of course the Survey has drawn on scholarship far beyond modern Bloomsbury in time and space: from continental giants of the past such as Jespersen and Kruisinga: from more recent continental giants in the Prague School of Mathesius, Trnka and Vachek – even to some extent from the Danish glossematics of Hjelmslev; from the French, such as Martinet and Adamczewski, and from Canadians as diverse as Wally Avis and W. H. Hirtle; and most obviously perhaps from Bloomfieldian structuralism, whether of Fries's brand or Pike's or Trager's or Hockett's, and from a succession of generative theories articulated by Chomsky et al. The nice thing about eclecticism is, as its etymology proclaims, that you can choose freely and widely what you need for a particular purpose, without boxing yourself into any single (and doubtless inevitably flawed) theoretical position. It's a matter of taste and personal intellectual bent, I suppose, but I have always found it liberating to be unconstrained by the very idea of an orthodoxy. In this, nothing would please me better than to be compared with a linguist friend I have particularly admired, Dwight Bolinger.

The Survey took up the bulk of my time in the 1960s and 1970s, but in addition I worked for the British Council, not only on committees but on report-writing after inspection and lecture visits to Russia, China, Korea, Japan, and a swathe of Commonwealth countries such as India, Ghana and Nigeria. In the only spell of sabbatical leave I ever had (1975–6), I took in Iraq and had a memorable few months in New Zealand. And I like to think I revolutionized linguistics at UCL by getting money together (thanks again to Tim Rix and Longman) and doing a spot of energetic head-hunting in Edinburgh. Thus it was that our English Department added a linguistics section headed by Michael Halliday and including Bob Dixon, Rodney Huddleston, Dick Hudson and Eugene Winter. In due course, this section moved out of English and ultimately joined Phonetics to become the Department of Phonetics and Linguistics. Oh yes, and there's another thing worth mentioning among the myriad of odds and ends I busied myself with during these years: I helped Tim Rix launch Longman into producing dictionaries – well, relaunch, really, since the Longman family were already on Johnson's title-page in 1755.

I was drawn outside academia on a couple of occasions to do jobs for Whitehall, for example to serve on a committee on school examinations (the 'Lockwood Report'; HMSO 1964), and once to chair a committee of inquiry into the speech therapy services (HMSO 1972) which I'm delighted to say totally revolutionized the profession, not least by making it an all-graduate career. But I wish I had done more, especially in relation to the teaching of English in schools. This was sharply brought home to me, oddly enough, when I was appointed Vice-Chancellor of London University (another job, like my very first, that I didn't apply for and was in this instance very reluctant to accept). After years of growth, the universities faced a sudden cut-back: in London's case, I had to implement a funding reduction of 17 per cent spread over three years. It was draconian, but in one of my chilly confrontations in the Senate House with the then Secretary of State, Sir Keith Joseph, he told me bluntly that if his department had the kind of money I was seeking, he wouldn't give it to me but to where it was infinitely more badly needed. 'When were you last in any of our inner city comprehensives?', he asked. Well, the following week he took me to one for a couple of hours, and the scales fell from my eyes. In all my years as a university teacher, I had of course known that we were selecting our students (little more than 10 per cent of the age group at that time) from obviously 'good' schools: the quality of intake was high, year after year. I was ashamed to realize that I had never bothered to find out what sort of quality education the *majority* of schools meted out.

Well, ever since, I've been trying to make restitution in whatever way I could. When I was President of the British Academy, I worked (as in so much these days, along with my wife, Gabriele Stein) at radically improving the new National Curriculum so as to ensure a better schooling 'for the many', as New Labour would say, without disrupting the kind of education expected of the growing numbers of students coming into the universities. We had some success in eradicating the emphasis on trivial aspects of grammar (such as the split infinitive) and introducing more serious attention to vocabulary, in the course of exposing the misplaced disdain for Standard English affected by many in the educational establishment.

Since entering the House of Lords, I have still further extended my interest in general educational issues to take up the disgracefully neglected matter of education and training for prisoners and 'young offenders' – the vast majority of them male and (even compared with our grossly undereducated population at large) disproportionately illiterate. In this respect too, I'm trying to make up for a happy, lucky life in the charmed circles of academia, though in another respect it's a return to an interest I indulged when I was in Durham. The Chief Constable was Alec Muir, brother of another friend Kenneth, who was Professor of English in Liverpool. Alec persuaded me to give a course of lectures for lifers and the like in Durham Gaol. I've never had more attentive and appreciative audiences!

Keith, I didn't want to do a piece for this volume, as you well know. In a letter on 30 June 2000, I wrote: 'I have become increasingly convinced that my own personal history would not be worth reading and that, by writing one, I would be implying that I thought it was.'

That remains my strongly held view and the grounds for continuing misgivings. But my letter to you went on: 'In your charity, you may well be tempted to reject my (I assure you) well-founded modesty, but I have to tell you firmly that my mind is made up.'

Well, 'in your charity' you would never have dreamed of rejecting my views; instead, you persuaded me to let you use precious time of your own to interview me. This is the result, and I can now admit that I'm glad and grateful that you did. You actually made me *enjoy* the unwonted experience of delving into (sometimes unwanted) memories of a pretty mixed personal past. If this were a self-assessment exercise, I'd give myself a beta minus: beta for undoubted hard work and a reasonable quota of good intentions; minus for spreading myself, my writing, my interests and my curiosity very much too widely; and hence for doing far too little at far too much.

REFERENCES

FRIES, C. C., 1952. *The Structure of English*, New York: Harcourt Brace.

HMSO, 1964. *The Examining of English Language*, 8th Report of the Secondary Schools Examinations Council, London: HMSO.

HMSO, 1972. *Speech Therapy Services*, Report of the Committee of Enquiry, London: HMSO.

QUIRK, R., 1951. 'Textual notes on *Hrafnkelssaga*', *London Medieval Studies* 2, 1–31.

QUIRK, R., 1954. *The Concessive Relation in Old English Poetry*, New Haven: Yale University Press.

QUIRK, R., 1960. 'Towards a description of English usage', *TPhS* 40–61.

QUIRK, R., 1962. *The Use of English*, London: Longman.

QUIRK, R. & FOOTE, P. G., 1957. *The Saga of Gunnlaug Serpent-Tongue*, London: Nelson.

QUIRK, R. & GREENBAUM, S., 1970. *Elicitation Experiments in English: Linguistic Studies in Use and Attitude*, London: Longman.

QUIRK, R. & KEMPSON, RUTH, 1971. 'Controlled activation of latent contrast', *Language* 47, 548–72.

QUIRK, R. & KUHN, SHERMAN M., 1953. 'Some recent interpretations of Old English digraph spellings', *Language* 29, 143–56.

QUIRK, R. & KUHN, SHERMAN M., 1955. 'The Old English digraphs: a reply', *Language* 31, 390–401.

QUIRK, R. & WRENN, C. L., 1955. *An Old English Grammar*, London: Methuen.

QUIRK, R., GREENBAUM, S., LEECH, G. & SVARTVIK, J., 1972. *A Grammar of Contemporary English*, London: Longman.

QUIRK, R., GREENBAUM, S., LEECH, G. & SVARTVIK, J., 1985. *A Comprehensive Grammar of the English Language*, London: Longman.

R. H. ROBINS

ROBINS, Robert Henry, FBA 1986; *b.* 1921; *d.* 2001; *m.* 1953 Sheila Marie Fynn (*d.* 1983); *Education:* Tonbridge School; New College, Oxford, 1940–1, 1945–8, MA 1948; DLit, London, 1968; *Career:* RAF Intelligence, 1942–5; Lecturer in Linguistics, School of Oriental and African Studies, London, 1948–55; Reader in General Linguistics, University of London, 1955–65; Professor of General Linguistics, 1966–86, Emeritus 1986–2001, Dean, Faculty of Arts, 1984–6, University of London; Head of Department of Phonetics and Linguistics, School of Oriental and African Studies, University of London, 1970–85; Member Senate, University of London, 1980–5; Research Fellow, University of California, 1951; Visiting Professor: Washington 1963, Hawaii 1968, Minnesota 1971, Florida 1975, Salzburg 1977, 1979; Leverhulme Emeritus Fellow 1990–1; President: Societas Linguistica Europaea 1974, CIPL 1977–97 (British Representative 1970–7), Philological Society 1988–92 (Hon. Secretary 1961–88); Member Academia Europaea 1991; Hon. Member Linguistic Society of America 1981–2001. *Major Publications: Ancient and Mediaeval Grammatical Theory in Europe* 1951; *The Yurok Language* 1958; *General Linguistics: An Introductory Survey* 1964; *A Short History of Linguistics* 1967; *Diversions of Bloomsbury* 1970; *Ideen- und Problemgeschichte der Sprachwissenschaft* 1973; *Sistem dan Struktur Bahasa Sunda* 1983; *The Byzantine Grammarians: Their Place in History* 1993; *Texts and Contexts: Selected Papers on the History of Linguistics* 1998.

* * *

For most people of my generation in Europe (b. 1921 in my case) the Second World War was an influential factor in the choice of a professional career. In too many cases the results were tragic, death or serious injury, but this article relates the life of one who, since the war, has made his living in university teaching.

I passed my schooldays in the manner then normal for children of middle-class families. My father was a medical practitioner in the county of Kent. By the time I was 14 I had been systematically taught Latin, French, mathematics, English, history, geography and divinity. At the age of 9 I was introduced to Ancient Greek, my father having already taught me the Greek alphabet. In my first school Latin was taught almost on medieval lines, as an essential part of education, entirely from English textbooks. Only after about three years were we actually introduced to Virgil's lovely poetry and to pompous old Cicero's turgid prose. But when I learned Greek I was immediately reading texts such as Plato's *Apology* and bits of Thucydides' *History*.

From my earliest days I have been fascinated by the languages of which I knew something. After my mother had told me that *pram* was a 'short form' and that the proper word was *perambulator* I proudly coined *terambulator* as the 'proper form' of *tram*, but this innovation in my *parole* never reached the stage of a change in *langue*. I also invented a comparative and superlative forms for English *rugger: ruggerior, ruggerrimus*, on the pattern of Latin adjectives like *miser*.

I was fascinated by the intricacies of Latin grammar and the peculiar terms used about it, which were never explained – 'ablative absolute' and so on. We were told that 'French came from Latin' and shown how; I was further struck by the way that English was 'like French' but also 'like German', but in a different sort of 'likeness'. Of course I knew nothing about linguistics as we have it today.

In 1935 I was fortunately awarded a scholarship to Tonbridge School, and immediately placed in the classical upper fifth, passing into the sixth form and the next year taking the School Certificate (today's GCSE). From that time in the sixth form on the classical side our studies were confined to Greek and Latin translation, prose and verse composition, literature and ancient history. Only an occasional English essay and a period of European (and one year American) history fell outside the ancient world. I continued my interest in linguistic relationships, particularly of Greek and Latin, supplementing it by reading the etymological headings in entries in Liddell and Scott's Greek and Lewis and Short's Latin dictionaries and acquiring certain bits of historical linguistics such as Grimm's Law from sporadic remarks from masters. By 1940 I had read, not always intelligently, Jespersen's *Language*.

In the autumn of 1939 I was successful in the scholarships examination at New College, Oxford, and 'went up' in October 1940. The syllabus for the first public examination, Moderations ('Mods'), was largely the continuation of what we had been doing at school, though one hoped at a higher level. I was fortunate to have come to New College where our academic tutor, E. C. Yorke, encouraged those who were interested to take comparative philology with Greek dialects as a special subject for the examinations. This was taught by Professor G. K. Braunholtz, whom I remember throughout my life for his scholarship and his charm, and for the old-fashioned Oxford hospitality of 'open house' for tea with him and his wife at their home every Sunday to any of his students.

Braunholtz's course was essentially the exposition on neogrammatical lines of the Indo-European family (with occasional excursions into Finno-Ugrian and others), with the major sound laws, analogical forms, and lexical borrowings. It was not itself historical; we had nothing on the neogrammarians' predecessors, nor any analysis of their theoretical stance, nor of the vigorous controversies about it at the end of the nineteenth century. I do not recall his actually mentioning the term *neogrammarian* at all. Our two textbooks were Buck (1928; 1933). Now I was able to reinforce the correspondences *sum eimí, es eílessí* and *est estí* with Sanskrit *ásmi, ási, ásti*, though to my lasting shame as a linguist I never properly learned Sanskrit, and my subsequent work on the history of linguistics has in this respect had to rely on secondary sources. I took the 'Mods' exams in June 1941, achieving my one straight alpha in comparative philology.

June 1940 to June 1941 were perhaps the most critical and perilous period in the Second World War as far as Britain was concerned, with the overrunning of continental Europe, Dunkirk, the 'Battle of Britain', and the air raids on British cities ('the Blitz'); looking back on school and university life at that time I find it surprisingly 'normal'. At Oxford some of the younger dons and college staff and some of the older students had left to join the forces or other war activities; we were expected to devote one morning a week to military training, in consideration of our being allowed to postpone our enlistment for about a year. But lecture lists were published and fulfilled, we had one-to-one tutorials, we wore gowns at lectures and tutorials and at dinner in Hall, where along with High Table we were waited on by college servants ('scouts').

Following 'Mods' I spent the Michaelmas term 1941 in college, attending various lectures and waiting for a call to Sandhurst or some other Officer Cadet Training Unit. But in December Japan entered the war. *More suo* the defence departments, having been assured that they had adequate resources and manpower for Far East intelligence work, found that they had not, and urgent appeals were sent out in February 1942 for young people in or outside the services with at least part of a degree course behind them to volunteer for a 'crash course' in military Japanese. I and about 20 others (mostly classics people) were accepted and sent to Bedford for the first of a series of Japanese courses, which in my case affected the whole of my working life.

We were in the charge of a retired naval captain, Oswald Tuck, whose service as a midshipman had started with helping the Japanese to run a modern navy, under the terms of the Anglo-Japanese alliance of 1902. He insisted on conventional politeness when we met each morning: 'Shokun ohayō' (Good morning, ladies and gentleman), 'Ohayō gozaimasu' (Good morning, Sir). But our courses themselves were entirely in what is now the hardly ever used 'classical Japanese', which in the war the Japanese exclusively used in official publications and messages, encrypted or *en clair*. Many of these were intercepted and copied for us at the Canadian naval base at Esquimault. As one example, the verb *to be* was *nari*, as against the modern *de aru* or *desu*. Our textbooks were Rose-Innes's character and Romaji dictionary (1942) and J. G. McIlroy's revised and abbreviated version of B. H. Chamberlain's grammar (1924). This was set out in a delightfully old-fashioned metalanguage. On page 16 we read 'Relative pronouns. The Japanese language has no relative pronouns.' The author then goes on to explain and exemplify the 'attributive' forms of verbs: *yukiki*, 'he went', *yukishi hito*, 'the man who went', *hisubeshi*, 'should keep secret', *hisubeki koto*, 'something that should be kept secret' (1924: 16). I was delighted to find a similar use of morphological inflection to embed a clause under a noun phrase in Yurok, a language of north California, on which I did fieldwork in 1951. We also learned, of course, the different writing systems, Romaji, katakana and hiragana, and the Japanese use of the Chinese character script. All this opened my eyes widely to the variety of language systems.

I was struck by the typology of Japanese, more distinct in the classical form than in modern colloquial from European languages. The inflexional systems of verbs and adjectives were highly developed, mostly by agglutinative suffixation, but representing different aspects of syntactic function from the languages I had been used to: no grammatical gender, no grammatical number (only lexically distinguished in some pronouns), and European conjunctival clauses (*although*, *because*, etc.), as well as modals like *want to*, *ought to*, all being expressed in the morphology of the verbs, along with the attributive forms already noticed. All these different forms were set out in tables rivalling Theodosius' *Kanónes* and numbering well over 2,000 different forms (McIlroy 1924: 113–38).

At the end of the first Bedford course in late summer 1942 we were assigned to the services; some went to Bletchley Park, then so secret but now public property. I was there briefly and then sent to London to enlist in the RAF and go to the School of Oriental and African Studies, rapidly becoming an armed services language training institute for the duration of the war, to take Firth's Japanese phonetics course, something largely ignored in Bedford. After this I went to an RAF station for a few weeks of 'boot camp' drill, and then back to London to join Firth's department as a teacher in another set of courses, phonetics for radiotelephony interception and translation for dealing with written intercepts and other texts, by stages building up for a 'conventional' war of a year or more against Japan. In due course I received a commission, ending the war in this same teaching job as a flight-lieutenant. With the sudden ending of the Japanese war the School was anxious to resume its normal work, and most of us service personnel, students and staff, were keen to get back to our interrupted university degree courses. Our early demobilization was part of a scheme for the quick release of essential civilian workers like miners, building workers and so on. I received an official form telling me that I was being discharged in advance on the strict understanding that I immediately took up work 'as an arts student with Messrs. New College'.

I retained two impressions from this wartime work: the obvious but exciting diversity of languages throughout the world and the pleasure to be derived from teaching. Life in the School had provided one or two instances of teacher-training. In my early days as an instructor with the lowly rank and uniform of an aircraftsman, second class, I had charge of a group that included some newly commissioned naval officers, proud of their status and given to a little alcoholic refreshment at lunchtime. Somehow I had to maintain my position: 'I am paid to teach you, and you are paid to listen and learn.' And in the later years of the war, attacks by flying bombs (V-1s – 'doodlebugs') drove us into the corridors away from glass windows to compete with each others' classes and maintain the attention of our students, who were more concerned with what was going on outside.

In the last year of the war the government turned its attention to the future of Oriental and African studies, and the Scarborough Commission was set up to make recommendations, which were quickly put into effect in the early post-war years. In 1944 Firth had been made the first Professor of General Linguistics in any British university. He was represented on the Commission and, on the basis of his war experience, insisted that linguistics should be properly maintained in the School, particularly in view of the relatively scantily studied and undocumented state of many of the languages involved. During the Japanese war years his department numbered around 10 teachers, civilian and servicemen, and in the wake of the Scarborough Report the department reached a complement of 14.

In October 1945 I took up my work for the second public examination in classics, 'Greats', graduating in 1948. The syllabus in those days might have been described in another university as a two-subject degree, Ancient History and Modern Philosophy. The old medieval continuity had long since gone. Ancient history stopped with the death of Marcus Aurelius (180), and ancient philosophy stopped with Aristotle. By convention, though lectures on figures from the period between might be given, modern philosophy started with Locke and Descartes, largely skipped Kant, wholly skipped Hegel, and started again with the nineteenth-century English philosophers, leading up to the twentieth century. A. J. Ayer and the Logical Positivists were in power; 'ordinary language philosophy' had hardly begun, but J. L. Austin, who had already established himself, was trying out such ideas in his lectures, suggesting that the problems of knowledge versus belief and reality against appearance could better be tackled by a semantic-syntactic analysis of *know* and *realize* in different collocations. He read a paper to the Philological Society, 'How to do things with words', but sadly he died young, leaving Searle, Grice and others to take up his thinking. My ancient history tutor was A. Andrews, who, with a command of modern Greek, had parachuted into occupied Greece and worked with the Resistance. In the face of this gallantry I felt rather humble after my own relatively comfortable war. To him I owe the obligation, in writing anything historical, to get back to the primary sources for any justification for my judgements.

Firth had made no secret of his intention to make his department in the post-war years a centre of general linguistics, co-operating with other departments, but organizationally independent in the School. It played an essential part in the re-creation of the Department of Southeast Asia and the training of their newly appointed staff. In the academic year 1947–8 I received a letter from Firth reporting the creation of a new Lectureship in Linguistics and saying 'There is no reason why you should not apply for it.' I did, and thus began my academic career at the School for the next 38 years, relieved at intervals by visiting appointments on the continent and in America varying between two and six months. My professional life in linguistics owes more to Firth than to any one other major figure. I was his younger colleague for 11 years in all, during the Japanese war and from 1948 until his retirement in 1956, and I acquired my personal outlook and ambitions in the subject from him.

Firth was a complex character (see further Scott 1961; Robins 1997). He was able and energetic; he knew just what he wanted and how to get it. In committees and occasionally in seminars he pressed his case to the point of discourtesy, and he was not ashamed of political lobbying and even intrigue to get his way. But the establishment and expansion of linguistics first in the School and then in other universities in the late 1950s and early 1960s owes more to him than to any one single other.

Within linguistics as a subject he had three major, one might almost say passionate, interests: the contextual theory of semantics, the history of linguistics, and prosodic phonology. As I moved through my professional years it was the history of linguistics that increasingly became my main research interest, and that stems directly from Firth.

During the creation and the running of the armed services Japanese courses his concept of the 'context of situation' was uppermost. The specialized demands of the services played into his own conception of 'a language' as, in fact, a complex of 'different languages', contextually determined and used and understood by speakers as such, sharing major lexical content and grammatical structures, but each exhibiting its own distinctive features. He was concentrating on official military Japanese, then written in the formal classical style, to the complete neglect of civilian usages and all literary writings. An analogy might be to organize the teaching of Latin on the basis of Caesar's *De bello Gallico*, and nothing else. Firth set out his wartime experiences in language teaching in an article in 1945.

From 1948, when he delivered his lecture to the Philological Society on 'Sounds and prosodies', prosodic phonology became his most prominent theme, very influential among his departmental colleagues (see Palmer 1970); but in the war his approach to the roman transcription of Japanese differed little from Daniel Jones's then standard phonemics. His writing of [tʃi] and [tsɯ] as /ti/ and /tu/, unlike the normal Japanese *chi* and *tsu*, was based on the complementary distribution of these two allophonic varieties of the consonant /t/ appearing as [t] before all other vowels.

Those of us who joined (or in my case rejoined) Firth's department between the years 1946 and 1951 had the interesting but uncomfortable experience of more or less simultaneously learning about the subject as a whole and being exposed to Firth's two theoretical convictions, that the context of situation was the only proper way to understand the function of language in society and the full meaning of what was said or written, and that prosodic theory was the best way of analysing the phonological structure of a language.

This is not the place to expound either of these theories (for which see Firth 1937: ch. 10; 1957; Palmer 1970); but between the years 1947 and 1956, as far as phonology was concerned, Firth was radically opposed to the dominant structuralist phonemics in America (cf. Harris 1951) and to the more traditional phoneme theory of Daniel Jones at University College, London: and in semantics he was equally hostile to the neglect of the study of meaning by most of the post-Bloomfieldians in America, and to the traditional equation of linguistic meaning as the 'expression of ideas'.

Of course he told us to read the classics of the subject: de Saussure, Sapir, Trubetzkoy, Bloomfield and others; 'soak yourself in the literature' was his advice to me. And he maintained a wide coverage in his department of the subject: with special but not exclusive reference to Oriental and African languages, phonetics and phonology received particular attention, with a laboratory and recording studio, and a post was established and maintained in comparative and historical linguistics, which was held by a succession of people and finally by Theodora Bynon, as Professor of Historical Linguistics up to her premature retirement in 1995, since when the post has been left unfilled. Firth always held the strength of the department for the role he expected. In the war, civilian and service staff numbered 14; from the late 1940s its teacher numbers ranged between 10 and 12, until the 1980s, when they fell sharply.

He very much encouraged publication on the lines of his own prime interests, and being without a basis of prior linguistic work, we were glad to follow him. We, his young colleagues, were mostly of the last generation of university teachers not to have read for a PhD, with its accompanying research programme; we came from first degrees in other subjects, which did not equip us seriously to challenge Firth's doctrines. Lyons (now Sir John, and Master of Trinity Hall, Cambridge), who was our colleague from 1957 to 1960, was the first one who felt able to do so (1966), though supporting his approach (cf. Lyons 1995).

Of Firth's two tenets, prosodic phonology received the more immediate attention, though Mitchell made a thorough contextual study of the language of commerce in a variety of Arabic (1957). Some 30 articles on prosodic phonology were published in the years 1949–56, of which 15 were selected by Palmer (1970). As we were in the School, these articles were concerned with parts of the phonology of languages little known to other linguists, which may have detracted from the notice of a wider linguistic public. The nearest to a prosodic analysis of the whole phonology of a language was Henderson's 'Prosodies in Siamese' (1949; cf. Palmer 1970: xiii). For some reason no written attention was paid to English, although much of Firth's programmatic article (1948) was illustrated from English, and Eileen Whitley gave some fascinating insights into the theory taken from English in her classes.

Firth himself never wrote a book setting out his principles of linguistics, though he talked about such a book sometimes. This was his tragedy; he felt that his ideas were original and important, but without a textbook he did not achieve the recognition that he considered he deserved in his lifetime. A generation later some of his proposals were taken up again, usually without acknowledgement, in post-Chomskian phonology and in current work on relevance and pragmatics.

Firth in fact wrote relatively little, but he was active in encouraging his colleagues to publish; he would seize on a topic, for example retroflexion and aspiration in Sanskrit, and get someone else to work it up (cf. Allen 1951; 1954). This was useful for those of us who still had to make our way to recognition. Until, after his retirement, first degrees, diplomas and taught-course Master's degrees were established, students were few and most of them were PhD candidates under supervision; in this context one of Firth's favourite boasts was 'We teach through our publications.'

Arising out of his insistence on the embedding of language in human social and personal contexts, the history of linguistics itself was a focus, at first a rather lonely focus, of Firth's general linguistics. Such then little-known figures as Dionysius Thrax, Priscian, the Scaligers, John Wilkins and Sir William Jones all receive mention, at least, in his deliberately popularizing book *The Tongues of Men* (1937). I well remember his astonishment and almost fury when, in answer to his question on what Oxford thought about Donatus and Priscian, I had to tell him that these two and the rest of the Late Latin grammarians were scarcely paid any attention: 'and that in one of the leading universities in classical learning!'

Two books published in the early 1950s illustrate two of Firth's characteristics: his interest in the history of his subject and his practice of working through his colleagues. During and after some teaching in India before the First World War he acquired a great interest in and respect for the Sanskritic tradition of linguistic scholarship, accompanied by a fairly limited knowledge of the Sanskrit language. Sidney Allen, later Professor of Comparative Philology at Cambridge, joined Firth's department in 1948 with a good knowledge of the language as the fruit of his 'Group E' work in that university. He was urged by Firth to write a generally accessible book on the historical evaluation of the works of the ancient Sanskrit phoneticians.

His *Phonetics in Ancient India* appeared in 1953, and Firth, always the politician, formally presented it to Pundit Nehru when he was on an official visit to Great Britain.

In 1950 Firth was asked to give some lectures on linguistic work in antiquity and the Middle Ages at Birkbeck College. He declined, but said 'Robins will do this for you.' I did, the lectures were well received, and I worked them up into a book that was published in 1951 with a subsidy from the School. This was a slight book (104 pages), and in its final chapter too 'Whig-historical' in evaluating our predecessors primarily in the light of their anticipation of the Euro-American linguistic scene at that time. But it did have the effect of encouraging others to follow it up, and two North American linguists, Francis Dinneen and Geoffrey Bursill-Hall, wrote their theses under my supervision on aspects of medieval linguistics (Bursill-Hall 1959; Dinneen 1961). Subsequently Dineen wrote various essays and a book dealing with linguistics in the ancient and the medieval world, and Bursill-Hall devoted much of his research to scholastic grammatical theory, leading to his critical study and translation of the *Grammatica Speculativa* of Thomas of Erfurt (1972) and his *Census of Medieval Latin Grammatical Manuscripts* (1981).

Firth retired in 1956 and died in 1960. His influence remained with me as I pursued my career in the University of London. I was already a Reader, and in 1966 I was made Professor of General Linguistics in the University of London. As the years progressed I was elected a Fellow of the British Academy in 1986 and a Member of the Academia Europaea in 1991.

So far I have tried to show how I came into linguistics as a career. Such an account relies on selective memories and written records, along with the intention of telling the truth as I saw it. It is therefore basically objective and factual. But a scholar's estimation of his contribution to his chosen subject is necessarily subjective, and this should properly belong to the judgement and assessment of others. I can only write about what I tried to do, how I tried to do it, and record what I have read of other people's reports of my achievement.

Scholars' work for and in their callings falls into three divisions: what they have written and published, what they have been able to do for their students, and what help they have given to their colleagues and their subject in their administrative capacity. This is no place to set out my own bibliography (for this up to 1996 see Law and Hüllen 1996: 27–42). My publications fall into three groups: general linguistic theory and methods, work on particular languages, and work on the history of linguistics, which has increasingly formed the major part of my research in the last three decades.

In 1964 I first published *General Linguistics: An Introductory Survey*, which I intended to be what its title suggests, an elementary one-volume exposition of the range of the subject; this ran through four editions (1964,

1971, 1980, 1989), and I now leave any successor to anyone willing to write such single-authored introductory textbooks. Apart from sundry articles on languages falling directly under the coverage of the School, I published my *Yurok Language: Grammar, Texts, Lexicon* in 1958, and I have used my fieldwork material for a few subsequent specialized articles. Though it is but a small part of my linguistic activities, I find particular pleasure in having recorded in text and on tape the grammar and some stories and songs of a language soon to be extinct, if it is not already so. The current Endangered Languages Project (CIPL and UNESCO) appears to me as one of the most urgent tasks for present-day linguists.

In the history of linguistics, when my first book (1951) went out of print, I incorporated what I had there written into a larger and more comprehensive *Short History of Linguistics* (1967), which became a widely used textbook, translated into several languages, and has run into a fourth edition (1997). I recently turned my attention to a group of grammarians whom I had long felt deserved more respect than they had been accorded, the linguistic scholars of the Byzantine Empire, maintaining classical Greek scholarship over a period of more than 1,000 years and providing the essential material, human and textual, for the revival of Greek studies in the western Renaissance (1993).

Overall, I would like to think that a reviewer of my conversation with Pierre Swiggers (1997), Margaret Thomas (1999: 179), has passed a fair characterization of my œuvre and my personality as a scholar:

> Robins's historical work probably overshadows his contributions to descriptive linguistics . . . Robins may come closest to Swiggers's characterization as an evader of dogmatism. He has an appreciative word for virtually all persons and ideas, seems dispositionally prone to see continuity, and is gracious even as he finds fault, for example, as he laments theoretical narrowness or insists on distinguishing endangered from threatened languages.

As a teacher, after Firth's retirement I took over his regular weekly lecture on general linguistics, together with a colleague, for much of the time Eugénie Henderson, who covered the details of phonetics and phonology. This constituted an annual first year course extending over three terms. Throughout it I set myself to cover or at least to mention authoritatively the whole comprehension of linguistics, synchronic and diachronic, leaving it to others to fill out the specialist details. Someone (I forget who) said that my treatment of English intonation by reference to Daniel Jones's 'two tunes' was 'palaeolithic'. Anyway, students would realize that intonation, so little noticed in everyday speech, was a relevant part of the subject. Specialists could take it over later, at least to no longer virginal ears. I dealt with the detailed history of linguistics in a second year course. I set store by my first year introductory lectures, from my own experience at Oxford studying philosophy for the first time. Subjects such as philosophy and linguistics, not generally studied at school, are challenging in a special way. Either there was not, or I just missed, a basic introductory course in the whole compass of philosophy, telling us what it was all about, before we were pitched into Locke and Descartes. This task I tried my best to fulfil through my general introductory lectures.

In scholarly administration I served as Secretary of the Philological Society and then as its President, 27 years in all, from 1961 to 1988, and as British representative and then as President of CIPL in the years 1970 to 1997, fully realizing how light are the duties of a President compared to the work done week in week out by the Secretaries-General, Professors 'Bob' Uhlenbeck and 'Piet' van Sterkenburg. From 1970 to 1985 I was Head of the Department of Phonetics and Linguistics in the School, resigning one year before my retirement in favour of Professor Theodora Bynon, the uniform choice of my colleagues. For me these were happy years academically and personally. Between us we were able to cover most of the theoretical and practical aspects of linguistics in teaching and research, including advanced experimental phonetics, structuralism, tagmemics, stratificational grammar, various aspects of generative grammar, historical linguistics, and the history of linguistics. I was and am proud of what was 'my Department', in which over the years were several colleagues whose level of advanced scholarship I would never claim to have attained. The Department produced three Fellows of the British Academy, and at the 1982 International Congress of Linguists in Tokyo two of the initial papers in the seven Plenary Lectures were given by my departmental colleagues, Professors Henderson, on phonetics and phonology, and Bynon, on historical linguistics.

I suppose that my single most important contribution to the subject was an enabling one. My two books (1951; 1967), my regular teaching in London, and my invited teaching for two years in Cambridge may have given support to the quite remarkable surge in interest in the history of linguistics manifested in Europe as a whole and in America during the last quarter of the twentieth century. Several specialist societies have come into being, among them the Henry Sweet Society for the History of Linguistic Ideas, the Société d'Histoire et d'Epistémologie des Sciences du Langage, which was kind enough to elect me Président d'Honneur, and more recently the North American Association for the History of the Language Sciences. In Great Britain the subject, which has unfortunately been dropped in London, is now fully taught and researched in Cambridge, where Dr Law is currently Reader in the History of Linguistic Thought, and also in Oxford, Sheffield and the new University of Luton, where I appreciate their invitation to take a part in the teaching of it.

Law (Law & Hüllen 1996: 9) kindly quotes a foreign scholar attributing to me the 'persona of "the perfect old-fashioned English gentleman"'. If this is a fair judgement I am pleased. In my Headship of my Department I do not recall any harsh words, given or received, between myself and my colleagues or students. During the silly years of the late 1960s and early 1970s in London or in America I never cancelled a class of mine, and I resorted to no more than a cheerful *badinage* with student 'strikers' and some colleagues who seemed to take all this nonsense (which has almost vanished from university life now) much too weightily. I coined and liked to use as a motto for the Department 'Good scholarship and good fellowship'.

I have always endeavoured, as I said in my inaugural address as Professor (1966), to keep my subject within the context of a liberal education. I find the exercise of 'pulling rank' unpleasant, and I have tried not to take myself (or others) too seriously. I am grateful to my good friend Vivien Law for drawing attention in her sketch of my academic life (Law & Hüllen 1996: 13) to the incident of Tony Klijnsmit's sand-and-oyster soup (further details in the text). In this connection and in a final reflection, I recall Firth's obvious enjoyment of our Christmas parties in the 1950s. We were a young department then, with plenty of young children. He loved dressing up as Father Christmas, and deceiving some of them as he distributed the presents with his Secretary as the Good Fairy. It reminds me of old Fezziwig's parties for his apprentices in Dickens's *Christmas Carol*, in Scrooge's youth before the iron bars of finance entered and darkened his soul. Perhaps this is not without relevance in these austere days when universities are encouraged and are even eager to adopt the principles and methods of limited liability companies.

REFERENCES

ALLEN, SIDNEY, 1951. 'Some prosodic aspects of retroflexion and aspiration in Sanskrit', *BSOAS* 13, 939–46.
ALLEN, SIDNEY, 1953. *Phonetics in Ancient India*, London: Oxford University Press.
ALLEN, SIDNEY, 1954. 'Retroflexion in Sanskrit: prosodic technique and its relevance to comparative statement', *BSOAS* 16, 556–65.
BAZELL, CHARLES ET AL., (eds.) 1966. *In Memory of J. R. Firth*, London: Longman.
BUCK, CHARLES, 1928. *Greek Dialects*, Ginn.
BUCK, CHARLES, 1933. *Comparative Grammar of Greek and Latin*, Chicago: University of Chicago Press.
BURSILL-HALL, GEOFFREY, 1959. *An Examination of the Doctrine of Partes Orationis in the Modistae*. PhD thesis, University of London.
BURSILL-HALL, GEOFFREY, 1972. *Thomas of Erfurt: Grammatica Speculativa*, London: Longman.
BURSILL-HALL, GEOFFREY, 1981. *A Census of Medieval Latin Grammatical Manuscripts*, Stuttgart: Frommann-Holzboog.
DINNEEN, FRANCIS, 1961. *The Linguistic Doctrine of Thomas Aquinas and its Relevance to Modern Linguistics*. PhD thesis, University of London.
FIRTH, JOHN R., 1937. *The Tongues of Men*, London: Watts.
FIRTH, JOHN R., 1945. 'Wartime experiences in linguistic training', *Modern Languages* 26.2, 38–46.
FIRTH, JOHN R., 1948. 'Sounds and prosodies', *TPhS* 1948, 127–52.
FIRTH, JOHN R., 1957. *Papers in Linguistics 1934–1951*, London: Oxford University Press.
HARRIS, ZELLIG, 1951. *Methods in Structural Linguistics*, Chicago: University of Chicago Press.

HENDERSON, EUGÉNIE, 1949. 'Prosodies in Siamese', *Asia Major* 1, 189–215.
JESPERSEN, OTTO, 1922. *Language*, London: Allen and Unwin.
LAW, VIVIEN & HÜLLEN, WERNER, 1996. *Linguists and their Diversions*, Münster: Nodus.
LYONS, JOHN, 1966. 'Firth's theory of "meaning"', in Charles Bazell et al. (eds.), *In Memory of J. R. Firth*, London: Longman, 288–302.
LYONS, JOHN, 1995. *Linguistic Semantics*, Cambridge: Cambridge University Press.
MCILROY, JAMES, 1924. *A Simplified Grammar of the Japanese Language*, Chicago: University of Chicago Press.
MITCHELL, TERENCE, 1957. 'The language of buying and selling in Cyrenaica', *Hespéris* 44, 31–71.
PALMER, FRANK, (ed.) 1970. *Prosodic Analysis*, London: Oxford University Press.
ROBINS, R. H., 1951. *Ancient and Mediaeval Grammatical Theory in Europe*, London: Bell.
ROBINS, R. H., 1964/1989. *General Linguistics: An Introductory Survey*, London: Longman.
ROBINS, R. H., 1966. *General Linguistics within a Liberal Education*, inaugural lecture, London: School of Oriental and African Studies.
ROBINS, R. H., 1967/1997. *A Short History of Linguistics*, London: Longman.
ROBINS, R. H., 1993. *The Byzantine Grammarians: Their Place in History*, Berlin: Mouton de Gruyter.
ROBINS, R. H., 1997. 'The contribution of John Rupert Firth to linguistics in the first fifty years of *Lingua*', *Lingua* 100, 205–22.
ROSE-INNES, ARTHUR, 1942. *Beginners' Dictionary of Chinese-Japanese Characters*, London: Lund Humphries.
SCOTT, NORMAN, 1961. 'Obituary, John Rupert Firth', *BSOAS* 24, 413–17.
SWIGGERS, PIERRE, (ed.) 1997. *Language and Linguistics*, Leuven: Peeters.
THOMAS, MARGARET, 1999. 'Review of Swiggers 1997', *Language* 75, 178–9.

NEIL SMITH

SMITH, Neilson Voyne, FBA 1999; Professor of Linguistics, University College, London, since 1981; *b.* 1939; *m.* 1966 Saraswati Keskar; *Education:* Tavistock Grammar School; Cheltenham Grammar School; Trinity College, Cambridge, BA 1961, MA 1964; University College, London, PhD 1964; *Career:* Lecturer in West African Languages, SOAS, 1964–70;Lecturer in Linguistics and West African Languages, SOAS, 1970–2; Reader in Linguistics, University College, London, 1972–81 (Head of Linguistics Section since 1972, Head of Department of Phonetics and Linguistics, 1983–90, Vice-Dean, Faculty of Arts, 1992–4, Postgraduate Tutor, Faculty of Arts, 1994–6; Member of Council 1987–93); Member Linguistics Panel, SSRC (Vice-Chairman 1977–8), ESRC (Vice-Chairman, Education and Human Development Committee); President: Linguistics Association of Great Britain 1980–6, Association of Heads and Professors of Linguistics 1993–4; Hon. Member Linguistic Society of America 1999; Senator, University of London 1989–93. *Major Publications: An Outline Grammar of Nupe* 1967; *The Acquisition of Phonology* 1973; *Modern Linguistics: The Results of Chomsky's Revolution* 1979 (with Deirdre Wilson); *The Twitter Machine: Reflections on Language* 1989; *The Mind of a Savant: Language Learning and Modularity* 1995 (with Ianthi Tsimpli); *Chomsky: Ideas and Ideals* 1999.

* * *

Nearing my final year as an undergraduate at Cambridge, I found myself selecting five optional subjects (out of some 77) to take for Part II of the Modern and Medieval Languages Tripos. I had selected the history of the French language, the history of the German language, German literature before 1500, Vulgar Latin and Romance philology, and was about to put down German literature in the twentieth century, when a close friend[1] asked if I knew what 'linguistics' was. After we had agreed that neither of us had the slightest idea, he then persuaded me to join him in adding it as our final option. I was sad to give up Bergengruen, Böll and Brecht, but I reasoned that I could always read these authors by myself, whereas linguistics was likely to be less amenable to dilettante study. So in October 1960 we enrolled on John Trim's course on 'The Principles of Linguistics', and I have been hooked ever since.

The bulk of the course consisted of phoneme theory, with a healthy admixture of morphemes and even a smattering of syntax in the form of immediate constituent analysis. Banal by today's standards, but Trim was an inspiring teacher and I was soon converted from my desire to be a medievalist to a desire to understand everything about the phoneme. In fact, my understanding even of that was minimal. I still remember with stark clarity at the end of the first term being given a passage and told to transcribe it both phonetically and phonemically. I had no idea what that meant. Similarly, I remember endlessly searching in my dictionary for some insight which would enable me to distinguish 'syntax' and 'semantics', but again to no avail. These memories have made me (try to be) tolerant of students today who have problems with a much more rebarbative jargon.

The year passed. We were entertained by some of the subject's luminaries – André Martinet, whose *Economie des changements phonétiques* had already captivated me, and Louis Hjelmslev, whose *Prolegomena to a Theory of Language* struck me (to the limited extent that I understood it) as offering the science I had often regretted abandoning for languages. We took finals. I got a distinctly mediocre 2.1, and was told unofficially that my worst paper had been linguistics, for which I got close to a third class mark. So I applied for jobs. Fortunately, none of librarianship, schoolteaching or the British Council would touch me and, *faute de mieux*, I started a PhD at UCL under the joint supervision of Dennis Fry and Gordon Arnold. I had no grant, but with fees at £42 a year and plenty of opportunities even then for teaching English as a foreign language, I survived.

At Cambridge I had been a contemporary of Dick Hudson, still my colleague 40 years on. He was starting a PhD at SOAS at the same time, and had been offered the opportunity to do fieldwork on the Beja of the Sudan. It seemed a wonderful idea, so thinking that if he could do it, I could do it, I planned to go up the Amazon and find my own unwritten language to study. I was advised that Nigeria was more likely to leave me alive at the end of my trip and I began to read about the area. I soon came across Siegfried Nadel's classic anthropology text *A Black Byzantium* about the Nupe. Nadel remarked that it was sad that no good grammar of Nupe existed: an invitation I couldn't resist. With some help from David Arnott and Evan Rowlands of SOAS, I was soon prepared, and in the summer of 1962 I hitch-hiked to Bida in Northern Nigeria (from Istanbul to Khartoum in the company of Dick).[2]

A year's fieldwork is wonderful training for any linguist. Being confronted with a complex tone language, whose syntax was unlike anything I had ever heard of, was chastening, exhilarating, illuminating, educative and fun. It was also intermittently very lonely and extremely hard work, but it set me up with stories to dine out on for life, and it also brought a PhD. When I returned to UCL after my fieldwork, the place had changed: Michael Halliday had arrived from Edinburgh and was offering elegant descriptive solutions to large numbers of problems I had been struggling with in my mud hut. My thesis transmogrified into a standard scale and category grammar of Nupe.[3] Better still, my new-found expertise as an Africanist seemed to have qualified me to become a Lecturer in West African Languages at SOAS. In 1964 appointing a new Lecturer was somewhat easier than indenting for a new carpet is now. There were 27 of us in the Department of Africa that year. The department now (2000) has about one-third that number of staff.

SOAS was strange. My colleagues were mostly a delight, but relations between the Linguistics Department[4] and the Africa Department were strained, and those between the Linguistics Department and the sister Department at UCL where I had come from were icy. It was 'not convenient' for me to use the library of the Linguistics Department or attend seminars there, and some of the students were warned not to talk to me 'in case they got confused'. Fortunately, I made two life-long friends and colleagues: Gilbert Ansre, the first black lecturer in the Africa Department, who taught me Ewe (see Smith 1968), and Yamuna Kachru,[5] Lecturer in Hindi and a talented generative grammarian. After I had graduated, John Trim had confided that the future was generative. Now I began to understand why, as Yamuna won all the syntactic arguments we had, and made me feel inadequate about my own grasp of theory. To learn a little about the new paradigm and to escape the suffocation of the rivalries at SOAS, I applied for a Harkness Fellowship and went to MIT and UCLA for a couple of years.

MIT was a revelation. There was huge enthusiasm, appallingly hard work, and remarkable talent. I found myself again a neophyte, but being a post-doctoral 'Visitor' I was spared the ignominy of having to turn in term papers proving my inadequacy. The worst embarrassment was discovering that the nice man I'd tried to explain 'generative grammar' to at a welcoming reception was Paul Kiparsky. I had gone to MIT because of Chomsky, but when I arrived, he was away. Fortunately, Morris Halle took me under his wing, and in due course I became a phonologist. The riches on offer were remarkable: courses by Roman Jakobson[6] on language and poetics, by J. R. (Haj) Ross and George Lakoff on English syntax and generative semantics, by Kiparsky on Indo-European and the structure of German, Jerrold Katz on the philosophy of language, Jerry Fodor on perception, Halle on phonology, Hugh Matthews on universal grammar (especially Hidatsa), Frits Staal on Sanskrit and the Paninian tradition. And after the first semester, Chomsky.

When I arrived, the place was buzzing with the ideas of generative semantics, and the demise of Chomsky's 'standard theory'[7] was widely assumed to be imminent. Chomsky's response was electrifying. In the spring semester of 1967 he delivered the lectures which became 'Remarks on mominalization' (Chomsky 1970). In fact these lectures were directed primarily against Bob Lees's *Grammar of English Nominalizations*,[8] but could be – and were – interpreted as a systematic attack on generative semantics. Chomsky's arguments were illuminating; at once critical, penetrating and innovative (X-bar theory first saw the light of day in these lectures), and ultimately set the scene for much of the linguistic theorizing of the next decade. Linguistics was not the only area in which I was being educated. While mounting an attack on 'transformationalism', Chomsky was devoting the major part of his time and energy to combating the Vietnam war: with endless teach-ins, meetings, demonstrations, lectures and conversations. From being a political innocent I became convinced that in this area too, Chomsky was more usually right than wrong.[9]

After 15 months at MIT, during which my first son (Amahl) was born,[10] we drove to UCLA for the last six months of the Fellowship.[11] The attraction of UCLA, apart from the Californian climate, was that it was the home of Vicki Fromkin and Paul Schachter, neither of whom I had met but whose work (Schachter & Fromkin 1968) on Akan (a language related to Nupe) I already knew. Moreover, I was familiar with Schachter's (1961) doctoral dissertation on Pangasinan: one of the earliest descriptive transformational grammars, and it was clear that I would be able to benefit hugely from working with him. It turned out that I did minimal work on Akan (or West African languages in general) but quite a lot on English. The department at UCLA was preoccupied with work on what turned into *The Major Syntactic Structures of English*,[12] a curious amalgamation of Fillmore's (1968) case grammar and Chomsky's 'nominalizations' framework. My contribution was negligible, but the experience of working on a detailed descriptive (but theoretically informed) grammar was an instructive complement to the addictive theory of MIT.

I returned to the UK and to SOAS to resume my post as Lecturer in West African Languages. I lectured at both SOAS and UCL, the latter at the invitation of Randolph Quirk and Michael Halliday, who already gave courses on 'An Introduction to Linguistic Studies' and 'English Structure and Usage' in the English Department. The political atmosphere was also gradually improving, and in 1970 my appointment was changed to include Linguistics in its title, and to give me an official foot in the Department of Phonetics and Linguistics – an unthinkable eventuality only a few years previously. I resumed work on West African languages, but my heart was really in linguistics, and my major research had begun to centre on language acquisition. Accordingly, when I was given the chance to return to UCL to be Head of the Linguistics Section of the recently[13] amalgamated Department of Phonetics and Linguistics (under the leadership of A. C. Gimson), I went back enthusiastically to (some of) my roots.

UCL held several attractions: it would enable me to concentrate on the subject I loved most, it would provide me with the chance to build up a department with the kind of theoretical orientation I was now committed to, and it already contained two outstanding linguists, Deirdre Wilson, another significant influence on my intellectual development, and Dick Hudson. I have been in the Department, and Head of Linguistics, ever since.

When I joined the Department in October 1972, there were only three of us in the Linguistics Section, and there was no single honours degree in linguistics: just combined honours degrees involving linguistics and any one of English, French, German, anthropology or philosophy, set up by my predecessor Halliday.[14] There was also a two-year postgraduate Diploma in Linguistics, and a sprinkling of research students. At this time all degrees were taught under the aegis of the Federal University, so we were able to take advantage of the linguists at SOAS and, to a lesser extent, at Birkbeck. None the less, there were three clear priorities: to increase the number of staff, to institute both a new MA and a single honours BA in Linguistics, and to attract enough students to justify the first two. The economic situation of the time (OPEC was becoming militant) meant that the only way to achieve the first two was to start by increasing student numbers.

The first new degree to be set up was the MA in Linguistics, with its first intake in 1973; the first new appointment, which gave the Section sufficient strength to make new programmes feasible, was Geoffrey Pullum, who joined in 1975 and stayed until 1981. Before this, it was not uncommon for people to be appointed because they were good clubbable types, or as a 'favour' to colleagues and friends; and there was a desire to pick someone who wouldn't 'rock the boat', in the words of A. C. Gimson. Fortunately Geoff's appointment – and all subsequent ones – were carried out in democratic fashion, with the overwhelming criterion being to get the best person. Democracy means that my role was only partial, but the ethos of the Department and the continued emphasis on theoretical excellence is something I have tried to foster.

With Pullum in post we now worked seriously on instituting the single honours Degree in Linguistics, and it started in 1977 with an intake of eight students. This development gave us some independence from the other departments with which we collaborated on combined honours degrees. This was just as well, because one of our most popular degrees, English and Linguistics, was unfortunately discontinued, with the last intake in 1976. Since then, the relative importance of the combined and single honours degrees has shifted systematically in favour of the latter. French and Linguistics followed English and Linguistics into limbo in 1983, and although we instituted combined honours degrees with Dutch (from 1985) and Italian (from 1986), the numbers of students never justified the organizational resources to make them viable. Even the introduction in 1990 of a joint Degree in Linguistics with Cognitive Science – an amalgam of linguistics, psychology and computer science – never attracted enough students to be successful. Now, all the joint degrees (except Italian and Linguistics) have been discontinued.

Fortunately, the single honours degree has flourished, and we currently have an intake of about 30 students per year. More importantly, the emphasis of the department, of UCL and of the elite research universities generally, is tending towards postgraduate programmes, and the MA has similarly expanded dramatically in the last few years. For a long time we had only a handful of MA students each year, but we now have up to 25 students per year. The success of this part of the programme, with its spin-off of providing a steady stream of first class research students, has led us to inaugurate (from 2002) two new advanced MAs with possible specialization in syntax or phonology. We hope to add a third degree with specialization in pragmatics soon.

Programmes of this kind can only be successful if they are attractive to the national and international linguistic community. UCL's linguistics is renowned[15] because we have staff who can attract students of the highest quality from around the world. After Pullum's resignation to go to the USA, we have been fortunate in being able to appoint a series of outstanding linguists from around the world: Michael Brody (from 1982), Robyn Carston (from 1985), John Harris (from 1986), Hans van de Koot (from 1989), Rita Manzini (from 1990 until 1998), Ad Neeleman (from 1998) and Moira Yip (from 2001). Linguistics is beautifully international: these people come from Hungary, New Zealand, Ireland, the Netherland, Italy and even England (via the USA). Until Ad joined us, we had been able to select each new appointment from a different country.

Core teaching in the Department has been systematically imbued by a desire for theoretical excellence. This has been manifest in three areas: generative syntax (where that includes word grammar, GPSG – which I used to teach), relevance-theoretic pragmatics, government phonology, and theory based language acquisition.

My perception of the field is that it has intermittently been bedevilled by woolly-mindedness and an eclecticism bordering on the amateurish. The best antidote to such sloppiness is rigorous theory. I have a passionate commitment to developing the best theory possible, in large part because I want to be pampered in a way that Joos thought no child should be.[16] The best explanations I have come across have systematically been the fruit of Chomsky's work. Every time I think I am in a position to understand what is going on, he has pushed the explanation one step further back. I have tried to couch my own work in the framework he has provided and build a department in which the construction of explanatory theories – and teaching them to each new generation – is central.

This has meant concentration on Chomskian theory simply because I think that that has been the most insightful. But Chomsky and his followers have no monopoly. My PhD thesis was 'Hallidayan' – a scale and category grammar of Nupe; my concentration on Chomskian syntax was replaced by GPSG (see e.g. Gazdar et al. 1985) for a couple of years (I taught it to all undergraduates and MA students for two years) until I became convinced that its concentration on descriptive rigour was bought at the cost of a lack of explanatory insight. In the department, we have always had the benefit of the maverick Dick Hudson and his word grammar (see e.g. Hudson 1990); and we currently have flexible syntax (see e.g. Neeleman & Weerman 1999), but the hard core has been 'Chomskian' syntax, as taught by Brody (e.g. Brody 1995), Manzini (see e.g. Manzini 1992), Neeleman and van de Koot (see e.g. Neeleman & van de Koot 1999) and myself. Similarly, my early commitment to phoneme theory was replaced by immersion in generative phonology: it just explained better what I could see going on. In the department this has resulted indirectly in the development of two off-shoots of generative phonology – government phonology as taught by John Harris (see e.g. Harris 1994), and optimality theory as taught by Moira Yip (see e.g. Yip in press).

Apart from generative syntax, the area for which the Linguistics Section of the Department is most renowned is pragmatics. Deirdre Wilson (in collaboration with Dan Sperber) has developed relevance theory (see e.g. Sperber & Wilson 1995) to a point where it is the default choice for pragmatics and has made UCL the world centre for the subject. As in many areas my contribution has been mainly that of facilitator, helping to create an ambience in which the theory and its adherents could flourish.

One can influence the field directly by one's research; slightly less directly through one's students, especially if one can help them to get jobs; and indirectly by the influence one can exert 'administratively'. This last includes developing the ethos of a department (especially in choosing whom to hire); influencing the theoretical direction to be taken by a journal; affecting the distribution of money by being on the relevant board of research councils or charities (or even acting as a reliable referee for them or for publishers); moulding national organizations such as the LAGB or AHPL; and inaugurating series like *UCL Working Papers in Linguistics*. There is a further form of influence that is even less tangible than the others: popularization, either writing for the general public, or appearing on radio and television. In none of these areas is it easy to identify the effects of oneself as opposed to that of one's colleagues. Making an appointment is no longer the gift of an autocratic Head – at best one has some power of veto; setting up a new degree programme involves the collaboration of one's colleagues; even influencing a journal or a publisher requires the acquiescence of an editorial board and the readiness of the public to buy the books and journals that result. I have been on the board of Cambridge Studies in Linguistics for over 20 years; I have been one of the editors of *Lingua* since 1986; and I am a founder editor of *Mind & Language*. At various times I have been on the editorial board of *Linguistics*, the *Journal of Linguistics and Phonology (Yearbook)*, but I often don't know where and to what extent I've made a difference. I have been blessed with collaborators who have inspired me and pushed me: they have made academic life a joy.[17] What I'm proudest of is my students, especially those whom I have guided as first or second supervisor to a PhD, and many of whom are now themselves academics.[18]

My own research has not been 'seminal' in the way that that of some of my colleagues has been. My work on African languages has been mostly useful as a tool for exposing generations of students to the task of analysing and formalizing data from a typologically unfamiliar tone language (Nupe), though when I look back at my field notes I am mildly surprised to see not only how many problems I came up against, but how many future solutions I dimly came up with. I think my best work was done on the acquisition of phonology, still widely cited a generation after I wrote it, and – with Ianthi Tsimpli – on the polyglot *savant*, Christopher. In each case, it is significant that the basis for insight was a huge mass of new data.

In teaching and in popularization, I have had two aims: on the one hand to explain and justify theory, and on the other hand to integrate the various parts of a discipline which is rapidly becoming overly specialized. In the 1960s it was reasonably easy to have 'read everything'. At the end of the first course I gave on generative grammar in 1964, one student asked me what to look at next, but my reading list already contained everything published. Those were the days. The expansion is wonderful, but it is now increasingly difficult to make connections between syntax, semantics, pragmatics and phonology, and decide, for instance, on the correct apportionment of responsibility among these components for the intonation of focused constituents. I am still exploring these interface areas in my ongoing work with Annabel Cormack.

There have been other influences that should not be passed over in silence. At Tavistock Grammar School, where I studied from 1950 to 1955, the major influence on me was Leonard Priestley (whose work on dislocation in French[19] is still of interest). He used to discuss astronomy in the French lessons, which so captivated me that I chose French in the sixth form, and started German, which he also taught, at the same time. My third subject was Latin. For family reasons, we moved to Gloucestershire and I attended Cheltenham Grammar School, where, for reasons that remain obscure, I was told that I should apply for Trinity to read 'Modern and Medieval Languages'. I got in the second time round, after three and a half years in the sixth form. Before going up to university I worked for six months on a farm, where I learnt a huge amount – from how to inoculate sheep to how to get the best out of people.

Neither of my parents went to university. My father[20] ran away from school when he was 13, and my mother[21] was forbidden to go to university when she decided to marry him. She was an infant teacher, and taught me at home for long periods, especially during the Second World War, when it was not possible to go to school. She was convinced that anyone with a BA must have some of the attributes of Einstein, and both my parents were imbued with a love of learning that made them do everything in their power to give me the opportunities they had not had. My father was creative in ways I am not, building fireplaces, taking out patents on a variety of toys and tools, starting his own companies and going bankrupt through a mixture of incompetence and soft-heartedness. It was a wonderful ambience for my sister[22] and me to grow up in.

Throughout my career I have been extremely fortunate to be a round peg in a round hole. Teaching, research and administration have all fascinated me, and have all extended me. I hope I have put back as much as I have taken out. I have tried to do something which will not stop my family and friends from respecting me.

NOTES

1 David Nice.

2 The Central Research Fund of the University of London had given me my air fare, but it seemed more interesting to go overland. The journey took two months.

3 (Smith 1964). Various chapters of this thesis were published as articles (Smith 1967a; 1967b; 1969). For the background theory, see Halliday (1961).

4 Actually the Department of Phonetics and Linguistics. The abbreviation reflects my own specialization and no disrespect to phonetics.

5 Née Keskar. She also obligingly let me marry her sister, Saras, on 2 July 1966.

6 Jakobson was at Harvard, but courses at both institutions were open to members of each.

7 As represented by his (1965).

8 Lees (1960). This was the first MIT PhD in Linguistics.

9 For some discussion of the relation between Chomsky's political and academic ideas, see Smith (1999).

10 On 4 June 1967. He later acquired phonology (Smith 1973) and, later still, became my co-author (Smith with Smith 1988). My second son, Ivan, was born in England on 13 July, 1973. He has been my mathematical and scientific advisor since shortly thereafter.

11 We arrived in LA on 31 December 1967, just in time for a party where I met many of the LA linguists.

12 Stockwell, Schachter & Partee (1973).

13 The amalgamation took place in 1970 after the resignation of Halliday.

14 These degrees enrolled their first students in 1969. One of the first cohort was Jane Grimshaw, reading anthropology and linguistics.

15 We have consistently received a top (5) rating in the research assessment exercises imposed by government.

16 'Children want explanations, and there is a child in each of us; descriptivism makes a virtue of not pampering that child' (Joos 1957: 96).

17 They are: Brenda Clarke, *Annabel Cormack, Chris Frith, Gary Morgan, John Morton, Neil O'Connor, Jamal Ouhalla, Amahl Smith, *Ianthi Tsimpli, *Deirdre Wilson and Bencie Woll. Those marked with an asterisk are the three with whom I have had the most prolonged and fruitful academic association.

18 I acted as first supervisor for the following students:

Abangma, S., 1992. *Empty Categories in Denya.*

Anderman, G., 1978. *Aspects of Complementation and its Implication for a Theory of Subordination: A Generative Study of Comparative Germanic Syntax with Special Reference to Swedish.*

Barton, D., 1976. *The Role of Perception in the Acquisition of Phonology.*

Betts, A., 1990. *German Impersonal Passives.*

Brody, M., 1984. *Conditions and NP-types.*

Bull, B., 1991. *The Non-Linear Phonological Structure of Moroccan Colloquial Arabic.*

Chan, B., 1999. *Aspects of the Syntax, Production and Pragmatics of Code-Switching – With Special Reference to Cantonese English.*

Chiat, S., 1978. *The Analysis of Children's Pronouns: An Investigation into the Prerequisites for Linguistic Knowledge.*
Cormack, A., 1989. *The Syntax and Semantics of Definitions.*
Curcó, C., 1997. *The Pragmatics of Humorous Interpretations: A Relevance-Theoretic Approach.*
Davies, L., 2001. *The Nature of Specific Language Impairment: Optionality and Principle Conflict.*
Dodd, B., 1975. *The Acquisition of Phonological Skills in Normal, Severely Subnormal and Deaf Children.*
Ejele, P., 1986. *Transitivity, Tense and Aspect in Esan (Ishan).*
Evans, B., 1999. *A Non-Coercing Account of Event Structure in Pular.*
Froud, K., 2001. *Agrammatism and the Minimalist Program: Evidence for the Morphology Interface from a Case of Acquired Language Pathology.*
Giejgo, J., 1981. *Movement Rules in Polish Syntax.*
Grimberg, M-L., 1997. *Against Rigidity: An Investigation of Semantics and Pragmatics of Indexicality.*
Haacke, W., 1993. *The Tonology of Khoekhoe (Nama/Damara).*
Kang, H.-K., 2000. *Aspects of the Acquisition of Quantification: Experimental Studies of English and Korean Children.*
Klavans, J., 1980. *Some Problems in a Theory of Clitics.*
Kumar, B. S., 1972. *Some Aspects of Sanskrit Syntax.* [SOAS]
Mapanje, J., 1983. *On the Interpretation of Aspect and Tense in Chiyao, Chichewa and English.*
McBrearty, J., 1980. *Initial Mutation in Modern Irish and its Implications for Phonological Theory.*
Morris, R., 1984. *Aspect, Case and Thematic Structure in English.*
Mtenje, A., 1986. *Issues in the Non-Linear Phonology of Chichewa.*
Osawa, F., 2000. *The Rise of Functional Categories: Syntactic Parallels between First Language Acquisition and Historical Change.*
Ouhalla, J., 1988. *The Syntax of Head Movement: A Study of Berber.*
Öztekin, H., 1987. *Clausal Complementation in Turkish.*
Paterson, S., 1983. *Voice and Transitivity.*
Pullum, G. K., 1976. *Rule Interaction and the Organization of a Grammar.*
Roberts, J., 1986. *Amele Grammar.*
Tsimpli, I.-M., 1992. *Functional Categories and Maturation: The Prefunctional Stage of Language Acquisition.*
Wilder, C., 1987. *The Syntax of German Infinitives.*
Zegarac, V., 1991. *Tense, Aspect and Relevance.*

I acted as second supervisor to the following students among many others:
Agouraki, Y., 1993. *Spec-Head Licensing: The Scope of the Theory.*
Ansre, G., 1966. *The Grammatical Units of Ewe.* [SOAS]
Benkaddour, A., 1982. *Nonlinear Analysis of some Aspects of the Phonology and Nonconcatenative Morphology of Arabic.* [SOAS]
Bhattacharya, T., 1999. *The Structure of the Bangla DP.*
Blass, R., 1988. *Discourse Connectivity and Constraints on Relevance in Sissala.*
Boadi, L., 1966. *The Syntax of the Twi Verb.* [SOAS]
Derbyshire, D., 1979. *Hixkaryana Syntax.*
Hiranburana, S., 1971. *The Role of Accent in Thai Grammar.* [SOAS]
Mittwoch, A., 1971. *Optional and Obligatory Verbal Complements in English.* [SOAS]
Nwachukwu, P., 1975. *Noun Phrase Sentential Complementation in Igbo.* [SOAS]
Papafragou, A. , 1998. *Modality and the Semantics–Pragmatics Interface.*
Wise, H., 1970. *Syntax of the Verb Phrase of Colloquial Egyptian Arabic: A Transformational Study.* [SOAS]
Xydopoulos, G., 1996. *Tense, Aspect and Adverbials in Modern Greek.*

19 Priestley (1956).
20 Voyne Smith – born 10 June 1910; died 18 January 1991.
21 Lilian Freda Smith (née Rose) – born 3 May 1913; died 6 August 1973.
22 Angela Dawn Cooper (née Smith) – born 15 October 1936.

REFERENCES

BRODY, M., 1995. *Lexico-Logical Form: A Radically Minimalist Theory*, Cambridge, MA: MIT Press.

CHOMSKY, N., 1965. *Aspects of the Theory of Syntax*, Cambridge, MA: MIT Press.

CHOMSKY, N., 1970. 'Remarks on nominalization', in R. Jacobs & P. Rosenbaum (eds.), *Readings in English Transformational Grammar*, Waltham, MA: Ginn, 184–221.

FILLMORE, C., 1968. 'The case for case', in E. Bach & R. Harms (eds.), *Universals in Linguistic Theory*, New York: Holt, Rinehart & Winston, 1–90.

GAZDAR, G., KLEIN, E., PULLUM G. & SAG, I., 1985. *Generalized Phrase Structure Grammar*, Oxford: Blackwell.

HALLIDAY, M. A. K., 1961. 'Categories of the theory of grammar', *Word* 17, 241–92.

HARRIS, J., 1994. *English Sound Structure*, Oxford: Blackwell.

HJELMSLEV, L., 1953. *Prolegomena to a Theory of Language*, Memoir 7 of the *International Journal of American Linguistics*. Rev. ed. 1961, Madison: University of Wisconsin Press.

HUDSON, R. A., 1990. *English Word Grammar*, Oxford: Blackwell.

JOOS, M., (ed.) 1957. *Readings in Linguistics*, Chicago: University of Chicago Press.

LEES, R., 1960. *The Grammar of English Nominalizations*, Bloomington: Indiana University Press.

MANZINI, R., 1992. *Locality: A Theory and Some of its Empirical Consequences*, Cambridge, MA: MIT Press.

MARTINET, A., 1955. *Economie des changements phonétiques: traité de phonologie diachronique*, Berne: A. Francke.

NADEL, S., 1942. *A Black Byzantium*, London: Oxford University Press.

NEELEMAN, A. & VAN DE KOOT, H., 1999. 'The configurational matrix', *UCL Working Papers in Linguistics* 11, 473–519.

NEELEMAN, A. & WEERMAN, F., 1999. *Flexible Syntax*, Dordrecht: Kluwer Academic.

PRIESTLEY, L., 1956. 'Reprise constructions in French', *Archivum Linguisticum* 7, 1–28.

SCHACHTER, P., 1961. *A Contrastive Analysis of English and Pangasinan*. PhD dissertation, UCLA.

SCHACHTER, P. & FROMKIN, V., 1968. *A Phonology of Akan: Akuapem, Asante and Fante*, Working Papers in Phonetics 9, Los Angeles: UCLA.

SMITH, N. V., 1964. *A Phonological and Grammatical Study of the Verb in Nupe*. PhD thesis, University of London.

SMITH, N. V., 1967a. *An Outline Grammar of Nupe*, London: SOAS.

SMITH, N. V., 1967b. 'The phonology of Nupe', *Journal of African Languages* 6, 89–98.

SMITH, N. V., 1968. 'Tone in Ewe', *MIT Research Laboratory of Electronics Quarterly Progress Report* 88, 290–304.

SMITH, N. V., 1969. 'The Nupe verb', *African Language Studies* 10, 90–160.

SMITH, N. V., 1970. 'Repetition of the verb in Nupe', *African Language Studies* 11, 319–39.

SMITH, N. V., 1973. *The Acquisition of Phonology*, Cambridge: Cambridge University Press.

SMITH, N. V., 1975. 'Universal tendencies in the child's acquisition of phonology', in N. O'Connor (ed.), *Language, Cognitive Deficits and Retardation: IRMMH Study Group 7*, London: Butterworth, 47–65.

SMITH, N. V., 1977. 'On generics', *TPhS* 27–48.

SMITH, N. V., 1978. 'Lexical representation and the acquisition of phonology', *Studies in the Linguistic Sciences* 8, 180–204.

SMITH, N. V., 1979. 'Syntax for psychologists', in J. Morton & J. Marshall (eds.), *Psycholinguistics Series 2*, 1–66.

SMITH, N. V., 1981a. 'Consistency, markedness and language change: on the notion "consistent language"', *Journal of Linguistics* 17, 39–54.

SMITH, N. V., 1981b. 'Grammaticality, time and tense', *Philosophical Transactions of the Royal Society London* B 295, 253–65.

SMITH, N. V., (ed.) 1982. *Mutual Knowledge*, London: Academic Press.

SMITH, N. V., 1983a. *Speculative Linguistics*, inaugural lecture delivered at UCL, published by the college.

SMITH, N. V., 1983b. 'On interpreting conditionals', *Australian Journal of Linguistics* 3, 1–23.

SMITH, N. V., 1987. 'Universals and typology', in S. Modgil & C. Modgil (eds.), *Noam Chomsky: Consensus and Controversy*, New York: Falmer Press, 57–66

SMITH, N. V., 1988a. 'First language acquisition and relevance theory', *Polyglot* 9. 2, 1–29.

SMITH, N. V., 1988b. 'Principles, parameters and pragmatics', review article on N. Chomsky, (1986), *Knowledge of Language: Its Nature, Origin and Use, Journal of Linguistics* 24, 189–201.

SMITH, N. V., 1989. *The Twitter Machine: Reflections on Language*, Oxford: Blackwell.

SMITH, N. V., 1990. 'Can pragmatics fix parameters?', in I. Roca (ed.), *Logical Issues in Language Acquisition*, Dordrecht: Foris, 277–89.

SMITH, N. V., 1999. *Chomsky: Ideas and Ideals*. Cambridge: Cambridge University Press.

SMITH, N. V., 2002. *Language, Bananas and Bonobos*, Oxford: Blackwell. (This is composed largely of a selection of essays written over the last few years for *Glot International*.)

SMITH, N. V. in press. 'Dissociation and modularity: reflections on language and mind', in M. Banich & M. Mack (eds.), *Mind, Brain and Language*, Mahuah, NJ: Lawrence Erlbaum.

SMITH, N. V. with CORMACK, ANNABEL, 1994. 'Serial verbs', *UCL Working Papers in Linguistics* 6, 63–88.

SMITH, N. V. with CORMACK, ANNABEL, 1999. 'Why are depictives different from resultatives?', *UCL Working Papers in Linguistics* 11, 251–84.

SMITH, N. V. with CORMACK, ANNABEL, 2000. 'Head movement and negation in English', *TPhS* 98, 49–85.

SMITH, N. V. with CORMACK, ANNABEL, in press. 'Modals and negation in English', in S. Barbiers & F. Beukema (eds.), *Modality in Generative Grammar*.

SMITH, N. V. with SMITH, AMAHL, 1988. 'A relevance-theoretic account of conditionals', in L. Hyman & C. Li (eds.), *Language, Speech and Mind: Studies in Honour of Victoria A. Fromkin*, London: Routledge, 322–52.

SMITH, N. V. with TSIMPLI, IANTHI, 1991. 'Linguistic modularity? A case-study of a *savant* linguist', *Lingua* 84, 315–51.

SMITH, N. V. with TSIMPLI, IANTHI, 1995. *The Mind of a Savant: Language Learning and Modularity*, Oxford: Blackwell.

SMITH, N. V. with TSIMPLI, IANTHI, 1998. 'Modules and quasi-modules: language and theory of mind in a polyglot savant', *Learning and Individual Differences* 10, 193–215.

SMITH, N. V. with WILSON, DEIRDRE, 1979. *Modern Linguistics: The Results of Chomsky's Revolution*, Harmondsworth: Penguin.

SMITH, N. V. with WILSON, DEIRDRE, (eds.) 1992. *Special Issue on Relevance Theory, Vol. 1, Lingua* 87, 1–202.

SMITH, N. V. with WILSON, DEIRDRE, (eds.) 1993. *Special Issue on Relevance Theory, Vol. 2, Lingua* 90, 1–220.

SMITH, N. V. with TSIMPLI, IANTHI & OUHALLA, JAMAL, 1993. 'Learning the impossible: the acquisition of possible and impossible languages by a polyglot *savant*', *Lingua* 91, 279–347.

SMITH, N. V. with O'CONNOR, NEIL, FRITH, CHRIS & TSIMPLI, IANTHI, 1994. 'Neuropsychology and linguistic talent', *Journal of Neurolinguistics* 8, 95–107.

SPERBER, D. & WILSON, D., 1995. *Relevance: Communication and Cognition*, 2nd ed. Oxford: Blackwell.

STOCKWELL, R., SCHACHTER, P. & PARTEE, B., 1973. *The Major Syntactic Structures of English*, New York: Holt, Rinehart & Winston.

YIP, M. in press. *Tone*, Cambridge: Cambridge University Press.

J. L. M. TRIM

TRIM, John, *b.* 1924; *Education:* University College, London, BA 1949; *Career:* Lecturer, University College, London, 1949–58; University Lecturer in Phonetics, University of Cambridge (founder Department of Linguistics and first Director), 1958–78; Fellow, Selwyn College, Cambridge, 1962–78; Visiting Professor, University of Cologne, 1973; Director, CILT, 1978–87; Director, Modern Languages Projects of the Council of Europe, 1971–97, and still engaged in this work; Organized Second International Congress of Applied Linguistics, 1969; Chairman, British Association of Applied Linguistics, 1985–8; Vice-President, Association International de Linguistique Appliqué, 1987–90. Hon. DLitt: Dublin, Prague, Wolverhampton, Oulu; Hon. Member: AILA, Association for Language Learning; Fellow Institute of Linguists; Fellow *h.c.* College of Preceptors; Comenius Fellow CILT; Adjunct Fellow National Foreign Languages Center, Washington, DC; Comenius Medal of the Czech Republic, *Officier dans l'Ordre des Palmes Académiques.*

* * *

It must be extremely difficult for scholars who have come into linguistics in the last years to conceive of the situation of academic life half a century ago. The Second World War had meant the total cessation of international scholarly contacts and publications, as of research not immediately related to the war effort. For linguistics in Britain, this meant that courses in relevant languages were energetically pursued at SOAS. For the Department of Phonetics at UCL, the consequences were dire. For the religious reasons which had originally brought him into the subject at the beginning of the century, Daniel Jones did not engage in war work and lost most of the younger people, who followed J. R. Firth to SOAS and remained there after the war. UCL itself was fragmented, with different departments evacuated to different provincial centres. D. J. and Hélène Coustenoble accompanied the French Department to Bangor. The German Department, in which I spent a year (1942–3) after leaving school before joining the infantry, was in Aberystwyth, with no contact with Bangor. On return to London after the end of the war, with the college a rebuilding site (75 per cent destroyed in air raids), D. J. had to rebuild a department virtually from scratch, recruiting Arnold, Gimson and O'Connor from the generation who had achieved first class results in French phonetics before going into the services, with Denis

Fry reorganizing a laboratory for experimental phonetics joined by Peter Denes.

I graduated in German in 1949, expecting to go on to postgraduate research in the literary field, though my best results were in the medieval paper. The syllabus for the BA (Hons) in German was 'German language and literature from its beginnings to the present day', encouraging a wide spread of interests. Unexpectedly, I was invited to meet Denis Fry, who offered me an Assistant Lectureship in Phonetics. Daniel Jones had just retired, leaving a gap in German phonetics, which he had himself taught, everybody else having come through Hélène Coustenoble's exacting, even terrifying hands. Fry invited me to develop the German side, and in due course to introduce courses in general linguistics. I would have no teaching duties in the first year. The choice was not an easy one. Though I could be given no assurances, I could expect a successful academic career in German. Professor Willoughby had arranged a *Lektorat* for me at a respected German university and my research plans were laid. However, an immediate entry into an academic post was even then an extraordinary opportunity. The introduction I had had to the neogrammarian legacy had interested me and I had had a practical training in German phonetics from Walter Kuhlmann during my semester in Freiburg. Above all, I was attracted by the social relevance of a proper understanding of the workings of language and speech. Phonetics had a tradition of service going back beyond Sweet to Ellis and Bell, and the Department had long accepted responsibilities to language teaching, the teaching and treatment of the deaf, speech therapy and communications engineering. I felt strongly that I would find fulfilment in such work and decided to take the plunge.

My initial salary was £500 p.a., payable quarterly in arrears. Fortunately, my wife's earnings as a health visitor supported us till the Christmas pay day arrived. The first year enabled me to read the German phonetic literature from Merkel and Brücke to Siebs, Vietor and Klinghardt, since when little seemed to have been added. In English phonetics, I read the tradition from Ellis and Sweet to Jones and Ward. In linguistics I read Herman Paul's *Prinzipien der Sprachgeschichte* and de Saussure's *Cours de linguistique générale*, and particularly Trubetzkoy's brilliant application of Saussurian principles to phonology. Within the Department I attended lectures, especially those of 'Doc' O'Connor on intonation, and the courses of Hélène Coustenoble, who rapidly dispelled any idea I might have that I could speak French acceptably but agreed at the end of the year that with some years of further training I might have the makings of a phonetician. I rose to the challenge of the staff ear-training sessions given by all colleagues in turn and acquired the basics of instrumental and experimental phonetics from Peter Denes and Denis Fry. I also went across to SOAS and attended courses by Eugenie Henderson and R. H. Robins and, of course, J. R. Firth.

Firth was at that time the dominant figure in British linguistics. On his return from India, he had taught in the UCL Phonetics Department under D. J., but thought it mere hack work, certainly by comparison with his co-operation with the anthropologist Malinowsky at LSE. To me, he seemed more a prophet than a scholar. He had great charisma as well as a forceful personality. His lectures were enthralling, his published writings giving little impression of their quality (Firth 1964). Above all, the abiding impression he left was of the infinite richness of human language and the intimacy of its relation to the life of the individual in society. He did not regard linguistics as a recent innovation, but traced, in broad outline, the sweep of linguistic inquiry through the ages. He dissented from structuralism, in both its Saussurian and American forms. For him, linguistic systems were not language itself but rather a set of tools for handling it. A favourite metaphor was to liken them to the scaffolding erected around a building, rather than the framework of steel girdering within it. American structuralism in particular he found an unacceptably reductionist and indeed impoverished view of language. He would have had no time for Chomsky's competence/performance distinction (Chomsky 1965: 10). In return, American linguists paid little attention to him, with the exception of Dell Hymes, who read him with care and may in some ways be regarded as a principal mediator of his basic message (Hymes 1974). Firth did not himself develop an integrative theory or descriptive model to match his insights – indeed, it may have been central to his ideology not to do so (Henderson 1987). Certainly, the early work of Halliday (1976), which might be seen in that light, seems to have received little support or encouragement from him.

If Firth's concern was with the social dimension of language, with links to social anthropology, that of Fry was with the individual as speaker and listener, with links to experimental psychology. He recognized the great wealth and complexity of the cognitive structures and processes, which an individual built up as a result of experiences of many different kinds, and in terms of which all experience, including that of language, was perceived and interpreted and behaviour organized (Fry 1977). Thus communication was assured despite great diversity in the actual behaviour of speakers. In the field of speech perception, it was not to be expected that a linguistic construct could be identified simply by programming a robotic device to recognize acoustic constants, e.g. a set of distinctive features physically present *in rebus*. On the other hand, a device equipped with a prior knowledge of a linguistic system (seen, pre-Chomsky, in terms of elements and structures) would be able to recognize a construct on the basis of a multiplicity of cues, no one of which was essential to recognition. During my years at UCL, a good deal of our research aimed to test this position (Trim 1962). It is interesting that in the passage from *Aspects of the Theory of Syntax* cited in the previous paragraph, Chomsky exempted phonetics from his general dismissal of previous work on the theory of performance. In the area of intonation, which was a focus of attention in the Department, I was able to show that the usual definition, in terms of changes in the fundamental frequency of the speech wave resulting from changes in the frequency of vibration of the vocal cords, was untenable, and that context-free tonal nuclei were readily identifiable in whispered speech (Trim 1970a). O'Connor and I also attempted to show (O'Connor and Trim 1953) that, as phonological units, consonant, vowel and syllable should be defined in phonotactic rather than phonetic terms.

Relations between UCL and SOAS, though in some cases affable on the personal level, were academically distant. One proposal for a series of joint seminars led to an initial meeting. Fry said: 'I take it that we are interested in finding out what happens when people speak to each other.' Firth retorted: 'No. Not at all. That is not what we are interested in at all.' After that there seemed little to say on either side and the meeting was not followed up. The phoneme theory (UCL) and the prosodic approach (SOAS) confronted each other like the trenches of the First World War. Rightly or wrongly, the UCL staff did not believe that any work not following the prosodic approach would be acceptable to a Board of Studies dominated by Firth. Only one member of staff offered a thesis for MA during my time. It was referred while the candidate was coached by an SOAS staff member in the presentation of the material in accordance with the prosodic approach. In any case, it was not felt that established academics should work for an examined qualification. Sidney Allen told me that, when he needed to finance his return to Trinity after the war, the Senior Tutor told him that there was 'nothing for it but to take one of those PhDs. But never mind, my boy, you can always live it down later.' How remote such attitudes now seem!

The 1950s were years of reconstruction, with a ferment of ideas. However, relatively little found its way into print, which may give an impression to later generations of stagnation and demands explanation. For one thing, there were relatively few outlets and no pressure towards continual publication. We at UCL fed into *Le Maître Phonétique*, still appearing in phonetic transcription and limited in size, scope and distribution. More importantly, ideas were exchanged by word of mouth, in seminars, small conferences and informally in personal encounters. In contributing to and benefiting from these exchanges, no one thought where their origins lay, or dreamt of claiming a new idea as one's 'intellectual property' or establishing a copyright. This has been a source of embarrassment to me in recent years, when I have drawn on this pool of experience, for example in the *Common European Framework for Languages: Learning, Teaching, Assessment* (Council of Europe 2001), and am expected to give references to support every proposal. I do not know where the stimuli came from and am obliged to cite more recent publications though I know their origins lie much further back. We expected to have to think a great deal out for ourselves. In my undergraduate days we were discouraged from reading secondary literature but encouraged rather to read and react to as much of the literature itself as possible. Daniel Jones was said to have discouraged his staff from reading about the phonetics and phonology of the languages they were investigating, because this would interpose a number of preconceptions between them and the actual phenomena. They should rather bring their highly trained perceptual, notational and analytic skills directly to bear on the speech of their informants, learning also to listen carefully and objectively to themselves as speakers and learners. There was therefore a concentration on professional development as an experiential dialectic between phonetician and speakers. Students were drawn into this dialectic of theory and practice and equipped to continue their development autonomously. During my years (1949–58) at UCL, I continuously developed my skills in, and understanding of, the processes of speech production and perception, especially in relation to English and German, but felt a need to publish only where I felt I had something new and significant to say, mainly in the field of intonation (Trim 1959c; 1964; 1970b). I was sure that the notations developed by Sweet and Palmer and later by Kingdon, followed by Arnold and O'Connor, were correct in eliminating the redundancy of continuous pitch curves by identifying the choices to be made and the points at which they were made. I found this to be as true of German as of English and suggested certain refinements to the system, once again showing that tonal units must be defined in functional rather than purely physical terms. On the other hand, I could not accept the American concept of 'pitch phonemes'. The categorial nature of phonemic distinctions is assured by the double articulation of language. /p/ and/b/ are phonemically distinct because *big* and *pig* are semantically unrelated. This is clearly not the case with the distinction, say, between low and high falls, or rises and fall–rises. With increasing experience and reflection, I became convinced that, while decisions were made only at certain points, the choice was not categorial. Rather than choosing from a closed inventory, a value had to be given to a parameter signalling the value of a semantic continuum, much as the height of mercury in a glass tube may signal temperature or atmospheric pressure. This gives intonation a different character from the rest of the linguistic system, more akin to pre- or paralinguistic communication: 'The louder, longer and higher-pitched I scream, the more I am hurt, terrified, etc.' I do not think the idea has been followed up, partly because of the problems it poses for notation.

At the same time, I developed my course in linguistics, attempting to bring together the neogrammarian heritage (Trim 1976) as propounded by Paul and mediated through Bloomfield (1933) (his behaviourism was late and inessential) with de Saussure's structuralism, in the light of Firth's social anthropological and Fry's psycholinguistic approaches (Trim 1959b). In the tradition of English phoneticians I also established contacts with speech therapists (Trim 1953; 1963), teachers of the deaf (Trim 1958), teachers of English (as mother tongue [Trim 1959a], as a foreign language [Trim 1961] and as a second language Trim 1977]) and communication engineers. In the abysmal state of public knowledge and understanding of language (which is still the case!), they found even elementary linguistic concepts both new and useful in their professional work.

In 1958, Sidney Allen, who had been elected to the Chair of Comparative Philology at Cambridge and had announced in his inaugural lecture that the introduction of linguistics would be his first priority, persuaded the Faculty of Classics, Modern and Medieval Languages (MML), Oriental Studies, Archaeology and Anthropology (A and A) and English to act as joint sponsors for a University Lectureship in Phonetics. Fry encouraged me to apply and, after an exhausting but exhilarating interview with a panel representing all these Faculties, I was appointed.

Coming to Cambridge in middle life, I found the workings of the dual university/college system hard to penetrate. Most dons led a double exist-ence, or more. Shackleton-Bailey held a University Lectureship in Tibetan, but was Bursar of his college and won a gold medal for his work in classics. As a University Lecturer in Phonetics I gave lectures and held practical classes in general phonetics and planned a phonetics laboratory. Incident-ally, when I presented my plans to equip the laboratory listening booths with twin-track tape-recorders (this was before the advent of the 'language laboratory') to the Colloquy of British Academic Phoneticians, they were greeted with horror. Students would break them. They should listen to discs through earphones. I should invest in a 78 r.p.m. disc cutter, for which Peter Strevens helpfully sent me a brochure, which I am afraid I ignored. At college level, however, my phonetics was of no interest, since it did not figure in the Tripos. Instead, I found my services in demand as a supervisor for the inter-faculty paper entitled 'Principles of Language', for which I became internal examiner. I developed it as a paper in linguistics and used it to attract promising young people from various faculties to the subject. Many of them were hooked. Among my earliest supervisees were John Wells and Eleanor Higginbottom (later Young) from Classics, Rodney Huddleston, Neil Smith and Dick Hudson from MML and Andrew Sinclair and Stephen Levinson from A and A. It is somewhat invidious to name particular names, since in all over the years more than 60 students went on to hold academic posts in different countries. In those early days, though enthusiastic students put more work into linguistics than was really appropriate to one seventh of a Part II Tripos, I did not consider that a single paper was an adequate basis for independent postgraduate research and sent students on to established departments in other universities. However, a small number of graduates from other universities came to Cambridge to work for PhDs under my supervision. When, on the move of Bob Auty to London in 1962, I was elected a Fellow of Selwyn College, it was as Director of Studies in Modern Languages and College Lecturer in German, again encouraging a wider scope rather than specialization.

In the early 1960s a Lectureship in Linguistics was instituted. The first holder was John Lyons. On his elevation to the Chair of Linguistics in Edinburgh, I moved to that post, the phonetics post being held first by Eleanor Higginbottom and then by Erik Fudge. In 1965, MML decided to set up a language laboratory and a Linguistic Computing Centre. William Bennett was appointed Assistant Director of Research in Applied Linguistics (the entire staff of the language laboratory!), and Frank Bott Senior Assistant in Research, responsible for computing programming. The General Board of the Faculties proposed that a Department of Linguistics be set up to include these developments as well as the existing lectureships in phonetics and linguistics. It was expected that Sidney Allen would assume the Headship of the new Department. However, MML voted to maintain the Computing Centre as an independent unit and Sidney Allen decided to devote himself to the duties of his Professorship within the Faculty of Classics. I was offered and accepted the Headship of the new Department, which was raised to a Directorship in 1970. A Postgraduate Diploma in Linguistics was instituted, which soon became a one-year MPhil. I insisted that all postgraduate students should follow the broad taught course before proceeding to independent doctoral research. I also insisted that all candidates should become proficient in practical phonetics as well as in theoretical linguistics, by including a small instrumental project as well as dictation exercises in English (RP), in a foreign language of choice from tape and in a general phonetic notation of meaningless sound sequences (including tones). This was not always popular, but I believe it to be a significant aspect of a professional linguist's education as well as proving to be of practical value in many cases. In general, I tried during the 1970s to develop the Department as a 'troika' of theoretical linguistics, phonetics and applied linguistics. I was and remain convinced that theory without practice becomes formalistic and sterile, and that practice without theory becomes dull, stagnant routine. Chomsky's drive to eradicate any dependence of linguistic theory upon the empirical, or, it sometimes seems, to acknowledge any relation between the two, has, in my view, had very serious long-term consequences for both. I also tried to cater for a wide diversity of interests (the 11 PhD students I supervised worked in very different fields) and to encourage the interaction of students both undergraduate and postgraduate across Faculty and disciplinary boundaries. I put the whole of my energy into creating a Department which would be a true academic community, within which young scholars could interact and develop in an atmosphere of keen, but many-sided intellectual inquiry, and to act as a focus for concern with language across the university. This aim required me to take an informed interest in all aspects of the work of the Department and took priority for me above my own publication record.

I also tried to play my part in university affairs and in the national life of the profession. Among other things I chaired the Joint Committee of

Management for the Cambridge Examinations in English as a Foreign Language and a government committee of inquiry into language laboratories. I was a member of the Hull Linguistics Circle and thus a founding member of the Linguistics Association and was a member of the Council of the Philological Society from 1968 to 1974. While I never really enjoyed giving marks to people, I frequently acted as external examiner. Over a period of some 20 years, for instance, I went to Edinburgh every June and eventually examined at every level in phonetics, linguistics and applied linguistics as well as in phonetics for the speech therapists. Edinburgh became for me the City of Eternal Sunlight – a view not, alas, shared by its residents!

My appointment as Director freed the post of University Lectureship in Linguistics, to which Pieter Seuren was appointed. His commitment to generative grammar had brought him into conflict with the Dutch establishment of the time, leading to his appointment to work in the Department on a project for an audiovisual course we developed in collaboration with first the Municipal, then the Free University of Amsterdam (Matter & Trim 1975). Seuren's clarity of exposition and the sense of intellectual excitement generated by theoretical linguistics at that time attracted some of the best minds in the undergraduate body. Bernard Comrie, John Hawkins, Andrew Radford, Nigel Vincent all pursued their Diploma and then doctoral studies in the Department and have gone on to distinguished academic careers. From 1963 to 1977 I directed a University Vacation Course in Linguistics and English Language, mainly for foreign students, again combining practical work in phonetics with lectures and intensive small group classes in theoretical linguistics, with lectures and seminars also on theoretical and practical aspects of language teaching. Many continental linguists had their first introduction to linguistics in these courses. There was a great hunger among language teachers internationally for a substantial initiation into communicative methodology. Their attendance in large numbers at lectures by such colleagues as Louis Alexander paid in fact for the small, high-level group work in theoretical grammar, given by the leading young linguists of the time, who were willing to come to Cambridge for three weeks for very modest fees, largely to meet each other and discuss the recent developments in a rapidly developing subject in some depth.

Meanwhile, a chain of events had led me to a closer involvement in applied linguistics. In setting up the university language laboratory I installed closed-circuit television, largely for the teaching of phonetics. The University Grants Committee, on the advice of its Audio-Visual Panel, refused to pay for the installation, considering television inappropriate in a language laboratory. Fortunately, the university was prepared to back my judgement and to meet the cost from its own funds. Following a TV series *I Hear, I See* in which Denis Fry, Frieda Goldman-Eisler and I were panellists, the producer and the chairman, Tony Benn, offered me a programme: *Look to the Future in Language Teaching*. This led to my acting as methodological consultant for *Parliamo Italiano*, the first BBC adult television language series, and as part-author of *Komm Mit!* This gave me a reputation as an expert on educational technology and I served for a year or two on the National Council for Educational Technology (NCET).

In 1965 I attended the foundation meeting of the British Association for Applied Linguistics (BAAL), where I successfully opposed the limitation of its aims to language teaching and machine translation and was elected its first treasurer. It turned out that BAAL was founded to host the Second International Congress of Applied Linguistics, which Peter Strevens had agreed to organize. When he withdrew for financial reasons, I seized the opportunity to replace him. I felt that the addition of a regular Congress of Applied Linguistics to the existing Congresses of Linguists and of Phonetic Sciences would consolidate the troika to which I was committed. As I explained in my Special Lecture to the Tokyo Congress (Trim 2001), I welcomed the opportunity to set a pattern for future Congresses representing the full breadth of the relevance of linguistic knowledge and understanding to the analysis and even solution of language problems in society. The organization of the Congress occupied the energies of Bill Bennett and myself from mid-1967 to 1969. The Congress attracted a very high level of participation and contribution (Perren & Trim 1971).

The Congress also brought me into the ambit of the Council of Europe, which had acted as midwife to the International Association for Applied Linguistics (AILA) and, unknown to me, was the sponsor of the Congress. The Council made a modest contribution towards its cost, requiring me to submit a written report. I became one of its 'experts' and in 1971 took the Chair of a small working group to examine the feasibility of a European unit-credit scheme for adult education. From my NCET days I took up the concept of educational technology propounded by its Director, Tony Becher. He considered its essence to be not the particulars of audiovisual hard- and software, but the 'systems approach' integrating needs analysis, objectives, methods, monitoring, feedback and evaluation into a continuous interactive process, in which the specification of worthwhile, appropriate and feasible objectives was the key element. I now had the opportunity to apply this approach to language teaching. It proved very appropriate to international co-operation, providing an integrative framework for contributions of the most diverse character. On the basis of a set of preliminary studies (Trim et al. 1980), a multidimensional descriptive model was proposed. In 1974 an intensive working meeting in Selwyn College produced long, unordered lists of categories within each parameter of the model, which were then brilliantly organized by J. A. van Ek in *Threshold Level English* (van Ek & Alexander 1980). This work had an immediate impact, providing a common point of reference for the various independently operating interests in the field. It gave substance to the 'communicative' approach and, by regarding function and meaning as primary rather than linguistic forms, which were treated as 'exponents' of the functional and notional categories, the model could be employed for any language. Over the past 25 years the Council of Europe has published versions for 25 European languages, with others in various stages of preparation.

In 1978, I decided that this work was of sufficient importance for me to give up the Directorship of the Department and to devote the final decade of my professional career to the language teaching field. On the retirement of George Perren I took up the post of Director of the Centre for Information on Language Teaching and Research (CILT), of which I have given accounts elsewhere (Trim 1996; 2000). My work for the Council of Europe continued. In 1981 I formulated the Committee of Ministers Recommendation R(81)18 to member governments on language teaching, and I devoted the 1980s to facilitating the consequent reforms of curricular guidelines, examination syllabuses, textbooks and, particularly, teacher-training, across Europe. The ministries in the countries of Central and Eastern Europe found R(82)18 and reports on its implementation of particular value in reorienting language teaching after the political changes around 1990. Following my retirement from the public service in 1987, the 1990s were mainly devoted to the development of two instruments, the *Common European Framework for Languages: Learning, Teaching, Assessment* (CEF) and the European Language Portfolio (ELP; Schärer 1999). In my contribution to CEF, I attempted a full taxonomy of language use and the competences (knowledge, skills, understanding) that underlie that use. It will no doubt be my last substantial contribution to the field.

Overall, I have found my work in phonetics, linguistics and applied linguistics rewarding both personally and professionally. I have felt enriched by the broad range of ideas and experiences to which I have been exposed and do not regret (while fully aware of the consequences) having passed on their benefit more in personal contact than in major publications. Of my output in the 1950s and 1960s, I do, however, regret not having published a study on the concept of 'Standard' in language, given to the National Association for the Teaching of English (NATE), and a paper on 'Accent and social prestige' given as a lunch-hour lecture at UCL, which Basil Bernstein considered to have influenced his thinking early in his career. Above all, I regret not having published the results of studies conducted over many years on the development of linguistic thought in Germany from the sixteenth to the eighteenth centuries, showing that the explosion of comparative philology in Germany in the early nineteenth century was inevitable and indeed overdue. I offered the paper for Willi Haas's Festschrift, but it was rejected as not conforming to the publisher's guidelines and I did not place it elsewhere.

I feel privileged to have played a part in the early formation of young scholars who have gone on to achieve distinction in the field. Perhaps I have derived most pleasure from creating an inclusive conceptual framework, within which I have been able to bring together members of the language teaching profession, from all over Europe and beyond, in such a way that a large group, consisting of one or two representatives from each of more than 30 countries, have settled in a few hours to develop close professional working relations and warm personal relations free from personal and national rivalries. I have enjoyed the free and unfettered exchange of ideas and experience in workshops, seminars and symposia. I am grateful for the professional collaborations and friendships this work has brought me, and for the recognition of my role by the French government, by the University of Dublin, the Charles University of Prague and the Universities of Wolverhampton and Oulu in their award of honorary doctorates, and by AILA, ALL, the Institute of Linguists and CILT in their Fellowships. Above all, I am profoundly grateful to the generations of students and fellow linguists in many countries who have enriched my life in so many ways. *Es sei wie es wolle, es war doch so schön. Pause.*

REFERENCES

BLOOMFIELD, L., 1993. *Language*, New York: Holt, Rinehart & Winston.
CHOMSKY, N., 1965. *Aspects of the Theory of Syntax*, Cambridge, MA: MIT Press.
COUNCIL OF EUROPE, 2001. *Common European Framework for Languages: Learning, Teaching, Assessment*, Cambridge: Cambridge University Press.
FIRTH, J. R., 1964. *The Tongues of Men* and *Speech*, London: Oxford University Press.
FRY, D. B., 1977. *Homo Loquens*, Cambridge: Cambridge University Press.
HALLIDAY, M. A. K., 1976. *System and Function in Language: Selected Papers*, G. T. Kress ed., London: Oxford University Press.
HENDERSON, E. J. A., 1987. 'J. R. Firth in retrospect: a view from the eighties', in R. Steele & T. Threadgold (eds.), *Language Topics: Essays in Honour of Michael Halliday*, Amsterdam: Benjamins, 57–68.
HYMES, D., 1974. *Foundations in Sociolinguistics: An Ethnographic Approach*, Philadelphia: University of Pennsylvania Press.
JONES, D., 1962a. *Outline of English Phonetics*, 9th ed. (repr., with further alterations), Cambridge: Heffer.
JONES, D., 1962b. *The Phoneme, its Nature and Use*, 2nd ed., Cambridge: Heffer.
JONES, W. & LAVER, J., (eds.) 1973. *Phonetics in Linguistics*, London: Longman.
MATTER, J. F. & TRIM, J. L. M., (eds.) 1975. *Levend Nederlands: Een Audio-Visuele Cursus Nederlands voor Buitenlanders*, Cambridge: Cambridge University Press.
O'CONNOR, J. D. & TRIM, J. L. M., 1953. 'Vowel, consonant and syllable – a phonological definition', *Word* 9.2, 103–22. Repr. in W. Jones and J. Laver (eds.), *Phonetics in Linguistics*, London: Longman (1973), 240–61.
PAUL, H., 1920. *Prinzipien der Sprachgeschichte*, 5th ed., Halle: Niemeyer.
PERREN, G. E. & TRIM, J. L. M., 1971. *Applications of Linguistics: Selected Papers of the Second International Congress of Applied Linguistics, Cambridge, 1969*, Cambridge: Cambridge University Press.
SAUSSURE, F. DE, 1955. *Cours de linguistique générale*, 5th ed., Paris: Payot.
SCHÄRER, R., (ed.) 1999. 'The European Language Portfolio', *Babylonia* 1/99, 1–80.
TRIM J. L. M., 1953. 'Some suggestions for the phonetic notation of sounds in defective speech', *Speech* 17.1, 21–4.
TRIM, J. L. M., 1958. 'Language and communication', *Teacher of the Deaf* August, 108–14.

TRIM, J. L. M., 1959a. 'Speech education', in R. Quirk & A. H. Smith, (eds.), *The Teaching of English*, Studies in Communication 3, London: Secker & Warburg, 60–86.

Trim, J. L. M., 1959b. 'Historical, descriptive and dynamic linguistics', *Language and Speech* 2.1, 9–15.

TRIM, J. L. M., 1959c. 'Major and minor tone-groups in English', *Le Maître Phonétique* July–Dec., 26. Repr. in W. Jones & J. Laver (eds.), *Phonetics in Linguistics*, London: Longman (1973), 320–3.

TRIM, J. L. M., 1961. 'English standard pronunciation', *English Language Teaching* 16.1, 28–37. Repr. in W. R. Lee, *ELT Selections 2*, London: Oxford University Press (1967), 233–42.

TRIM, J. L. M., 1962. 'The identification of phonological units', *Proceedings of the Fourth International Congress of Phonetic Sciences, Helsinki, 1961*, The Hague: Mouton.

TRIM, J. L. M., 1963. 'Linguistics and speech pathology', in S. E. Mason & L. Stein (eds.), *Signs, Signals and Symbols*, London: Methuen, 33–43.

TRIM, J. L. M., 1964. 'Tonetic stress marks for German', in D. Abercrombie, D. B. Fry, P. A. D. MacCarthy, N. C. Scott & J. L. M. Trim (eds.), *In Honour of Daniel Jones: Papers Contributed on the Occasion of his Eightieth Birthday, 12 September 1961*, London: Longman, 374–83.

TRIM, J. L. M., 1970a. 'Cues to the recognition of whispered speech', *Proceedings of the Sixth International Congress of Phonetic Sciences, Prague, 1967*, Munich: Hueber.

TRIM, J. L. M., 1970b. 'Some continuously variable features in British English intonation', *Actes du Xe Congrès International des Linguistes, Bucarest, 1967*, Bucharest: Editions de l'Académie de la République Socialiste de Roumanie, 263–7.

TRIM, J. L. M., 1976. 'Die Junggrammatiker nach 100 Jahren', in 'Akten des V. Internationalen Germanisten-Kongresses, Cambridge 1975', *Jahrbuch für Internationale Germanistik*, Reihe A, B and 2.1, 75–96.

TRIM, J. L. M., 1977. 'Helping migrant children to communicate: some implications of the Council of Europe's work in language systems construction', in M. de Greve & E. Rosseel (eds.), *Problèmes linguistiques des enfants de travailleurs migrants. 10e Colloque de l'AIMAV en collaboration avec la Commission des Communautés Européennes*, Brussels: AIMAV.

TRIM, J. L. M., 1980. *Developing a Unit/Credit Scheme of Adult Language Learning*, Oxford: Pergamon Press.

TRIM, J. L. M., 1987. 'Daniel Jones' "classical" model of pronunciation training: an applied linguistic revaluation', in R. Steele & T. Threadgold (eds.), *Language Topics: Essays in Honour of Michael Halliday*, 69–78. Amsterdam: Benjamins.

TRIM, J. L. M., 1992. 'Where have all the phoneticians gone?', in A. van Essen & E. I. Burkart (eds.), *Homage to W. R. Lee: Essays in English as a Foreign or Second Language*, Berlin: Foris, 261–71.

TRIM, J. L. M., 1996. 'View from the Bridge', in E. W. Hawkins, *30 Years of Language Teaching*, London: CILT, 321–30.

TRIM, J. L. M., 2000. 'CILT and the legacy of Comenius', in *Comenius Fellowship Papers 2000*, London: CILT, 8–11.

TRIM, J. L. M., 2001. 'The birth and early development of AILA', in AILA, *Selected Papers from AILA '99 Tokyo*, Tokyo: Waseda University Press, 261–76.

TRIM, J. L. M., RICHTERICH,R., VAN EK, J. A. & WILKINS, D. A., 1980. *Systems Development in Adult Language Learning*, Oxford: Pergamon Press.

TRUBETZKOY, N. S., 1958. *Grundzüge der Phonologie*, 2nd ed., Göttingen: Vandenhoeck & Ruprecht.

VAN EK, J. A. & ALEXANDER, L. G., 1980. *Threshold Level English*, Oxford: Pergamon Press.

VAN EK, J. A. & TRIM, J. L. M., 1991a. *Threshold Level 1990*, Cambridge: Cambridge University Press.

VAN EK, J. A. & TRIM, J. L. M., 1991b. *Waystage 1990*, Cambridge: Cambridge University Press.

VAN EK, J. A. & TRIM, J. L. M., 2000. *Vantage*, Cambridge: Cambridge University Press.

VAN EK, J. A., ALEXANDER, L. G. & FITZPATRICK, M. A., 1980. *Waystage English*, Oxford: Pergamon Press.

PETER TRUDGILL

TRUDGILL, Peter John, FBA 1989; Professor of English Linguistics, University of Fribourg, since 1998; *b.* 1943; *m.* (i) 1968 Sandra Walker, (ii) 1980 Jean Marie Hannah; *Education:* City of Norwich School; King's College, Cambridge, BA (MA) in Modern and Mediaeval Languages, 1963–6; Postgraduate Diploma in General Linguistics, University of Edinburgh, 1967, PhD 1971; *Career:* Department of Linguistic Science, University of Reading: Assistant Lecturer 1970–3, Lecturer 1973–8, Reader 1978–83, Professor (Personal Chair) 1983–6; Department of Language and Linguistics, University of Essex: Reader in Sociolinguistics 1986–7, Professor of Sociolinguistics (Personal Chair) 1987–92; Department of English, University of Lausanne: Professor of English Language and Linguistics 1993–8. Doctorate Honoris Causa, Faculty of Letters, Uppsala University, 1995; President Societas Linguistica Europaea, 1992–3; Vice-President Societas Linguistica Europaea 1993–4; Fellow: Norwegian Academy of Sciences and Letters 1995, Royal Norwegian Society of Sciences 1996; Member: Social Science Research Council Linguistics Panel 1975–8, Academic Advisory Board, Linguistic Minorities Project, London University Institute of Education, 1979–82, Advisory Group, European Science Foundation, Adult Language Acquisition Project, 1981–3, Longman's Advisory Panel on Linguistics and Lexicography 1981–99, Social Science Research Council, Education and Human Development Committee, 1982, Institute for Functional Research of Language and Language Use, University of Amsterdam, 1988–, CNAA Advisory Panel 1988–90, Evaluation Committee on Linguistics, University of East Anglia, 1989, Committee for Swiss Association of Applied Linguistics 1993–8, Appointment Committee for Swedish Chair in Sociolinguistics 1980, Appointment Committee for Tromsø University Chair of English 1989; Member Editorial Boards: *English World Wide* 1980–91, *American Speech* 1981–5, *Language Sciences* 1981–, *Papers in Geolinguistics* 1986–, *Oxford International Encyclopaedia of Linguistics* 1986–90, *Norsk Lingvistisk Tidsskrift* 1987–, *Language Variation and Change* 1989–, *Nordic Journal of Linguistics* 1990–, *International Journal of Applied Linguistics* 1990–, *Atlas Linguarum Europae* 1990–3, *Multilingua* 1993–, *Zeitschrift für Anglistik und Amerikanistik* 1995–, *Journal of Sociolinguistics* 1996–, *Journal of Multilingual and Multicultural Development* 1996–, *European Journal of English Studies* 1997–, *Journal of Greek Linguistics* 1999–, *Poznan Studies in Contemporary Linguistics* 1999–. *Major Publications: Sociolinguistic Patterns in British English*, 1978; *Language in the British*

Isles; *Applied Sociolinguistics*; *English Dialects: Studies in Grammatical Variation* (with J. K. Chambers); *The Sociolinguistics Reader* (with J. Cheshire); *Language Myths* (with L. Bauer); *The Social Differentiation of English in Norwich* 1974; *Sociolinguistics: An Introduction to Language and Society* 1974; *Accent, Dialect and the School* 1975; *English Accents and Dialects: An Introduction to Social and Regional Varieties of British English* (with A. Hughes); *Dialectology* (with J. K. Chambers); *International English: A Guide to Varieties of Standard English* (with J. Hannah); *On Dialect: Social and Geographical Perspectives*; *Coping with America: A Beginner's Guide to the USA*; *Dialects in Contact*; *The Dialects of England*; *Bad Language* (with L. G. Andersson); *Introducing Language and Society*; *Dialects, Sociolinguistic Variation and Change*.

* * *

It was sort of a secret schoolboy vice that I had. I read all the foreign language grammars in the local library, and collected as much information as I could find about the languages of the world. Having started French, German and Latin at grammar school, I then asked for, and got, *Teach Yourself Spanish* and *Teach Yourself Malay* as birthday and Christmas presents. Together with my school friend John Sandford, now Professor of German at Reading University, I became, as we hitch-hiked round Europe in the 1960s, interested in Flemish and Luxemburgish and Plattdeutsch and Swiss German as well as other languages we encountered, such as Italian and Greek and Macedonian. Thus, like many other people of my generation, I became interested in linguistics without knowing that there was any such thing.

In spite of having some very good teachers at the City of Norwich Grammar School, I knew nothing about linguistics and went up to Cambridge to study French and German at King's believing that this was the only way to pursue my interests. I was not a naturally gifted practical linguist – although once at Cambridge I took additional classes in Polish for a while out of interest – and hopeless as a literary scholar. One of the most important things ever to happen to me, therefore, was to find quite by chance a copy of Hockett (1958) lying around on a table in the Modern Languages Library at Sidgwick Avenue. This, I realized as I turned the pages, was what I was really interested in. Talking to other students, I then learnt that it was actually possible to study this topic. Soon afterwards, at the beginning of my second year, my tutor, the very distinguished literary scholar R. R. Bolgar, asked me to write an essay on the novel *A Rebours* by Joris-Karl Huysmans. I sat down to read it and had an overwhelming sense that not only did I really not want to read it at all but that I was not going to. (I still have this book on my shelves, its pages uncut.) Very nervous and self-effacing Norfolkman that I was, I went timidly back to Bolgar and said that I believed that there was a subject called general linguistics and that I was considering dropping French literature in favour of that. He smiled and replied: 'I think that would be a very good idea.'

In due course, then, I ended up studying general linguistics at Cambridge – under the supervision of, first, John Trim and, later, Eleanor Higginbottom – as well as the histories of the English, French and German languages. Particularly instructive were supervisions on the history of French from Jim Laidlaw (see below) and classes on the history of English from John Bromwich. John Lyons, recently departed for Edinburgh, also made impressive guest appearances giving lectures on Chomsky.

Wanting to continue my linguistics studies after graduation, during my last undergraduate year at Cambridge I applied to the Australian National University in Canberra for a scholarship to work on Aboriginal languages. As part of my application, I sent them a description I had written – which I had been too nervous and self-effacing to show to anybody in Cambridge – of the phonology of Norfolk English. I eventually got cold feet, however, and withdrew my application, timidly but probably correctly believing that I was ill-equipped to work on Australian languages. Instead, at the suggestion of Eleanor Higginbottom, whom I was eventually brave enough to confide in about my interest in dialectology and my desire to continue in that field, I applied to join the two-year MA course at UCL – for which I was interviewed by a very amiable Bob Dixon – and for the one-year Diploma in General Linguistics at Edinburgh. I was accepted for both, but my fate was decided by some nameless official in the Department of Education, who decided to award me a one-year rather than a two-year state studentship.

I initially floundered somewhat on the Diploma course, on which we had excellent training from, amongst others, John Lyons, Ron Asher, Erik Fudge, Keith Brown and John Laver, and felt rather intimidated by my failure to understand what generative grammar was for – a problem solved for me by Dinneen's excellent textbook (Dinneen 1967). John Lyons was later kind enough to refer to the 1966–7 group of Diploma students at Edinburgh as his '*annus mirabilis*'. We were all of us people who had not known what linguistics was until we became undergraduates; who had been fortunate enough to benefit from the state studentship postgraduate grant system; and who were later able to obtain posts as universities rapidly expanded their linguistics teaching in the 1960s and 1970s. We included amongst others Mike Garman, now Professor at Reading; Gerry Knowles, now at Lancaster University, who had been with me (and Martin Harris) at Cambridge, and who was very influential in developing my thinking; and Barbara Bird, an excellent phonetician, who teaches English linguistics at the University of Oslo.

In the week after my graduation from Cambridge I had had another happy encounter, by chance, with a book. Walking around Heffers bookshop in Cambridge, I came across Capell's *Studies in Socio-linguistics* (1966) and bought it, having been seduced by the title: I was not sure what it meant. but was very attracted to the idea that linguistics could in some way be related to the study of society. It turned out that Capell's book, which is very anthropological-linguistic in emphasis, was not quite what I thought it was going to be, although I could not at that time have said exactly what I was expecting. There was not much sociolinguistics taught as part of the Edinburgh course.

A third happy chance encounter with a book was therefore very fortunate. In Bauermeister's bookshop in Edinburgh, in November 1966, I came across the volume edited by Bill Bright, arising out of the first ever sociolinguistics conference, at UCLA in 1964, entitled *Sociolinguistics* – this time, significantly, without a hyphen. It contained an early Labov article 'Hypercorrection by the lower middle-class as a factor in linguistic change'. I immediately bought the book, even though it was much more than I could afford (£5 16s 6d), and discovered, on reading Labov, that this was what I was expecting under the heading of 'sociolinguistics', and this was what I wanted to do with my academic life.

John Lyons encouraged us as Diploma students to work on linguistic topics of our own choice, and at some stage during 1967 I wrote an essay for him on sociolinguistics, including references to the work of Labov, McDavid and others who appeared in the Bright volume. This kind of work was new to him too, and he was extremely encouraging about and supportive of my interest in it. I later, therefore, plucked up courage to ask him, again rather nervously, if I could do a PhD in the area I had written on – the sociolinguistic study of linguistic change – and he agreed. I had not yet seen Labov's *The Social Stratification of English in New York City* (1966) but I knew enough about it to be sure that I wanted to do a sociolinguistic urban dialect study according to this model. I thought – for reasons that I now fail to understand altogether but which probably had to do with a timid assumption that no one could possibly be interested in Norwich – that I would be expected as an Edinburgh student to work on the dialect of Edinburgh, until one day when Keith Brown said that, surely, I would be much better off working on my own dialect. And so, of course, that is what, with considerable relief and undying gratitude to him, I decided to do, rather anxiously worrying that, given this exciting new field of Labovian sociolinguistics, someone else might get in there and do it before me.

I was a PhD student at Edinburgh, then, from 1967 to 1970. The financial details of my career are, I believe, rather salutory. I was not successful in an application for a further state studentship. However, as there were then no fees of any significance to pay, I believed that I ought to try and make a start and, with help from my parents, and feeling rather panicky, I did so. John Lyons then came to the rescue. He found departmental money to pay for me to do some office work and to give undergraduate tutorials – some of my students turned out to be rather successful, notably Alison White, later

Eliot, who went on to teach linguistics at Sussex, and Gregory James, who is now teaching linguistics in Hong Kong. Chance also again played a part in my further progress: I wrote to my Cambridge tutor in the history of the French language, Jim Laidlaw of Clare College, who later became Professor at Aberdeen, and told him – out of gratitude for the encouragement he had given me earlier – what I was doing. He wrote back and reminded me that my college, King's, might be prepared to help me financially. I had foolishly not even considered this. I wrote to the Bursar at King's, the late Ken Polack, who immediately agreed that the college would make me an award for my first year. My problems were finally solved when, for my last two years, Edinburgh University, no doubt encouraged by the example of King's, awarded me a university scholarship. I think it is rather obvious that, had I been a student today, I would have had no chance of a career in academic linguistics.

People often describe me as the first British sociolinguist. Actually this is a title that should probably be accorded to R. B. Le Page, unless it should go to Halliday or Firth. However, when I started work on my PhD, I was not familiar with Bob's work at all, and, without having any real awareness that this was the case, I became the first student in Britain to start to work in the Labovian linguistic-variation-and-change paradigm (though I believe that Gerry Knowles with his work on Liverpool was not far behind). I was therefore very much on my own in making decisions as to how to carry out my research and what my objectives were. John Lyons, saying that he knew nothing about my research area, handed over responsibility for me to the phonetician and dialectologist Bill Jones, and the Scottish dialectologist Jim Mather. Of course, they knew nothing about what I was doing either, although they were very helpful and encouraging. If in later years some of my PhD students have thought that I have taken a rather 'hands-off' approach to their supervision, this undoubtedly dates from my own experiences of working almost entirely by myself, a very educational although, I suppose, not entirely to be recommended experience. What I should have done, of course, was to contact Labov himself to tell him what I was doing, but naturally I was too nervous and self-effacing to do that. This was something else which never even occurred to me.

I was due to run out of grant money at the end of my three years in June 1970, and was planning to finish my thesis by then (which indeed I did). It was therefore with great interest that I saw, in January that year, that the Department of Linguistic Science at Reading University was advertising a lectureship in sociolinguistics – the timing, another stroke of good fortune, could not have been better. On my way down to Reading to be interviewed for the job, I suddenly realized, somewhere around Newcastle, that I might actually get the post. What on earth would I teach if I did get it? I had never attended a course in sociolinguistics as such – there weren't any – and I had never read a textbook on sociolinguistics – there weren't any of those either.

So as I travelled south, I worked out what I thought a lecture course in sociolinguistics might look like. The final form, arrived at somewhere around Peterborough, looked very much like the contents of the first edition of my Penguin book (see below). At Reading, I was interviewed by Frank Palmer, David Crystal, David Wilkins and, sitting rather disconcertingly behind me, Peter Matthews. One of the first questions Palmer asked me was: 'If you got this job, and we asked you to teach a course in sociolinguistics, what would you teach?' Crystal vouchsafed afterwards that I had been the only candidate able to answer that question at length and in clear sequential detail, a sign I suppose of the extent to which those of us working in the field were very much breaking new ground.

I began teaching in the Department of Linguistic Science at Reading University in the autumn of 1970. One important thing that has stayed with me, from my four years at Edinburgh and my 16 years at Reading, is the insistence of both Lyons and Palmer that their departments be 'school neutral'. There was, of course, in the 1960s and early 1970s a lot of emphasis on the work of Chomsky and his associates, but in both departments at that time it was felt to be important that students should know about other approaches to linguistics as well. In this kind of atmosphere, and with the approval of Palmer, it was easy for me to develop teaching and research at Reading in sociolinguistics and dialectology as I wished. I had valuable advice and encouragement from Crystal and from Malcolm Petyt, but essentially I was a 26-year-old sociolinguist making it up as I went along.

Towards the end of my first year at Reading, in July 1971, I was awarded an Edinburgh PhD for my thesis *The Social Differentiation of English in Norwich*, later published by Cambridge University Press (1974a), with Le Page as my external examiner. I was also during this year required to make a presentation at a staff seminar, for which I wrote my paper 'Sex, covert prestige and linguistic change in the urban British English of Norwich' (1972). Crystal, who was on the editorial board of the newly formed journal *Language in Society*, heard the paper and immediately sent it off to the editor Dell Hymes to suggest publication. During the summer of 1971 I was on holiday in Norway when I received a letter from my mother. Did I, she asked, know someone called William Labov? Labov, it emerged, was on the editorial board of *Language in Society*, and had seen my submitted paper. He is, of course, not at all nervous or self-effacing and, while on a field trip around Britain, figuring that all proud parents would have copies of their offspring's PhD dissertations to hand, arrived in Norwich, looked in the phone-book, and telephoned my parents. He had tea with them, and while enjoying, as everyone does, my mother's cake, scanned through my thesis. The contact that I should have initiated much earlier was thus made. I finally met Labov the following year in Philadelphia, and there followed an academic friendship which has lasted to the present and which has been enormously helpful and inspirational to me. There also followed invitations to attend conferences in the United States, and my work – no thanks to any initiatives from my reticent Norfolk self – began to be known internationally. I have always since then taken pains to assure students that it is not only in order but actually polite to get in touch with well-known scholars whose field they are working in to inform them of what they, as students, are doing. Such scholars are, after all, as we all soon come to realize, just people.

I will, then, admit to being instrumental in introducing Labovian linguistics to Britain. I believe, however, that from very early on there was a distinctively British flavour to the work of sociolinguists in this country. This owes much to Bob Le Page, whose influence is clear in the work of other British sociolinguists such as Jim Milroy and Lesley Milroy, as well as in the work of the British-based American Suzanne Romaine. This influence is particularly noticeable in the extent to which research in Britain has very often focused on the role of identity, and on the extent to which notions such as language, dialect, variety and speech community are problematical. This is clear already in my edited book *Sociolinguistic Patterns in British English* (1978), the title of which was intended to be a homage to Labov, reflecting the title of his own book *Sociolinguistic Patterns*, and which contained papers by the leading British-based sociolinguists of the time, including the Milroys, Romaine, Knowles and Jenny Cheshire.

I think that if I personally have had any influence, it has been along the two main lines already visible in my book *Sociolinguistics: An Introduction to Language and Society* (1974b). This, incidentally, was commissioned by Crystal for his new series immediately after I had made my first staff seminar pesentation (see above). Obviously, once again I was fortunate enough to be in the right place at the right time. It was one of the very first textbooks exclusively on sociolinguistics ever written. It owed a lot to my PhD, and to Labov, especially to his insistence on sociolinguistics as a way of doing linguistics and his emphasis on the necessity for the empirical study of the speech of ordinary speakers in a social context. It was also based on other reading I had done in the area of work by scholars such as Fishman and Gumperz, as well as on conversations I had had with my fellow Edinburgh PhD students, such as Mike Garman, who had been working in India, and Arne Kjell Foldvik from Norway (now teaching linguistics at the University of Trondheim), who had fascinating tales to tell about the sociolinguistic situation in that country. One contribution I have been able to make subsequently to sociolinguistics has been that my knowledge of Norwegian – learnt mainly from Arne Kjell's parents over a number of summer vacations – has enabled me to incorporate much Scandinavian sociolinguistic research into my own work (see Trudgill 1986, for instance) and to help to introduce this research to other sociolinguists in Britain and elsewhere. I was also keen to promote the idea of linguistic human rights – as we would now call it. This was something which had struck me as a vitally important issue when Lyons, in his first introductory lecture to us on the Edinburgh diploma course, had argued that all languages and dialects were equally complex and structured, expressive systems. The perception of the importance of this issue was reinforced by the distress I felt at the extent to which it had become apparent to me that many of the people I interviewed and recorded in Norwich for my PhD research had been made to feel ashamed and humiliated by their local dialect and accent. My first two PhD students at Reading were Viv Edwards, now once again at Reading as Professor of Language and Education, and Jenny Cheshire, now Professor of Linguistics at Queen Mary College, London University. It is interesting to see that they, too, and in their turn their students, have both been very concerned with linguistic human rights, and with the study of the vernacular – and in fact these issues have been characteristic of British work in sociolinguistics in general in the last 30 years – so perhaps I had a hand in that.

These two issues – sociolinguistics as a form of linguistics, and linguistic human rights (particularly for minority language and dialect speakers) – came together early in my career in a rather surprising way. As I began to work my way into the sociolinguistics milieu and tradition, it never occurred to me that sociolinguistics was anything other than a way of doing linguistics. Firth was obviously a linguist. So were Le Page and Labov. Their linguistics was socially informed and socially sensitive, but it was linguistics. However, it gradually became clear to me in those early years that there were many other scholars doing what was, in my young opinion, very good work that they referred to as sociolinguistics, which, however, seemed to have very little to do with what Le Page or Labov or I were doing. I am thinking here, for example, of work in the social psychology of language, the sociology of language, discourse analysis, ethnomethodology and the like. This did not appear to me to be a particularly problematical matter, except in so far as it was perhaps giving rise to misunderstandings, not least on the part of the growing number of students who were being attracted to courses in sociolinguistics. The point was that much of the work by people who were carrying out research under the rubric of 'sociolinguistics' was valuable and insightful, but it seemed that not everybody involved was clear about the fact that scholars were working with different – sometimes very different – objectives. These enterprises could interact in ways that were mutually beneficial, but I felt it was as well to point out that the umbrella term 'sociolinguistics' had become at least potentially confusing.

I therefore gave a short presentation at the 1977 International Congress of Linguists in Vienna on this topic. I had been invited to contribute to a panel discussion following a paper by the leading ethnomethodologist Aaron Cicourel, and this seemed an appropriate moment. I simply suggested, rather nervously, to the 3,000 or so people present that it was well to be clear about the fact that some sociolinguistics, like Labov's, was aimed at answering questions which were, quite legitimately, of no professional concern to Aaron Cicourel, such as why human languages are as they are, how and why languages change, and so on. Other people, such as Cicourel himself, were doing research which was aimed at answering questions which were, quite legitimately, of no professional concern to me (though as a human being I might be very interested), such as why human societies are as they are, and why human social interaction is as it is. I also pointed out that some work had mixed objectives – to find out more simultaneously about both language and society and their interrelationships. This point was immediately misunderstood. (It has also been misunderstood subsequently, so I suppose that has to be my own fault.) Tove Skutnabb-Kangas, someone whose work I have subsequently come to know and appreciate, stood up and accused me of disparaging work in applied sociolinguistics, i.e. work in the application of the results of sociolinguistic research to the solution of real-world (educational, political, social) problems. This was not what I meant at all. I had felt since my Edinburgh days that sociolinguists had a duty to help to solve whatever social problems they could. (And if I had been less surprised by her attack, I would have pointed to my *Accent, Dialect and the School* [1975] – a book which incidentally was rather influential amongst teachers and in education colleges for many years – as evidence of this!) I was therefore very grateful to Michael Halliday for standing up and arguing that what I had said was quite valid and that both types of academic sociolinguistic work had applications in the non-academic world; and that to point out that social-scientifically oriented sociolinguistics was different from linguistically oriented sociolinguistics was in no way to argue against the social mobilization of sociolinguistic research findings.

I no longer work in Britain, having been attracted to Switzerland in the early 1990s – with the encouragement of Jenny Cheshire – by the fascinating sociolinguistic situation, the research tradition in anglistics, the respect – and therefore time made available – for scholarship and research, the wonderfully liberating absence of bureaucracy and formal evaluation, and, yes, the high salaries. I like to think, however, that I remain very much in touch with the British sociolinguistic scene; and I believe that the following history is very relevant. In the late 1970s, a group of British-based sociolinguists started an informal organization which arranged small conferences which we called Sociolinguistic Symposia. Early participants included Bob Le Page, Euan Reid, Suzanne Romaine, Jim Milroy, Lesley Milroy, Jenny Cheshire, and a number of others including myself and, as an influential overseas visitor, Jack Chambers. These meetings were initially set up because sociolinguists in Britain felt that the meetings of the Linguistics Association of Great Britain, excellent as they were, continued to be dominated by non-sociolinguistic concerns, and we wanted a forum where we could meet and discuss issues of concern to ourselves intensively and in depth. Present at these meetings were practitioners of sociolinguistics with linguistic, social scientific and mixed objectives and motivations, although the former probably dominated. And of course there were also papers dealing with applied sociolinguistic themes. These meetings as, eventually, annual events gradually became bigger and bigger and attracted international attention, particularly when we were able to invite distinguished speakers from abroad, most notably Labov himself. More recently, there has been another interesting development. The Sociolinguistic Symposium at Cardiff in 1997 was by common consent a very successful meeting. It was also very large – at one point there were 10 parallel sessions. It was, however, the perception of many, particularly younger scholars, that work in linguistically motivated sociolinguistics was at this meeting very much dominated, in numerical terms, by work in sociolinguistics which had social-scientific and/or social-interactional objectives, notably various forms of discourse analysis. Interestingly, this led to the formation by younger British scholars of another breakaway organization, which had its first small conference on Linguistic Variation and Change at the University of Reading later in 1997. The second, called VIEW (Variation is EveryWhere), took place at Essex in September 2000, and the third in York in 2001.

My point in narrating this bit of British academic sociology is that I hope very much that, in spite of the fact that linguistically motivated work in sociolinguistics can be time-consuming and expensive, it will not be swamped by other sorts of research also labelled sociolinguistics. It is most encouraging to note, therefore, that work in Britain in Labovian sociolinguistics is currently undergoing a renaissance, led by people such as Paul Kerswill, my successor at Reading, and my former students David Britain and Enam Al-Wer at the University of Essex. The book *Urban Voices* (Foulkes & Docherty 1999), which includes work by what we can perhaps call a third generation of secular linguistics scholars in Britain, is an excellent illustration of this point. If I have played any part at all over the past 30 years in the development of such work, I shall be very pleased indeed.

REFERENCES

BRIGHT, WILLIAM, 1966. *Sociolinguistics*, The Hague: Mouton.
CAPELL, ARTHUR, 1966. *Studies in Socio-linguistics*, The Hague: Mouton.
DINNEEN, FRANCIS, 1967. *An Introduction to General Linguistics*, New York: Holt, Rinehart & Winston.
FOULKES, PAUL & DOCHERTY, GERRY, (eds.) 1999. *Urban Voices*, London: Edward Arnold.
HOCKETT, CHARLES, 1958. *A Course in Modern Linguistics*, New York: Macmillan.
LABOV, WILLIAM, 1966. *The Social Stratification of English in New York City*, Washington, DC: Center for Applied Linguistics.
LABOV, WILLIAM, 1972. *Sociolinguistic Patterns*, Oxford: Blackwell.
TRUDGILL, PETER, 1972. 'Sex, covert prestige and linguistic change in the urban British English of Norwich', *Language in Society* 1, 179–95.
TRUDGILL, PETER, 1974a. *The Social Differentiation of English in Norwich*, Cambridge: Cambridge University Press.

TRUDGILL, PETER, 1974b. *Sociolinguistics: An Introduction to Language and Society*, 4th ed. 2000, London: Penguin.
TRUDGILL, PETER, 1975. *Accent, Dialect and the School*, London: Edward Arnold.
TRUDGILL, PETER, (ed.) 1978. *Sociolinguistic Patterns in British English*, London: Edward Arnold.
TRUDGILL, PETER, 1986. *Dialects in Contact*, Oxford: Blackwell.

JOHN WELLS

WELLS, John Christopher, FBA 1996; Professor of Phonetics, UCL, since 1988; *b.* 1939; *Education:* St John's School, Leatherhead; Trinity College, Cambridge, BA 1960, MA 1964; UCL, MA 1962, PhD 1971; *Career:* Assistant Lecturer in Phonetics, UCL, 1962–5, Lecturer 1965–82, Reader 1982–8, Head of Department of Phonetics and Linguistics 1990–2000; Member: Council of the IPA 1970– (Secretary 1973–86; Editor *JIPA* 1971–87); Council of the Philological Society 1989–1995; Academy of Esperanto 1971–; President World Esperanto Association 1989–95. *Major Publications: Longman Pronunciation Dictionary* 1990 [2nd ed. 2000], *Accents of English* 1982; *Lingvistikaj Aspektoj de Esperanto* 1978 [2nd ed. 1989]; *Jamaican Pronunciation in London* 1973; *Practical Phonetics* 1971 (with G. Colson); *Concise Esperanto and English Dictionary* 1969.

* * *

For the purposes of my future career, I think I chose my parents well. My father was an Anglican clergyman, my mother a teacher of physical education and mathematics. Both were university graduates, both read widely, and both were accustomed to speaking in public and to putting across difficult topics in accessible terms.

I had a happy though impecunious childhood. My parents could not have afforded from their own resources to educate me at independent schools, but I was supported from the age of nine onwards by scholarships. I am grateful to the long-dead benefactors who made this possible.

I have always been interested in languages. I started French in primary school and then Latin at prep school. There I also came across an old copy of Hugo's *Learn Italian in Three Months*, and for my twelfth birthday asked for, and received, an Italian–English dictionary. By then my Latin teacher was giving me Virgil to read in the original. I started Ancient Greek the same year, when I moved to St John's, Leatherhead. At the age of 14 I passed my O-levels (equivalent of today's GCSEs) in French, Latin, Greek and English language; my other subjects included English literature, maths and additional maths.

Like several other contributors to this volume, I started out as a classicist. My choice of classics flowed really from a decision I had to make on arrival at St John's, where I was required to choose between science, Spanish and Greek: I chose Greek. When I came to enter the sixth form, my best two subjects (French and maths) could not be combined, whereas my two next best (Greek and Latin) could. I went on to do classics at A- and S-levels and then at university.

At age 16 I decided to teach myself Esperanto. I quickly attained fluency, and read widely: not only original works of literature (yes, they do exist) but also translations, which gave me a nodding acquaintance at least, via Esperanto, with some of the masterpieces of the literatures of Italian, Polish, Hungarian, Finnish and Japanese. By the time I went up to Cambridge I had read Mickiewicz and Madách and knew what a haiku was.

I also taught myself shorthand: not the Pitman shorthand commonly used in Britain, but Gregg shorthand, as used in the USA. I quickly achieved a respectable speed in writing it. The snag was that in class I tended to write down everything the teacher said, instead of producing a précis as the longhand user has to. This made my notes too prolix. Once I realized the problem I decided to use shorthand only on the rare occasions when a verbatim note is required.

As a teenager I borrowed several books a week from the public library, including some on phonetics and linguistics. I remember puzzling over Daniel Jones's description of the articulation of English /r/ and concluding that he and I articulated it in different ways.

Leaving school in 1957, I had a few months to spare before going up to university. Given that I was interested in languages and anxious to travel, my parents very sensibly arranged an exchange with a German family. I spent six weeks in Kiel with the von Briskorns, and then their son Klaus spent six weeks with us in England. This was my first trip abroad, and I was determined to put it to good use. It offered ideal conditions for *ab initio* language learning – total immersion. Both Klaus and I took the task of my learning German very seriously. While he was at school during the day, I was left at home with Frau v. Briskorn, who knew no English but took me shopping with her and kept up a constant flow of conversation. In this way I acquired a fluency in German which has been useful to me ever since. On re-establishing contact with Klaus 30 years later, I was interested to observe that I had based my German pronunciation exactly on his, not on that of his siblings or parents. For example, I still tend to pronounce *Zug* as [tsʊx] rather than the standard [tsuːk].

It was at Cambridge that I first came seriously into contact with phonetics and linguistics. For the third year of the Classical Tripos we had to choose between philosophy, archaeology, history, literature and language. I chose language. This mainly meant comparative philology, under the guidance of Sidney Allen, who like me was at Trinity. He introduced us to linguistics. Latin and Greek had hitherto been purely written languages for me, and it was a revelation to be taught that they had phonemic systems and allophones. I remember constructing vowel diagrams for him of the vowel systems of both languages. We were also taught Italic dialects by Oswald Szemerenyi and some Sanskrit by Sir Harold Bailey. I found Gleason's

Introduction (1955) in the library, and read it with fascination. I even purchased a copy of Bloomfield's *Language*. All six of us who were in the 1959–60 language group became academics; among us were Jean Aitchison, Eleanor Higginbottom (who was briefly to become Lecturer in Phonetics at Cambridge; her surname subsequently became Young and then Jackson) and Wynn Roberts (the first native speaker of Welsh I had met; now Professor of Linguistics at Simon Fraser). John Lyons and Peter Matthews were postgraduates ahead of us, and seemed to know an awful lot more than I did.

Meanwhile John Trim was in his second year as a Lecturer in the Department of Other Languages. I attended his course on phonetics, and found the subject enthralling. It is to Trim that I owe all my basic phonetic training. He not only taught us phonetic theory but also provided ample practice in ear-training and sound production in accordance with the Daniel Jones tradition. When, due to graduate, I expressed a wish to study phonetics further, he recommended to me A. C. Gimson at University College London, who accepted me for the two-year MA (as it then was) in General Linguistics and Phonetics. I was lucky enough to win a state scholarship to finance me for these two years, so that both my undergraduate and my taught postgraduate study were financed by the government. I had to live very frugally as a student, but at least I did not emerge with a burden of debt such as today's students typically incur.

At the end of my final undergraduate year I won a travel scholarship that enabled me to visit Greece. I studied Pring's phonetics-based *Grammar of Modern Greek* (1950) and tried to acquire as much knowledge of the modern language as I could, building on the extensive knowledge of Ancient Greek that I already had. This was before the days of mass tourism in Greece, and I was able to explore the Parthenon in Athens and to sit on the supposed throne of King Minos in Crete in a way that would be quite impossible today.

At the Cambridge University Esperanto Club I got to know Victor Sadler, reading psychology one year ahead of me. He preceded me to the UCL Phonetics Department as a postgraduate to work on psychoacoustics, so that when I arrived there was already someone in the Department that I knew. (In later life, after a spell running the World Esperanto Association office in Rotterdam, he was to become a software engineer working on machine translation and the millennium bug.) Eleanor Higginbottom also transferred from Cambridge to UCL Phonetics at the same time as I did. David Crystal, then an undergraduate in the UCL English Department, used to be waiting outside O'Connor's room for his hour of supervision as I came out from mine.

As postgraduates at UCL, Eleanor and I were taught phonetics by Gimson and O'Connor, and experimental phonetics by Fry and Fourcin. We were sent to Robins at the School of Oriental and African Studies for linguistics supervision. (I was, however, warned not to take too seriously everything I might come across at SOAS, because 'they have some very strange ideas there'.) I also attended Jack Carnochan's course on the phonetics of Ibo. Firth died three months after I reached UCL, and I never met him.

Back at UCL, Gimson set Eleanor and me the tutorial assignment of describing the phonetics of our own idiolects. He was so pleased with the results that he published both our essays in *Le Maître Phonétique*. Anyone who seeks out this, my first published article (Wells 1962), will be struck by my choice of phonemicization: American-style structuralist, demonstrating the striking extent to which I was under the influence of the now deeply unfashionable neo-Bloomfieldians (see for example Trager and Smith 1951; Hockett 1958). In fact I exchanged letters with both Gleason and Henry Lee Smith Jr at this time.

Dennis Fry rightly insisted that if I wanted to make a career as a phonetician I must get to grips with laboratory phonetics. Coming as I did from an arts background, I did not find this easy. With Adrian Fourcin's help I nevertheless managed to complete a spectrographic project measuring the formants of the English monophthongs. Having once demonstrated that I could carry out an experimental-phonetic project, though, I have since steered clear of laboratory work.

Upon my completion of the MA, Fry offered me a post as Assistant Lecturer in Phonetics at UCL. Clearly I was lucky to be in the right place at the right time. I have remained on the academic staff at UCL ever since.

Shortly after my appointment I was summoned to meet Daniel Jones at his home. I found him sitting at a desk in his study, a somewhat shrunken old man surrounded by electric fires. There was no small talk: he got straight down to business. 'Ah, Wells, good of you to come. Now sit down here, will you, and read to me from this.' It was a passage of Hindi in phonetic transcription: Jones was putting me through my paces. But Trim, Fry, Gimson and O'Connor had trained me well. I was able to produce satisfactory monophthongal [e:] and [o:], to control aspiration at will, to distinguish retroflex stops from dental, to articulate a retroflex flap and a nasalized [i]. I realized with relief that I had passed the test. We moved on to an animated discussion about his *English Pronouncing Dictionary*.

I remain a great admirer of the Daniel Jones tradition in phonetics (see Collins and Mees 1999: 421–4). I continue to regard it as important for budding phoneticians to learn not only to recognize but also to perform all the sound-types of the world's languages.

In 1963 Michael Halliday set up a linguistics department at UCL. Like Dick Hudson and Neil Smith, I attended his course on the grammar of English, and found much to admire in his approach, particularly in the way he was able to integrate intonation into the description of clause structure.

From 1958 onwards I had attended a number of international Esperanto conferences. By 1963 these meetings had taken me not only to France, Germany, Belgium, the Netherlands and Denmark, but also to Poland, Czechoslovakia, Yugoslavia and Bulgaria, which in those days were pretty exotic destinations for a young Englishman. In each of these countries I took the opportunity to acquaint myself with the phonetics of the local language. The 1959 World Esperanto Youth Congress was held in a suburb of Gdańsk called *Wrzeszcz*, and I vividly remember getting Polish friends to demonstrate the differences between its final consonant cluster and that of *Brześć*, the Polish name of Brest-Litovsk. Few non-Polish participants could perceive and make the difference.

By 1963, then, I had become thoroughly proficient in Esperanto (which remains the only language beside English in which I can lecture absolutely fluently and confidently). I had also come to realize how out of touch with current international usage the English–Esperanto dictionaries then available were. So when the publishers of the Teach Yourself series approached me with the suggestion that I should compile a two-way Esperanto dictionary, I leapt at the opportunity. In its compilation I made extensive use of monolingual Esperanto and English dictionaries and of bilingual dictionaries of these languages and French, German, Spanish and Russian, checking forms and senses through chains of languages. The grammatical preamble I wrote for my dictionary reveals Halliday's influence in the use of such terms as 'nominal group' (for which one would nowadays say 'noun phrase'). It was published in early 1969, and remains in print to this day. Its success led to my being elected to the Academy of Esperanto shortly afterwards.

But if the Esperanto dictionary forced me into a crash course of self-taught lexicology and improved my knowledge of modern languages, it was not very relevant to my career in phonetics. Only after I had finished work on it did I get round to completing my PhD.

The topic of my doctoral dissertation reveals a further influence on my academic development, namely my sexuality. Shortly after my appointment to the staff at UCL the Home Office (or was it MI6?) approached me with the suggestion that I should do some work for them on speaker identification. I would need to sign the Official Secrets Act. This was a time when the Burgess and Maclean scandals were fresh in people's minds, and when being homosexual (or gay, as we were just beginning to call ourselves) was seen as not only criminal but tantamount to being of suspect loyalty. I had realized while at Cambridge that my sexual interests were indeed directed only towards other men. If I accepted the spooks' invitation they would surely run a security check on me and I might face the same fate as Oscar Wilde and Alan Turing. Self-preservation meant that I had little hesitation in turning them down.

My first serious boyfriend, Pagro, was a Jamaican who had come to the UK as a teenager a few years earlier. His education had been pretty limited, and his language was definitely in the lower-mesolectal part of the creole continuum. I quickly acquired some knowledge of Jamaican Creole, helped in this task by spending a good deal of time not only with him but also with his friends and extended family. (I had no relatives in London. He seemed to have hundreds.)

I had for some time been thinking about questions of bidialectalism and of the extent to which people can and do change their accent. For my doctoral work I decided to focus on the pronunciation of Jamaicans who had, like Pagro, come to London as adolescents or young adults. How would they adjust their phonetics to their new situation? First, I had to understand their point of departure. With the help of a grant from the University of London I spent two months in Jamaica in 1966, taking Pagro with me. Through the entrée he afforded me, I was able to live close to the common people, partly in a slum in Kingston and partly in the rural poverty of Westmoreland, where he had grown up. I found the best informants to help me get a grasp of Jamaican Creole were children of 11 or 12, old enough to know their language thoroughly but young enough not to be affected by the sense of linguistic shame and embarrassment that characterized adult speakers.

It was not till 1969–70 that I got round to organizing my survey of Jamaicans in London, for which I recruited respondents largely among people I had met through Pagro (though by now he and I were no longer together). I found that they readily made superficial realizational adjustments to their original pronunciation, but had great difficulty in acquiring new phonological contrasts. I recorded plenty of hypercorrections such as [fʊθ] for *foot*, as well as interesting forms such as [bʌʊʔ ə dem] *both of them*, which can result only from the intersection of Jamaican and London phonology. Bob Le Page both advised me before I set off for Jamaica and acted as my external examiner. The dissertation was subsequently published by the Society (Wells 1973).

I have maintained an interest in Caribbean English. My life partner, Gabriel, comes from Montserrat. We have been together since 1968.

In the late 1960s Greta Colson, a teacher of speech and drama, persuaded me to teach a phonetics course at Ivy House (now part of the University of Middlesex). I found drama students very different from the speech therapy students who formed the bulk of my teaching at UCL: intellectually weaker, but fired with boundless and exhausting enthusiasm. Greta sat in on my classes and wrote the content up. Our collaboration resulted in the textbook *Practical Phonetics* (Wells & Colson 1971), which strangely enough has proved to be popular particularly among students of speech therapy.

In 1975–6 I attended an introductory Zulu course taught by David Rycroft at SOAS. I was impressed by his analysis of depressor consonants and tone, which had the effect of reducing Doke's incoherent nine-tone-level analysis to a simple High versus Low with rather complicated realization rules. I satisfied myself that the output of Rycroft's rules agreed exactly with what the native speaker pronounced. This convinced me of the virtues of a phonological analysis more abstract than that allowed in Jonesian or structuralist phonemics.

Every summer vacation since my postgraduate days I have taught on summer courses for English for overseas students, first in Cambridge and Leeds, latterly in London. For many years John Trim ran an excellent linguistic summer course in Cambridge, where Neil Smith, Erik Fudge, Ken Albrow and Bernard Comrie were among my fellow tutors. One year Trim asked me to do some sessions on English local accents, a challenge I accepted. I realized that there was no published comprehensive introduction to this topic, and put together an article summarizing such knowledge as I had. It helped that I was a northerner educated in the south. David Crystal accepted this article for the *Journal of Linguistics* (Wells 1970).

Shortly after it was published two things happened. Peter Trudgill, someone I had not then heard of, wrote to me about my neglect of East Anglian speech, and Cambridge University Press approached me to expand the article into a book. I am grateful to both. The book was 12 years in gestation, years during which I published very little – which under today's circumstances would probably mean losing my job. What I attempted to do in *Accents of English* (Wells 1982) was to bring together all the information I could find on the pronunciation of English as a first language and present it in a unified framework. American scholars had struck me as knowing very little about British accents other than RP, while the British seemed equally ignorant of American phonetics. Neither seemed to know anything at all about everyday Irish or West Indian pronunciation. In this work I found it necessary to introduce a number of new terms, many of which have since been generally adopted by colleagues in the field: *rhotic, yod dropping, smoothing, TH Fronting, glottalling, diphthong shift.*

From time to time I had encountered British students whose native language was not English but Welsh. I came to feel that I really ought to learn something of that language. I started attending evening classes, and progressed as far as the A-level examination. In 1985 the British Esperanto Association was due to hold a conference in Llandudno, and I took the opportunity to produce a small two-way Welsh–Esperanto dictionary (Wells 1985), with the help, needless to say, of a number of native Welsh speakers. It includes a structural sketch of Welsh in Esperanto and one of Esperanto in Welsh. The peak of my attainment in spoken Welsh came when I was interviewed live in that language by BBC Radio Cymru.

I had also done a fair amount of broadcasting in English by this time. René Quinault, an English specialist working as a producer with BBC English by Radio (as it then was), had attended a lunchtime lecture I had given at UCL, and recruited me for a radio series on EFL phonetics. Latterly, like my mentor Gimson in his day, I have become something of a regular radio commentator on linguistic topics, no doubt helped by the fact that I work only 10 minutes' walk from Broadcasting House. I hate writing scripts but am happy to launch into unscripted discussion.

Another work of popularization was my linguistic account of Esperanto, written in that language (Wells 1978). It has since been translated into German, Danish and Korean. One of the issues I discuss is the nature of the neutral, international pronunciation standard and the sociolinguistic question of how it might have arisen. I take the view, by the way, that Esperanto is no more 'artificial' than EFL; for the small group of its native speakers it is of course not artificial at all. The linguist's task is to describe it as an interesting linguistic phenomenon (see Wells 1994).

Ever since I came to UCL I had known Randolph Quirk (now Lord Quirk), the Quain Professor of English Language and Literature and always a lively commentator on linguistic affairs. In the early 1980s Della Summers, at the publishers Longman, had the idea of commissioning a pronunciation dictionary, and I believe it was Randolph who suggested to her that I might be the person to compile it. I had long been in the habit of suggesting amendments and improvements to Daniel Jones's *English Pronouncing Dictionary*, sending them first to Jones himself and then to Gimson, who succeeded him as its editor. When Gimson died in 1985 the publishers of *EPD*, Dent, approached me to take it over; but they were not prepared to make the major changes that I considered necessary, and I decided instead to accept Longman's invitation. (Subsequently my colleague Susan Ramsaran took over as editor of *EPD*. When she left academic life to enter the Anglican ministry, Dent sold the title to Cambridge University Press, who, with Peter Roach and James Hartman as the new editors, did introduce the long-needed changes.)

My *Longman Pronunciation Dictionary* appeared in 1990, with a second edition in 2000. It differs from the Jones–Gimson *EPD* in various ways, in particular by covering American as well as British pronunciation, in not restricting the British pronunciation to Received Pronunciation, and in redefining RP to include a wider range of possibilities (such as a tenser final vowel in *happy*, [ə] in the final syllable of *careless* and *kindness*, and the potentiality of an intrusive r in *thawing*). I analyse all syllabic consonants as reflecting an underlying sequence of schwa plus consonant. (Jones and Gimson, pre-Chomskian in their theoretical approach, had no concept of an 'underlying' representation. I do, but the requirements of EFL pedagogy mean that I keep it in the background.) I propose a unified and rule-governed treatment of the compression phenomenon evidenced in the varisyllabicity of words such as *lenient, influence, reference* and *national*. I propose a heretical but to me convincing theory of syllabification. And for various words of uncertain or controversial pronunciation I adduce evidence from polling surveys that I have conducted (Wells 1995; 2000).

My other main activity in the EFL field is that of being Director of the annual UCL Summer Course in English Phonetics, a role I took over from

Gimson in 1983. While other courses have been discontinued as no longer viable, the UCL course has more than doubled in size and become an important source of departmental income as well as a potent vehicle for the dissemination internationally of information about English phonetics and how to teach it.

I have supplied pronunciations for a number of English dictionaries and encyclopedias. Publishing houses in Britain (though not in the USA) have over the last quarter-century gradually adopted the International Phonetic Alphabet, a trend I favour. Where publishers rejected IPA in favour of a respelling system, I have at least made sure that the system is as logical, consistent and self-explanatory as possible (see for example *Encarta World English Dictionary* 1999).

In 1990 I took over from Neil Smith as Head of the Department of Phonetics and Linguistics at UCL, and served in this role for 10 years. Administration is not my strong point, but at least the Department remained financially viable and emerged unscathed from the ever more frequent assessments, audits and appraisals to which we are all nowadays subject.

I have also served for some years as President of the British Association of Academic Phoneticians, whose main role is to organize a biennial colloquium.

Through Gimson's sponsorship I was elected to the Council of the International Phonetic Association. In time I took over from him as Editor of its *Journal* and as Secretary. I oversaw the gradual modernization of the IPA alphabet (e.g. the redesign of the Chart, the introduction of the symbols [ɟ] and [ɥ] and the withdrawal of recognition from various little-used symbols). But it was only when I resigned and Ladefoged succeeded that the IPA finally held a proper Convention (in Kiel, 1989) and set about a comprehensive revision of the Alphabet.

One of the classes I regularly teach deals with the phonetics of ten or a dozen languages each year, using native-speaking informants (including members of the class). As various informants offered themselves, I have become familiar with the phonetics of a large number of languages. I was able to put this kind of knowledge to practical use when the need arose to co-ordinate the computer-readable phonetic transcription of several European languages as part of the Speech Assessment Methods (SAM) research project chaired by Adrian Fourcin in the late 1980s. It was necessary to negotiate tactfully with speech technologists and phoneticians representing many different international partners. In this way we produced the SAM Phonetic Alphabet (SAMPA), an ASCIIization of the IPA now widely adopted as an international standard. I imagine it will be superseded by Unicode if and when the Unicode standard becomes a practical reality: but we have not yet reached that point. In extended form SAMPA, still using only ASCII symbols, can cater for the phonemic and 'phonotypical' notation of any language (see the website www.phon.ucl.ac.uk/home/sampa).

In 1995 I launched my personal homepage on the departmental website. Guided by my colleagues Mark Huckvale and Warwick Smith, I learnt HTML and have become an enthusiastic webmaster. Amongst other web initiatives, I created a site devoted to the topic of Estuary English (www.phon.ucl.ac.uk/home/estuary), which has succeeded in bringing together the academic research on this topic, not to mention a mass of popular journalism. The website also contains a slightly longer version of this article, with pictures: http://www.phon.ucl.ac.uk/home/wells/philsoc-bio.htm.

REFERENCES

BLOOMFIELD, L., 1933. *Language*, British ed., 1935, London: George Allen & Unwin.
COLLINS, BEVERLEY & MEES, INGER, 1999. *The Real Professor Higgins: The Life and Career of Daniel Jones*, Berlin: Mouton de Gruyter.
Encarta World English Dictionary, 1999. London: Bloomsbury.
GLEASON, HENRY A. JR, 1955. *Introduction to Descriptive Linguistics*, New York: Holt, Rinehart & Winstone.
HOCKETT, CHARLES F., 1958. *A Course in Modern Linguistics*, New York: Macmillan.
PRING, JULIAN T., 1950. *A Grammar of Modern Greek on a Phonetic Basis*, London: University of London Press.
TRAGER, GEORGE L. & SMITH, HENRY L. JR, 1951. *An Outline of English Structure*, Studies in Linguistics Occasional Papers 3, Norman, OK: Battenberg Press.
WELLS, JOHN C., 1962. ə spesəmin əv britiʃ iŋgliʃ, *Le Maître Phonétique* 117, 2–5.
WELLS, J. C., 1969. *Concise Esperanto and English Dictionary*, London: English Universities Press, Teach Yourself Books.
WELLS, J. C., 1970. 'Local accents in England and Wales', *Journal of Linguistics* 6, 231–52.
WELLS, J. C., 1973. *Jamaican Pronunciation in London*, Oxford: Blackwell, for the Philological Society.
WELLS, J. C., 1978. *Lingvistikaj Aspektoj de Esperanto*, 2nd ed. 1989, Rotterdam: Universala Esperanto-Asocio.
WELLS, J. C., 1982. *Accents of English*, 3 vols. plus cassette, Cambridge: Cambridge University Press.
WELLS, J. C., 1985. *Geiriadur Esperanto/Kimra Vortaro*, Teddington: Group Five.
WELLS, J. C., 1990. *Longman Pronunciation Dictionary*, Harlow: Longman, 2nd ed. 2000, Harlow: Pearson Education.
WELLS, J. C., 1994. 'Esperanto', in R. E. Asher (ed.), *Encyclopedia of Language and Linguistics*, Oxford: Pergamon Press, 1143–5.
WELLS, J. C., 1995. 'Age grading in English pronunciation preferences', *Proceedings of the XIIIth International Congress of Phonetic Sciences*, Stockholm, 13–19 August 1995, 3, 696–9.
WELLS, J. C., 2000. 'British English pronunciation preferences: a changing scene', *Journal of the International Phonetic Association* 29.1, 33–50.
WELLS, J. C. & COLSON, GRETA, 1971. *Practical Phonetics*, London: Pitman.

GENERAL INDEX